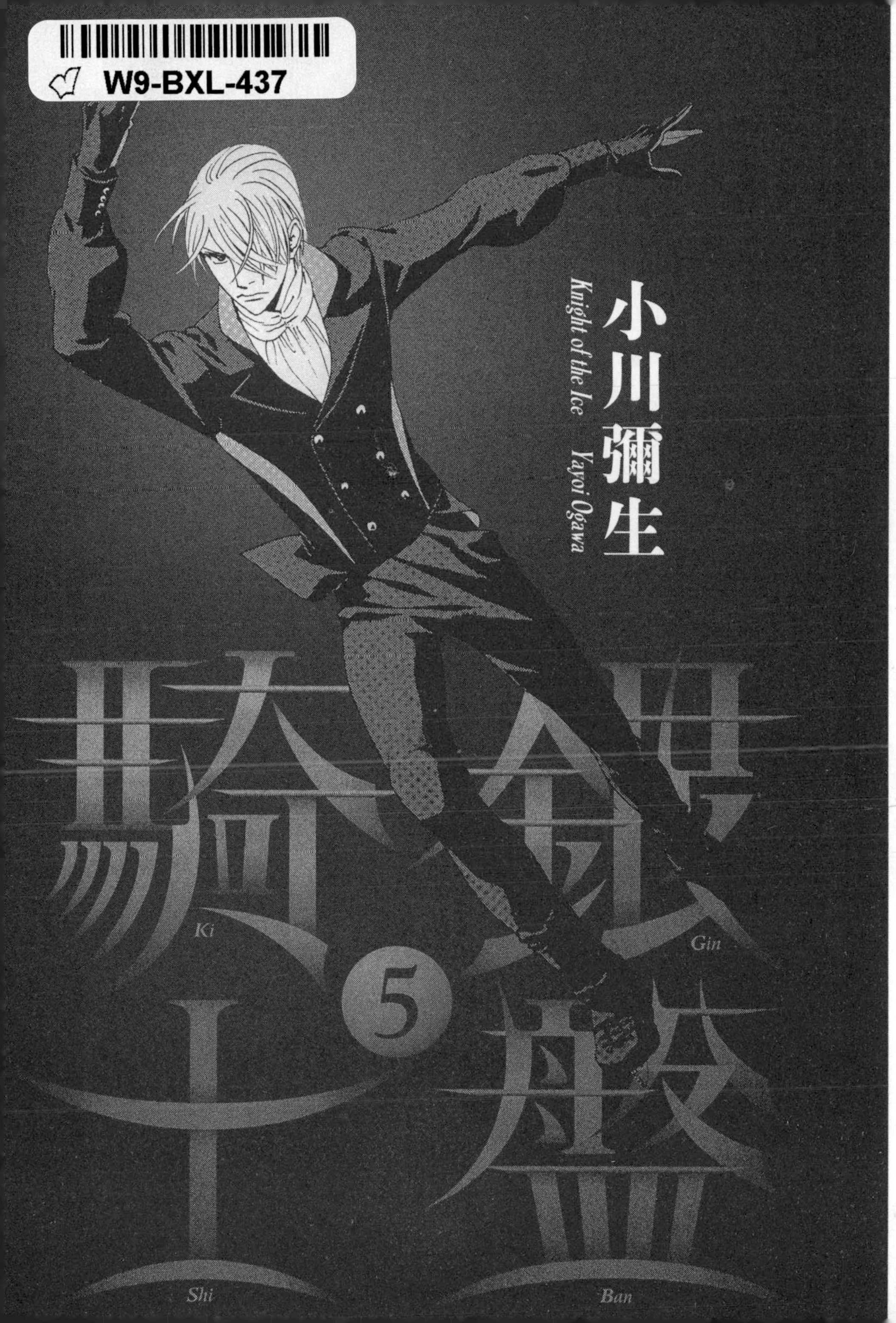
小川彌生
Knight of the Ice
Yayoi Ogawa
銀盤
Gin Ban
騎士
Ki Shi
5

Characters

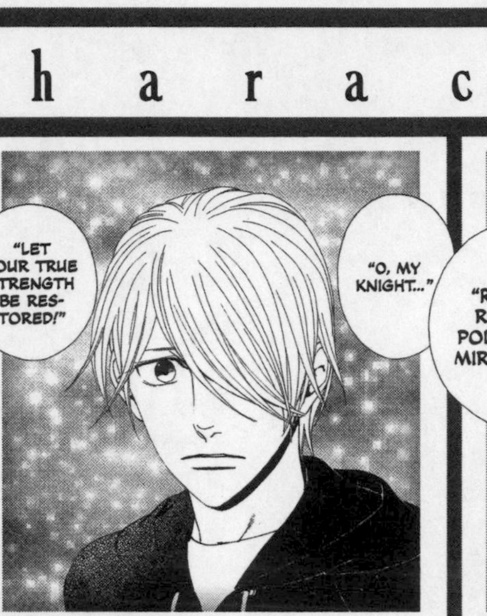
"O, MY KNIGHT..."
"LET YOUR TRUE STRENGTH BE RESTORED!"

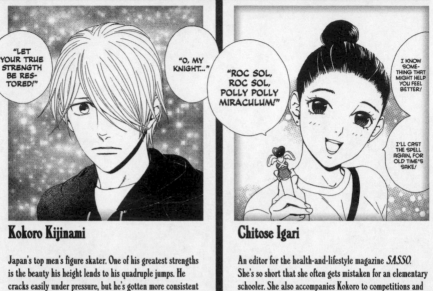

Kokoro Kijinami

Japan's top men's figure skater. One of his greatest strengths is the beauty his height lends to his quadruple jumps. He cracks easily under pressure, but he's gotten more consistent since Chitose started reciting their magic spell for him. He and Chitose have been friends since childhood, and he was two years behind her in school.

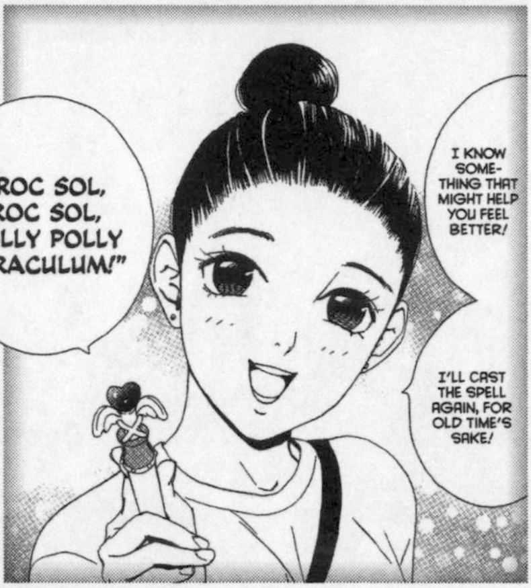
I KNOW SOMETHING THAT MIGHT HELP YOU FEEL BETTER!
I'LL CAST THE SPELL AGAIN, FOR OLD TIME'S SAKE!
"ROC SOL, ROC SOL, POLLY POLLY MIRACULUM!"

Chitose Igari

An editor for the health-and-lifestyle magazine *SASSO*. She's so short that she often gets mistaken for an elementary schooler. She also accompanies Kokoro to competitions and pretends to be his personal trainer. It was Moriyama's idea. She and Kokoro are finally taking the first steps in their relationship now.

Magical Princess Lady Lala is a magical girl anime that used to air on TV. Chitose and Kokoro loved it, and they often played pretend as the characters.

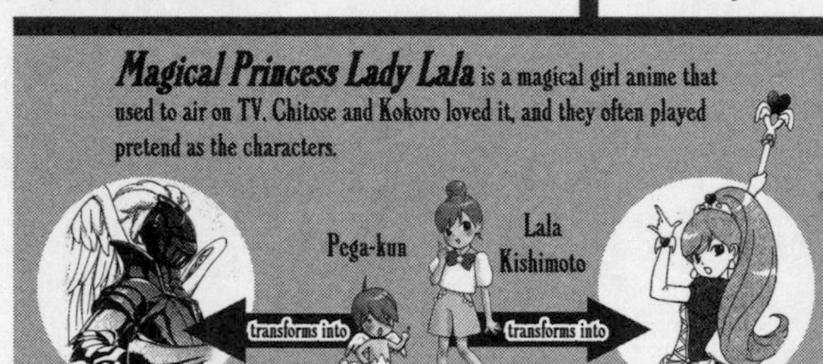
Pegasus Knight
transforms into
Pega-kun
Lala Kishimoto
transforms into
Lady Lala

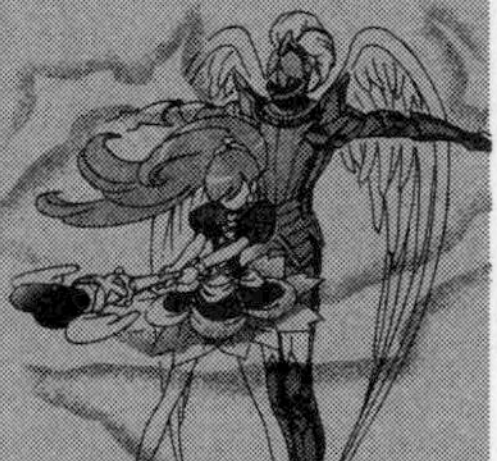

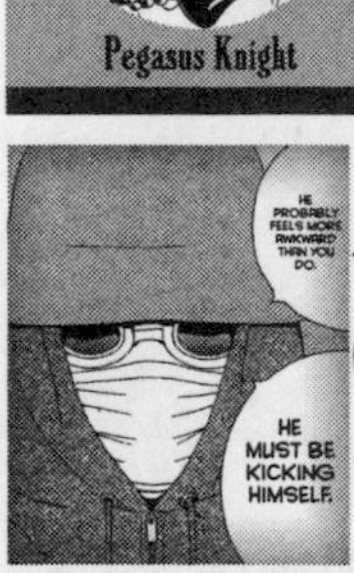
HE PROBABLY FEELS MORE AWKWARD THAN YOU DO.
HE MUST BE KICKING HIMSELF.

Yayoi Ogata

A manga artist. She went to the same college as Chitose and knows about her relationship to Kokoro.

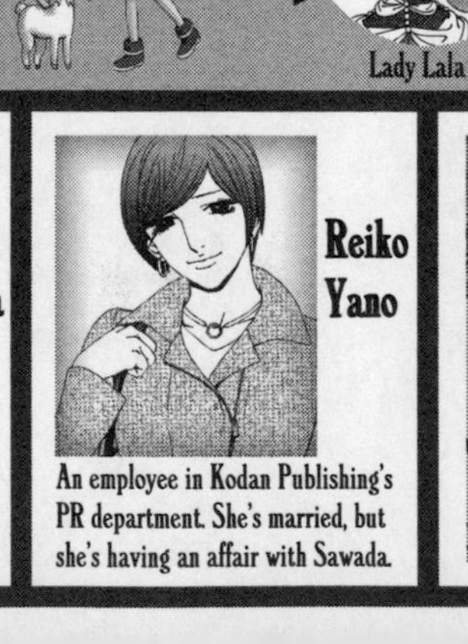

Reiko Yano

An employee in Kodan Publishing's PR department. She's married, but she's having an affair with Sawada.

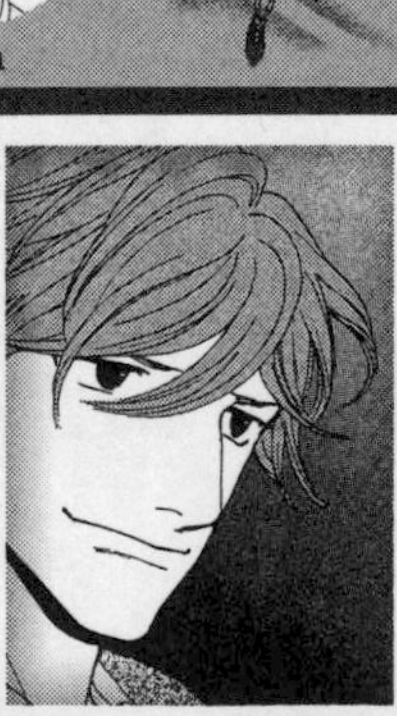

Koichi Sawada

The head of the editorial department for Kodan Publishing's magazine *SASSO*. He's good at his job, but can be somewhat lacking in delicacy...

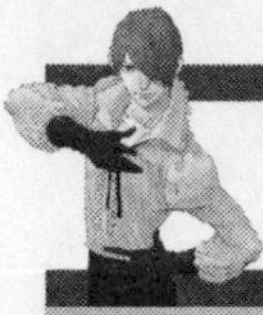

Knight of the Ice

Kokoro's Staff

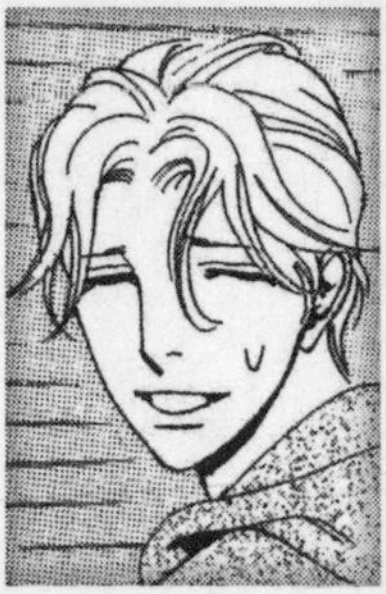

Kenzo Dominic Takiguchi

Kokoro's personal trainer.

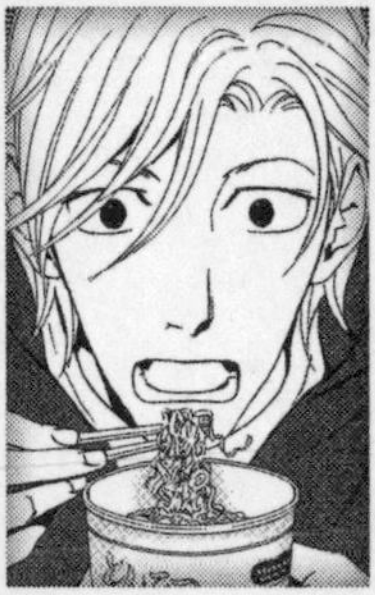

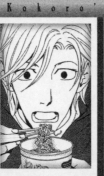

Hikaru Yomota

Kokoro's assistant coach and a former ice dancer.

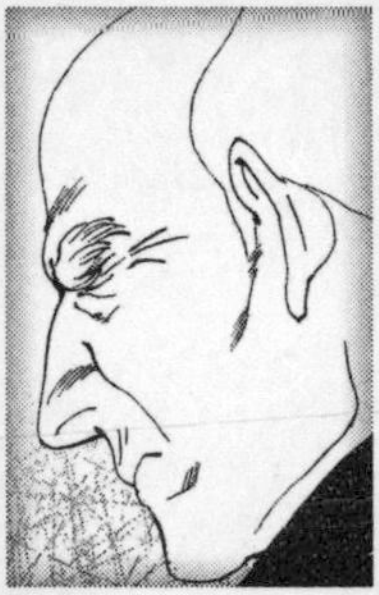

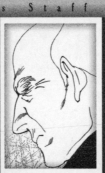

Takejiro Honda

Kokoro's coach. Masato Tamura, Raito Tamura's grandfather and coach, is his longtime rival.

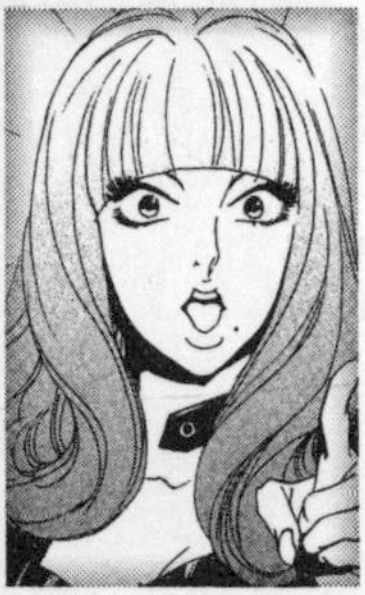

Moriyama

Kokoro's manager. She's not afraid to get a little pushy if that's what it takes to get results.

Kokoro's Rivals

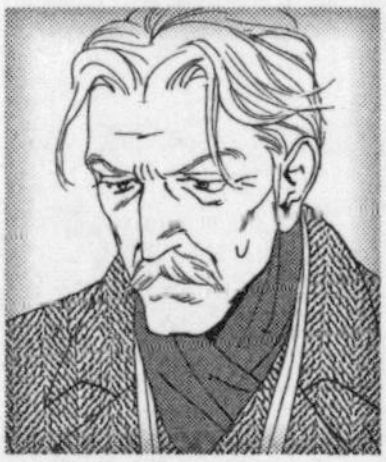

Masato Tamura

Raito Tamura's grandfather. He's his coach, as well as Fuuta Kumano's.

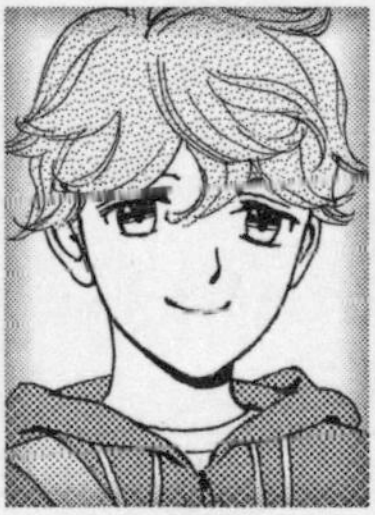

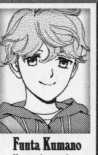

Fuuta Kumano

He can always rely on his speed and his devilish cuteness.

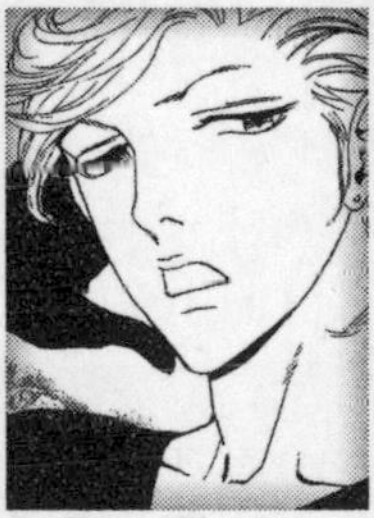

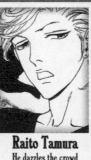

Raito Tamura

He dazzles the crowd with his passion and expressiveness.

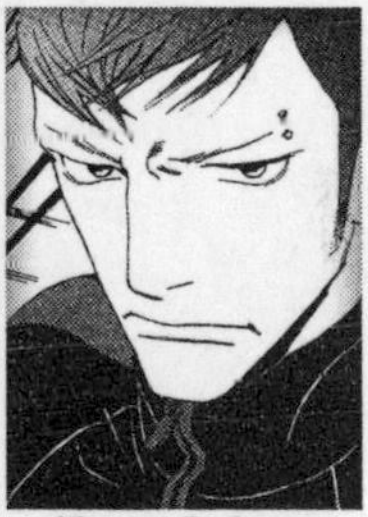

Taiga Aoki

His greatest strength is his ability to land two different quad jumps.

Liza Shibata

A model. Could the reports of her and Kokoro's relationship be part of her plot?

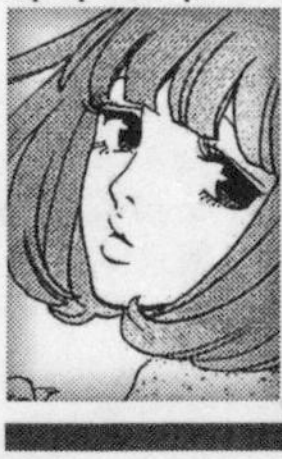

Lilika

An avid fan of Kokoro's.

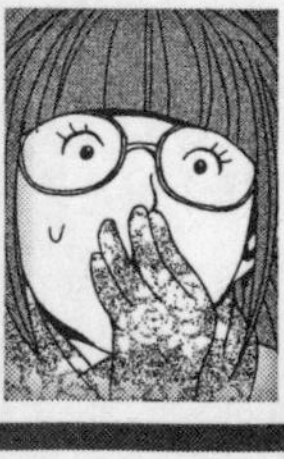

Kokoro's Family

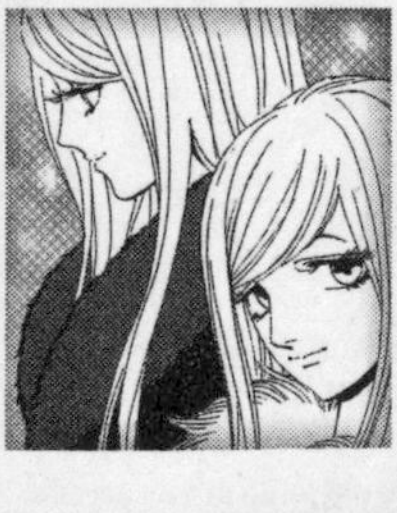

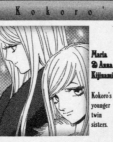

Maria & Anna Kijinami

Kokoro's younger twin sisters.

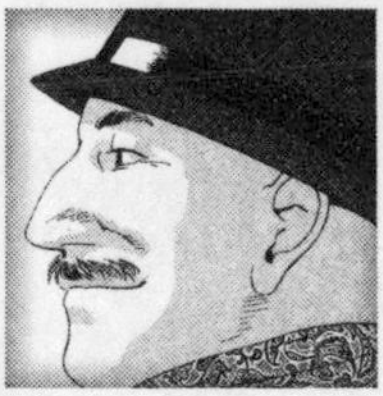

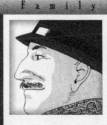

Kokoro's Father

President of the Kijinami Group, a company that runs a number of boutique ryokan.

Contents

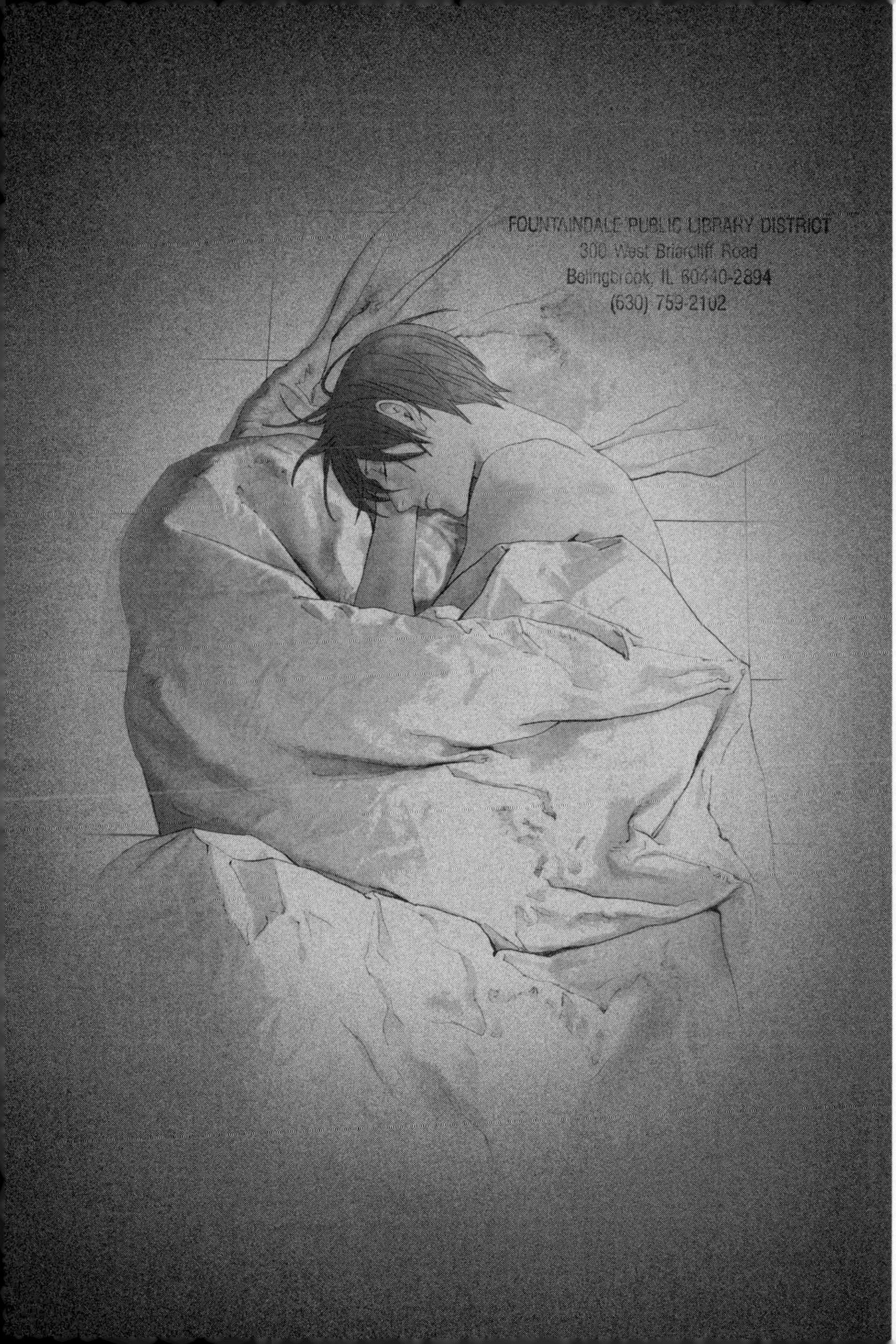

Spell 22
My Wish

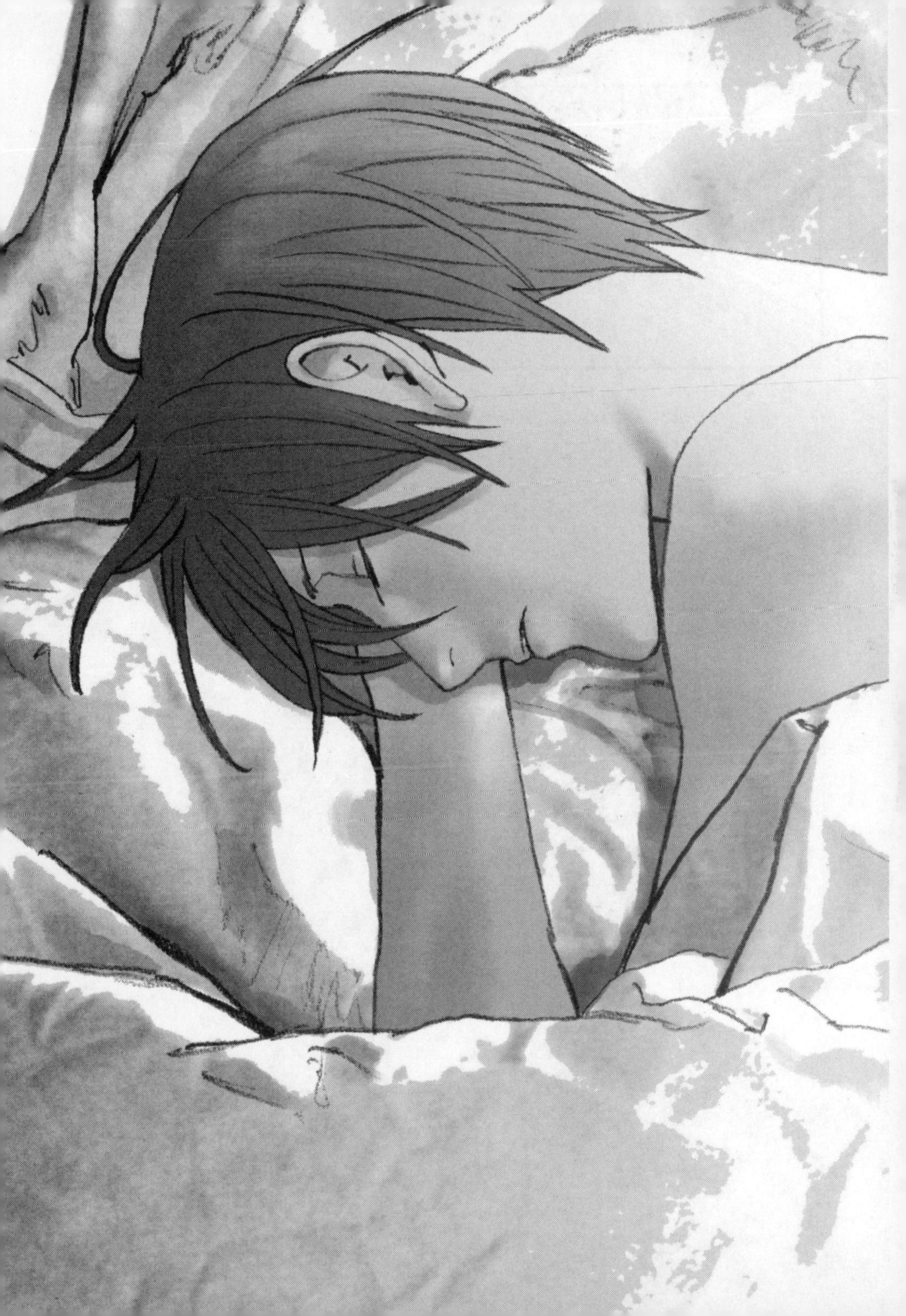

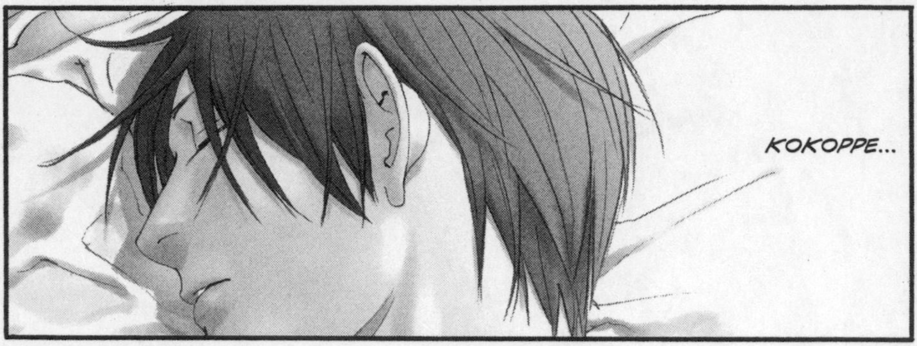
KOKOPPE...

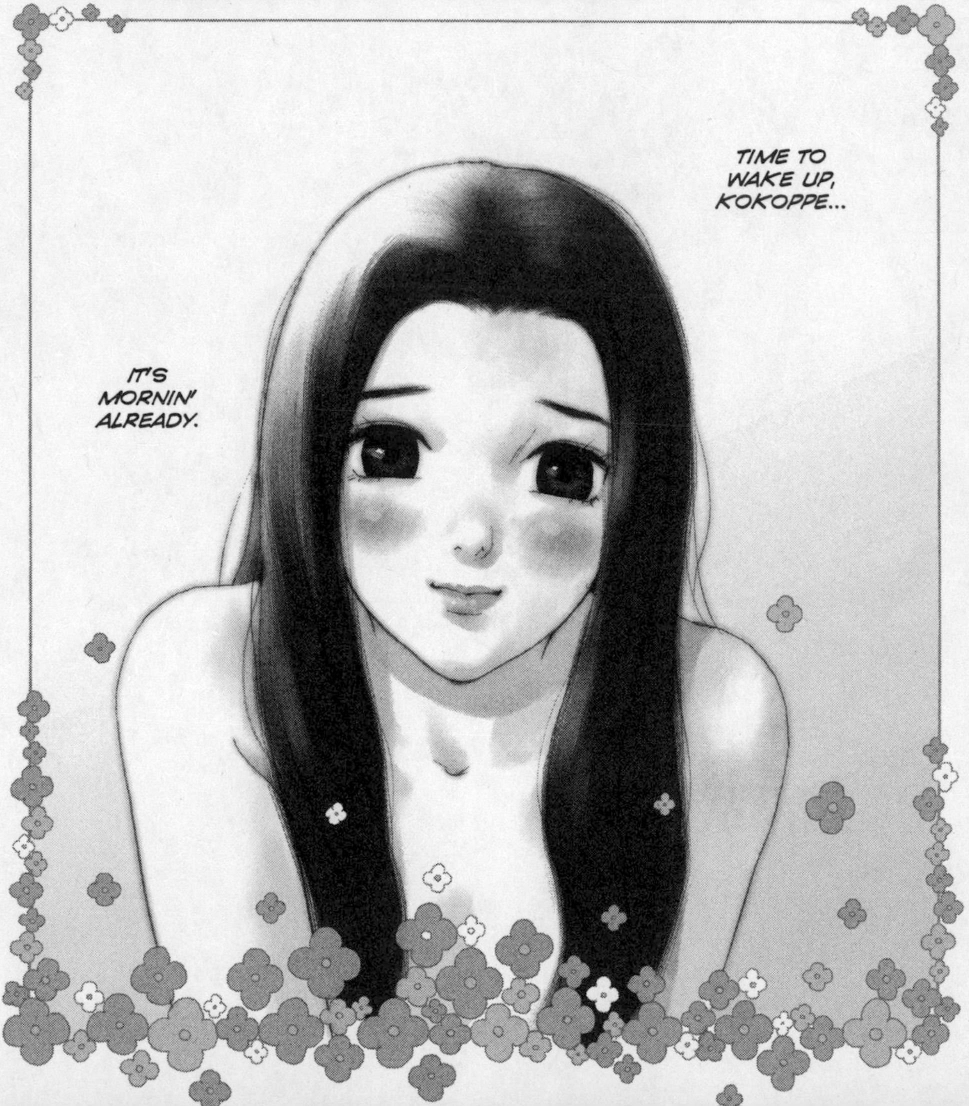
TIME TO WAKE UP, KOKOPPE...
IT'S MORNIN' ALREADY.

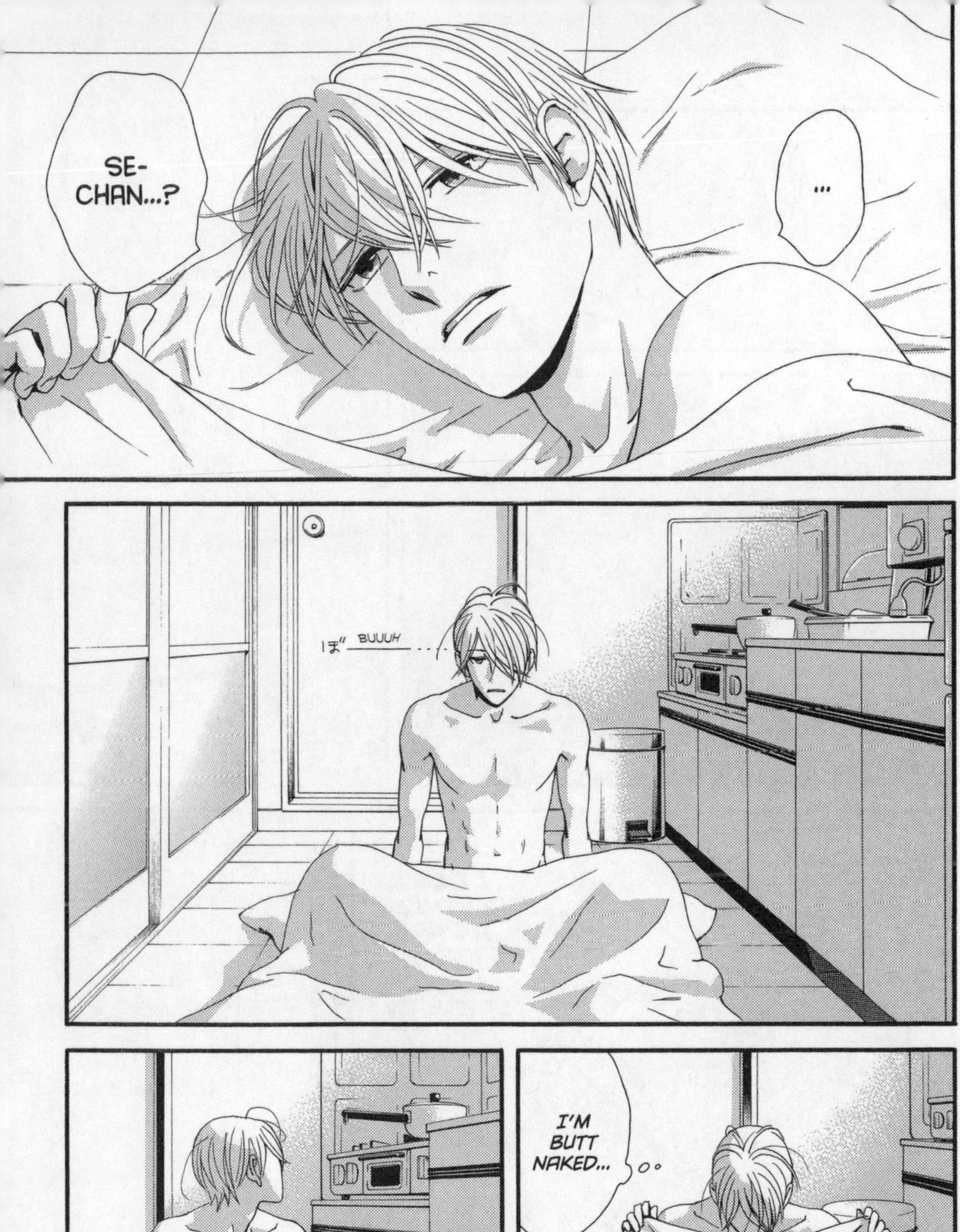
...
SE-CHAN...?
ぼ"
BUUUH
I'M BUTT NAKED...
AND... I SLEPT IN THE KITCHEN?

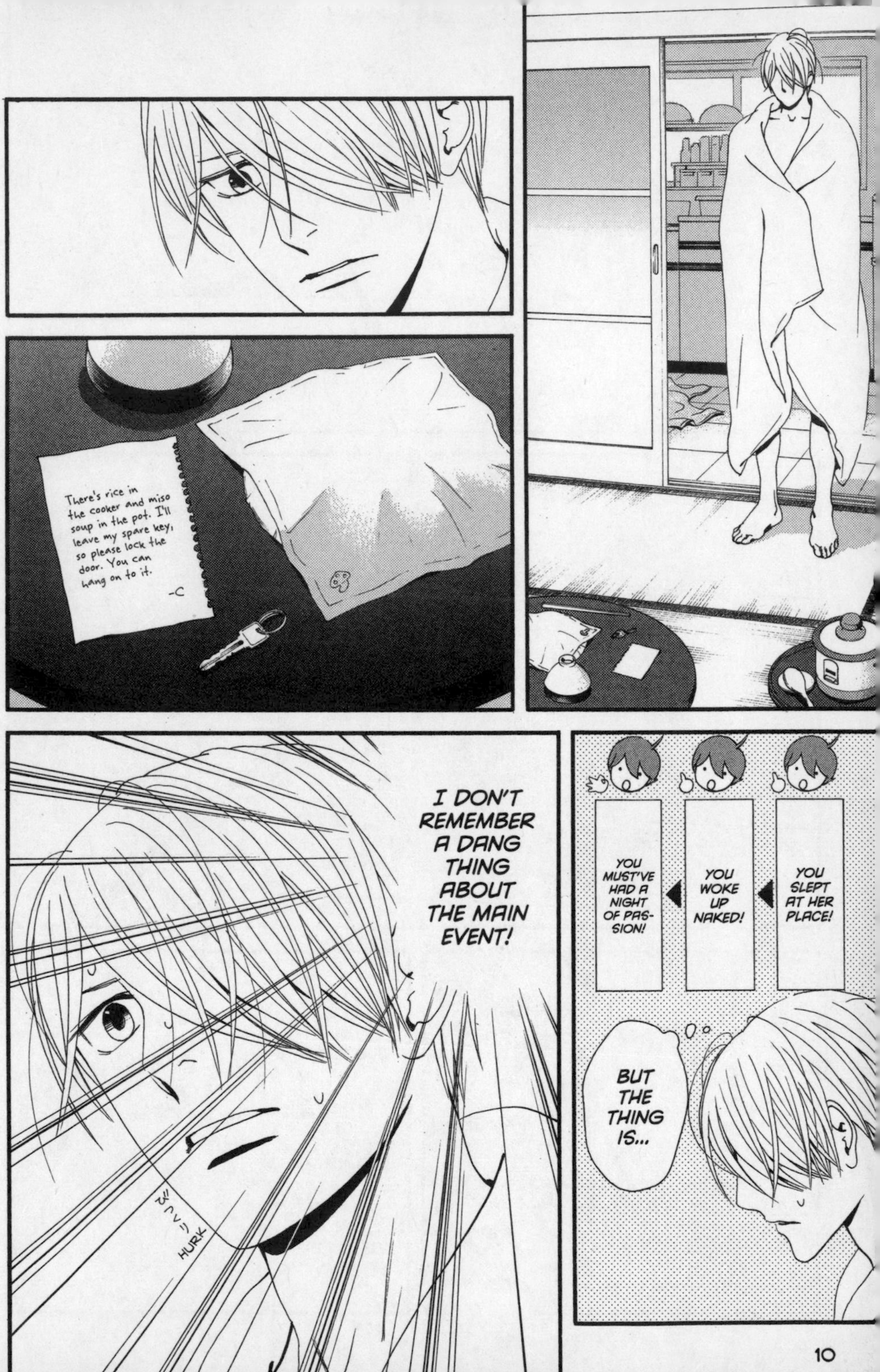
There's rice in the cooker and miso soup in the pot. I'll leave my spare key, so please lock the door. You can hang on to it.
-C
YOU SLEPT AT HER PLACE!
YOU WOKE UP NAKED!
YOU MUST'VE HAD A NIGHT OF PAS-SION!
BUT THE THING IS...
I DON'T REMEMBER A DANG THING ABOUT THE MAIN EVENT!
びっくり
HURK

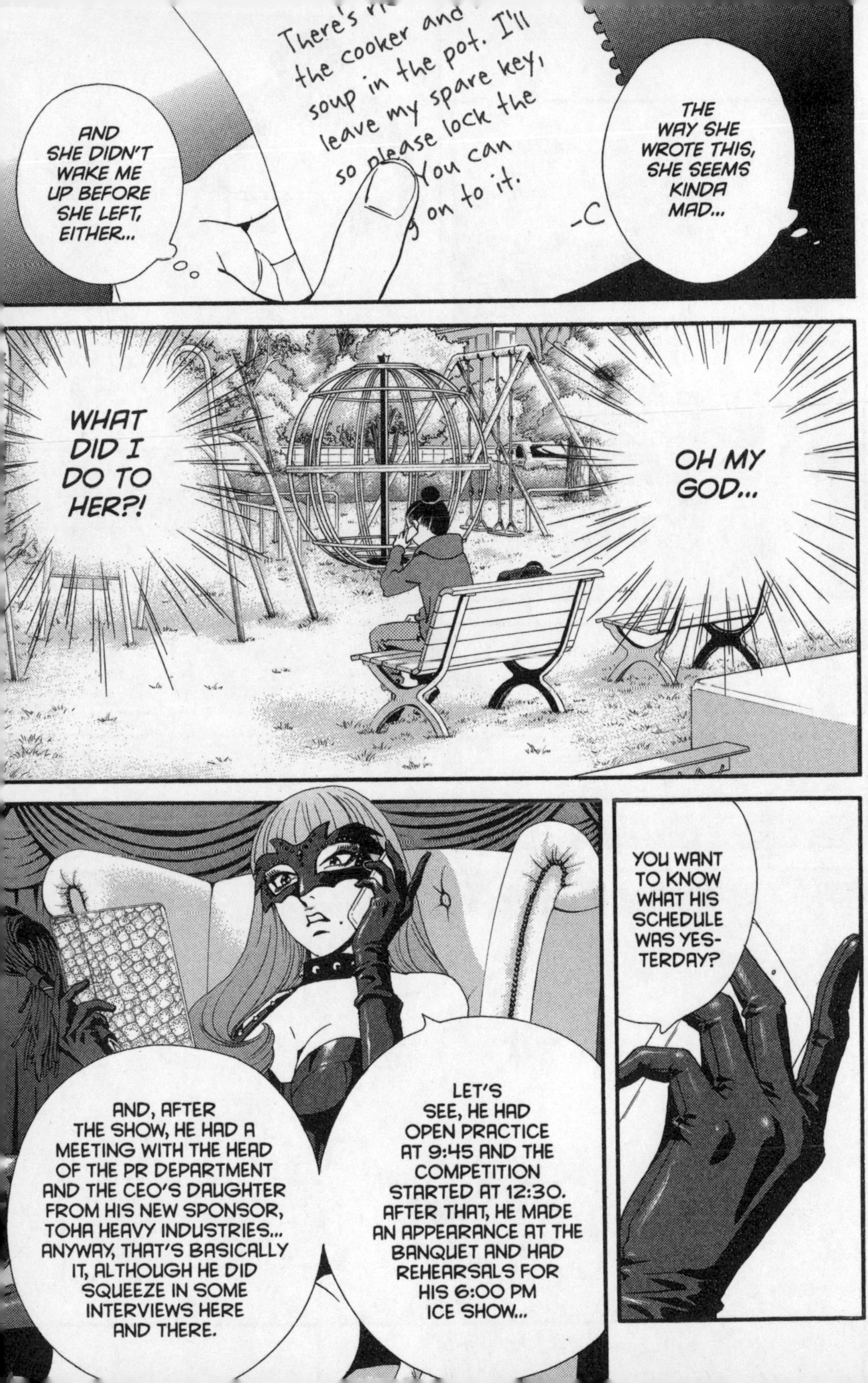
There's
the cooker and
soup in the pot. I'll
leave my spare key,
so please lock the
You can
on to it.
-C
THE WAY SHE WROTE THIS, SHE SEEMS KINDA MAD...
AND SHE DIDN'T WAKE ME UP BEFORE SHE LEFT, EITHER...
OH MY GOD...
WHAT DID I DO TO HER?!
YOU WANT TO KNOW WHAT HIS SCHEDULE WAS YES-TERDAY?
LET'S SEE, HE HAD OPEN PRACTICE AT 9:45 AND THE COMPETITION STARTED AT 12:30. AFTER THAT, HE MADE AN APPEARANCE AT THE BANQUET AND HAD REHEARSALS FOR HIS 6:00 PM ICE SHOW...
AND, AFTER THE SHOW, HE HAD A MEETING WITH THE HEAD OF THE PR DEPARTMENT AND THE CEO'S DAUGHTER FROM HIS NEW SPONSOR, TOHA HEAVY INDUSTRIES... ANYWAY, THAT'S BASICALLY IT, ALTHOUGH HE DID SQUEEZE IN SOME INTERVIEWS HERE AND THERE.

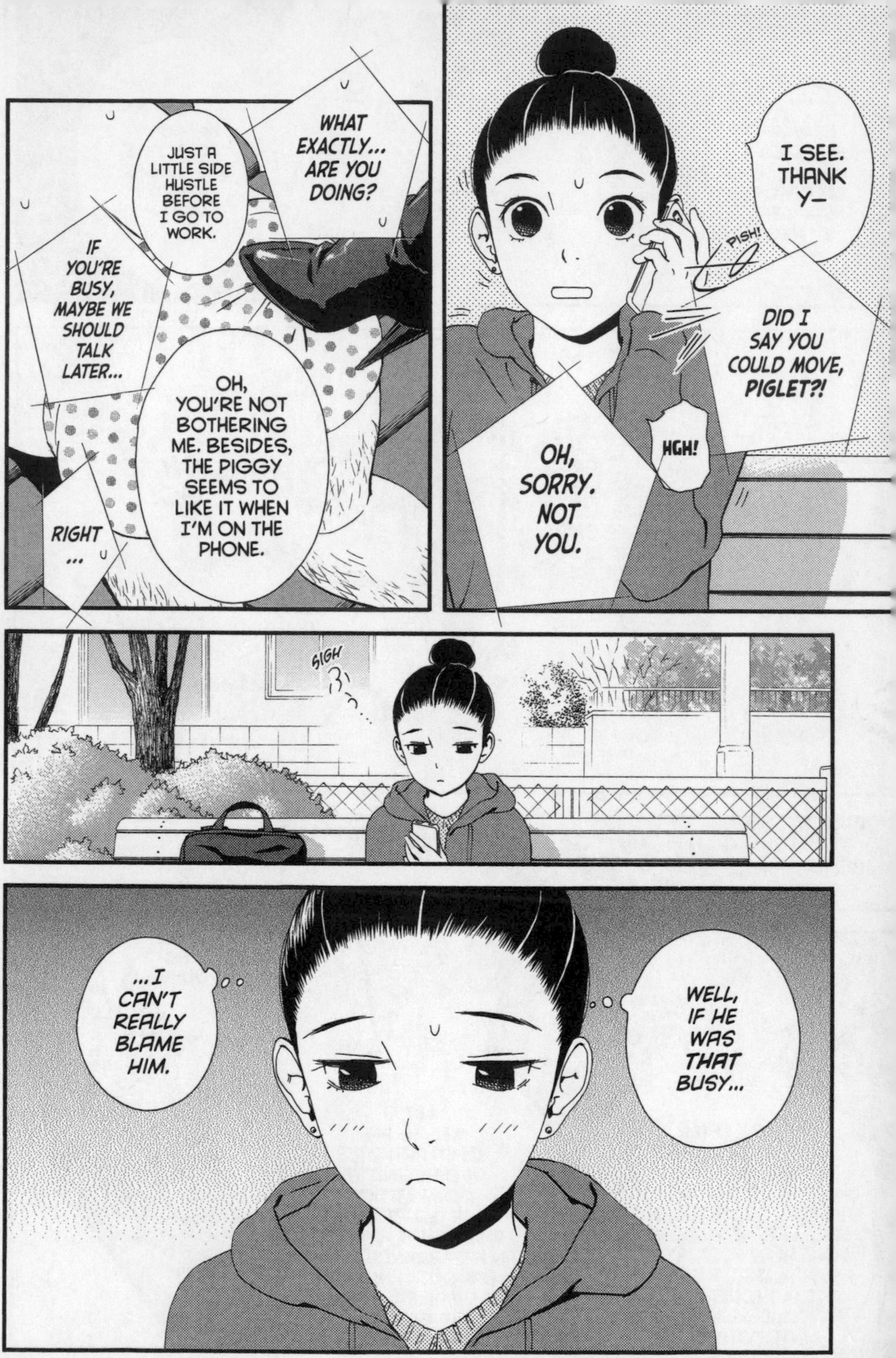
I SEE. THANK Y—
PISH!
DID I SAY YOU COULD MOVE, PIGLET?!
HGH!
OH, SORRY. NOT YOU.
WHAT EXACTLY... ARE YOU DOING?
JUST A LITTLE SIDE HUSTLE BEFORE I GO TO WORK.
IF YOU'RE BUSY, MAYBE WE SHOULD TALK LATER...
OH, YOU'RE NOT BOTHERING ME. BESIDES, THE PIGGY SEEMS TO LIKE IT WHEN I'M ON THE PHONE.
RIGHT...
SIGH
WELL, IF HE WAS THAT BUSY...
...I CAN'T REALLY BLAME HIM.

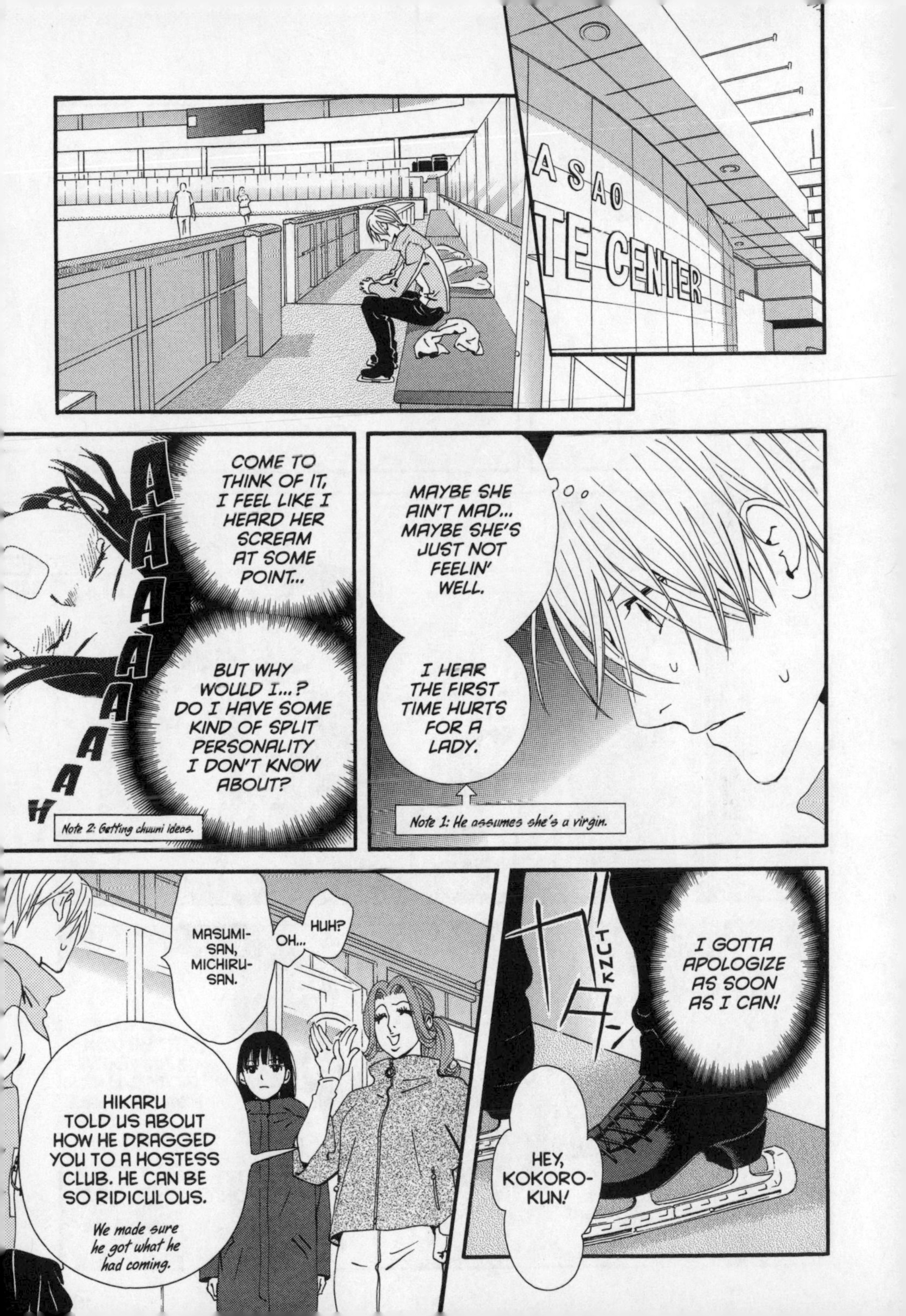
ASAO
TE CENTER
MAYBE SHE AIN'T MAD... MAYBE SHE'S JUST NOT FEELIN' WELL.
I HEAR THE FIRST TIME HURTS FOR A LADY.
Note 1: He assumes she's a virgin.
AAAAAAAH
COME TO THINK OF IT, I FEEL LIKE I HEARD HER SCREAM AT SOME POINT...
BUT WHY WOULD I...? DO I HAVE SOME KIND OF SPLIT PERSONALITY I DON'T KNOW ABOUT?
Note 2: Getting chuuni ideas.
I GOTTA APOLOGIZE AS SOON AS I CAN!
TUNK
HEY, KOKORO-KUN!
HUH?
OH...
MASUMI-SAN, MICHIRU-SAN.
HIKARU TOLD US ABOUT HOW HE DRAGGED YOU TO A HOSTESS CLUB. HE CAN BE SO RIDICULOUS.
We made sure he got what he had coming.

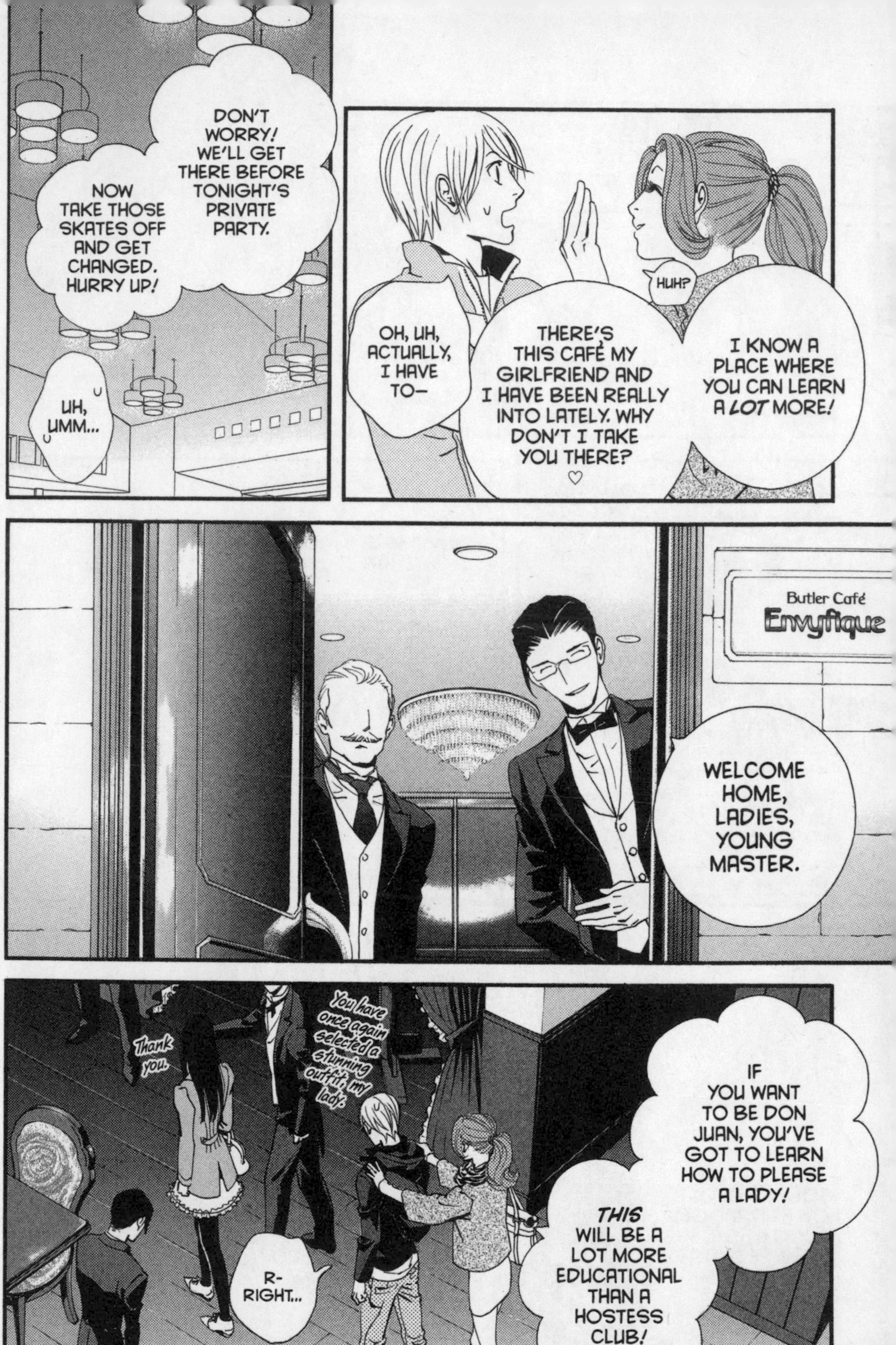
I KNOW A PLACE WHERE YOU CAN LEARN A *LOT* MORE!
HUH?
THERE'S THIS CAFÉ MY GIRLFRIEND AND I HAVE BEEN REALLY INTO LATELY. WHY DON'T I TAKE YOU THERE? ♡
OH, UH, ACTUALLY, I HAVE TO—
DON'T WORRY! WE'LL GET THERE BEFORE TONIGHT'S PRIVATE PARTY.
NOW TAKE THOSE SKATES OFF AND GET CHANGED. HURRY UP!
UH, UMM...
Butler Café
Envyfique
WELCOME HOME, LADIES, YOUNG MASTER.
IF YOU WANT TO BE DON JUAN, YOU'VE GOT TO LEARN HOW TO PLEASE A LADY!
THIS WILL BE A LOT MORE EDUCATIONAL THAN A HOSTESS CLUB! ♡
You have once again selected a stunning outfit, my lady.
Thank you.
R-RIGHT...

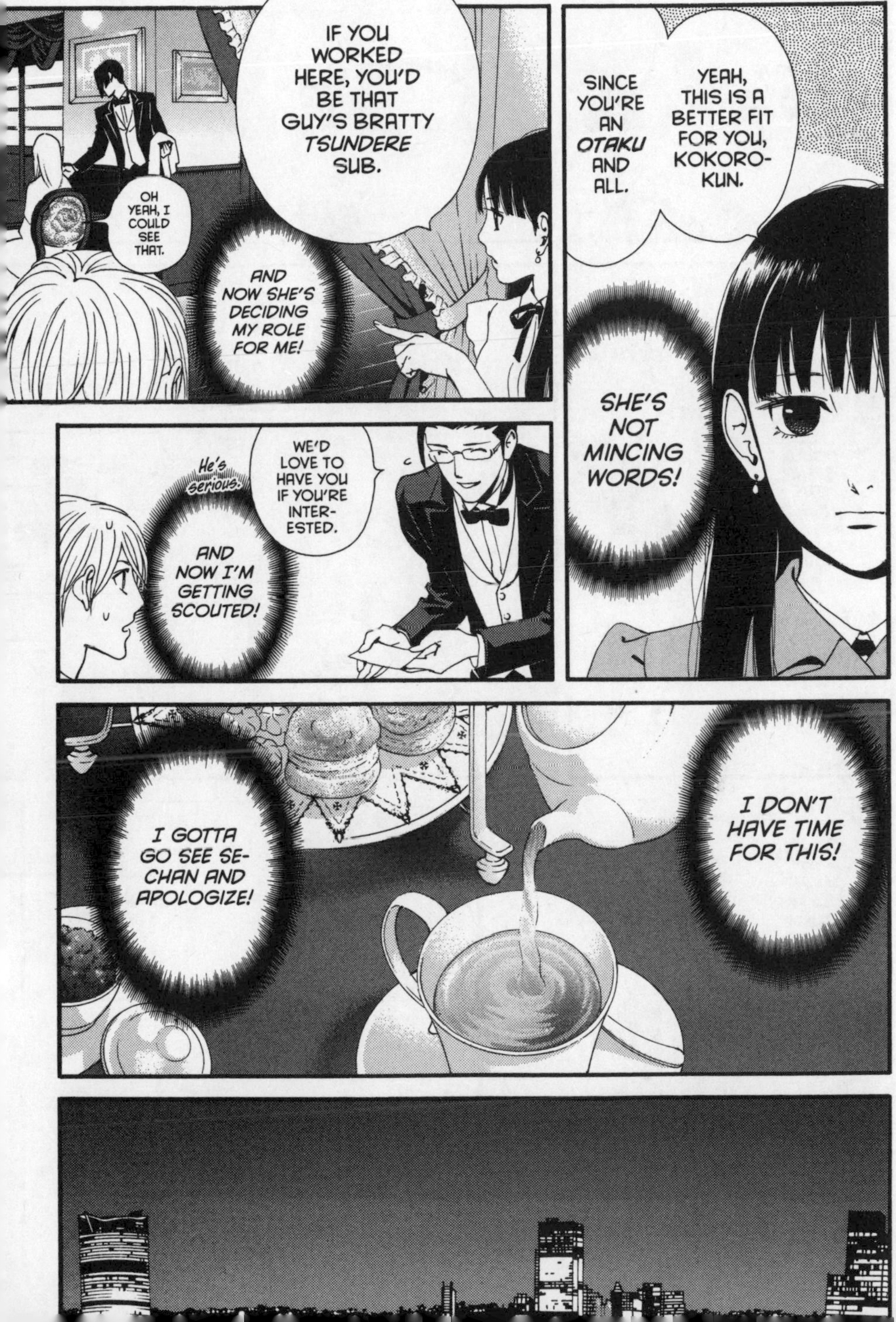
YEAH, THIS IS A BETTER FIT FOR YOU, KOKORO-KUN.
SINCE YOU'RE AN OTAKU AND ALL.
SHE'S NOT MINCING WORDS!
IF YOU WORKED HERE, YOU'D BE THAT GUY'S BRATTY TSUNDERE SUB.
AND NOW SHE'S DECIDING MY ROLE FOR ME!
OH YEAH, I COULD SEE THAT.
WE'D LOVE TO HAVE YOU IF YOU'RE INTER-ESTED.
He's serious.
AND NOW I'M GETTING SCOUTED!
I DON'T HAVE TIME FOR THIS!
I GOTTA GO SEE SE-CHAN AND APOLOGIZE!

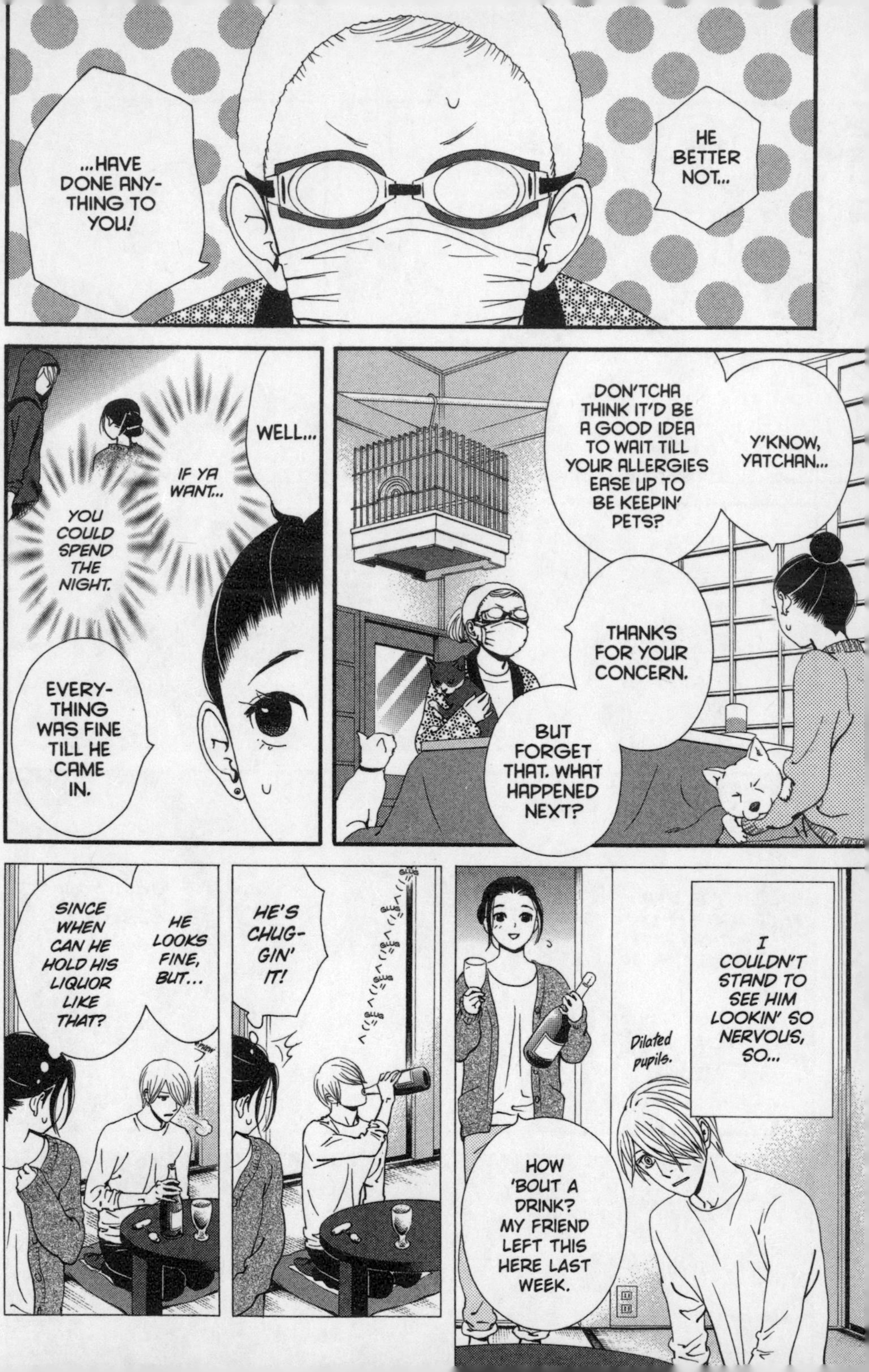
HE BETTER NOT...
...HAVE DONE ANY-THING TO YOU!
Y'KNOW, YATCHAN...
DON'TCHA THINK IT'D BE A GOOD IDEA TO WAIT TILL YOUR ALLERGIES EASE UP TO BE KEEPIN' PETS?
THANKS FOR YOUR CONCERN.
BUT FORGET THAT. WHAT HAPPENED NEXT?
WELL...
IF YA WANT...
YOU COULD SPEND THE NIGHT.
EVERY-THING WAS FINE TILL HE CAME IN.
I COULDN'T STAND TO SEE HIM LOOKIN' SO NERVOUS, SO...
Dilated pupils.
HOW 'BOUT A DRINK? MY FRIEND LEFT THIS HERE LAST WEEK.
GLUG
GLUG
GLUG
GLUG
GLUG
HE'S CHUG-GIN' IT!
HE LOOKS FINE, BUT...
SINCE WHEN CAN HE HOLD HIS LIQUOR LIKE THAT?

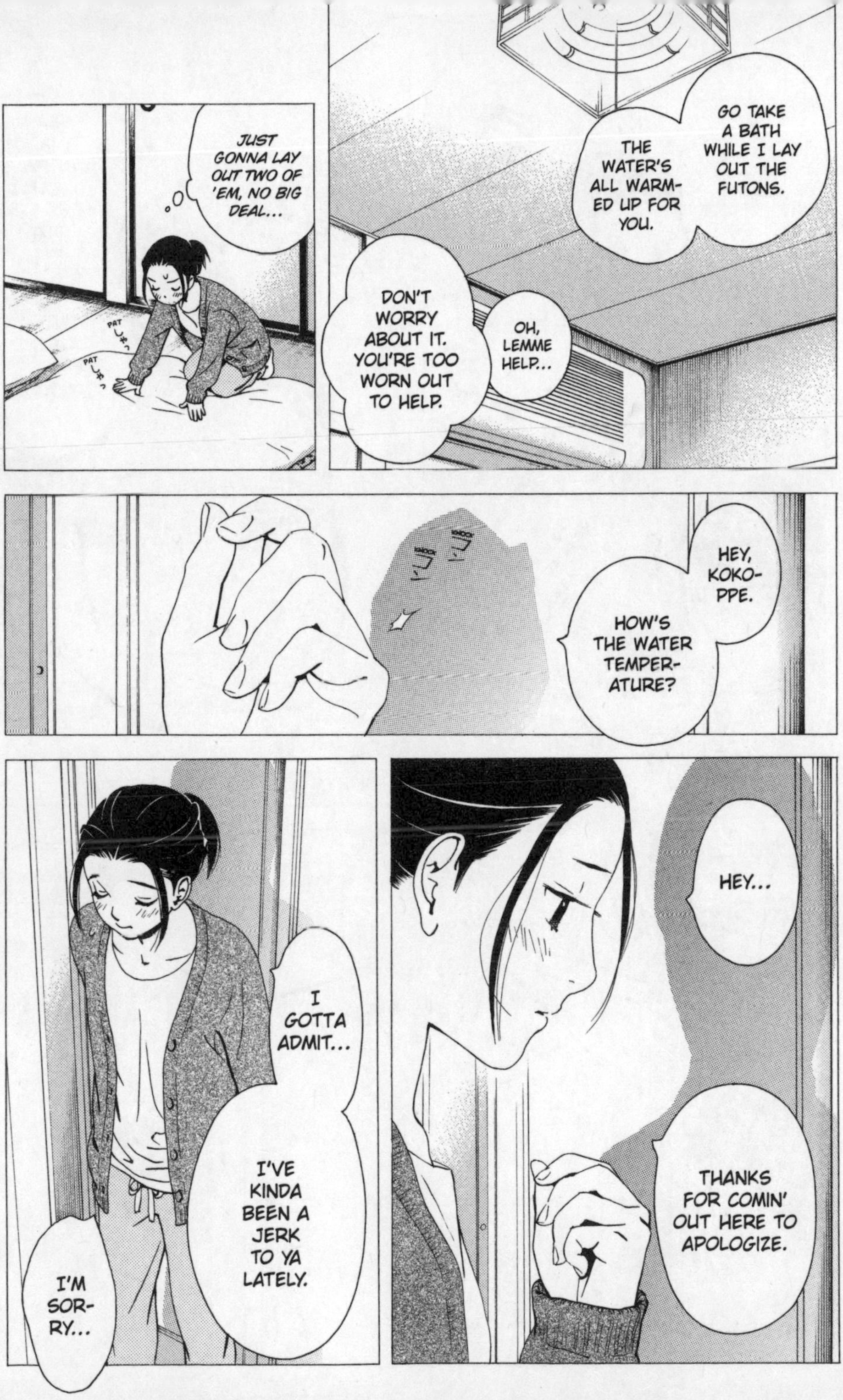
GO TAKE A BATH WHILE I LAY OUT THE FUTONS.
THE WATER'S ALL WARM-ED UP FOR YOU.
OH, LEMME HELP...
DON'T WORRY ABOUT IT. YOU'RE TOO WORN OUT TO HELP.
JUST GONNA LAY OUT TWO OF 'EM, NO BIG DEAL...
PAT
PAT
HEY, KOKO-PPE.
KNOCK
KNOCK
HOW'S THE WATER TEMPER-ATURE?
HEY...
THANKS FOR COMIN' OUT HERE TO APOLOGIZE.
I GOTTA ADMIT...
I'VE KINDA BEEN A JERK TO YA LATELY.
I'M SOR-RY...

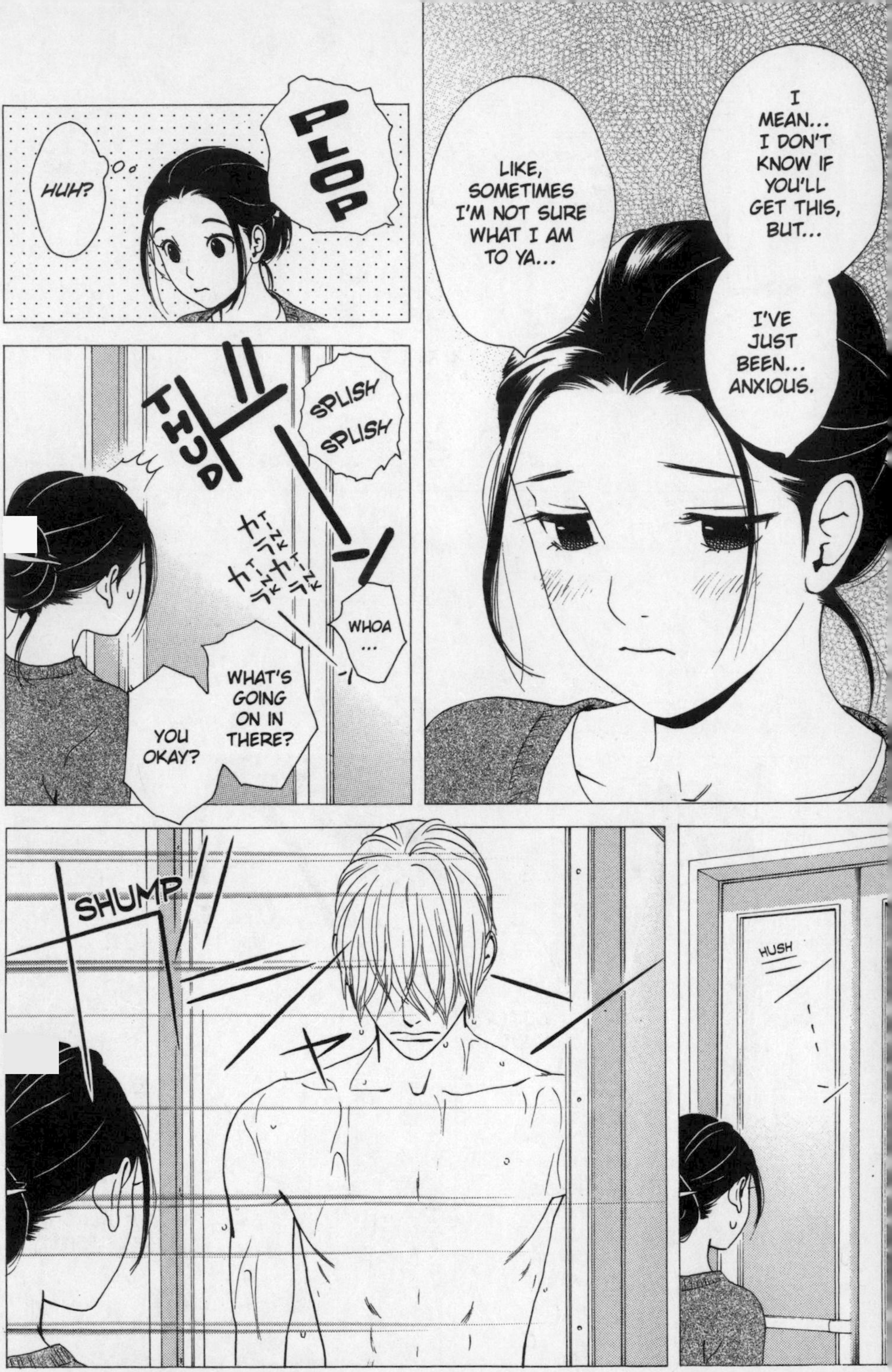
I MEAN... I DON'T KNOW IF YOU'LL GET THIS, BUT...
LIKE, SOMETIMES I'M NOT SURE WHAT I AM TO YA...
I'VE JUST BEEN... ANXIOUS.
PLOP
HUH?
THUD
SPLISH SPLISH
WHOA ...
WHAT'S GOING ON IN THERE?
YOU OKAY?
HUSH
SHUMP

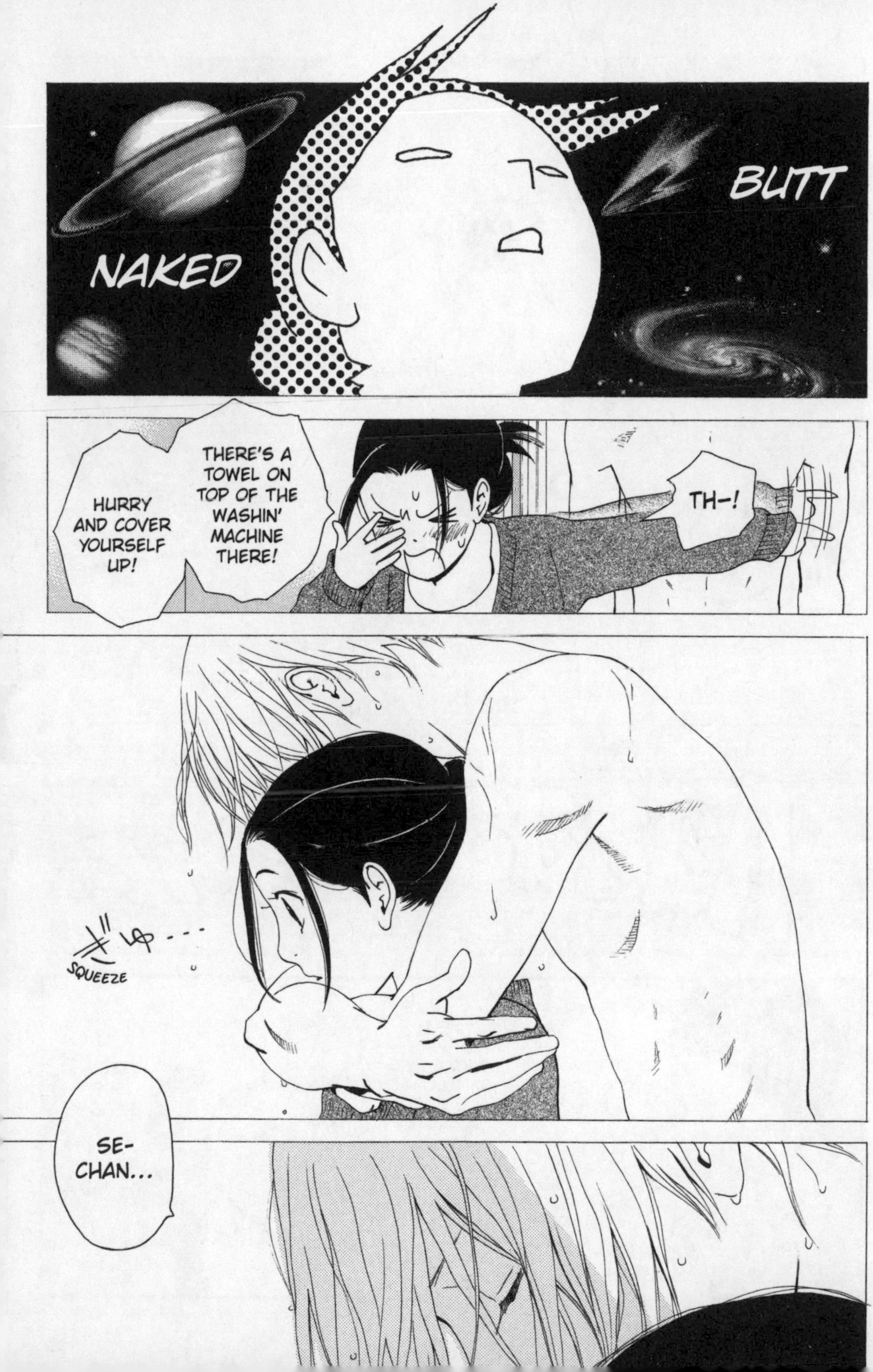

BUTT
NAKED
TH-!
THERE'S A TOWEL ON TOP OF THE WASHIN' MACHINE THERE!
HURRY AND COVER YOURSELF UP!
ぎゅ…
SQUEEZE
SE-CHAN...

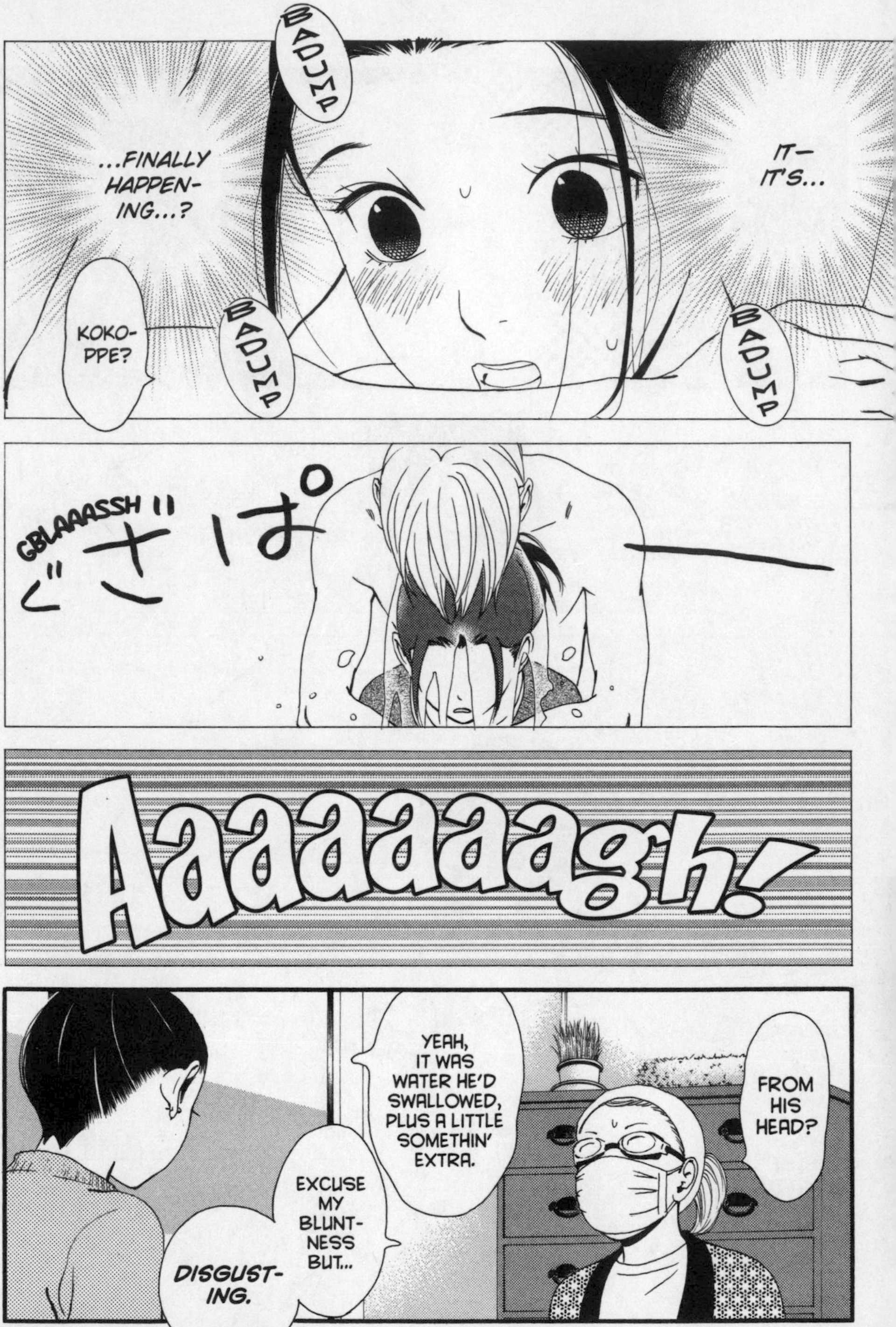
BADUMP
IT— IT'S...
...FINALLY HAPPEN-ING...?
BADUMP
BADUMP
KOKOPPE?
GBLAAASSH!!
ぐざぱー
Aaaaaaaagh!
FROM HIS HEAD?
YEAH, IT WAS WATER HE'D SWALLOWED, PLUS A LITTLE SOMETHIN' EXTRA.
EXCUSE MY BLUNT-NESS BUT...
DISGUST-ING.

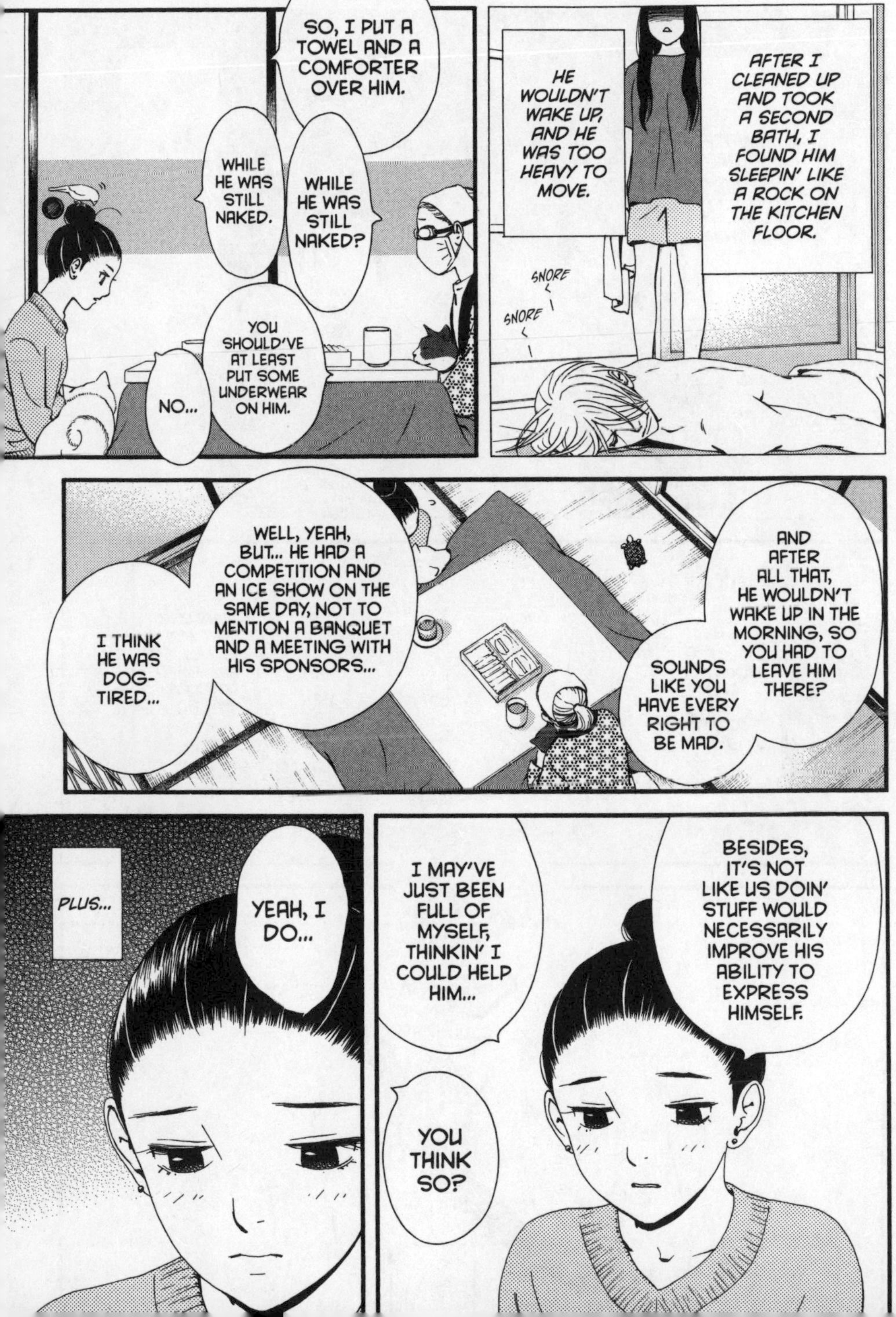
AFTER I CLEANED UP AND TOOK A SECOND BATH, I FOUND HIM SLEEPIN' LIKE A ROCK ON THE KITCHEN FLOOR.
HE WOULDN'T WAKE UP, AND HE WAS TOO HEAVY TO MOVE.
SNORE
SNORE
SO, I PUT A TOWEL AND A COMFORTER OVER HIM.
WHILE HE WAS STILL NAKED?
WHILE HE WAS STILL NAKED.
YOU SHOULD'VE AT LEAST PUT SOME UNDERWEAR ON HIM.
NO...
AND AFTER ALL THAT, HE WOULDN'T WAKE UP IN THE MORNING, SO YOU HAD TO LEAVE HIM THERE?
SOUNDS LIKE YOU HAVE EVERY RIGHT TO BE MAD.
WELL, YEAH, BUT... HE HAD A COMPETITION AND AN ICE SHOW ON THE SAME DAY, NOT TO MENTION A BANQUET AND A MEETING WITH HIS SPONSORS...
I THINK HE WAS DOG-TIRED...
BESIDES, IT'S NOT LIKE US DOIN' STUFF WOULD NECESSARILY IMPROVE HIS ABILITY TO EXPRESS HIMSELF.
I MAY'VE JUST BEEN FULL OF MYSELF, THINKIN' I COULD HELP HIM...
YOU THINK SO?
YEAH, I DO...
PLUS...

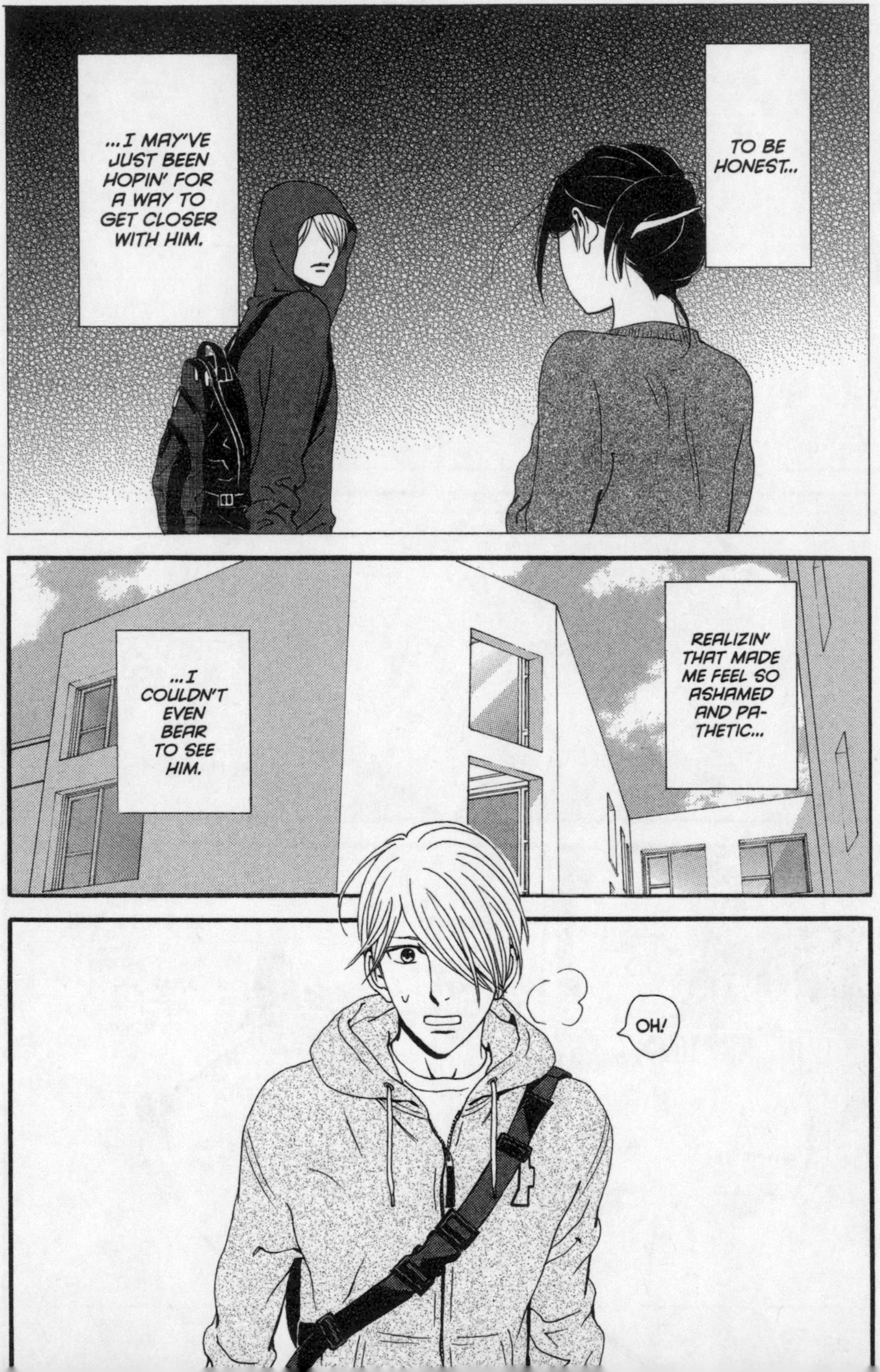
TO BE HONEST...
...I MAY'VE JUST BEEN HOPIN' FOR A WAY TO GET CLOSER WITH HIM.
REALIZIN' THAT MADE ME FEEL SO ASHAMED AND PA-THETIC...
...I COULDN'T EVEN BEAR TO SEE HIM.
OH!

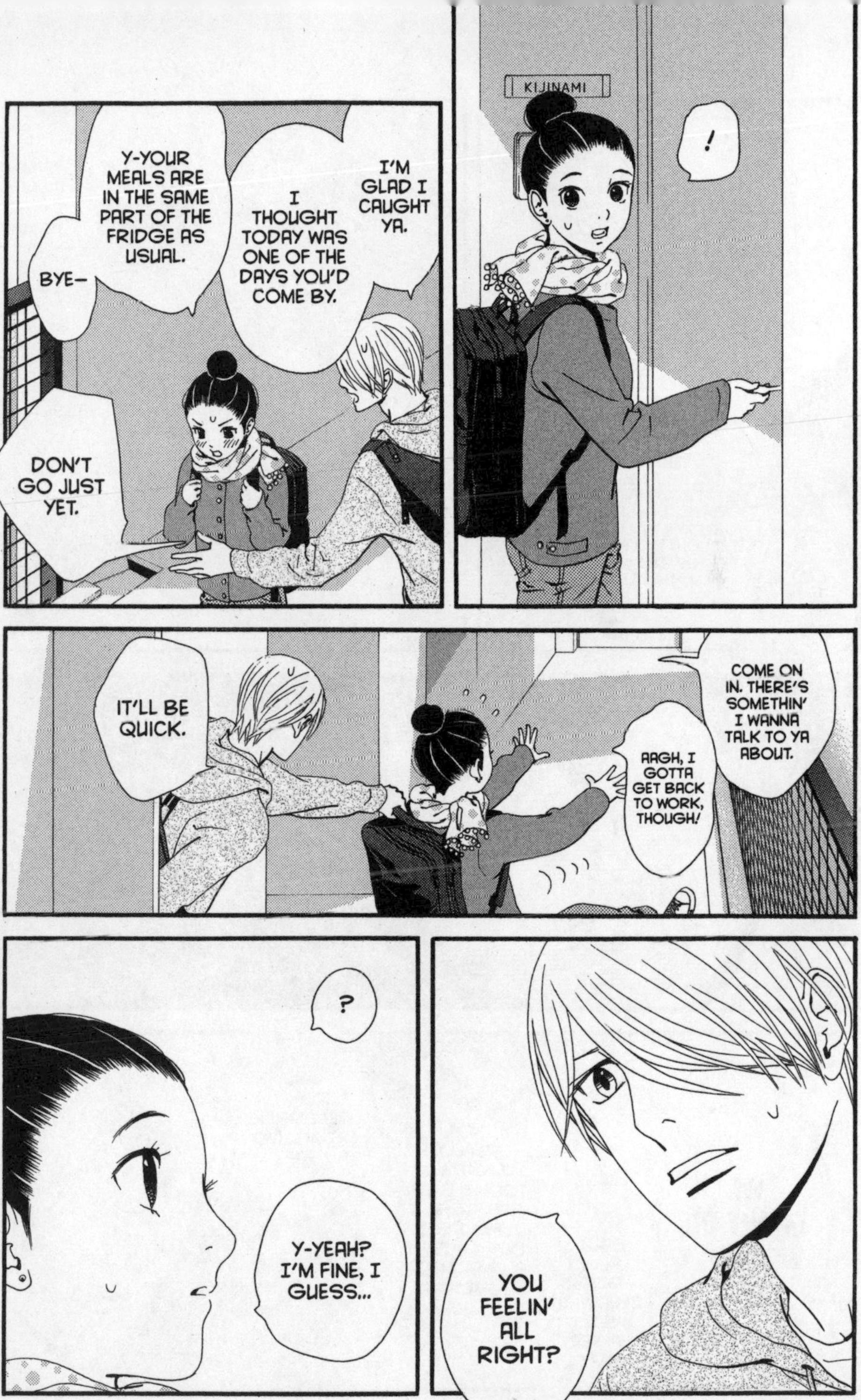
KIJINAMI
!
I'M GLAD I CAUGHT YA.
I THOUGHT TODAY WAS ONE OF THE DAYS YOU'D COME BY.
Y-YOUR MEALS ARE IN THE SAME PART OF THE FRIDGE AS USUAL.
BYE—
DON'T GO JUST YET.
COME ON IN. THERE'S SOMETHIN' I WANNA TALK TO YA ABOUT.
ARGH, I GOTTA GET BACK TO WORK, THOUGH!
IT'LL BE QUICK.
YOU FEELIN' ALL RIGHT?
?
Y-YEAH? I'M FINE, I GUESS...

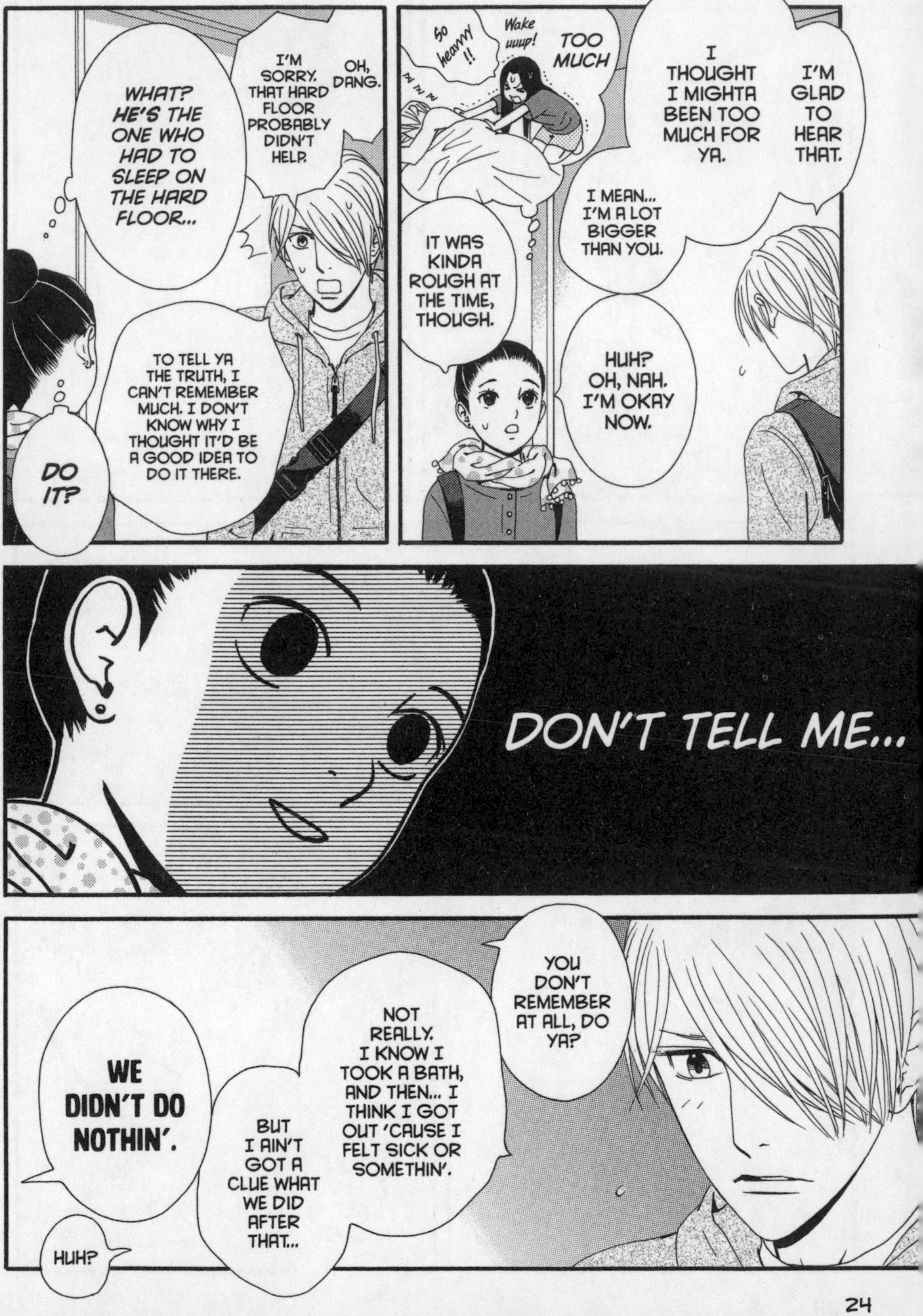
I'M GLAD TO HEAR THAT.
I THOUGHT I MIGHTA BEEN TOO MUCH FOR YA.
I MEAN... I'M A LOT BIGGER THAN YOU.
HUH? OH, NAH. I'M OKAY NOW.
IT WAS KINDA ROUGH AT THE TIME, THOUGH.
TOO MUCH
Wake uuup!
So heavvvy !!
OH, DANG.
I'M SORRY. THAT HARD FLOOR PROBABLY DIDN'T HELP.
WHAT? HE'S THE ONE WHO HAD TO SLEEP ON THE HARD FLOOR...
TO TELL YA THE TRUTH, I CAN'T REMEMBER MUCH. I DON'T KNOW WHY I THOUGHT IT'D BE A GOOD IDEA TO DO IT THERE.
DO IT?
DON'T TELL ME...
YOU DON'T REMEMBER AT ALL, DO YA?
NOT REALLY. I KNOW I TOOK A BATH, AND THEN... I THINK I GOT OUT 'CAUSE I FELT SICK OR SOMETHIN'.
BUT I AIN'T GOT A CLUE WHAT WE DID AFTER THAT...
WE DIDN'T DO NOTHIN'.
HUH?

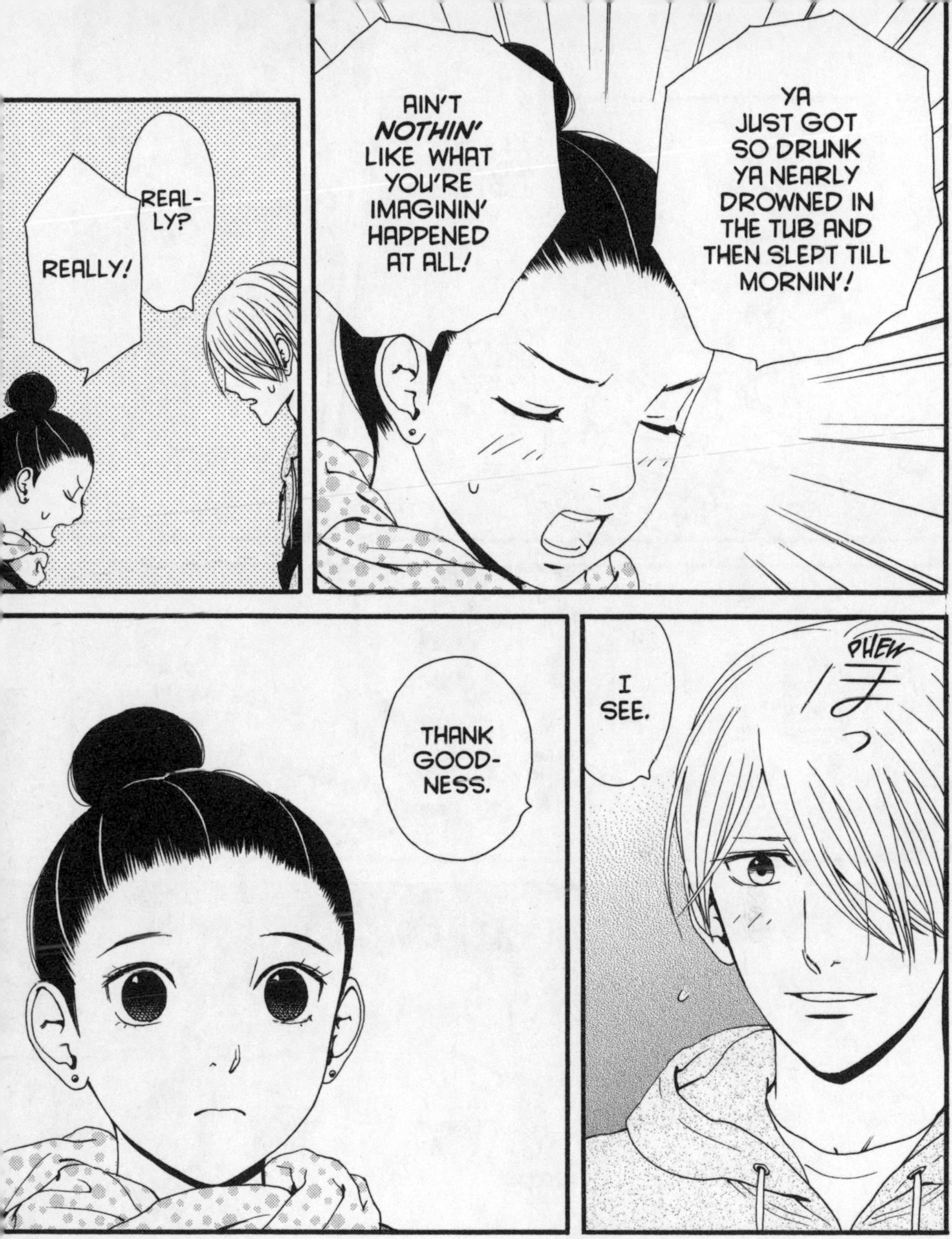
YA JUST GOT SO DRUNK YA NEARLY DROWNED IN THE TUB AND THEN SLEPT TILL MORNIN'!
AIN'T *NOTHIN'* LIKE WHAT YOU'RE IMAGININ' HAPPENED AT ALL!
REAL-LY?
REALLY!
PHEW
ほっ
I SEE.
THANK GOOD-NESS.
SO I DIDN'T FORGET IT. ♡
And I don't have a split personality.
"THANK GOOD-NESS"...?

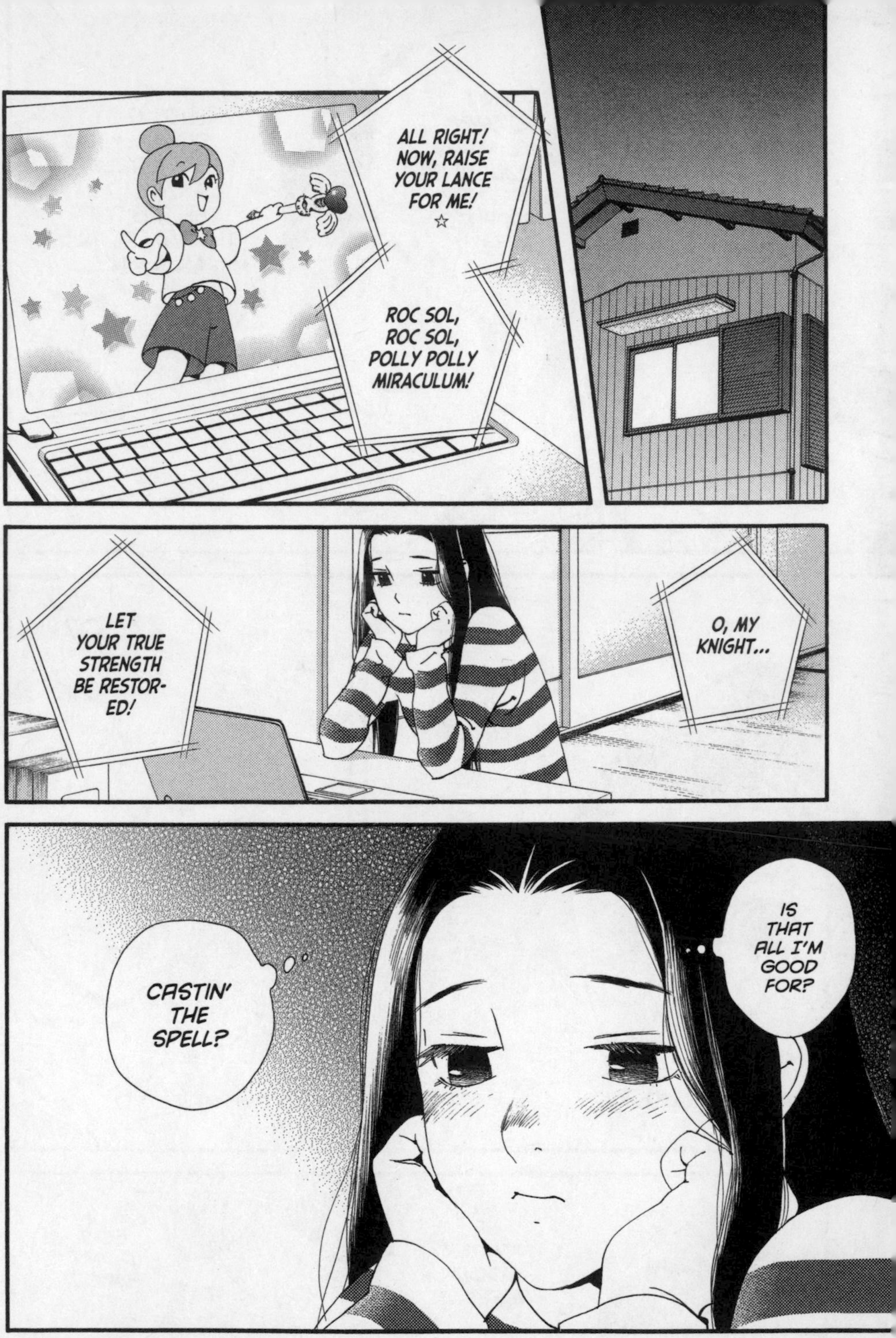
ALL RIGHT! NOW, RAISE YOUR LANCE FOR ME! ☆
ROC SOL, ROC SOL, POLLY POLLY MIRACULUM!
O, MY KNIGHT...
LET YOUR TRUE STRENGTH BE RESTOR-ED!
IS THAT ALL I'M GOOD FOR?
CASTIN' THE SPELL?

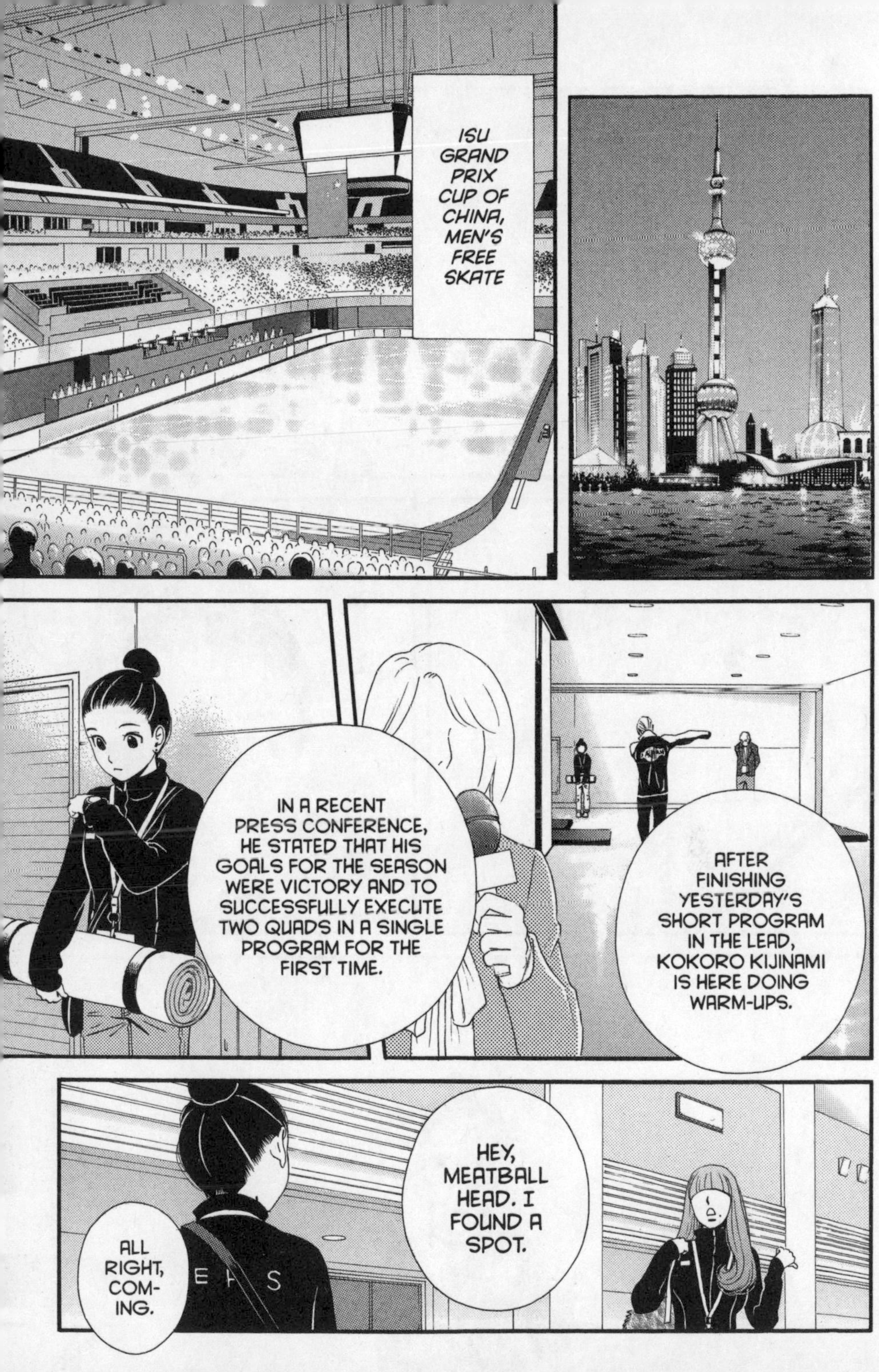
ISU GRAND PRIX CUP OF CHINA, MEN'S FREE SKATE
AFTER FINISHING YESTERDAY'S SHORT PROGRAM IN THE LEAD, KOKORO KIJINAMI IS HERE DOING WARM-UPS.
IN A RECENT PRESS CONFERENCE, HE STATED THAT HIS GOALS FOR THE SEASON WERE VICTORY AND TO SUCCESSFULLY EXECUTE TWO QUADS IN A SINGLE PROGRAM FOR THE FIRST TIME.
HEY, MEATBALL HEAD. I FOUND A SPOT.
ALL RIGHT, COM-ING.

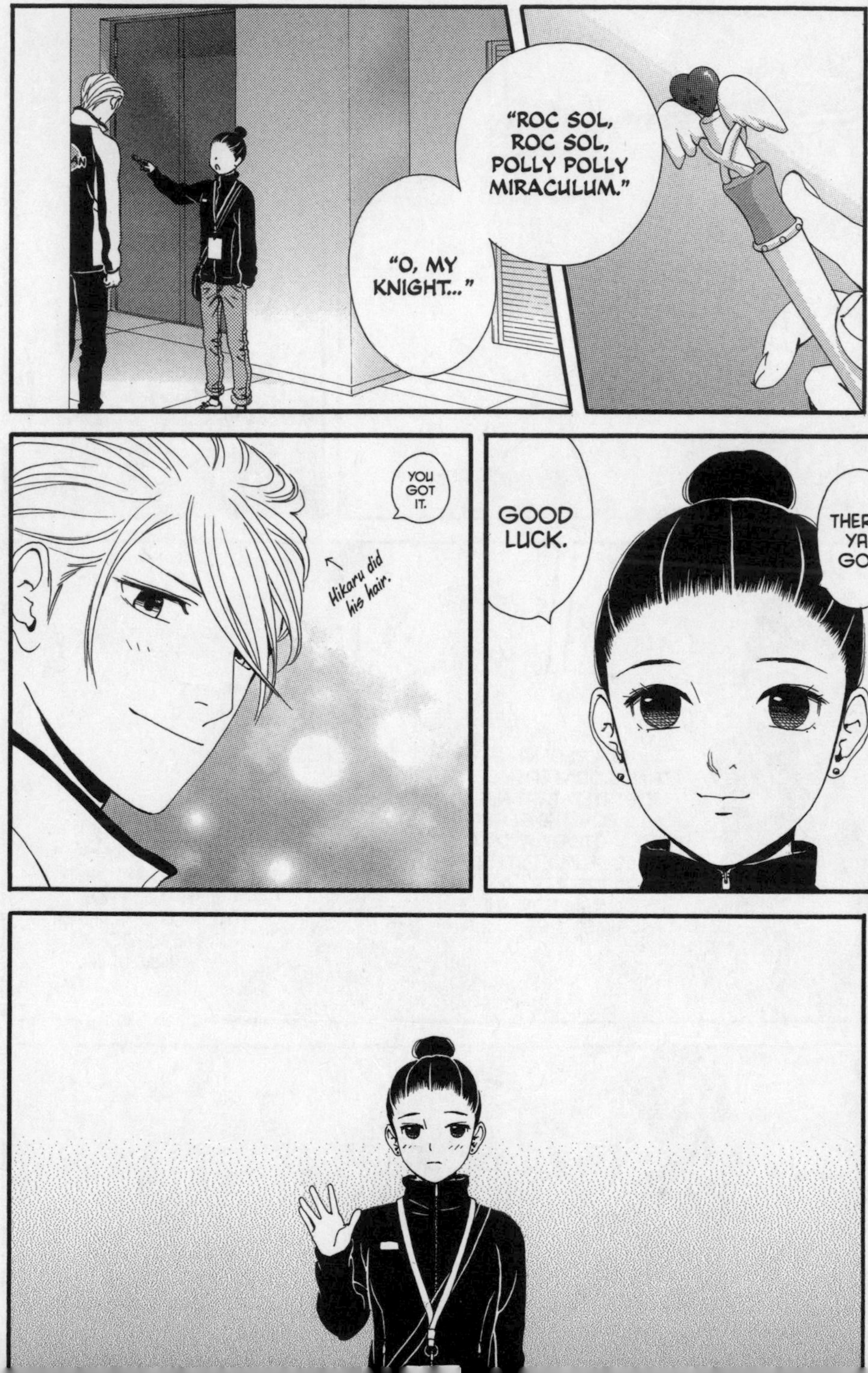
"ROC SOL, ROC SOL, POLLY POLLY MIRACULUM."
"O, MY KNIGHT..."
THERE YA GO.
GOOD LUCK.
YOU GOT IT.
Hikaru did his hair.

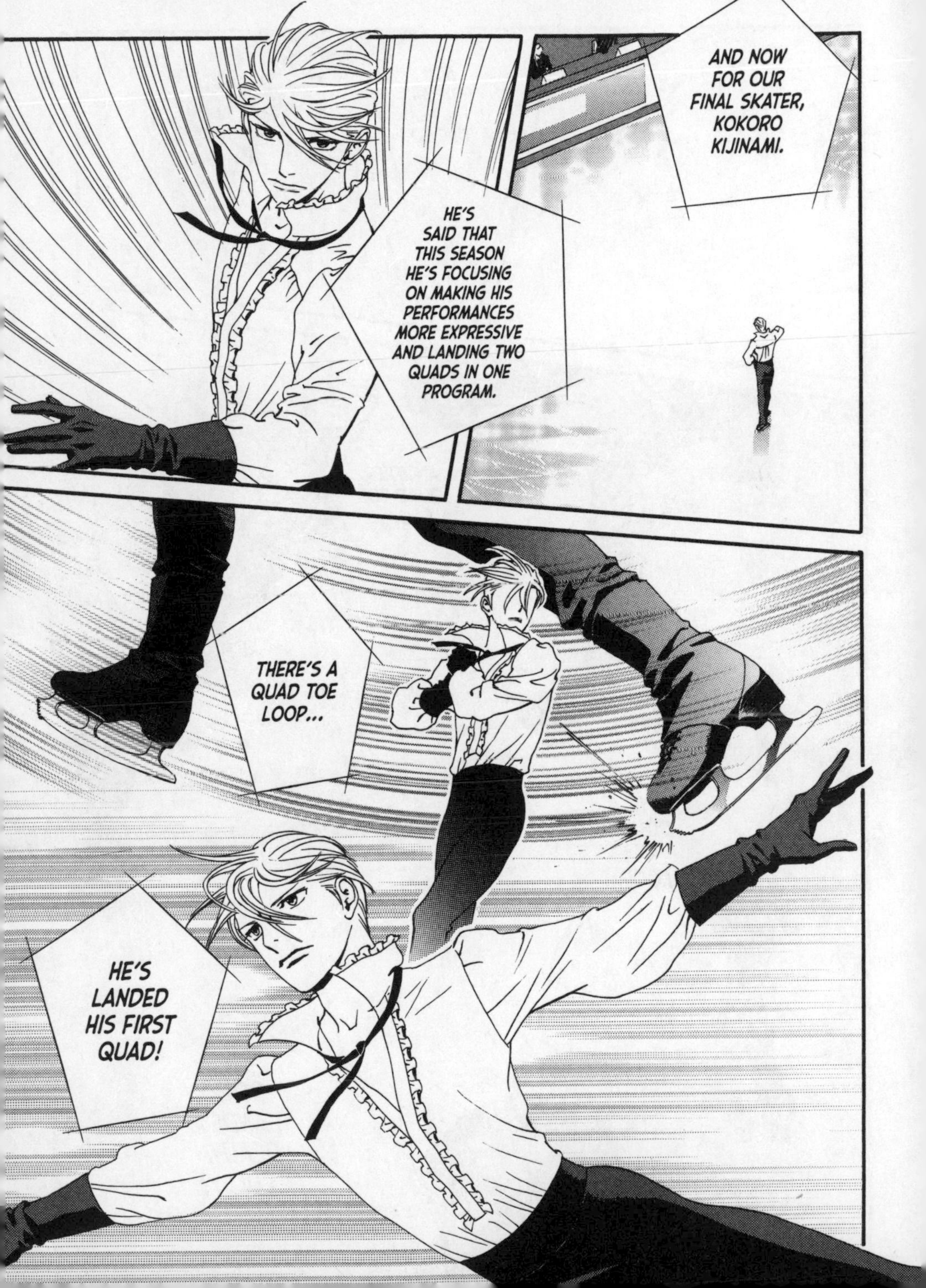
AND NOW FOR OUR FINAL SKATER, KOKORO KIJINAMI.
HE'S SAID THAT THIS SEASON HE'S FOCUSING ON MAKING HIS PERFORMANCES MORE EXPRESSIVE AND LANDING TWO QUADS IN ONE PROGRAM.
THERE'S A QUAD TOE LOOP...
HE'S LANDED HIS FIRST QUAD!

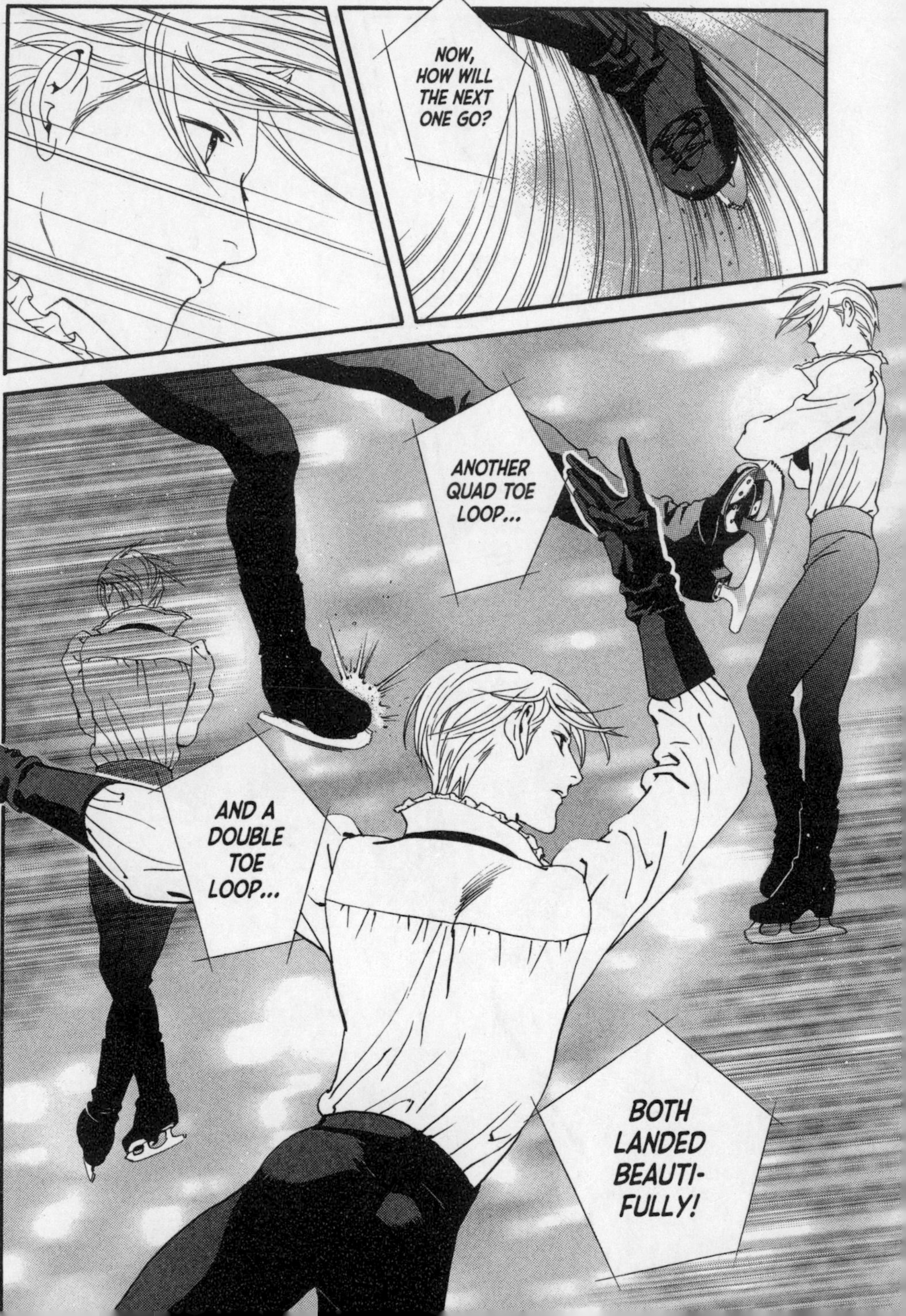
NOW, HOW WILL THE NEXT ONE GO?
ANOTHER QUAD TOE LOOP...
AND A DOUBLE TOE LOOP...
BOTH LANDED BEAUTI-FULLY!

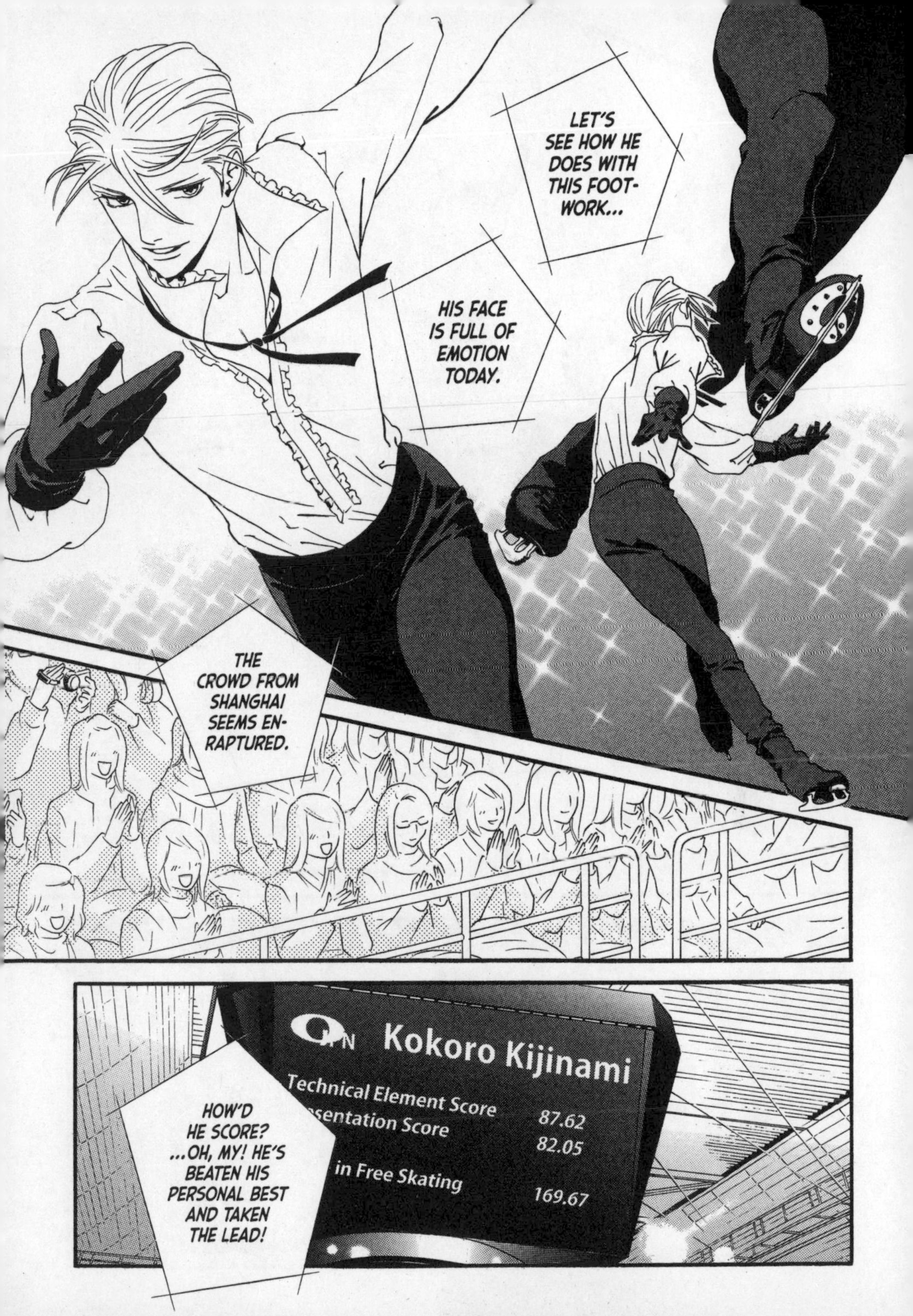
LET'S SEE HOW HE DOES WITH THIS FOOT-WORK...
HIS FACE IS FULL OF EMOTION TODAY.
THE CROWD FROM SHANGHAI SEEMS EN-RAPTURED.
Kokoro Kijinami
Technical Element Score
sentation Score
in Free Skating
87.62
82.05
169.67
HOW'D HE SCORE? ...OH, MY! HE'S BEATEN HIS PERSONAL BEST AND TAKEN THE LEAD!

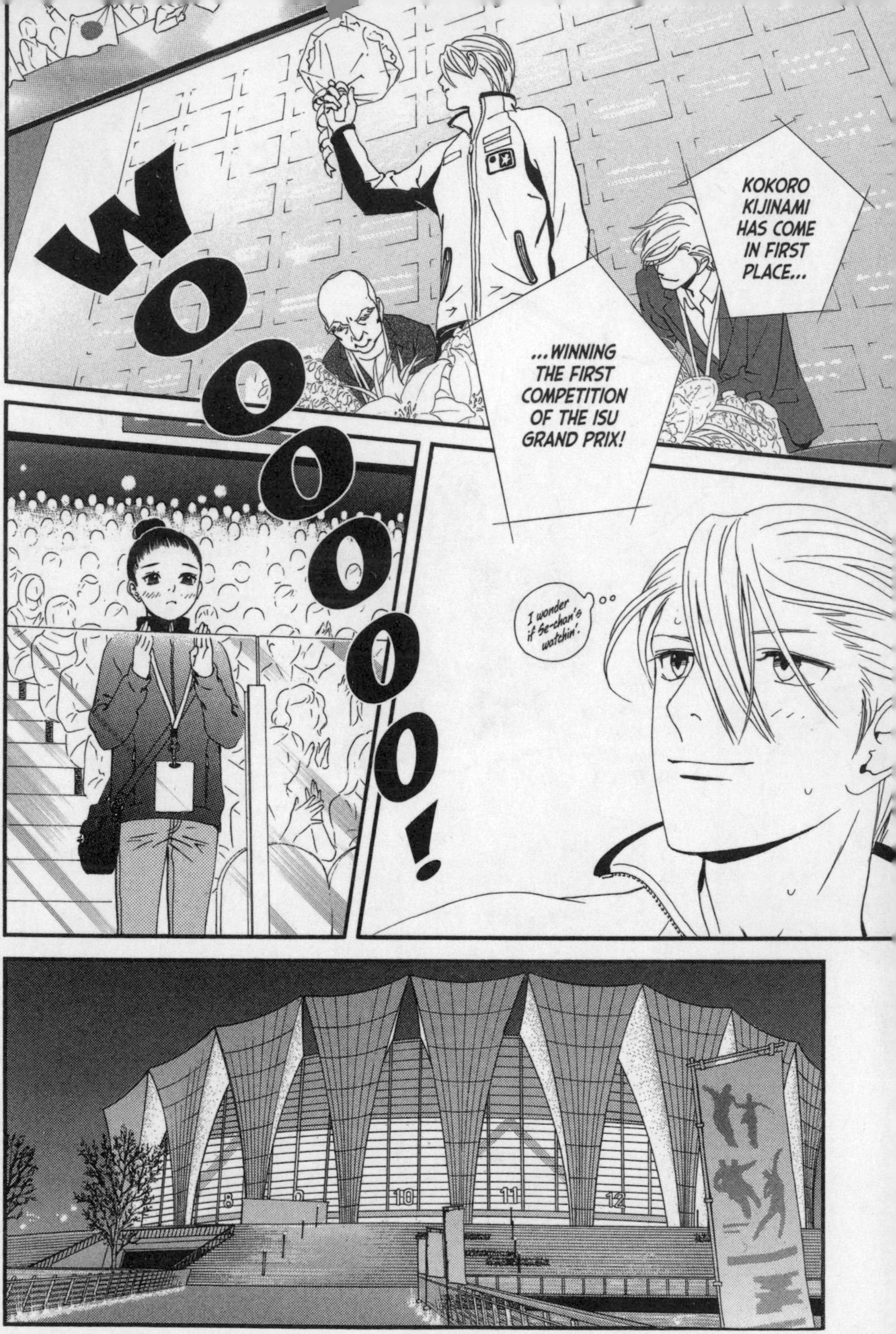
KOKORO KIJINAMI HAS COME IN FIRST PLACE...
...WINNING THE FIRST COMPETITION OF THE ISU GRAND PRIX!
WOOOOOO!
I wonder if Se-chan's watchin'.

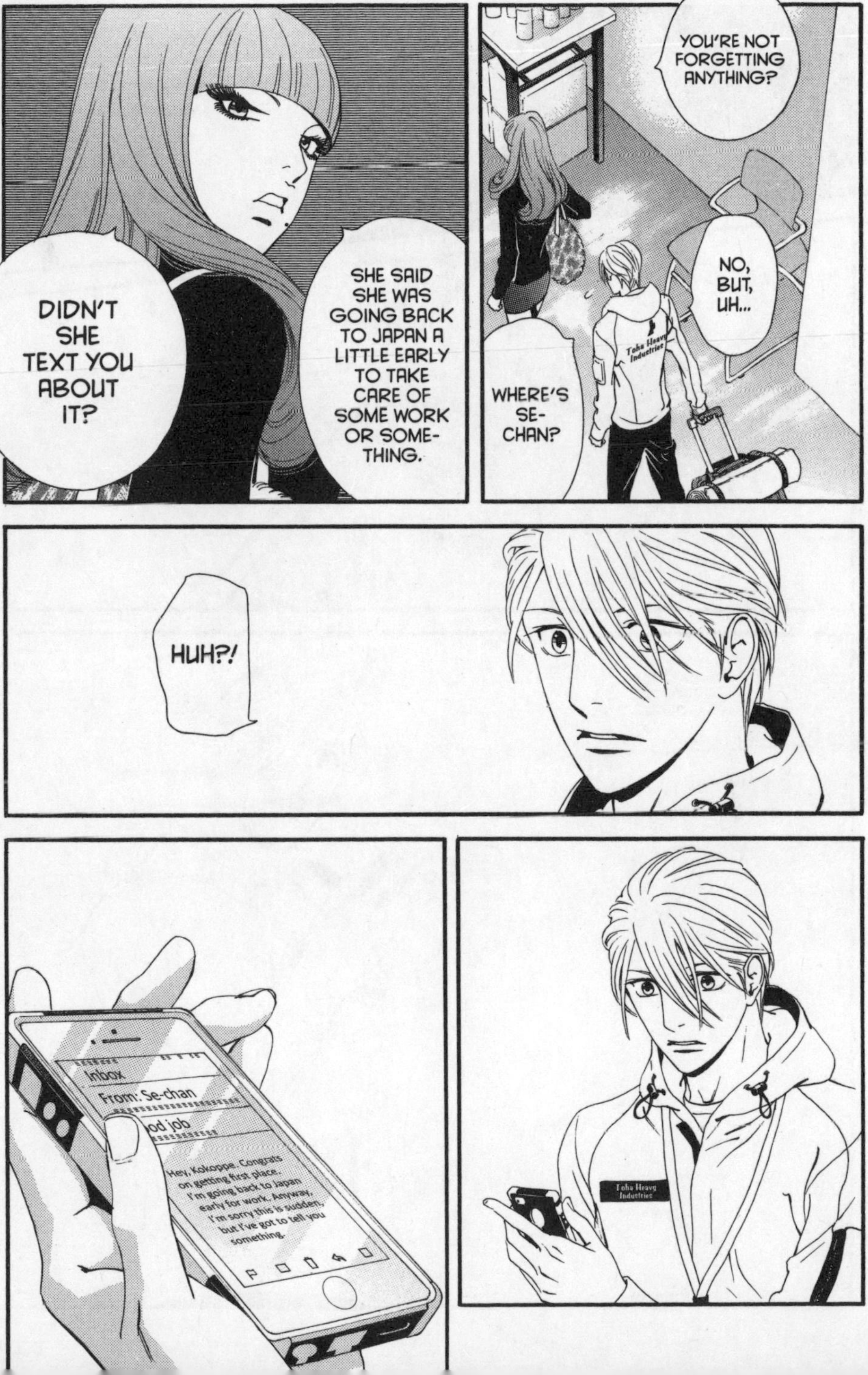
YOU'RE NOT FORGETTING ANYTHING?
NO, BUT, UH...
WHERE'S SE-CHAN?
Toha Heavy Industries
SHE SAID SHE WAS GOING BACK TO JAPAN A LITTLE EARLY TO TAKE CARE OF SOME WORK OR SOMETHING.
DIDN'T SHE TEXT YOU ABOUT IT?
HUH?!
Toha Heavy Industries
Inbox
From: Se-chan
Hey, Kokoppe. Congrats on getting first place. I'm going back to Japan early for work. Anyway, I'm sorry this is sudden, but I've got to tell you something.

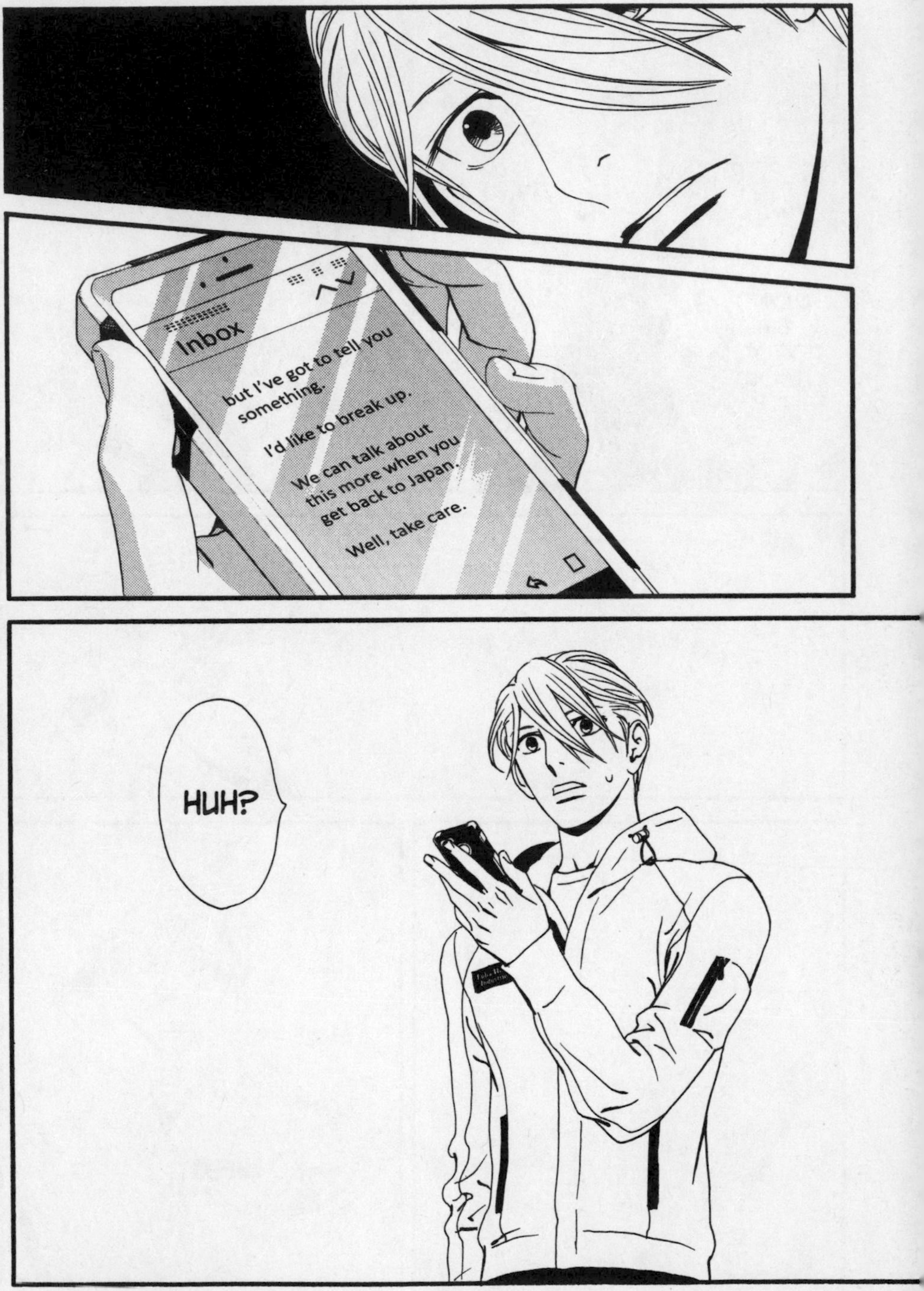
Inbox
but I've got to tell you something.
I'd like to break up.
We can talk about this more when you get back to Japan.
Well, take care.
HUH?

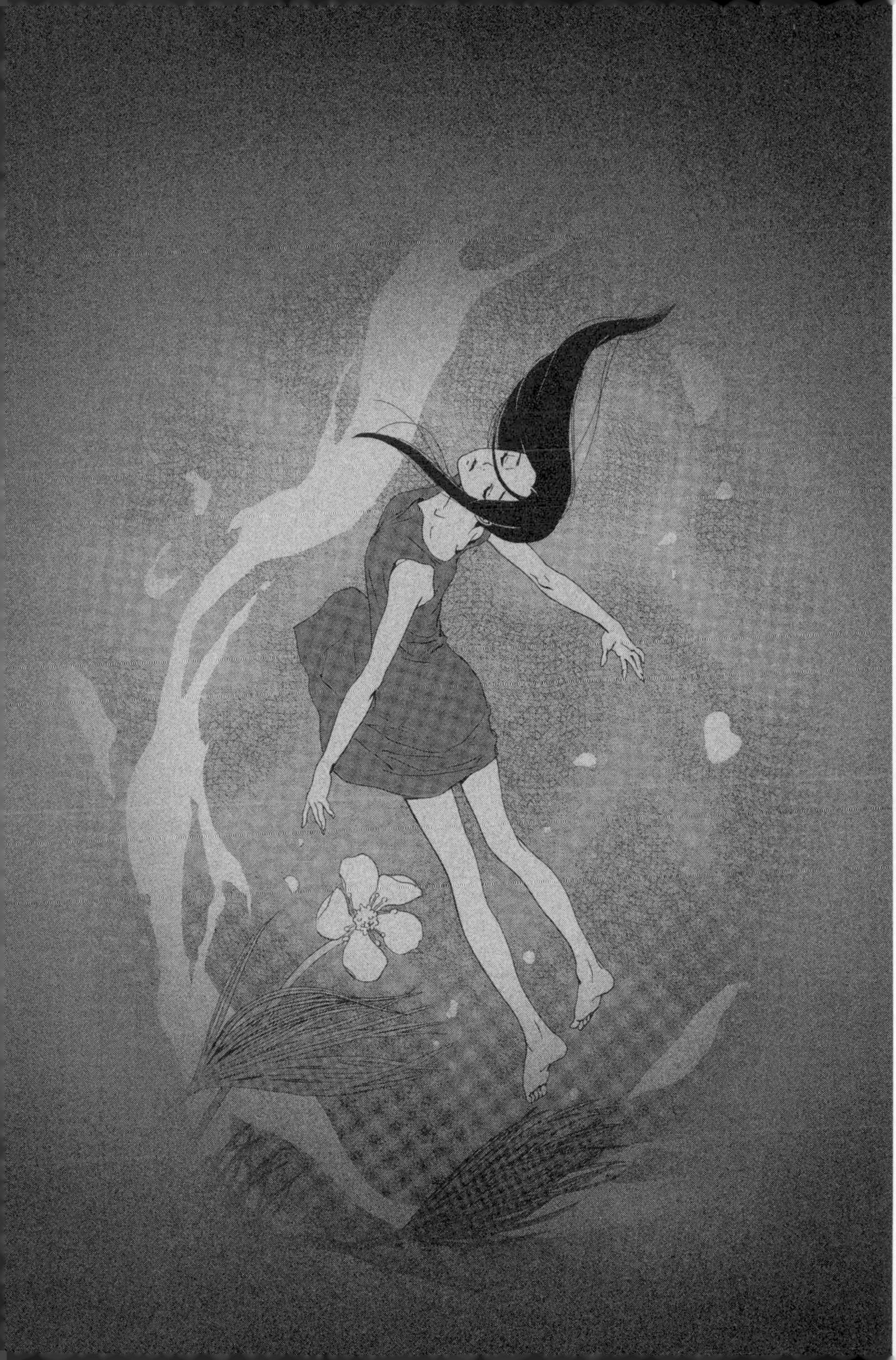

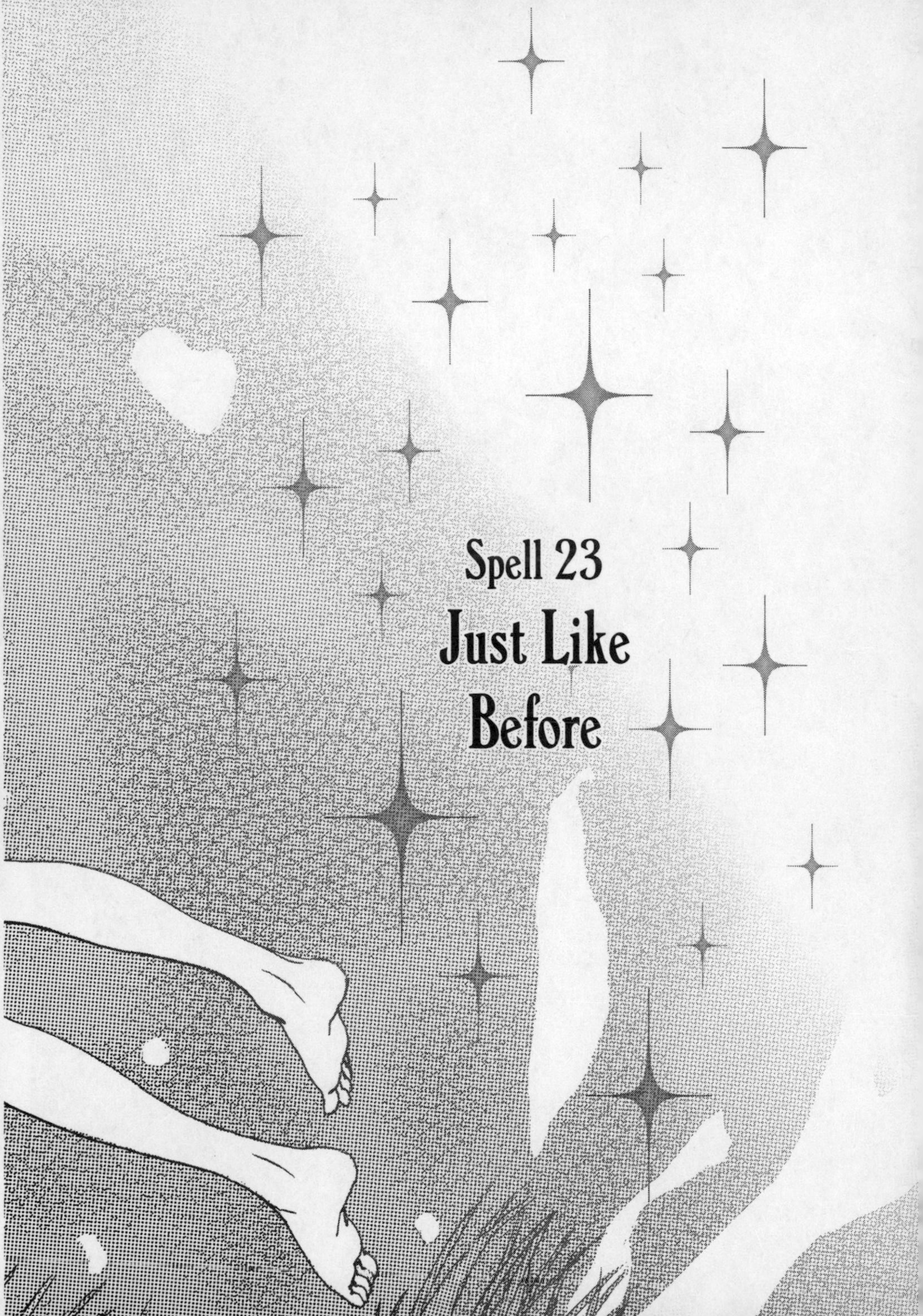
Spell 23
Just Like
Before

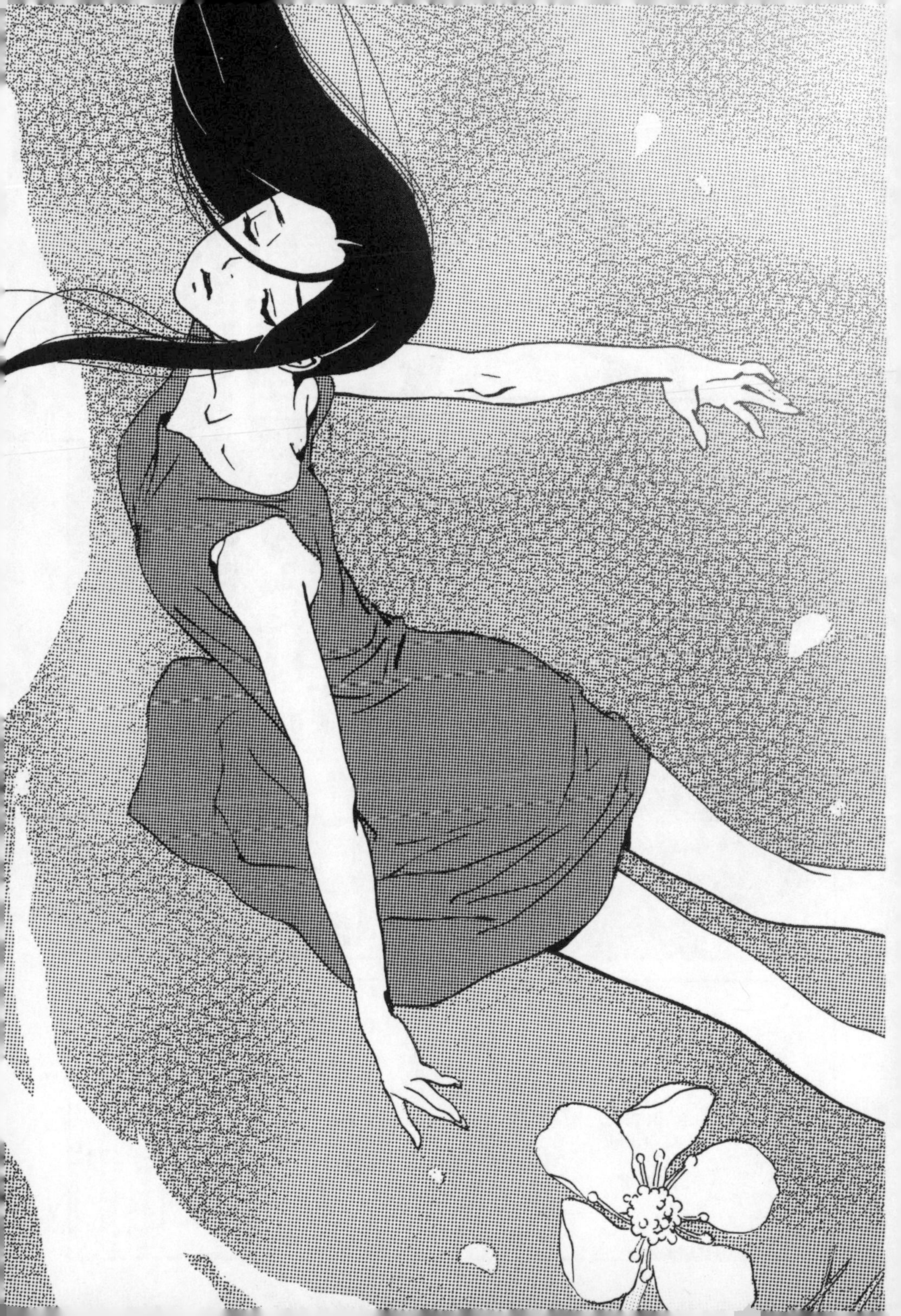

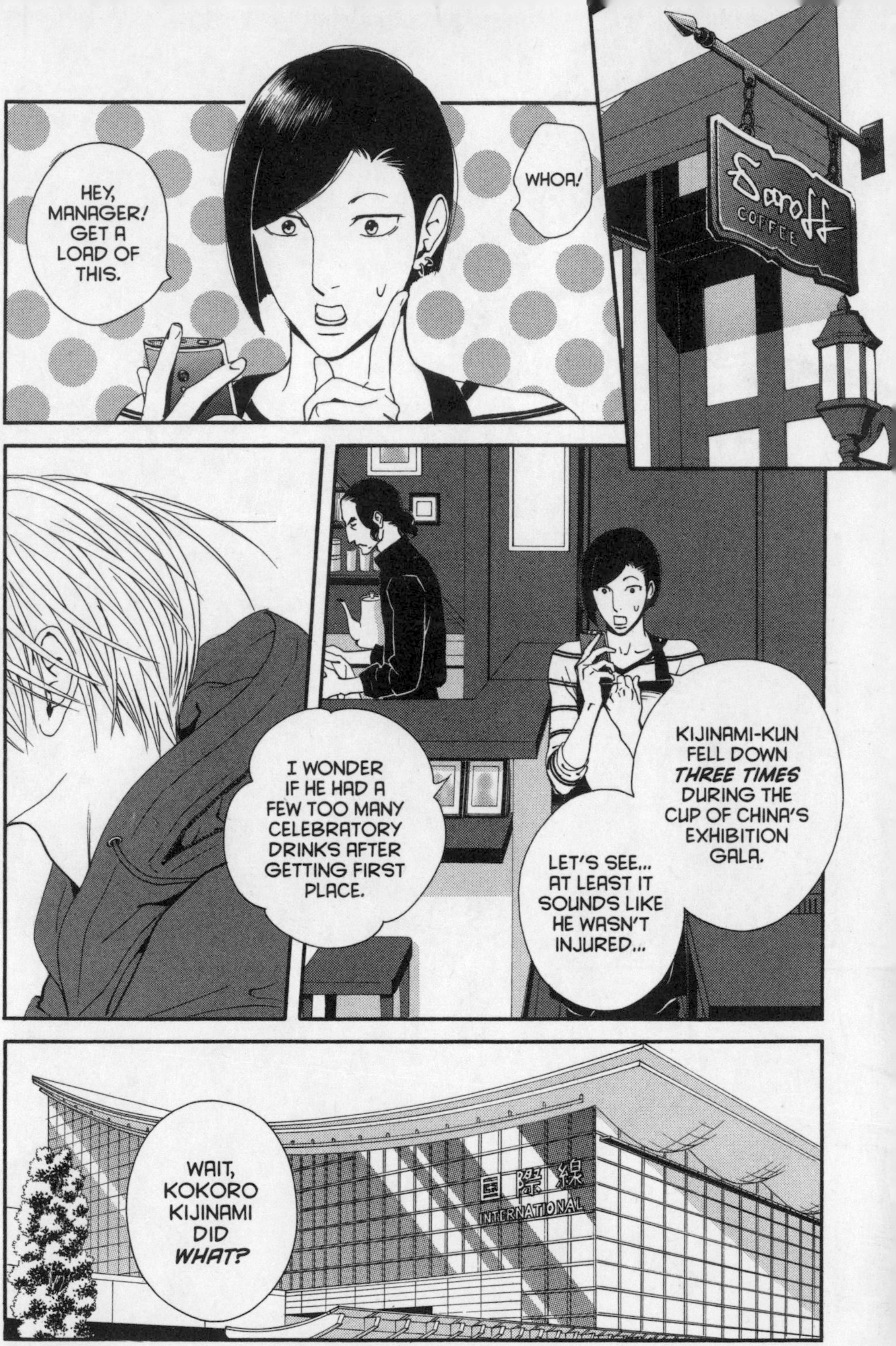
Saroff
COFFEE
WHOA!
HEY, MANAGER! GET A LOAD OF THIS.
KIJINAMI-KUN FELL DOWN *THREE TIMES* DURING THE CUP OF CHINA'S EXHIBITION GALA.
LET'S SEE... AT LEAST IT SOUNDS LIKE HE WASN'T INJURED...
I WONDER IF HE HAD A FEW TOO MANY CELEBRATORY DRINKS AFTER GETTING FIRST PLACE.
国際線
INTERNATIONAL
WAIT, KOKORO KIJINAMI DID *WHAT?*

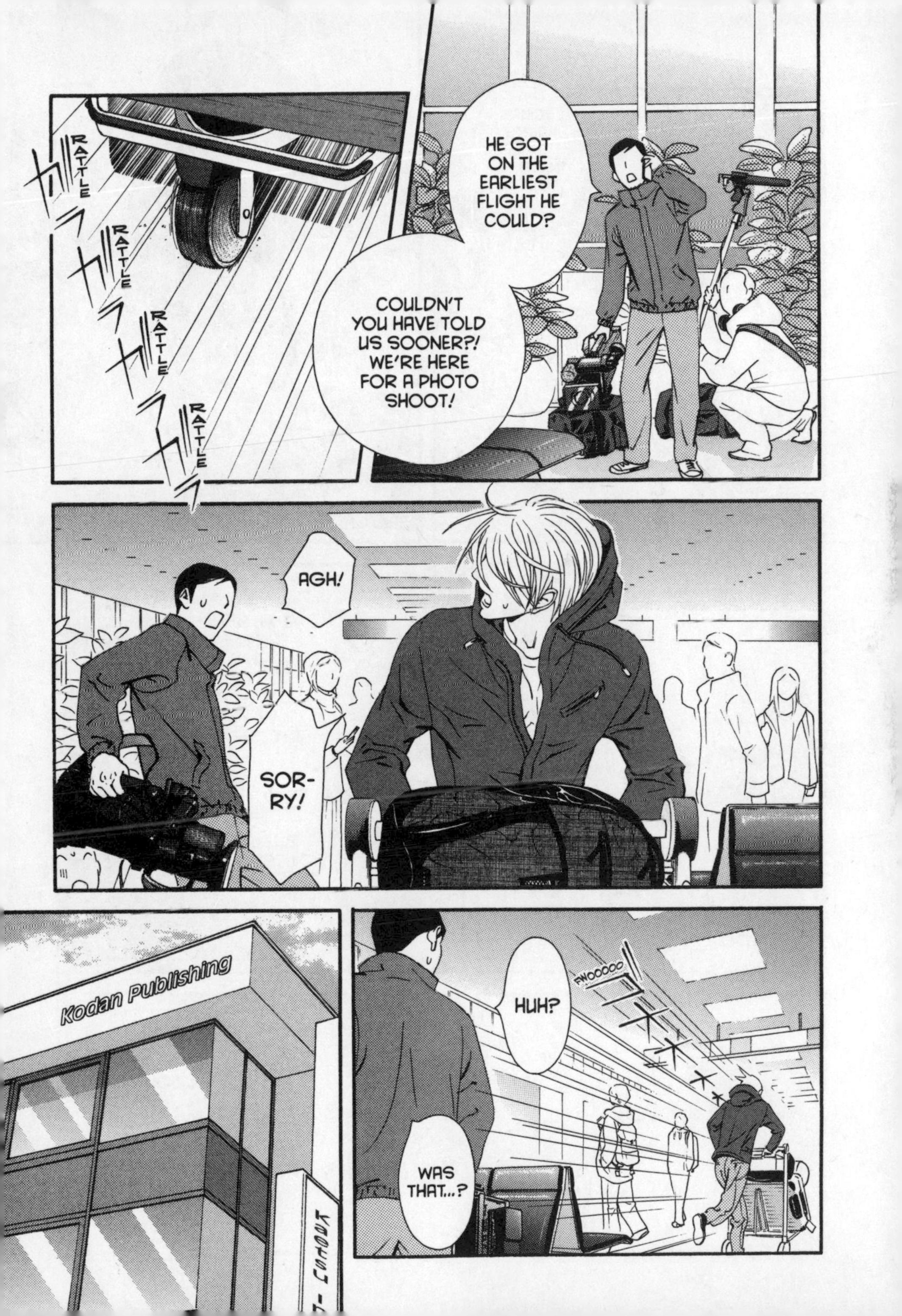
HE GOT ON THE EARLIEST FLIGHT HE COULD?
COULDN'T YOU HAVE TOLD US SOONER?! WE'RE HERE FOR A PHOTO SHOOT!
RATTLE
RATTLE
RATTLE
RATTLE
AGH!
SOR-RY!
FWOOOOO
HUH?
WAS THAT...?
Kodan Publishing

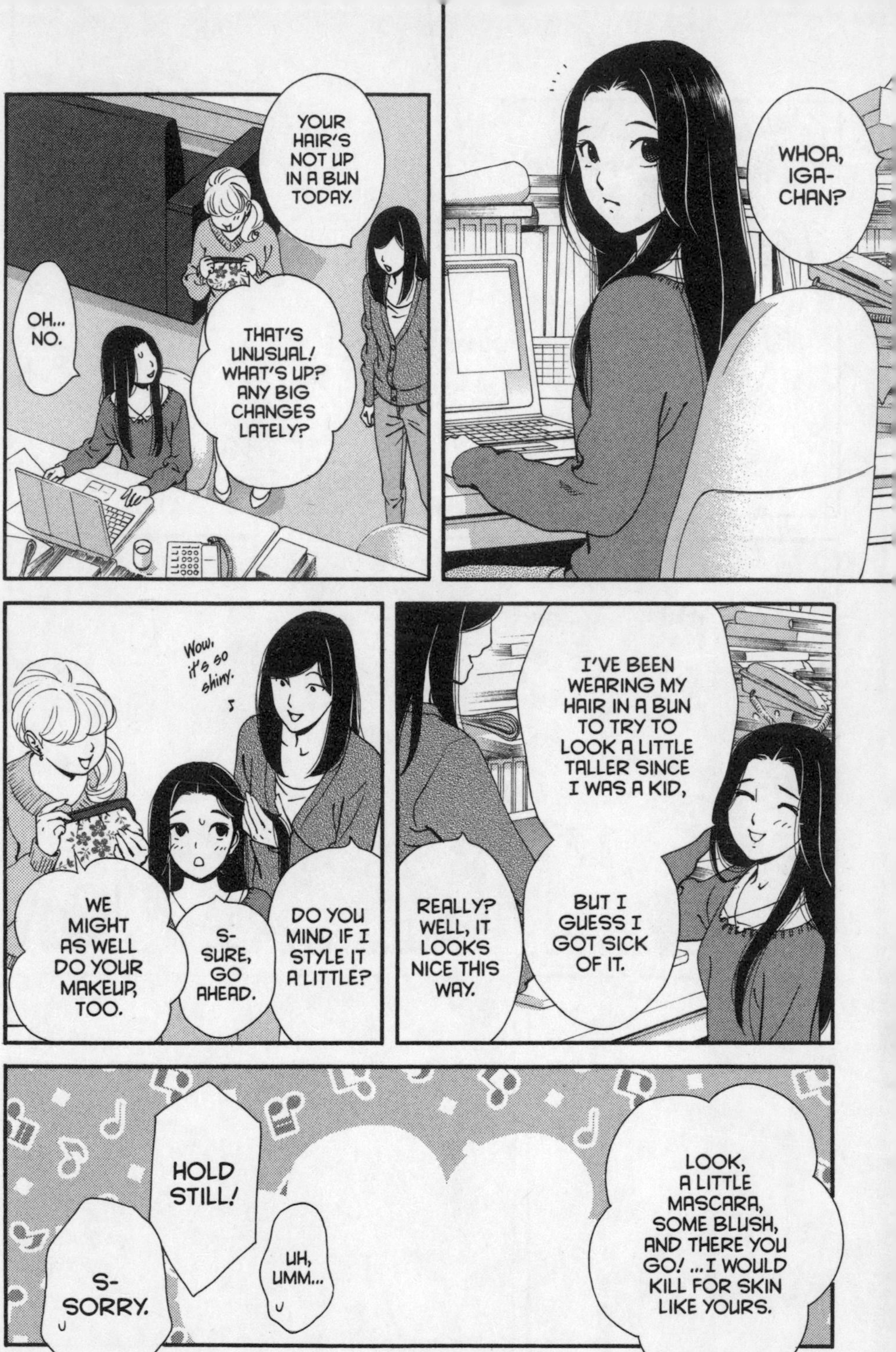
WHOA, IGA-CHAN?
YOUR HAIR'S NOT UP IN A BUN TODAY.
OH... NO.
THAT'S UNUSUAL! WHAT'S UP? ANY BIG CHANGES LATELY?
I'VE BEEN WEARING MY HAIR IN A BUN TO TRY TO LOOK A LITTLE TALLER SINCE I WAS A KID,
BUT I GUESS I GOT SICK OF IT.
REALLY? WELL, IT LOOKS NICE THIS WAY.
Wow, it's so shiny.
DO YOU MIND IF I STYLE IT A LITTLE?
S-SURE, GO AHEAD.
WE MIGHT AS WELL DO YOUR MAKEUP, TOO.
LOOK, A LITTLE MASCARA, SOME BLUSH, AND THERE YOU GO! ...I WOULD KILL FOR SKIN LIKE YOURS.
HOLD STILL!
UH, UMM...
S-SORRY.

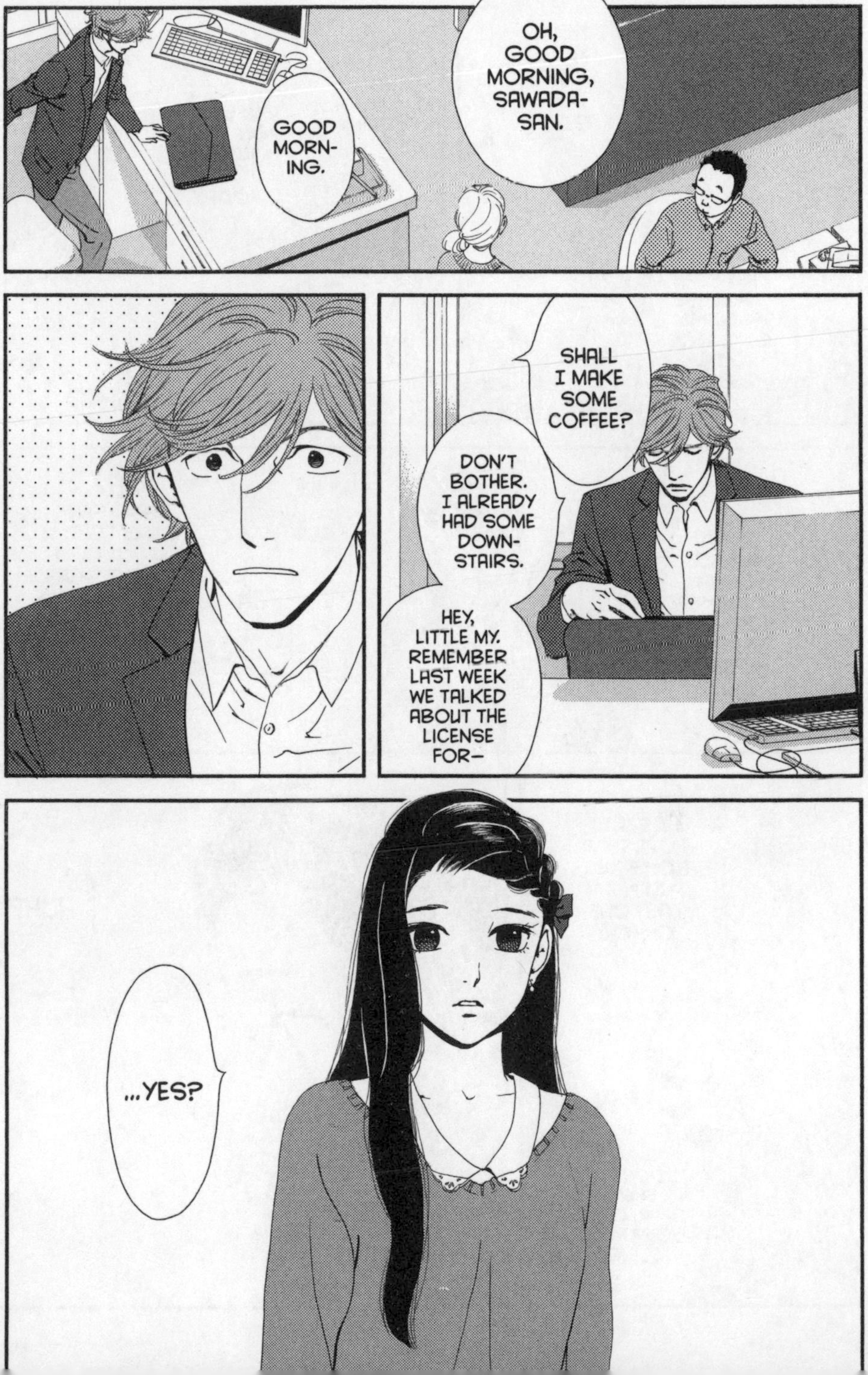
OH, GOOD MORNING, SAWADA-SAN.
GOOD MORNING.
SHALL I MAKE SOME COFFEE?
DON'T BOTHER. I ALREADY HAD SOME DOWNSTAIRS.
HEY, LITTLE MY. REMEMBER LAST WEEK WE TALKED ABOUT THE LICENSE FOR–
...YES?

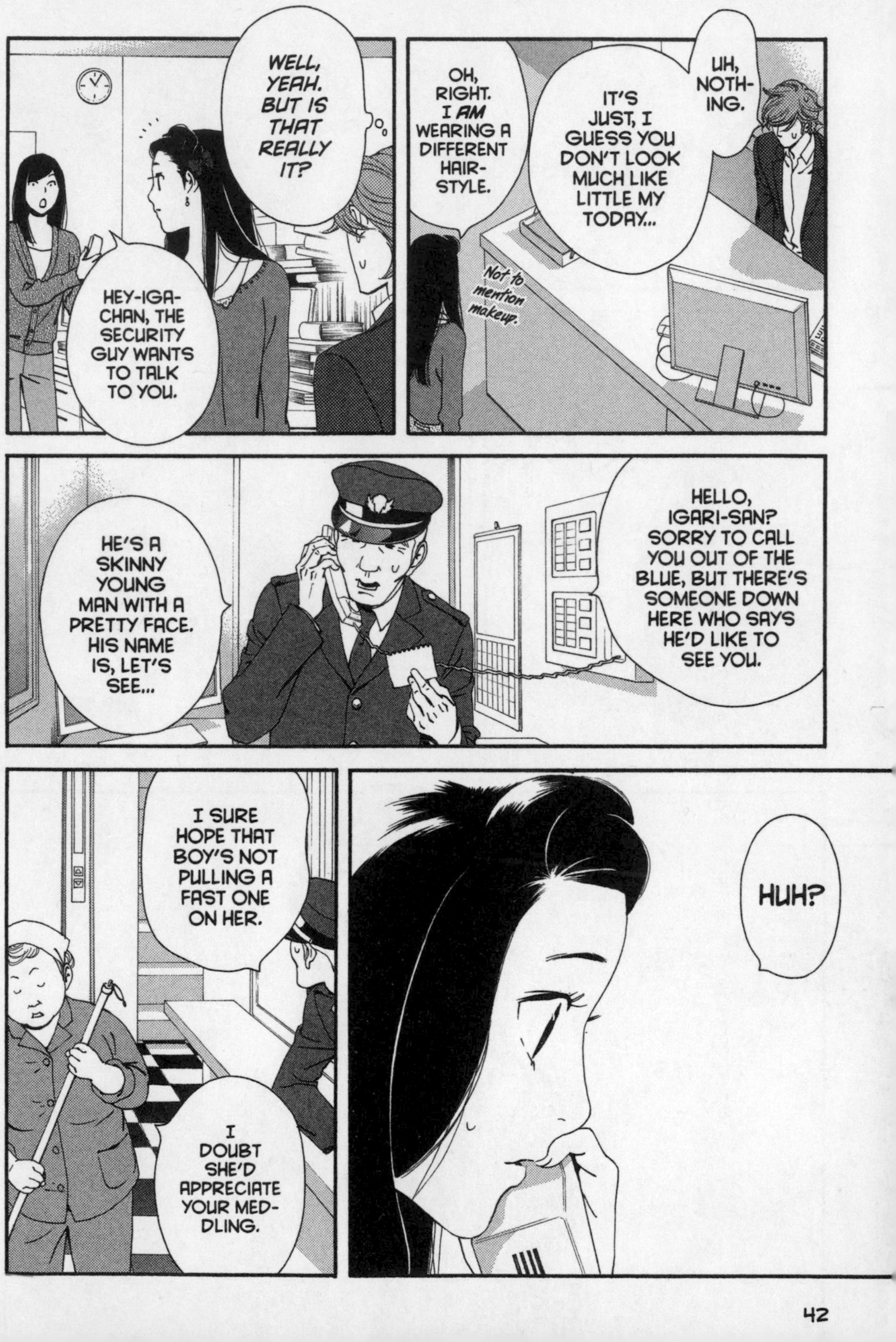
UH, NOTHING.
IT'S JUST, I GUESS YOU DON'T LOOK MUCH LIKE LITTLE MY TODAY...
OH, RIGHT. I *AM* WEARING A DIFFERENT HAIRSTYLE.
Not to mention makeup.
WELL, YEAH. BUT IS THAT REALLY IT?
HEY-IGA-CHAN, THE SECURITY GUY WANTS TO TALK TO YOU.
HELLO, IGARI-SAN? SORRY TO CALL YOU OUT OF THE BLUE, BUT THERE'S SOMEONE DOWN HERE WHO SAYS HE'D LIKE TO SEE YOU.
HE'S A SKINNY YOUNG MAN WITH A PRETTY FACE. HIS NAME IS, LET'S SEE...
HUH?
I SURE HOPE THAT BOY'S NOT PULLING A FAST ONE ON HER.
I DOUBT SHE'D APPRECIATE YOUR MEDDLING.

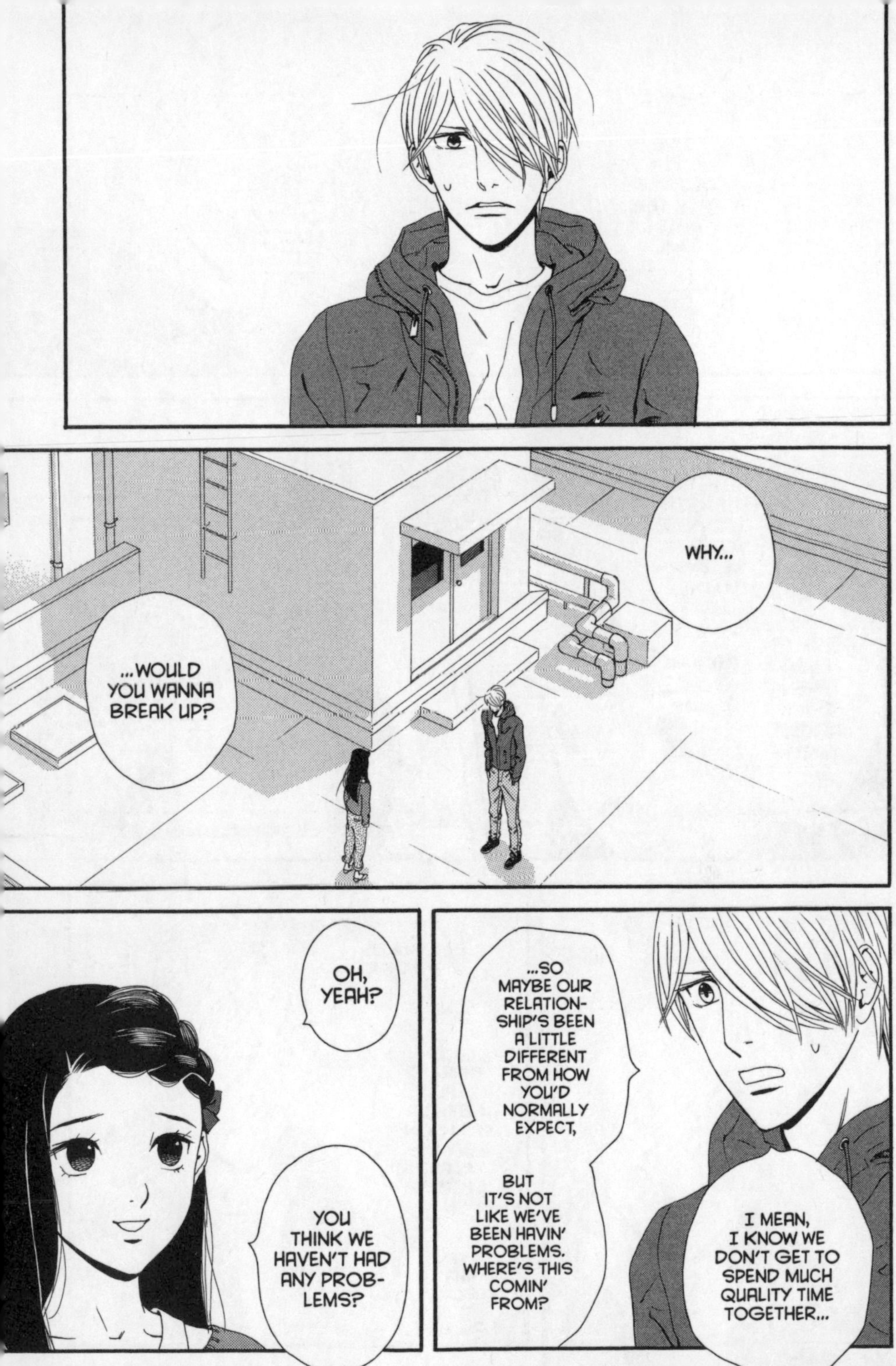
WHY...
...WOULD YOU WANNA BREAK UP?
I MEAN, I KNOW WE DON'T GET TO SPEND MUCH QUALITY TIME TOGETHER...
...SO MAYBE OUR RELATIONSHIP'S BEEN A LITTLE DIFFERENT FROM HOW YOU'D NORMALLY EXPECT,
BUT IT'S NOT LIKE WE'VE BEEN HAVIN' PROBLEMS. WHERE'S THIS COMIN' FROM?
OH, YEAH?
YOU THINK WE HAVEN'T HAD ANY PROB-LEMS?

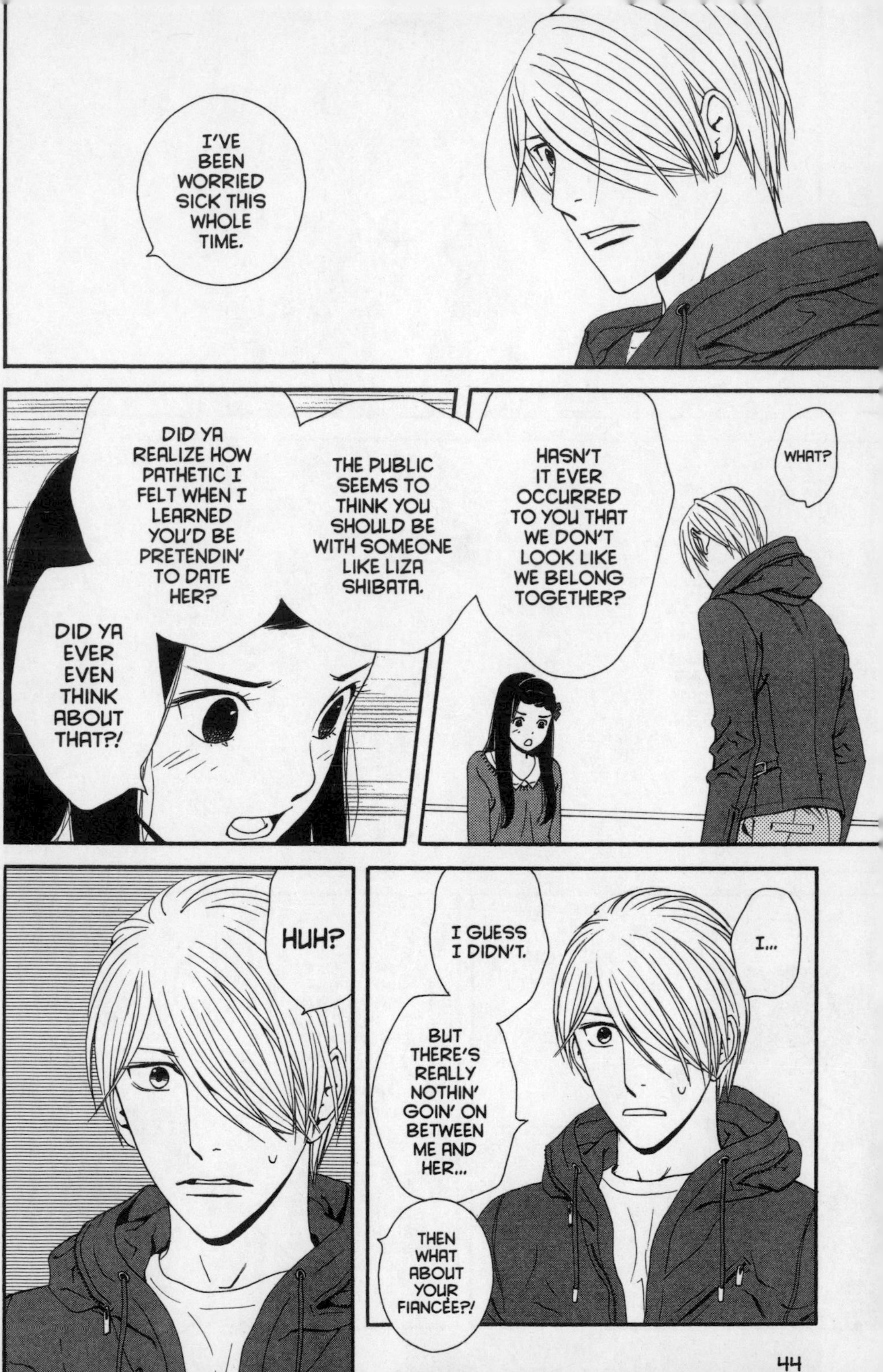

I'VE BEEN WORRIED SICK THIS WHOLE TIME.
WHAT?
HASN'T IT EVER OCCURRED TO YOU THAT WE DON'T LOOK LIKE WE BELONG TOGETHER?
THE PUBLIC SEEMS TO THINK YOU SHOULD BE WITH SOMEONE LIKE LIZA SHIBATA.
DID YA REALIZE HOW PATHETIC I FELT WHEN I LEARNED YOU'D BE PRETENDIN' TO DATE HER?
DID YA EVER EVEN THINK ABOUT THAT?!
I...
I GUESS I DIDN'T.
BUT THERE'S REALLY NOTHIN' GOIN' ON BETWEEN ME AND HER...
THEN WHAT ABOUT YOUR FIANCÉE?!
HUH?

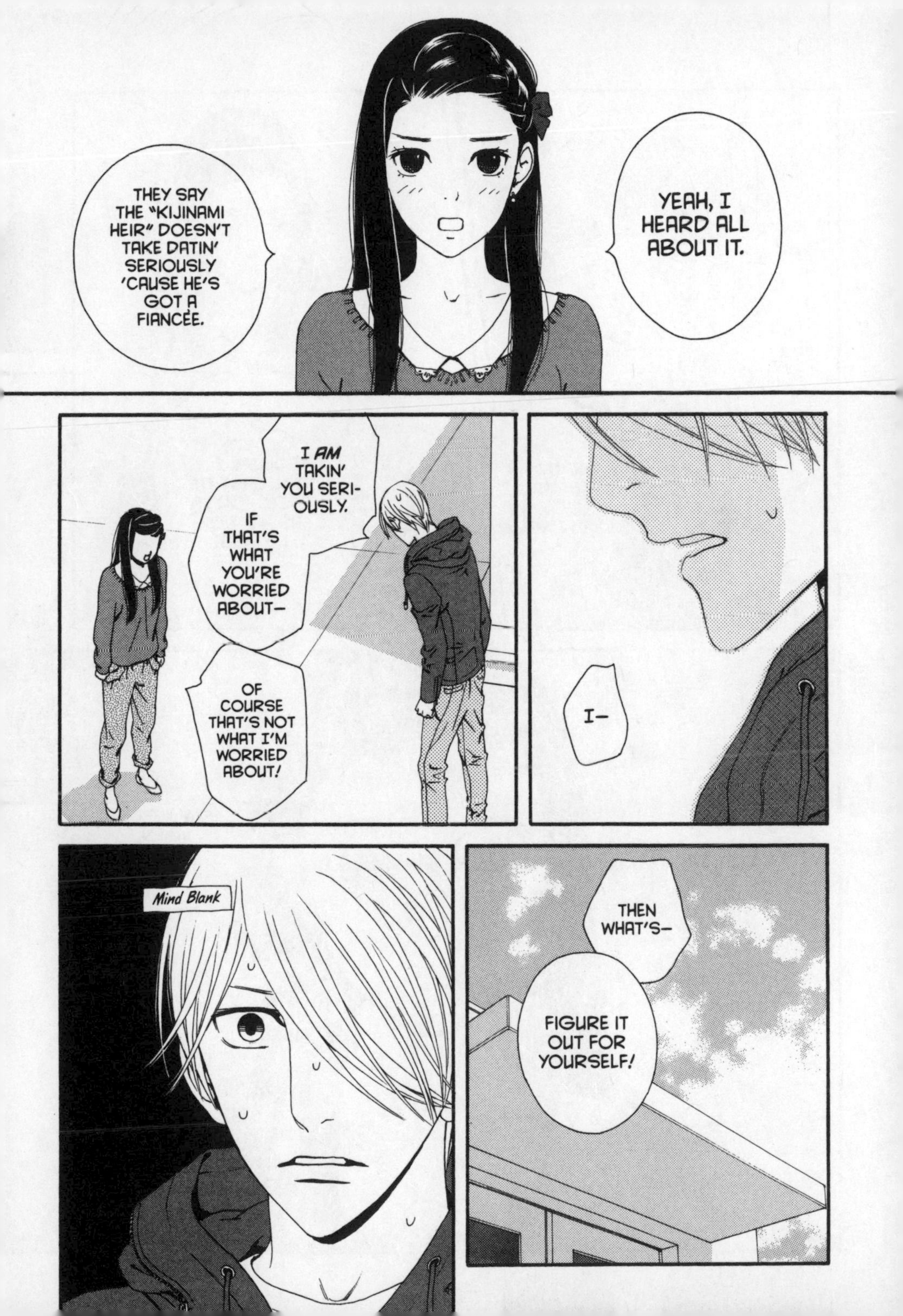
YEAH, I HEARD ALL ABOUT IT.
THEY SAY THE "KIJINAMI HEIR" DOESN'T TAKE DATIN' SERIOUSLY 'CAUSE HE'S GOT A FIANCÉE.
I–
I *AM* TAKIN' YOU SERIOUSLY.
IF THAT'S WHAT YOU'RE WORRIED ABOUT—
OF COURSE THAT'S NOT WHAT I'M WORRIED ABOUT!
THEN WHAT'S—
FIGURE IT OUT FOR YOURSELF!
Mind Blank

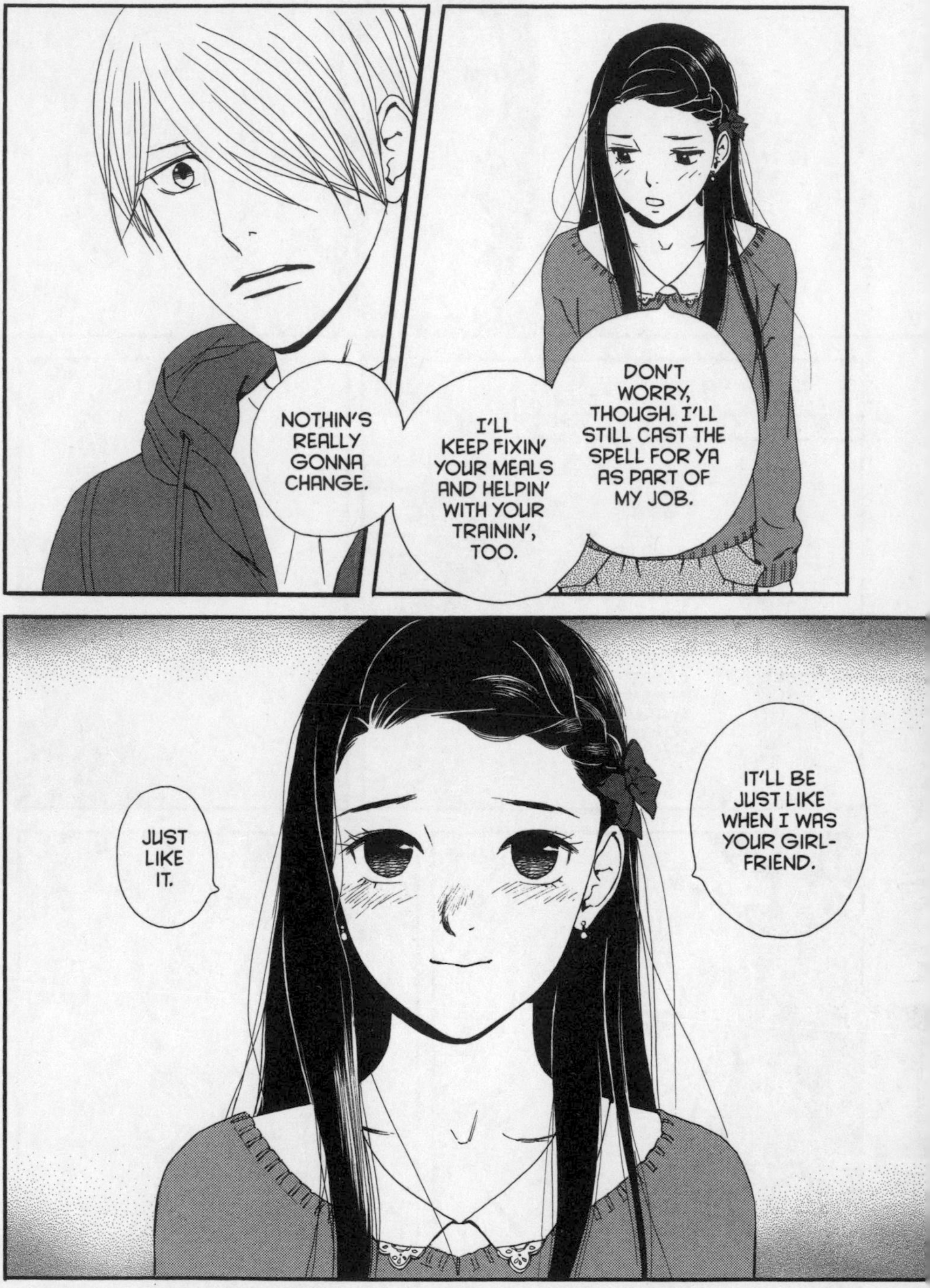
DON'T WORRY, THOUGH. I'LL STILL CAST THE SPELL FOR YA AS PART OF MY JOB.
I'LL KEEP FIXIN' YOUR MEALS AND HELPIN' WITH YOUR TRAININ', TOO.
NOTHIN'S REALLY GONNA CHANGE.
IT'LL BE JUST LIKE WHEN I WAS YOUR GIRL-FRIEND.
JUST LIKE IT.

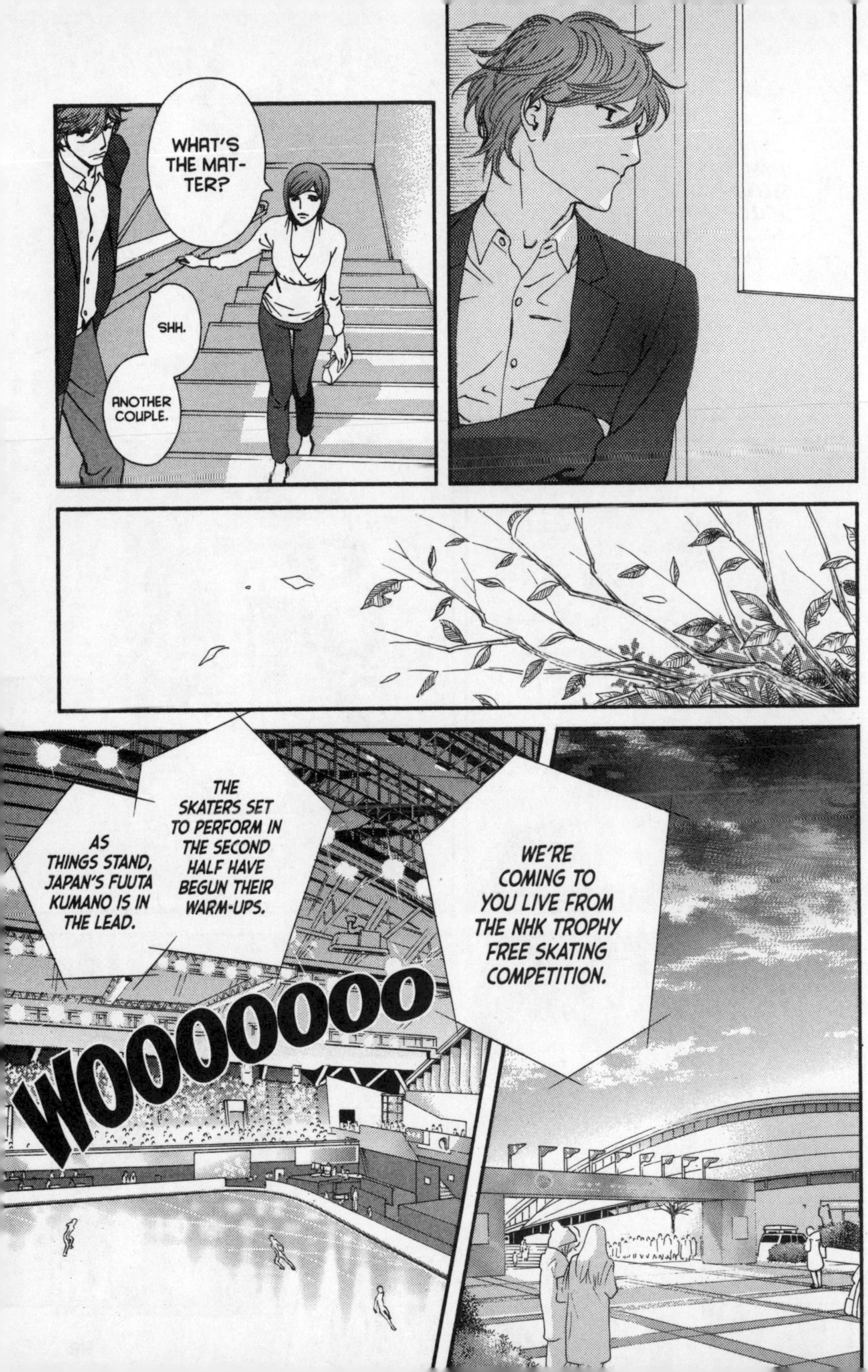
WHAT'S THE MATTER?
SHH.
ANOTHER COUPLE.
WE'RE COMING TO YOU LIVE FROM THE NHK TROPHY FREE SKATING COMPETITION.
THE SKATERS SET TO PERFORM IN THE SECOND HALF HAVE BEGUN THEIR WARM-UPS.
AS THINGS STAND, JAPAN'S FUUTA KUMANO IS IN THE LEAD.
WOOOOOOO

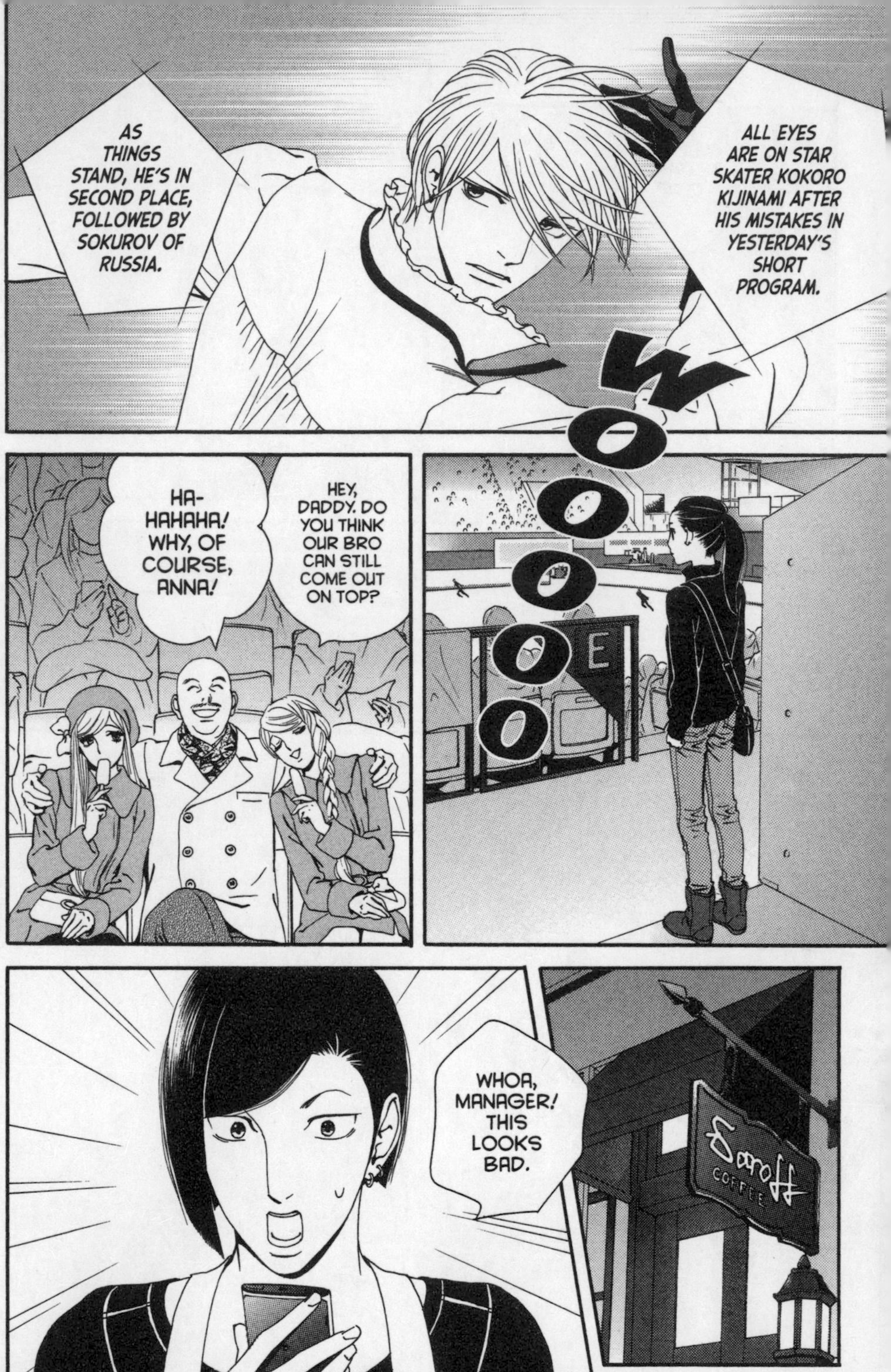
ALL EYES ARE ON STAR SKATER KOKORO KIJINAMI AFTER HIS MISTAKES IN YESTERDAY'S SHORT PROGRAM.
AS THINGS STAND, HE'S IN SECOND PLACE, FOLLOWED BY SOKUROV OF RUSSIA.
WOOOOOOO
HEY, DADDY. DO YOU THINK OUR BRO CAN STILL COME OUT ON TOP?
HA-HAHAHA! WHY, OF COURSE, ANNA!
COFFEE
WHOA, MANAGER! THIS LOOKS BAD.

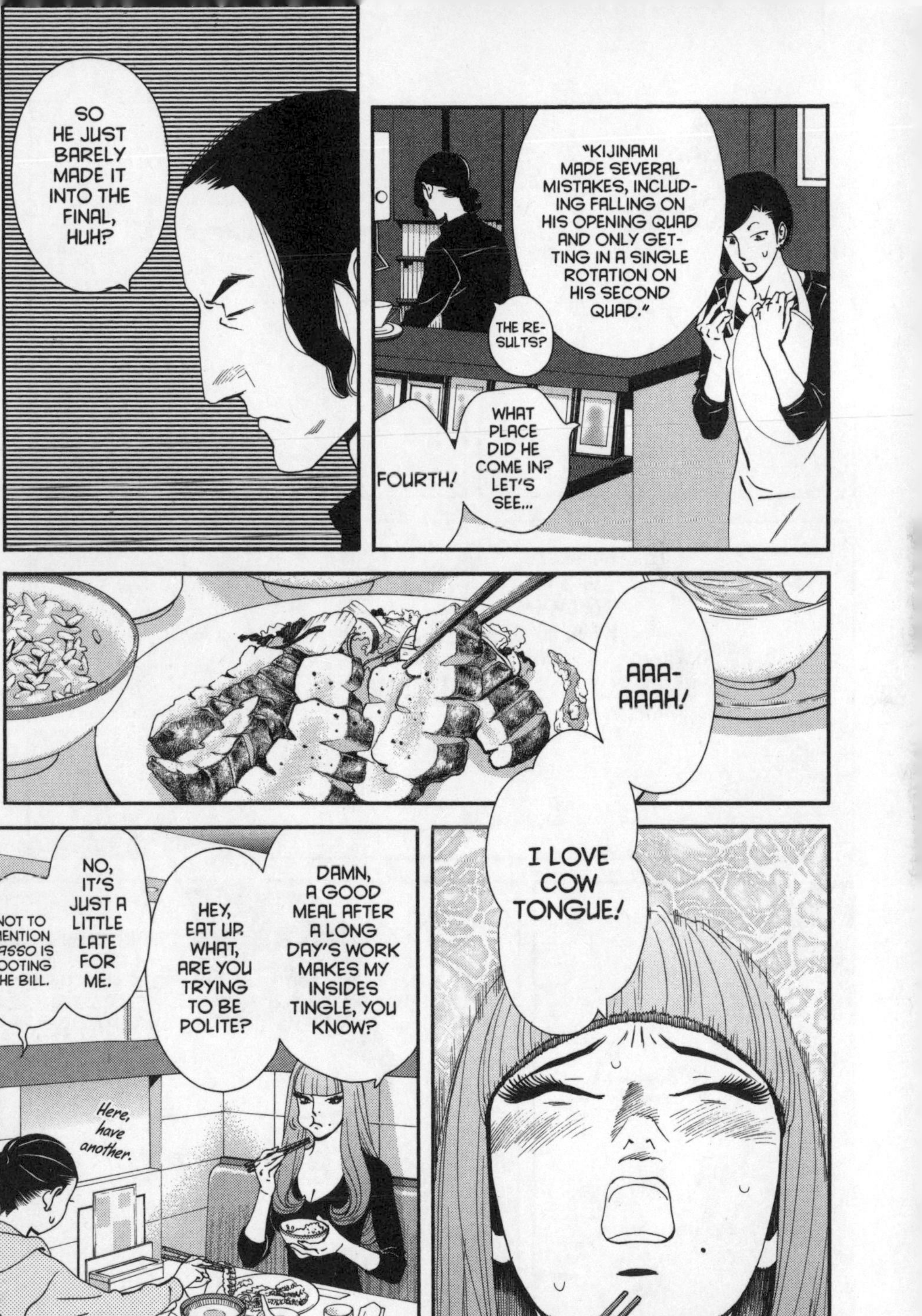
"KIJINAMI MADE SEVERAL MISTAKES, INCLUDING FALLING ON HIS OPENING QUAD AND ONLY GETTING IN A SINGLE ROTATION ON HIS SECOND QUAD."
THE RESULTS?
WHAT PLACE DID HE COME IN? LET'S SEE...
FOURTH!
SO HE JUST BARELY MADE IT INTO THE FINAL, HUH?
AAA-AAAH!
I LOVE COW TONGUE!
DAMN, A GOOD MEAL AFTER A LONG DAY'S WORK MAKES MY INSIDES TINGLE, YOU KNOW?
HEY, EAT UP. WHAT, ARE YOU TRYING TO BE POLITE?
NO, IT'S JUST A LITTLE LATE FOR ME.
NOT TO MENTION *SASSO* IS FOOTING THE BILL.
Here, have another.

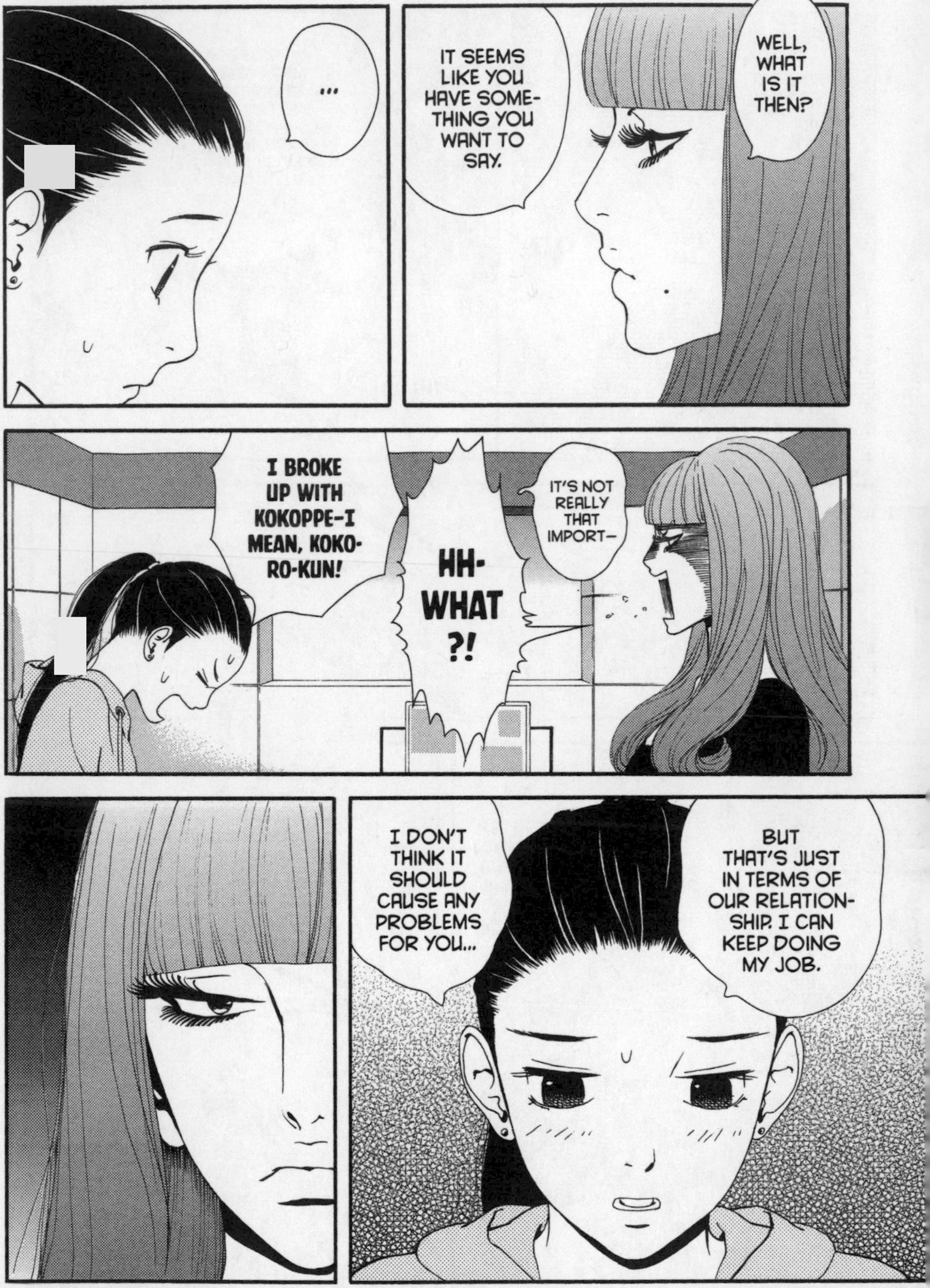
WELL, WHAT IS IT THEN?
IT SEEMS LIKE YOU HAVE SOME-THING YOU WANT TO SAY.
...
IT'S NOT REALLY THAT IMPORT—
I BROKE UP WITH KOKOPPE—I MEAN, KOKO-RO-KUN!
HH-WHAT?!
BUT THAT'S JUST IN TERMS OF OUR RELATION-SHIP. I CAN KEEP DOING MY JOB.
I DON'T THINK IT SHOULD CAUSE ANY PROBLEMS FOR YOU...

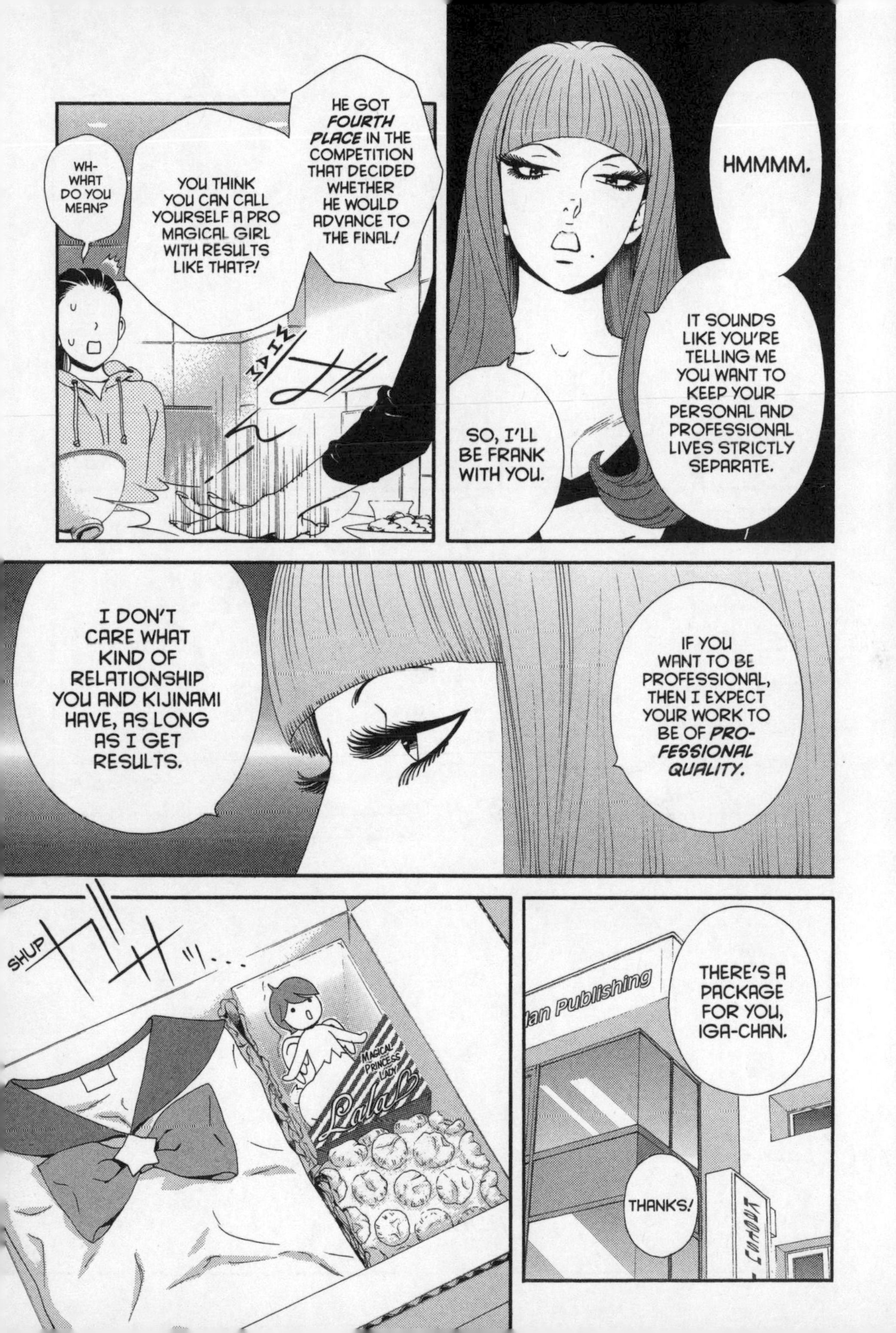
HMMMM.
IT SOUNDS LIKE YOU'RE TELLING ME YOU WANT TO KEEP YOUR PERSONAL AND PROFESSIONAL LIVES STRICTLY SEPARATE.
SO, I'LL BE FRANK WITH YOU.
HE GOT *FOURTH PLACE* IN THE COMPETITION THAT DECIDED WHETHER HE WOULD ADVANCE TO THE FINAL!
YOU THINK YOU CAN CALL YOURSELF A PRO MAGICAL GIRL WITH RESULTS LIKE THAT?!
WH-WHAT DO YOU MEAN?
IF YOU WANT TO BE PROFESSIONAL, THEN I EXPECT YOUR WORK TO BE OF *PRO-FESSIONAL QUALITY.*
I DON'T CARE WHAT KIND OF RELATIONSHIP YOU AND KIJINAMI HAVE, AS LONG AS I GET RESULTS.
THERE'S A PACKAGE FOR YOU, IGA-CHAN.
THANKS!
SHUP
MAGICAL PRINCESS LADY
Lala

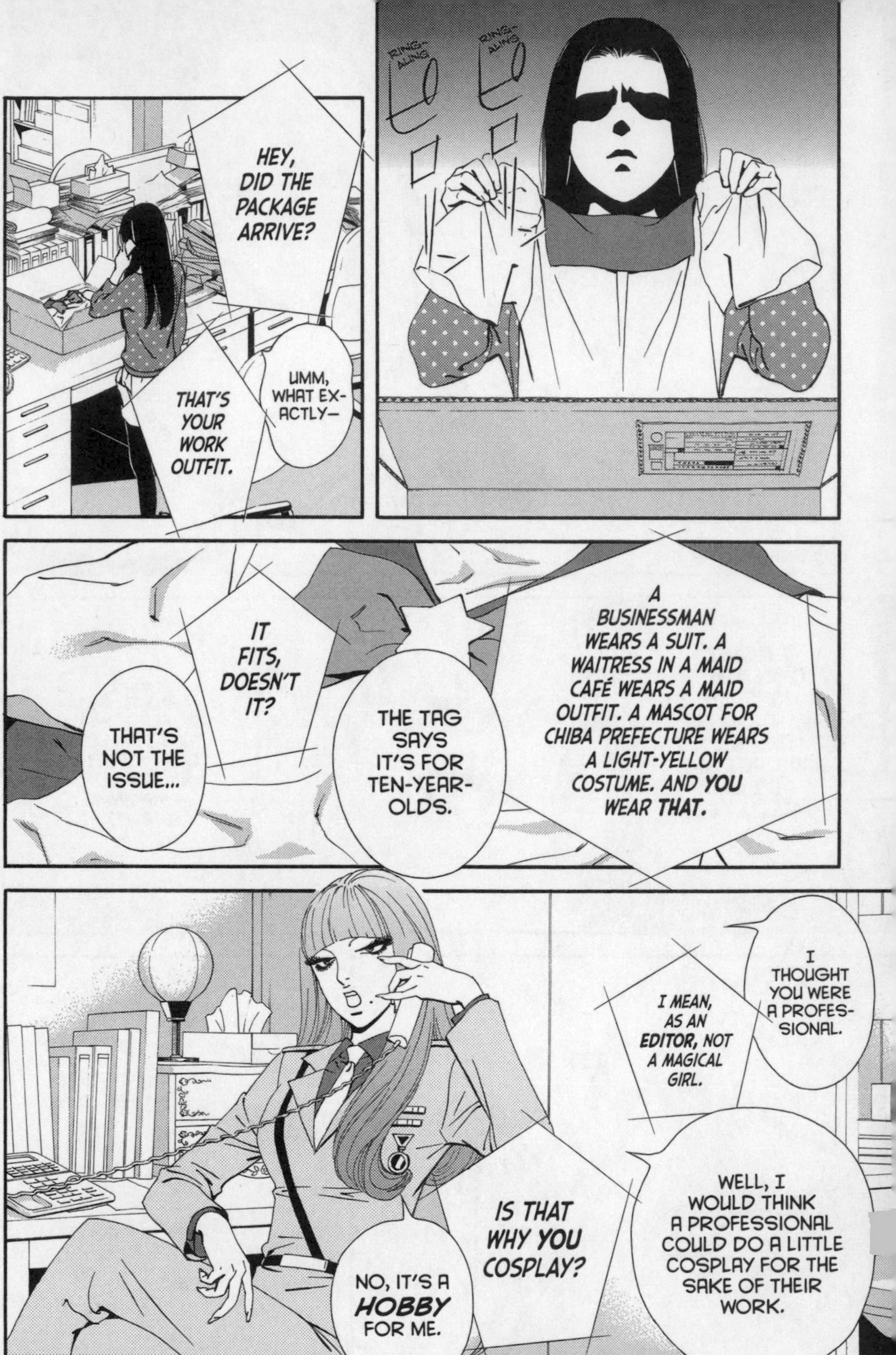
RING-ALING
RING-ALING
HEY, DID THE PACKAGE ARRIVE?
UMM, WHAT EX-ACTLY—
THAT'S YOUR WORK OUTFIT.
A BUSINESSMAN WEARS A SUIT. A WAITRESS IN A MAID CAFÉ WEARS A MAID OUTFIT. A MASCOT FOR CHIBA PREFECTURE WEARS A LIGHT-YELLOW COSTUME. AND YOU WEAR THAT.
IT FITS, DOESN'T IT?
THE TAG SAYS IT'S FOR TEN-YEAR-OLDS.
THAT'S NOT THE ISSUE...
I THOUGHT YOU WERE A PROFES-SIONAL.
I MEAN, AS AN EDITOR, NOT A MAGICAL GIRL.
WELL, I WOULD THINK A PROFESSIONAL COULD DO A LITTLE COSPLAY FOR THE SAKE OF THEIR WORK.
IS THAT WHY YOU COSPLAY?
NO, IT'S A HOBBY FOR ME.

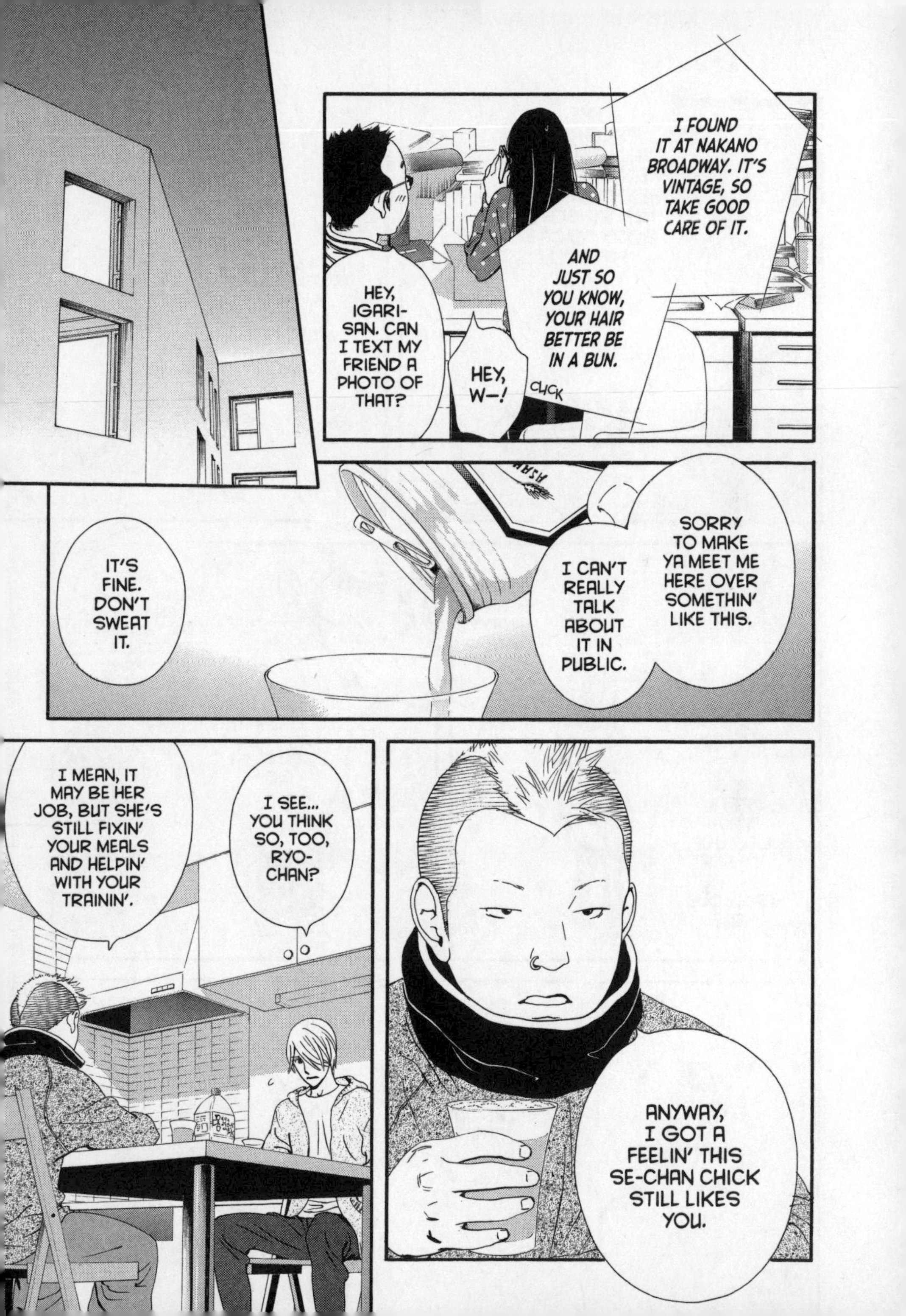
I FOUND IT AT NAKANO BROADWAY. IT'S VINTAGE, SO TAKE GOOD CARE OF IT.
AND JUST SO YOU KNOW, YOUR HAIR BETTER BE IN A BUN.
HEY, IGARI-SAN. CAN I TEXT MY FRIEND A PHOTO OF THAT?
CLICK
HEY, W—!
SORRY TO MAKE YA MEET ME HERE OVER SOMETHIN' LIKE THIS.
I CAN'T REALLY TALK ABOUT IT IN PUBLIC.
IT'S FINE. DON'T SWEAT IT.
ANYWAY, I GOT A FEELIN' THIS SE-CHAN CHICK STILL LIKES YOU.
I SEE... YOU THINK SO, TOO, RYO-CHAN?
I MEAN, IT MAY BE HER JOB, BUT SHE'S STILL FIXIN' YOUR MEALS AND HELPIN' WITH YOUR TRAININ'.

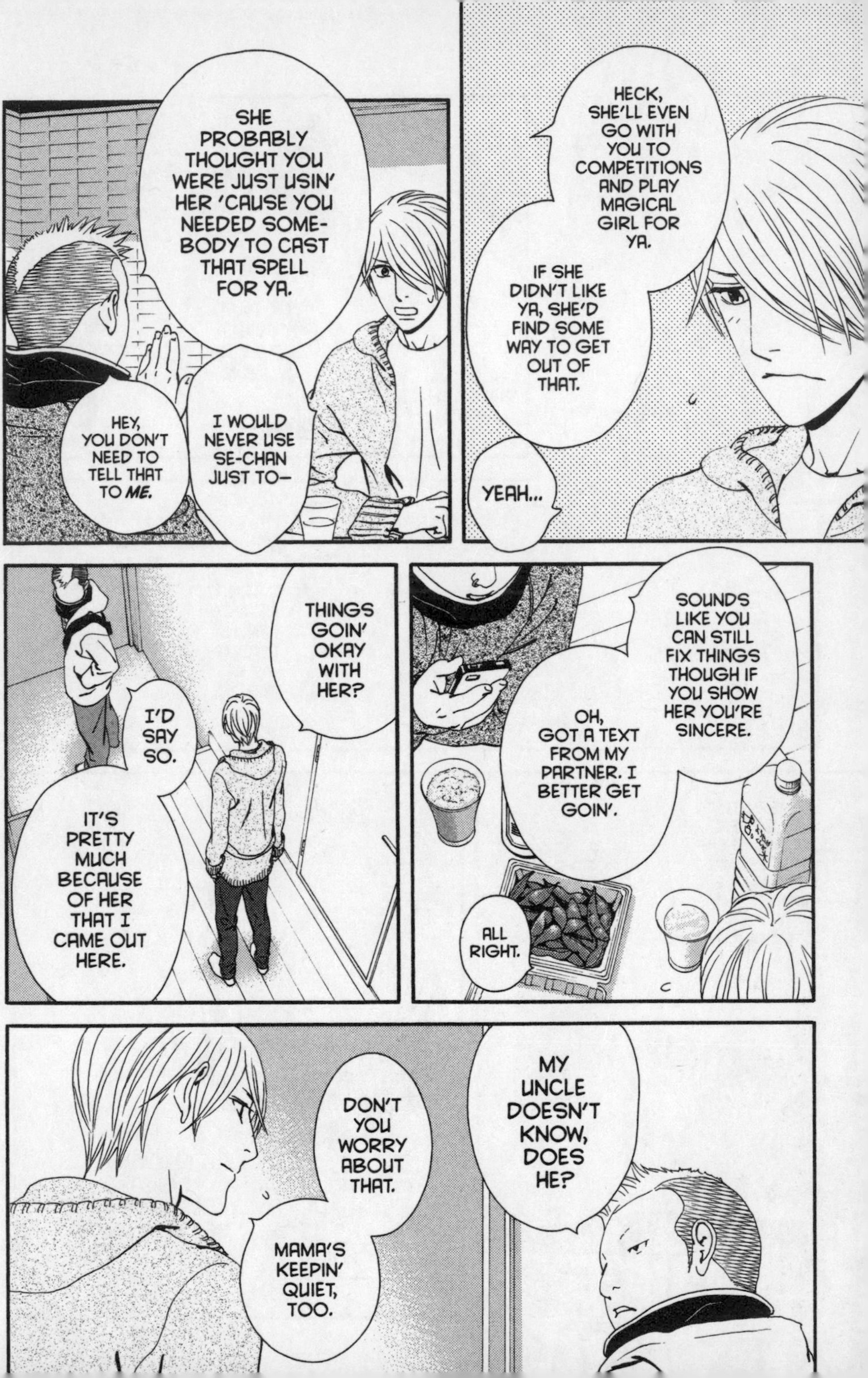
HECK, SHE'LL EVEN GO WITH YOU TO COMPETITIONS AND PLAY MAGICAL GIRL FOR YA.
IF SHE DIDN'T LIKE YA, SHE'D FIND SOME WAY TO GET OUT OF THAT.
YEAH...
SHE PROBABLY THOUGHT YOU WERE JUST USIN' HER 'CAUSE YOU NEEDED SOME-BODY TO CAST THAT SPELL FOR YA.
I WOULD NEVER USE SE-CHAN JUST TO—
HEY, YOU DON'T NEED TO TELL THAT TO *ME.*
SOUNDS LIKE YOU CAN STILL FIX THINGS THOUGH IF YOU SHOW HER YOU'RE SINCERE.
OH, GOT A TEXT FROM MY PARTNER. I BETTER GET GOIN'.
ALL RIGHT.
THINGS GOIN' OKAY WITH HER?
I'D SAY SO.
IT'S PRETTY MUCH BECAUSE OF HER THAT I CAME OUT HERE.
MY UNCLE DOESN'T KNOW, DOES HE?
DON'T YOU WORRY ABOUT THAT.
MAMA'S KEEPIN' QUIET, TOO.

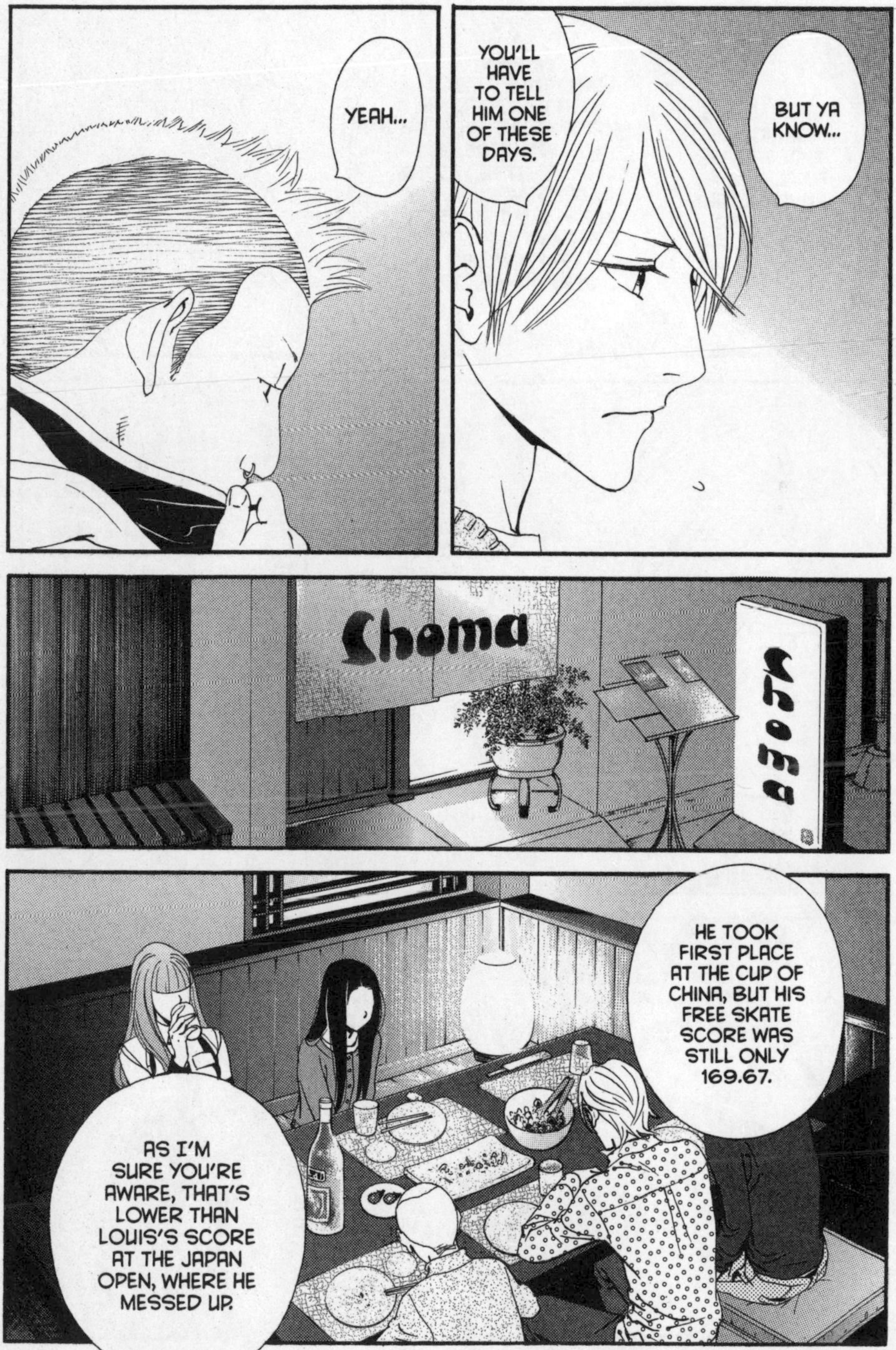
BUT YA KNOW...
YOU'LL HAVE TO TELL HIM ONE OF THESE DAYS.
YEAH...
Shoma
Shoma
HE TOOK FIRST PLACE AT THE CUP OF CHINA, BUT HIS FREE SKATE SCORE WAS STILL ONLY 169.67.
AS I'M SURE YOU'RE AWARE, THAT'S LOWER THAN LOUIS'S SCORE AT THE JAPAN OPEN, WHERE HE MESSED UP.

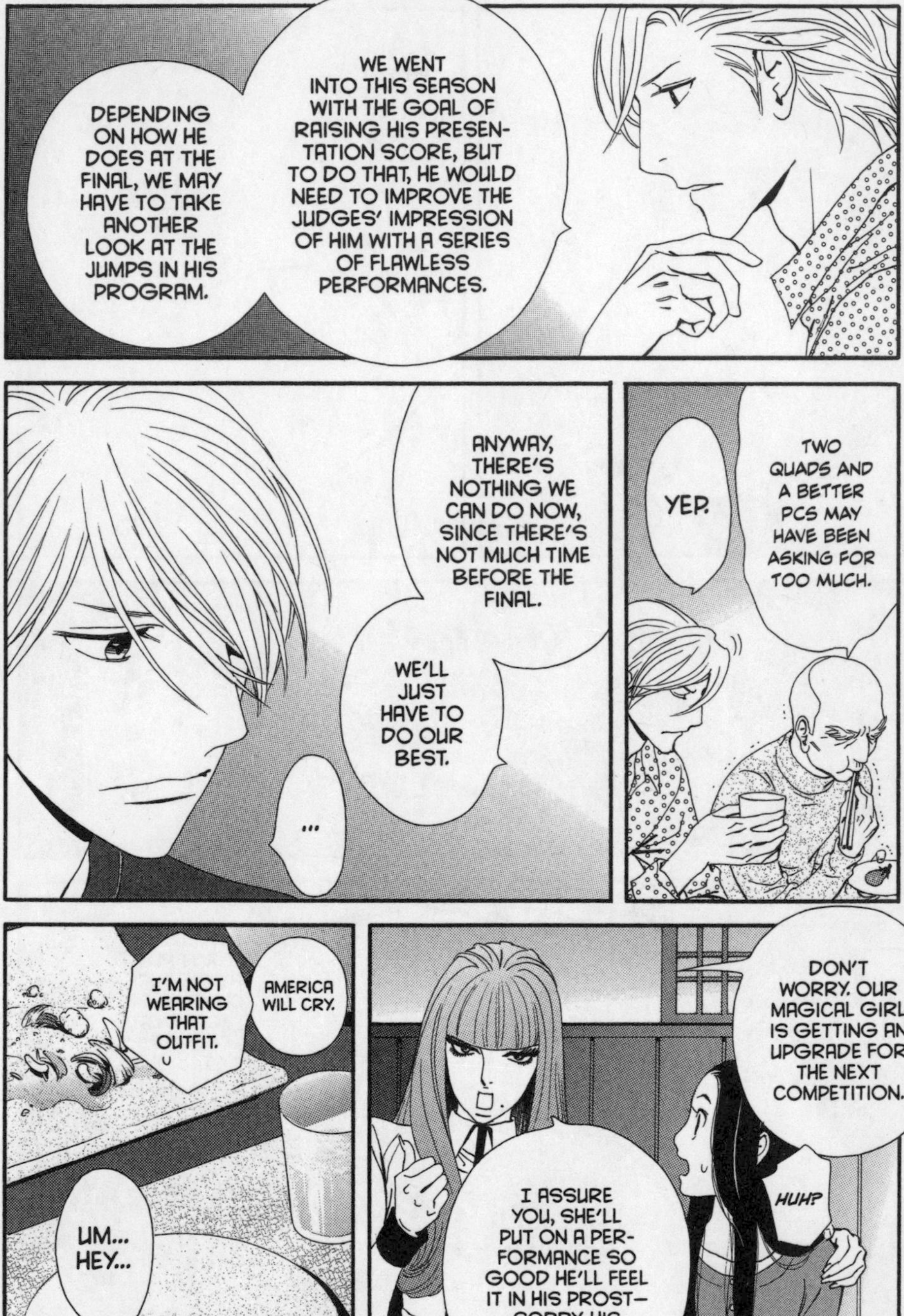
WE WENT INTO THIS SEASON WITH THE GOAL OF RAISING HIS PRESEN-TATION SCORE, BUT TO DO THAT, HE WOULD NEED TO IMPROVE THE JUDGES' IMPRESSION OF HIM WITH A SERIES OF FLAWLESS PERFORMANCES.
DEPENDING ON HOW HE DOES AT THE FINAL, WE MAY HAVE TO TAKE ANOTHER LOOK AT THE JUMPS IN HIS PROGRAM.
TWO QUADS AND A BETTER PCS MAY HAVE BEEN ASKING FOR TOO MUCH.
YEP.
ANYWAY, THERE'S NOTHING WE CAN DO NOW, SINCE THERE'S NOT MUCH TIME BEFORE THE FINAL.
WE'LL JUST HAVE TO DO OUR BEST.
...
DON'T WORRY. OUR MAGICAL GIRL IS GETTING AN UPGRADE FOR THE NEXT COMPETITION.
HUH?
I ASSURE YOU, SHE'LL PUT ON A PER-FORMANCE SO GOOD HE'LL FEEL IT IN HIS PROST–SORRY, HIS HEART.
AMERICA WILL CRY.
I'M NOT WEARING THAT OUTFIT.
UM... HEY...

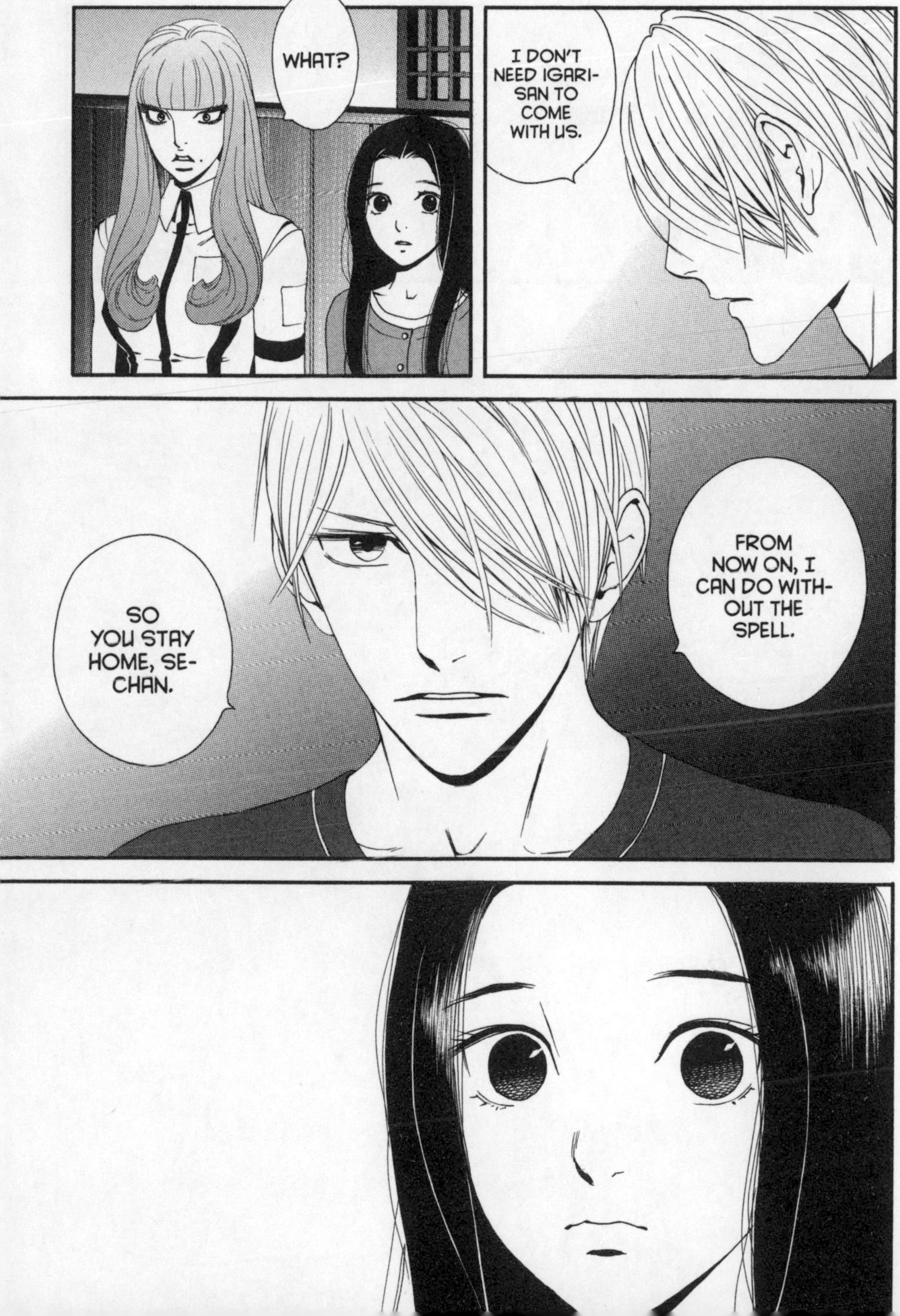
I DON'T NEED IGARI-SAN TO COME WITH US.
WHAT?
FROM NOW ON, I CAN DO WITH-OUT THE SPELL.
SO YOU STAY HOME, SE-CHAN.

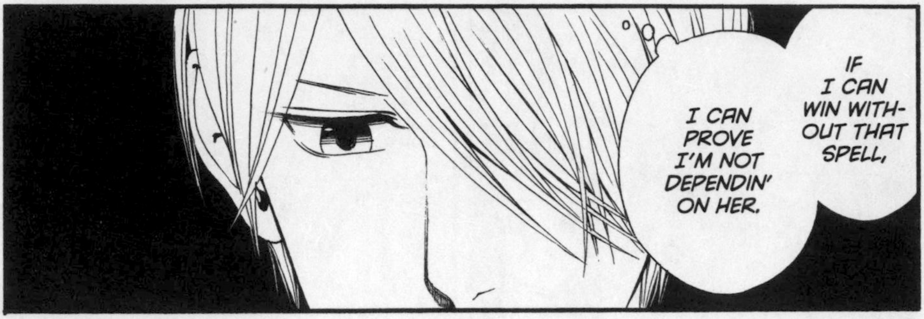
IF I CAN WIN WITH-OUT THAT SPELL,
I CAN PROVE I'M NOT DEPENDIN' ON HER.

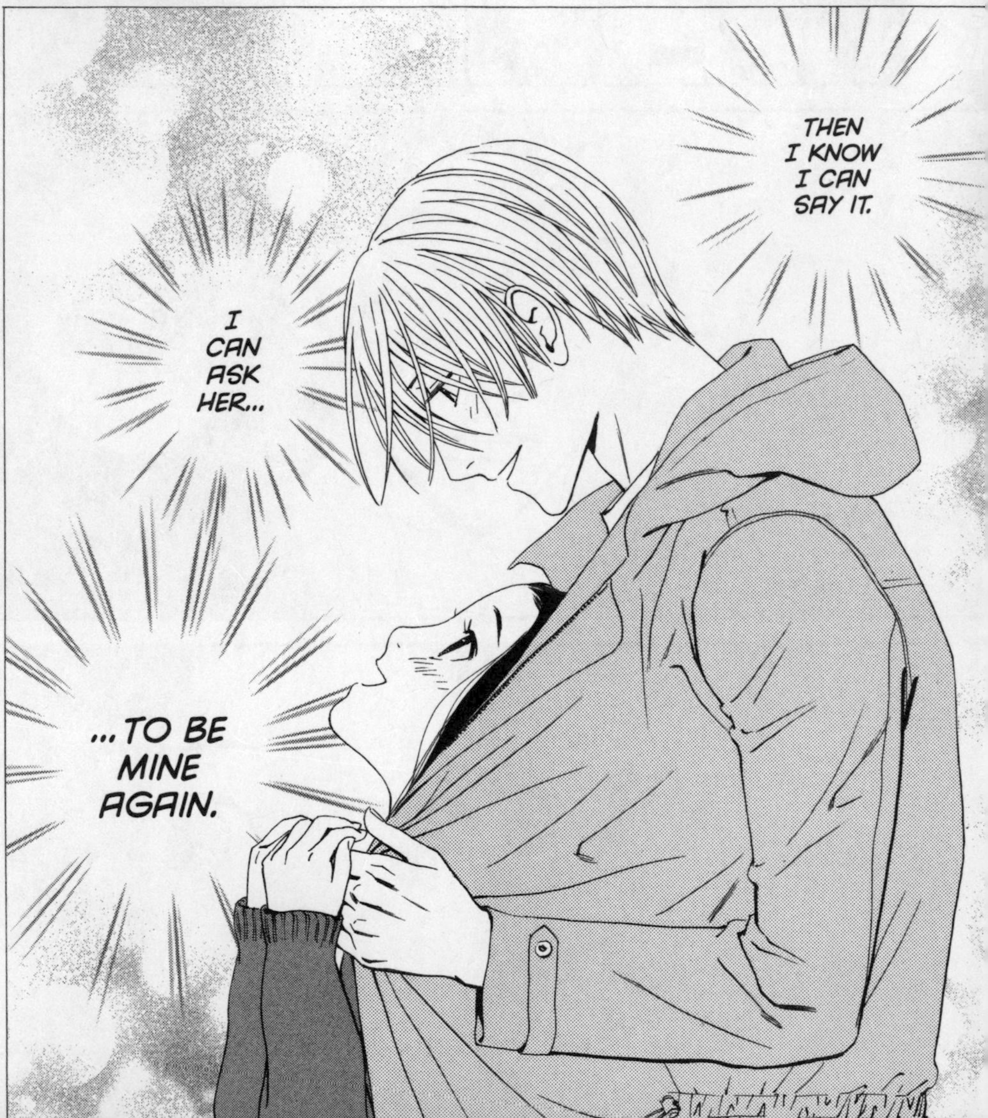
THEN I KNOW I CAN SAY IT.
I CAN ASK HER...
...TO BE MINE AGAIN.

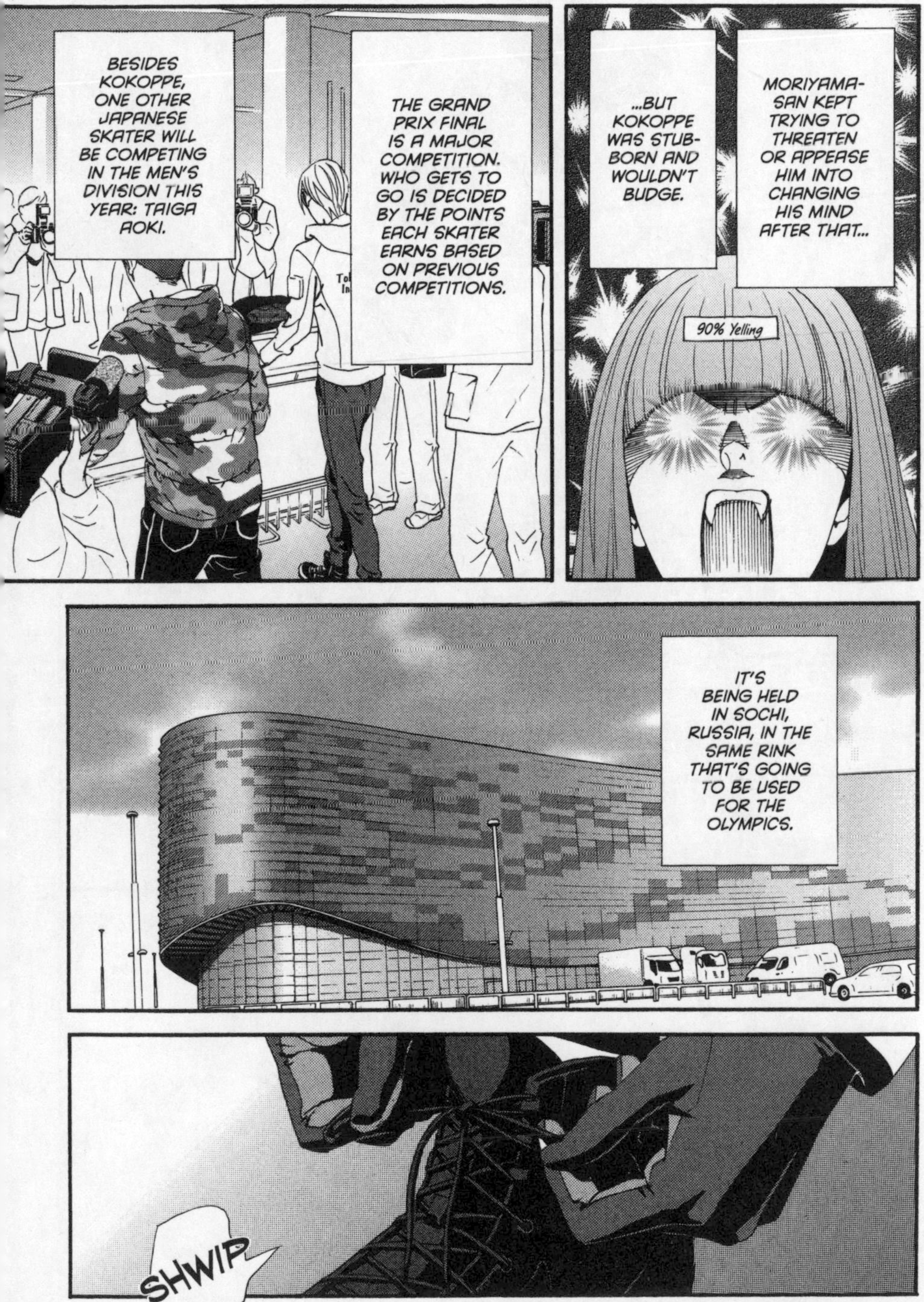
MORIYAMA-SAN KEPT TRYING TO THREATEN OR APPEASE HIM INTO CHANGING HIS MIND AFTER THAT...
...BUT KOKOPPE WAS STUBBORN AND WOULDN'T BUDGE.
90% Yelling
THE GRAND PRIX FINAL IS A MAJOR COMPETITION. WHO GETS TO GO IS DECIDED BY THE POINTS EACH SKATER EARNS BASED ON PREVIOUS COMPETITIONS.
BESIDES KOKOPPE, ONE OTHER JAPANESE SKATER WILL BE COMPETING IN THE MEN'S DIVISION THIS YEAR: TAIGA AOKI.
IT'S BEING HELD IN SOCHI, RUSSIA, IN THE SAME RINK THAT'S GOING TO BE USED FOR THE OLYMPICS.
SHWIP

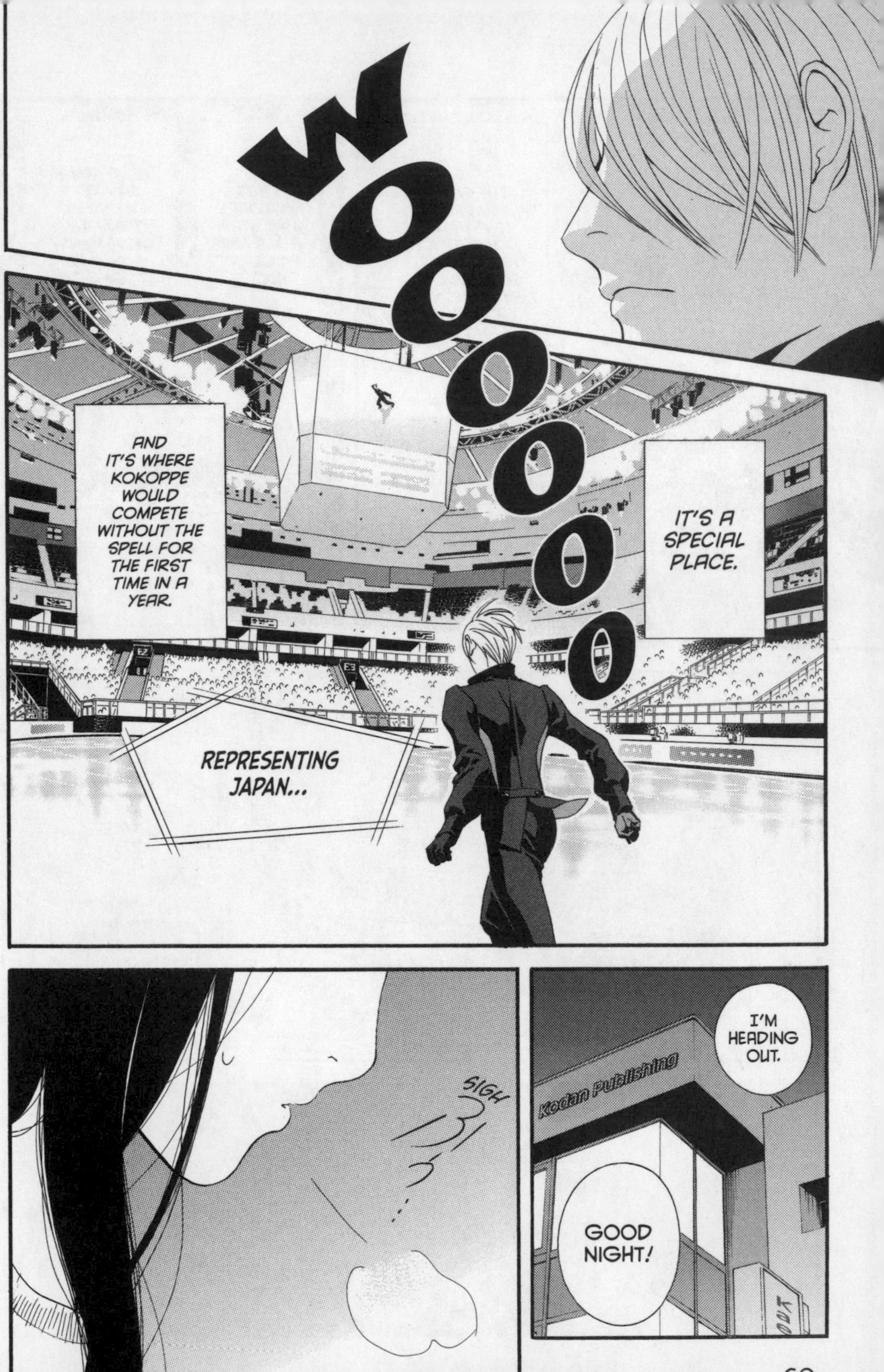
WOOOOOO
IT'S A SPECIAL PLACE.
AND IT'S WHERE KOKOPPE WOULD COMPETE WITHOUT THE SPELL FOR THE FIRST TIME IN A YEAR.
REPRESENTING JAPAN...
I'M HEADING OUT.
Kodan Publishing
GOOD NIGHT!
SIGH

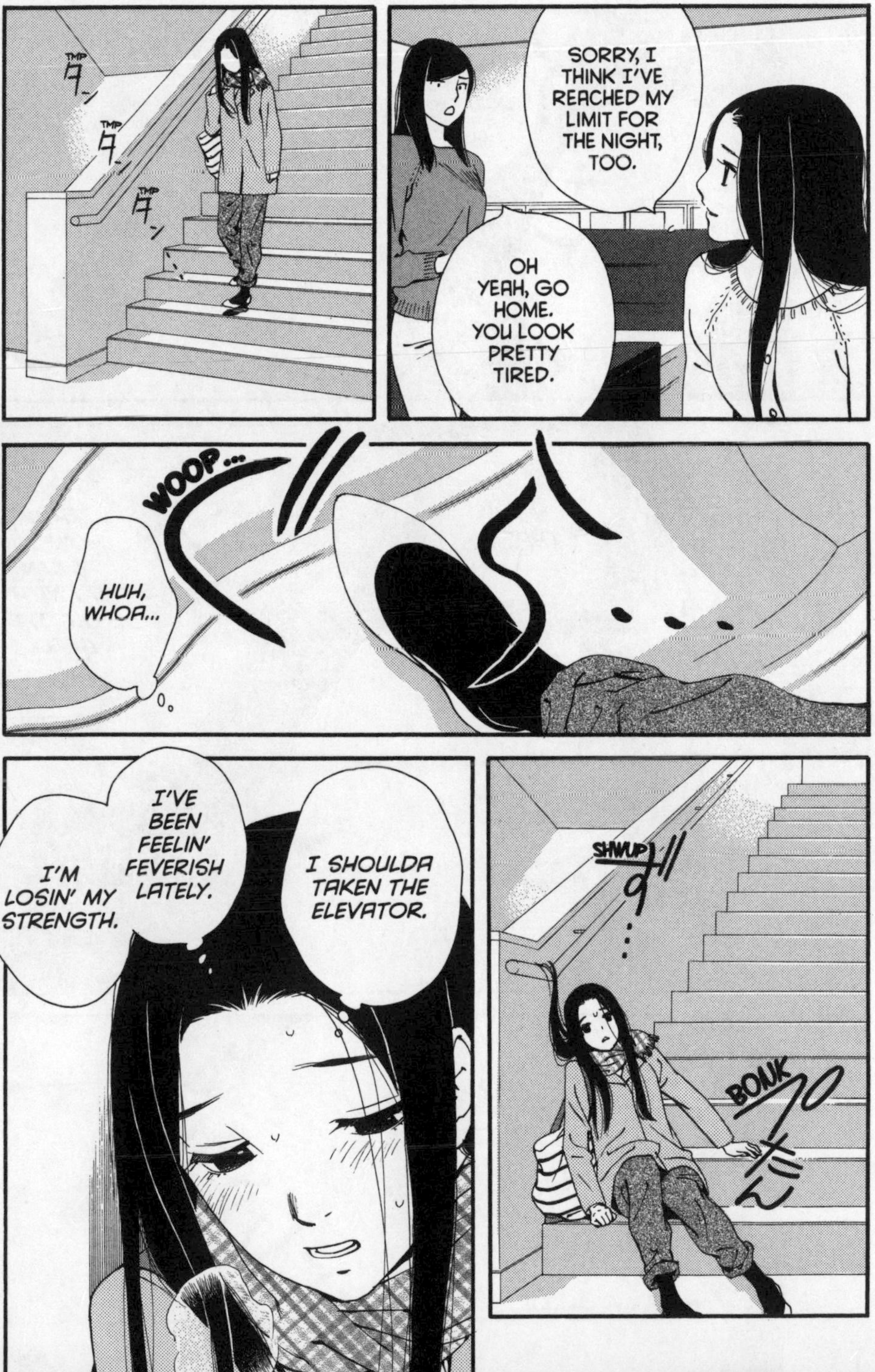
SORRY, I THINK I'VE REACHED MY LIMIT FOR THE NIGHT, TOO.
OH YEAH, GO HOME. YOU LOOK PRETTY TIRED.
TMP
TMP
TMP
WOOP...
HUH, WHOA...
SHWUP
BONK
I SHOULDA TAKEN THE ELEVATOR.
I'VE BEEN FEELIN' FEVERISH LATELY.
I'M LOSIN' MY STRENGTH.

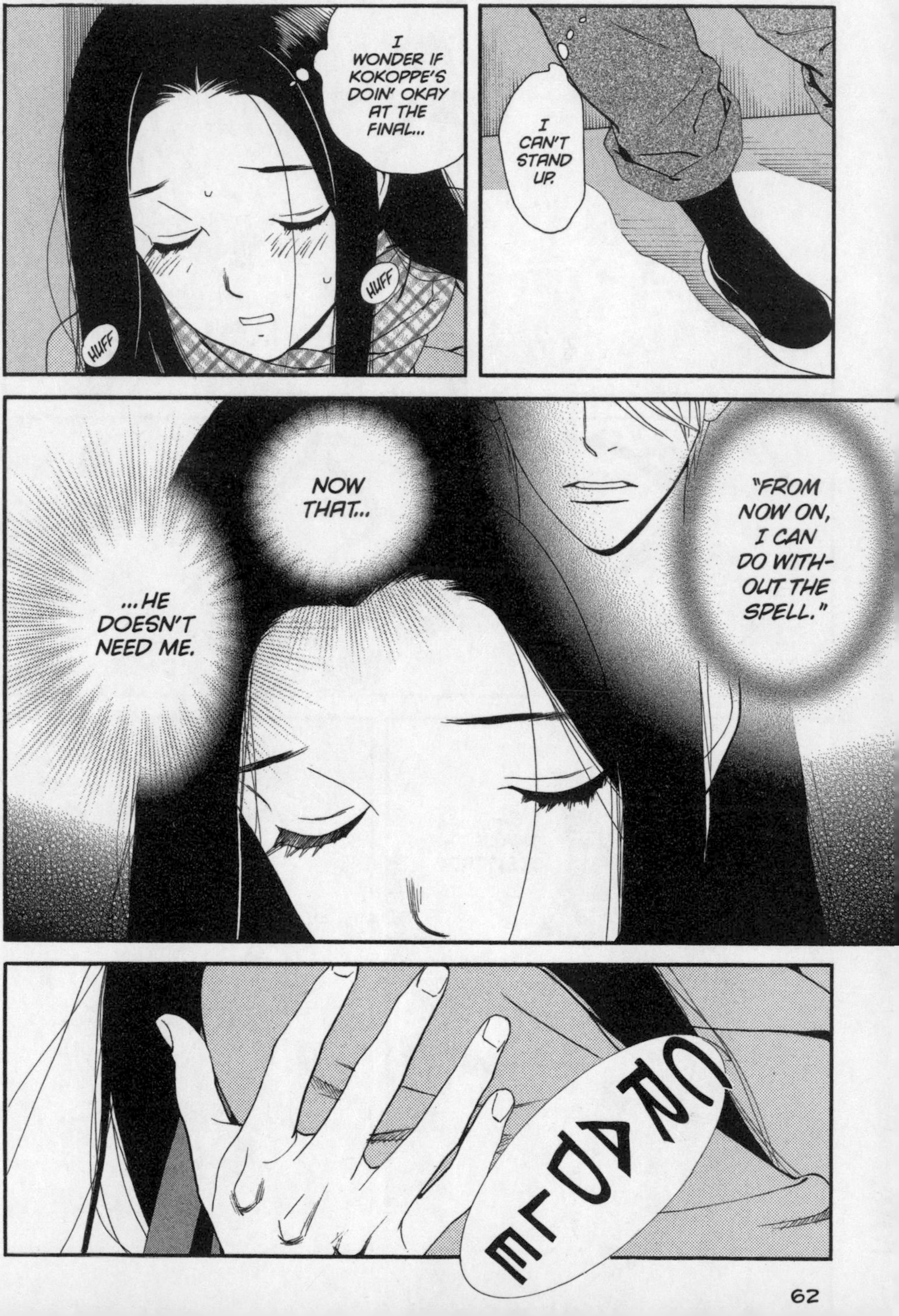
I CAN'T STAND UP.
I WONDER IF KOKOPPE'S DOIN' OKAY AT THE FINAL...
HUFF
HUFF
"FROM NOW ON, I CAN DO WITH-OUT THE SPELL."
NOW THAT...
...HE DOESN'T NEED ME.

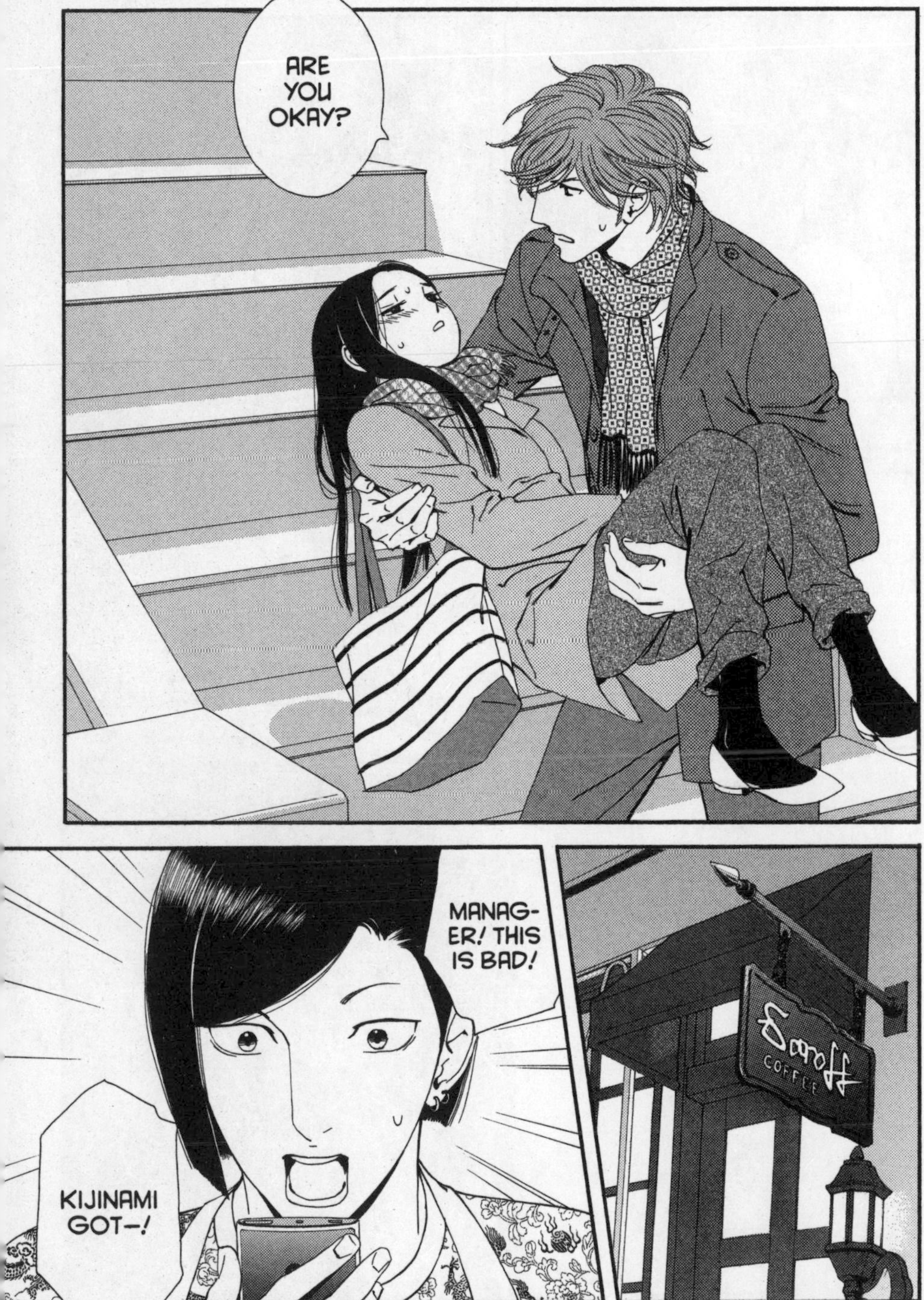
ARE YOU OKAY?
MANAG-ER! THIS IS BAD!
KIJINAMI GOT—!

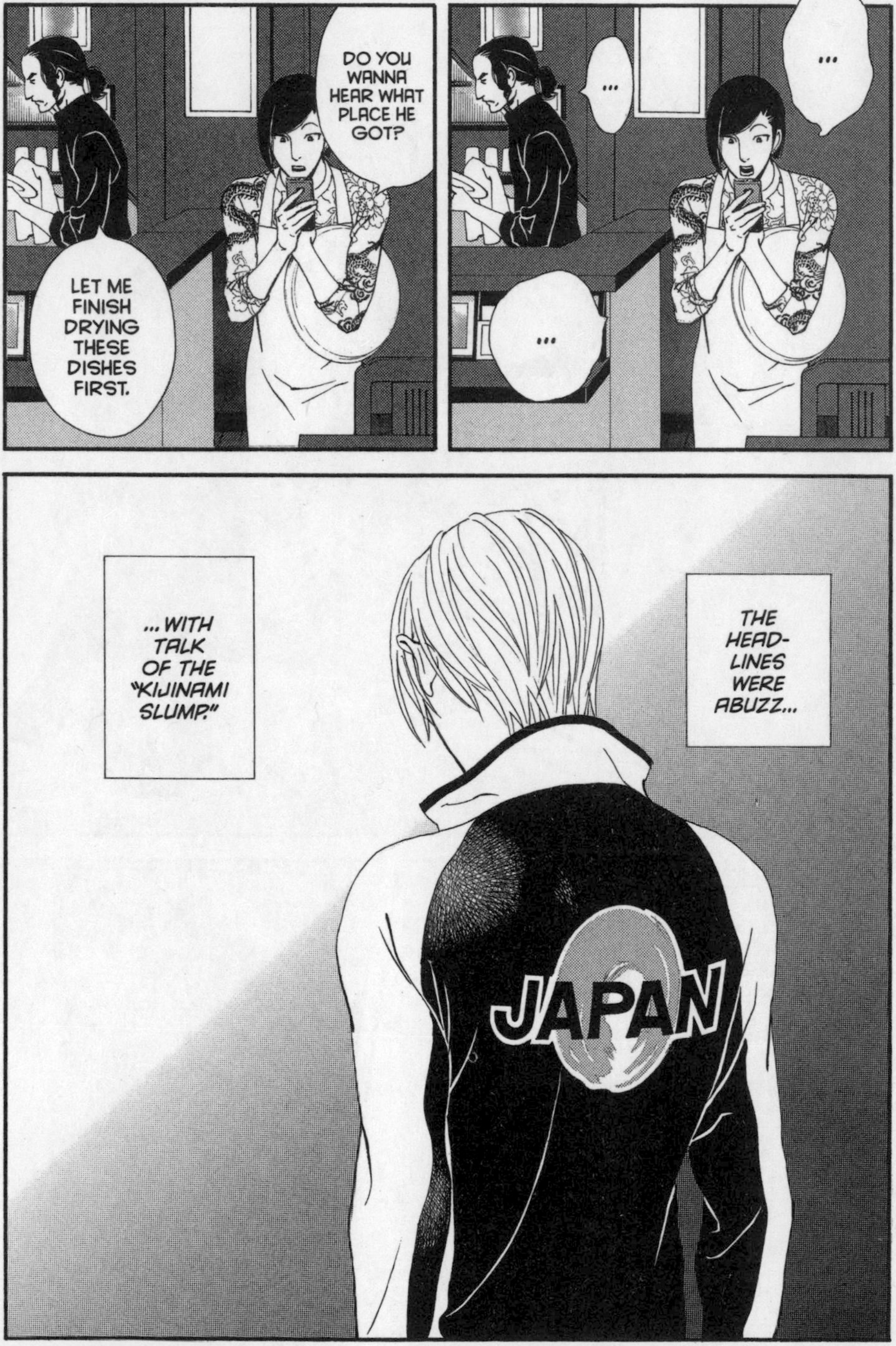
...
...
...
DO YOU WANNA HEAR WHAT PLACE HE GOT?
LET ME FINISH DRYING THESE DISHES FIRST.
THE HEAD-LINES WERE ABUZZ...
...WITH TALK OF THE "KIJINAMI SLUMP."
JAPAN

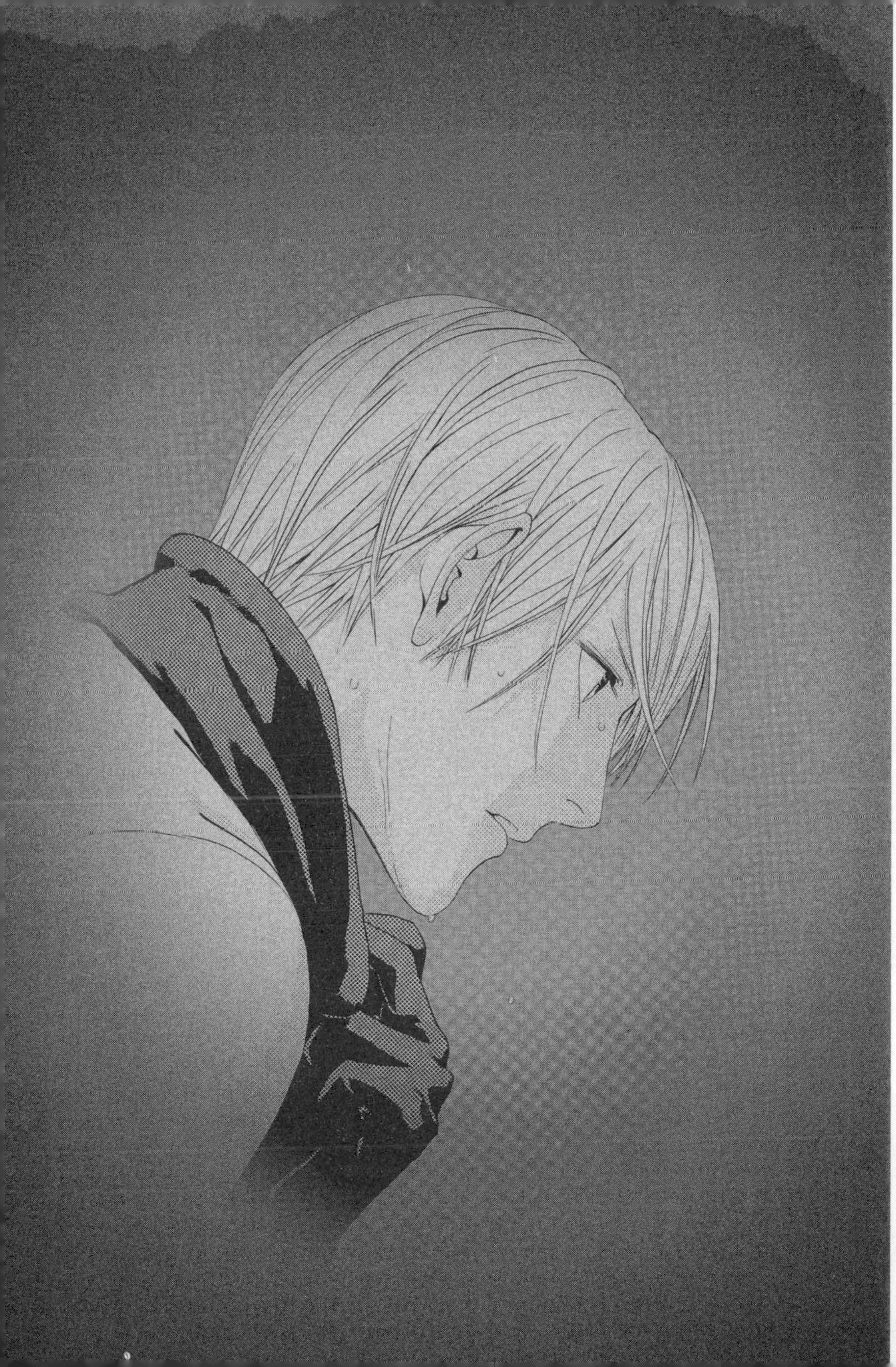

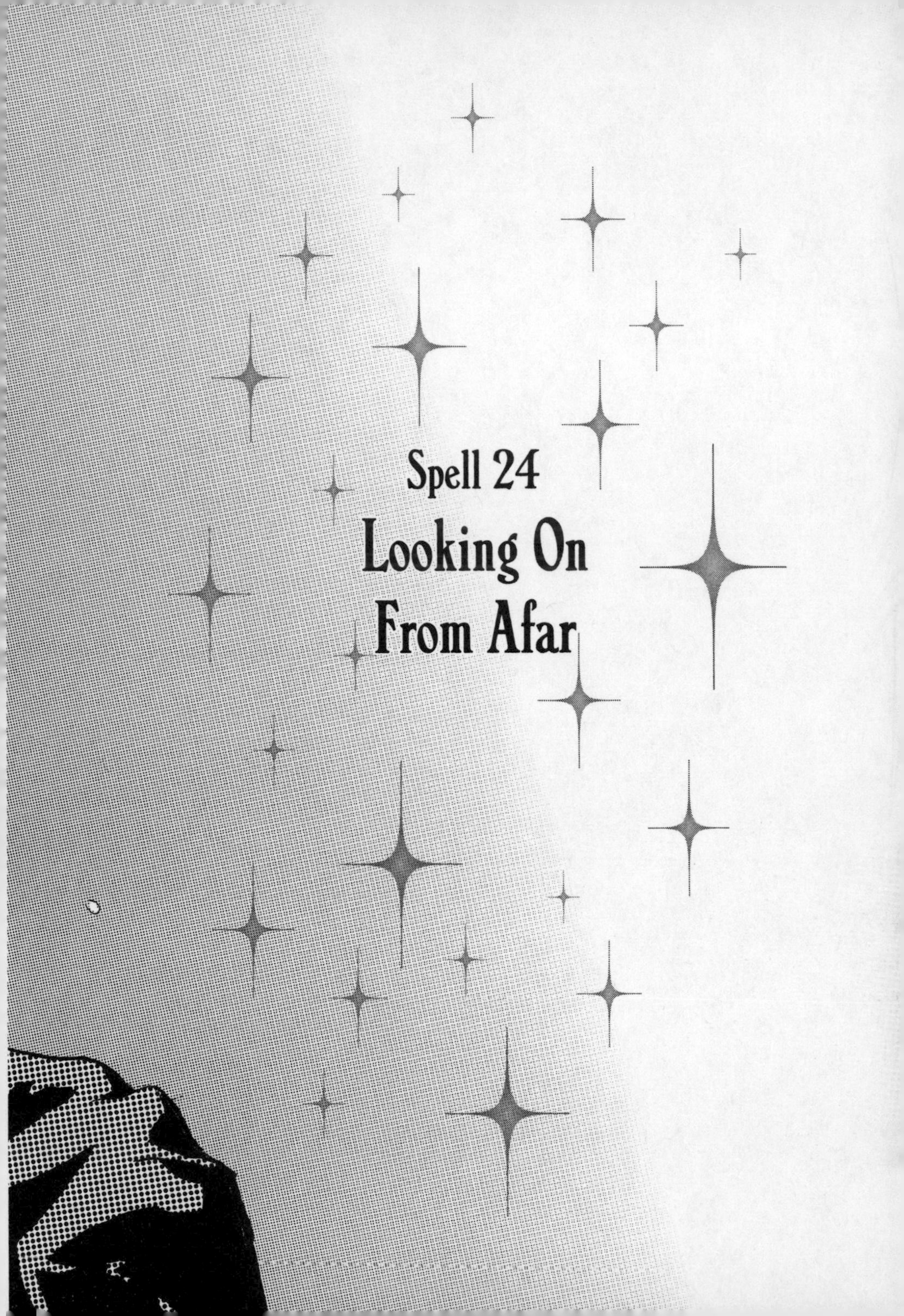
Spell 24
Looking On
From Afar

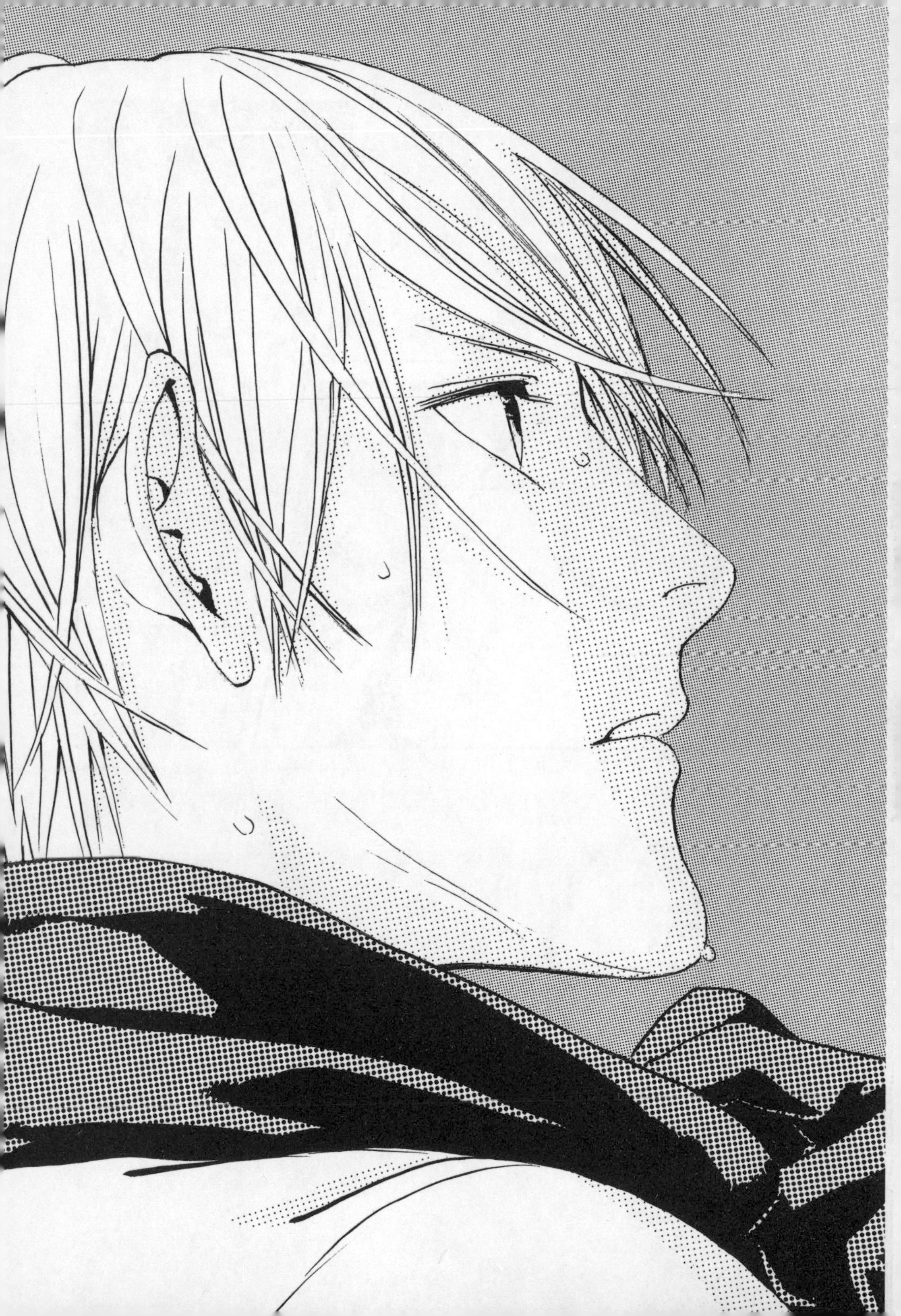

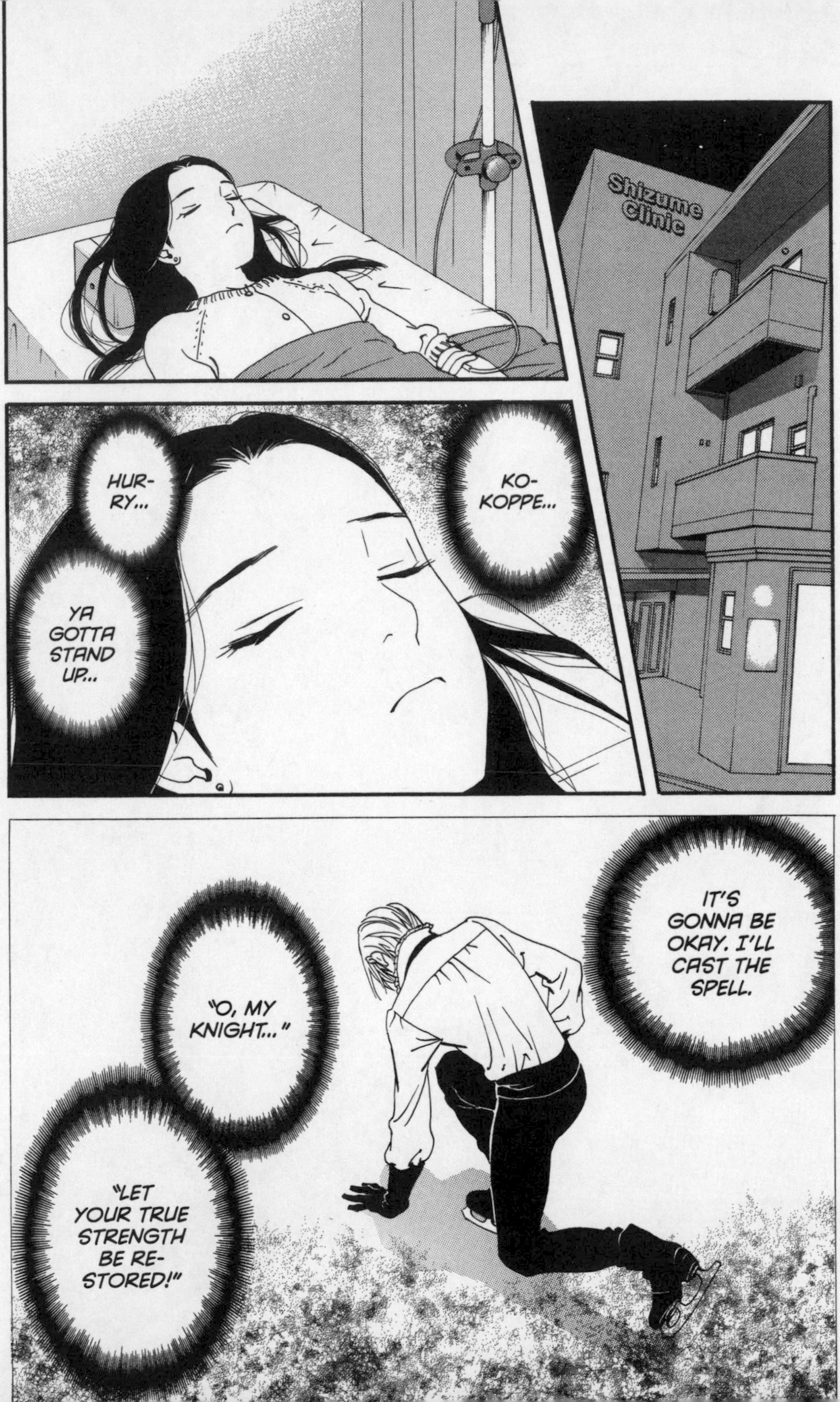
Shizume Clinic
KO-KOPPE...
HURRY...
YA GOTTA STAND UP...
IT'S GONNA BE OKAY. I'LL CAST THE SPELL.
"O, MY KNIGHT..."
"LET YOUR TRUE STRENGTH BE RESTORED!"

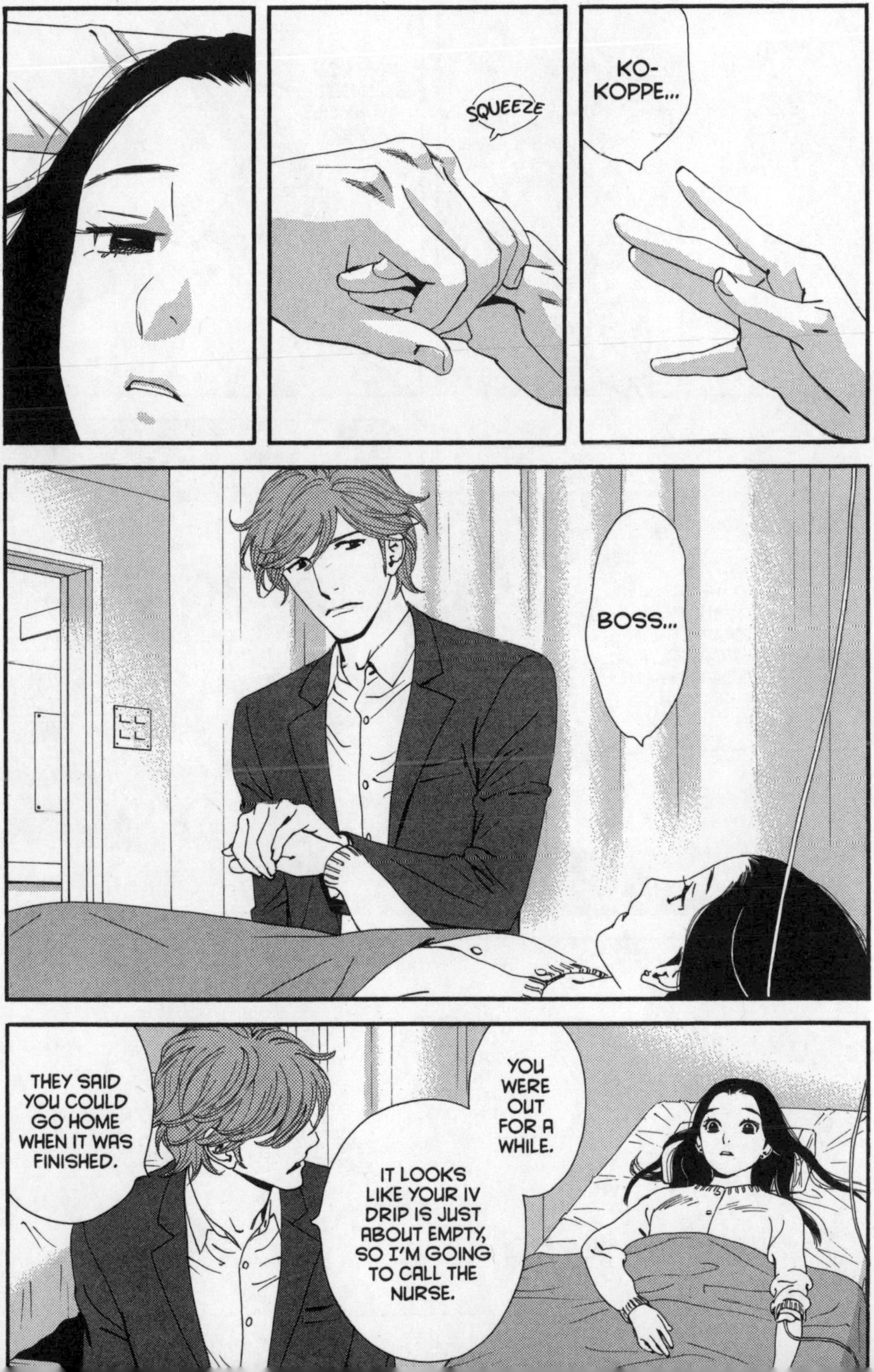
KO-
KOPPE...
SQUEEZE
BOSS...
YOU WERE OUT FOR A WHILE.
IT LOOKS LIKE YOUR IV DRIP IS JUST ABOUT EMPTY, SO I'M GOING TO CALL THE NURSE.
THEY SAID YOU COULD GO HOME WHEN IT WAS FINISHED.

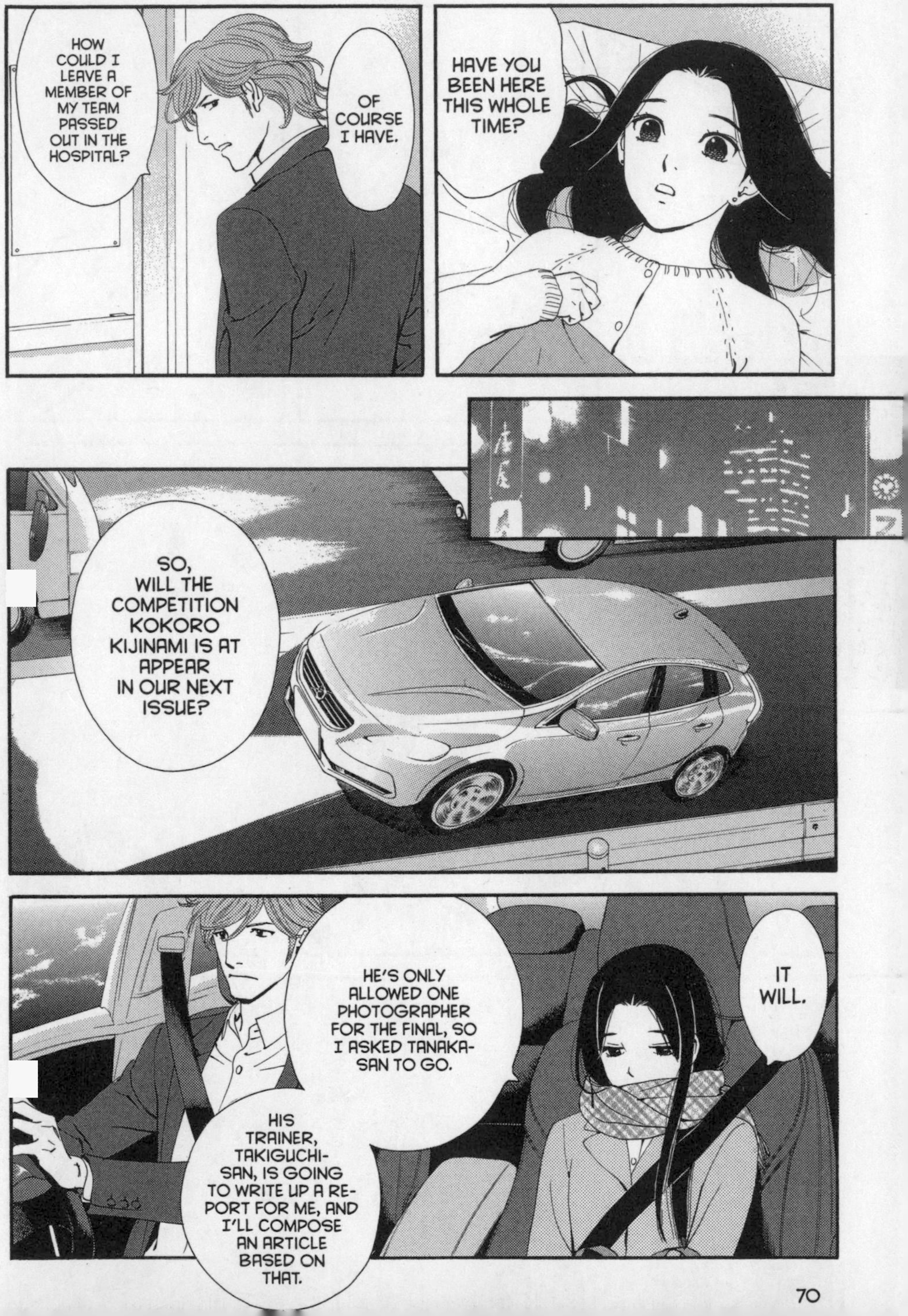
HAVE YOU BEEN HERE THIS WHOLE TIME?
OF COURSE I HAVE.
HOW COULD I LEAVE A MEMBER OF MY TEAM PASSED OUT IN THE HOSPITAL?
SO, WILL THE COMPETITION KOKORO KIJINAMI IS AT APPEAR IN OUR NEXT ISSUE?
IT WILL.
HE'S ONLY ALLOWED ONE PHOTOGRAPHER FOR THE FINAL, SO I ASKED TANAKA-SAN TO GO.
HIS TRAINER, TAKIGUCHI-SAN, IS GOING TO WRITE UP A RE-PORT FOR ME, AND I'LL COMPOSE AN ARTICLE BASED ON THAT.

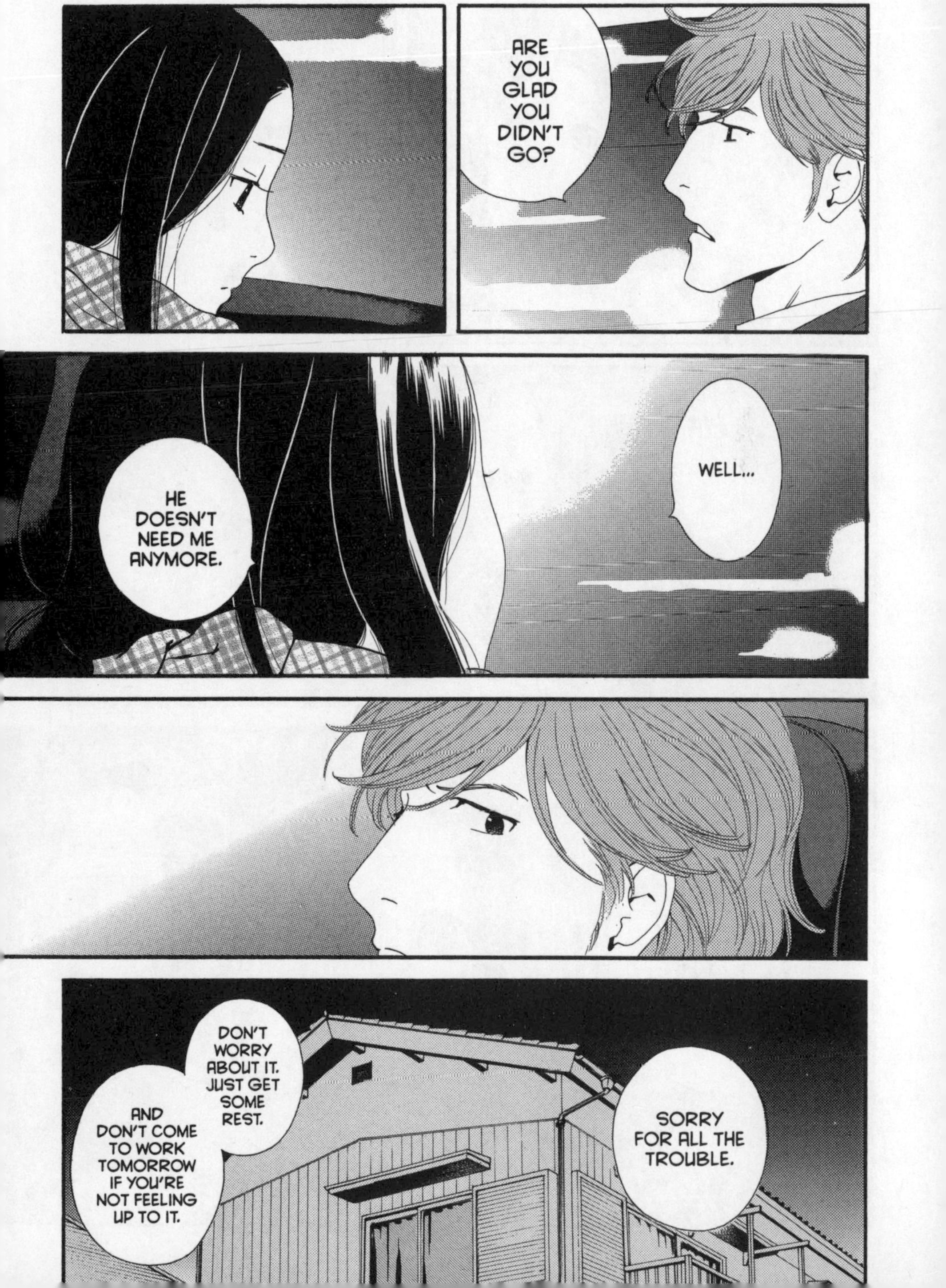
ARE YOU GLAD YOU DIDN'T GO?
WELL...
HE DOESN'T NEED ME ANYMORE.
SORRY FOR ALL THE TROUBLE.
DON'T WORRY ABOUT IT. JUST GET SOME REST.
AND DON'T COME TO WORK TOMORROW IF YOU'RE NOT FEELING UP TO IT.

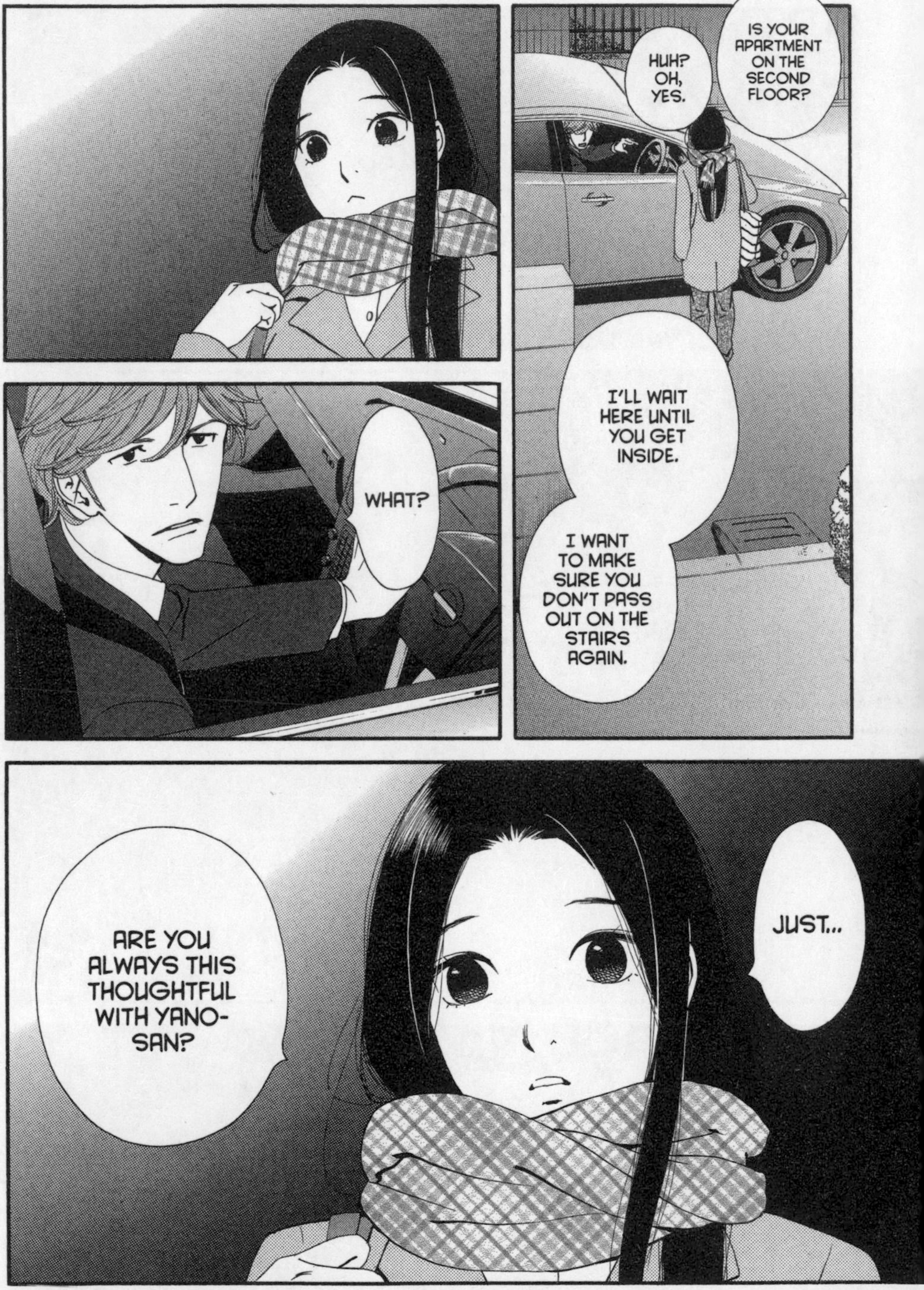
IS YOUR APARTMENT ON THE SECOND FLOOR?
HUH? OH, YES.
I'LL WAIT HERE UNTIL YOU GET INSIDE.
I WANT TO MAKE SURE YOU DON'T PASS OUT ON THE STAIRS AGAIN.
WHAT?
JUST...
ARE YOU ALWAYS THIS THOUGHTFUL WITH YANO-SAN?

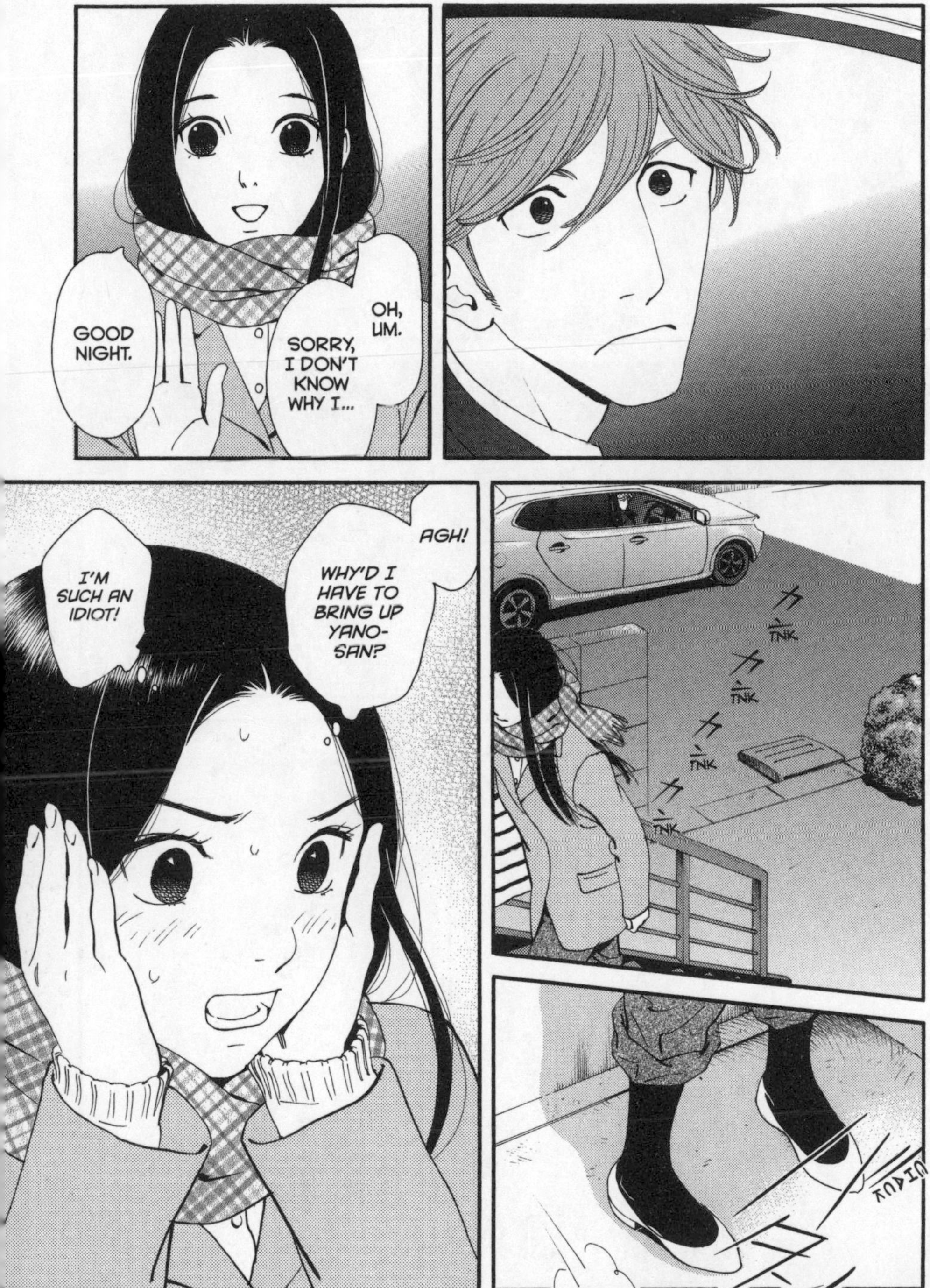
OH, UM. SORRY, I DON'T KNOW WHY I...
GOOD NIGHT.
TNK
TNK
TNK
TNK
AGH! WHY'D I HAVE TO BRING UP YANO-SAN?
I'M SUCH AN IDIOT!

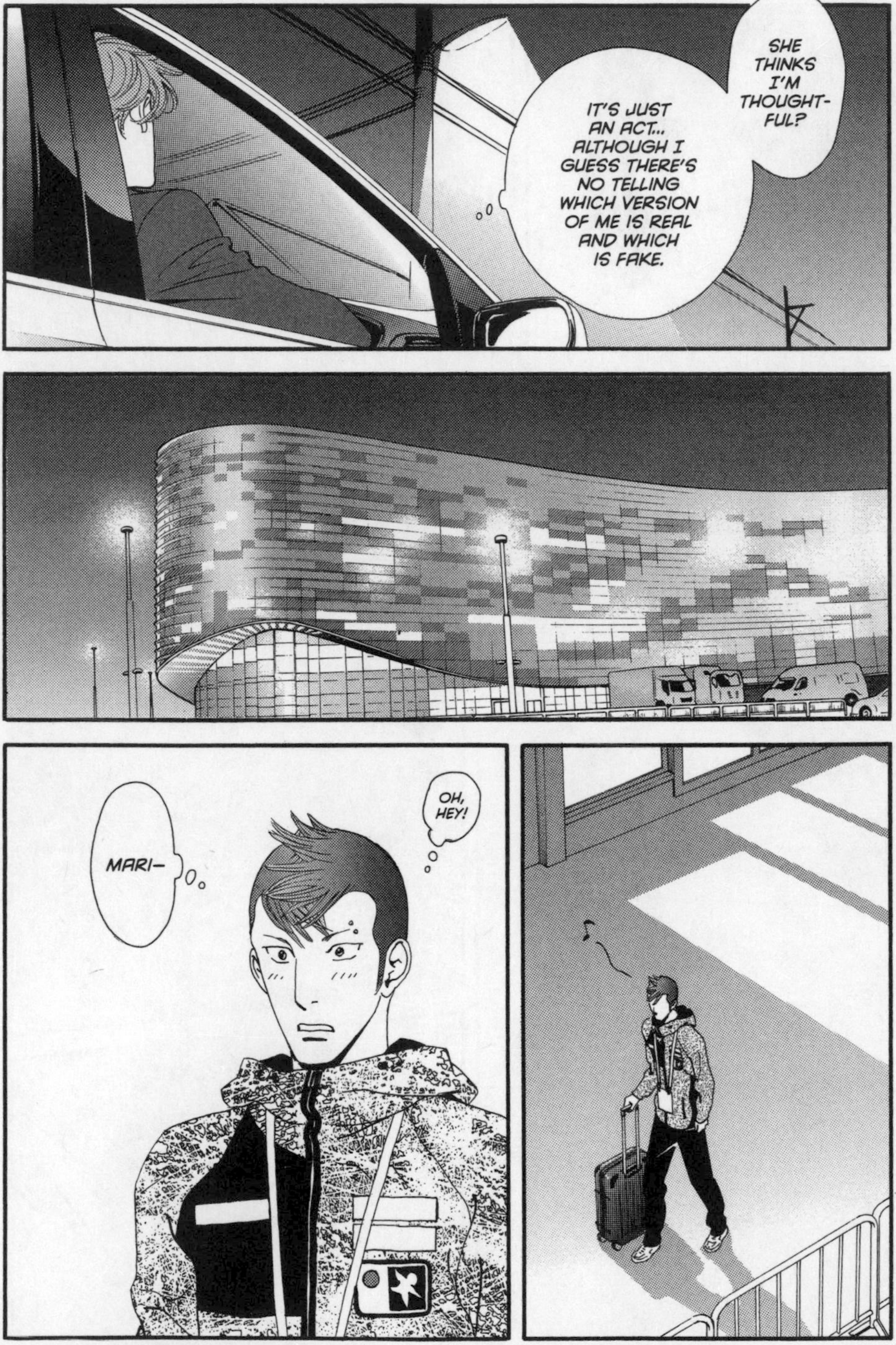
SHE THINKS I'M THOUGHT-FUL?
IT'S JUST AN ACT... ALTHOUGH I GUESS THERE'S NO TELLING WHICH VERSION OF ME IS REAL AND WHICH IS FAKE.
OH, HEY!
MARI—

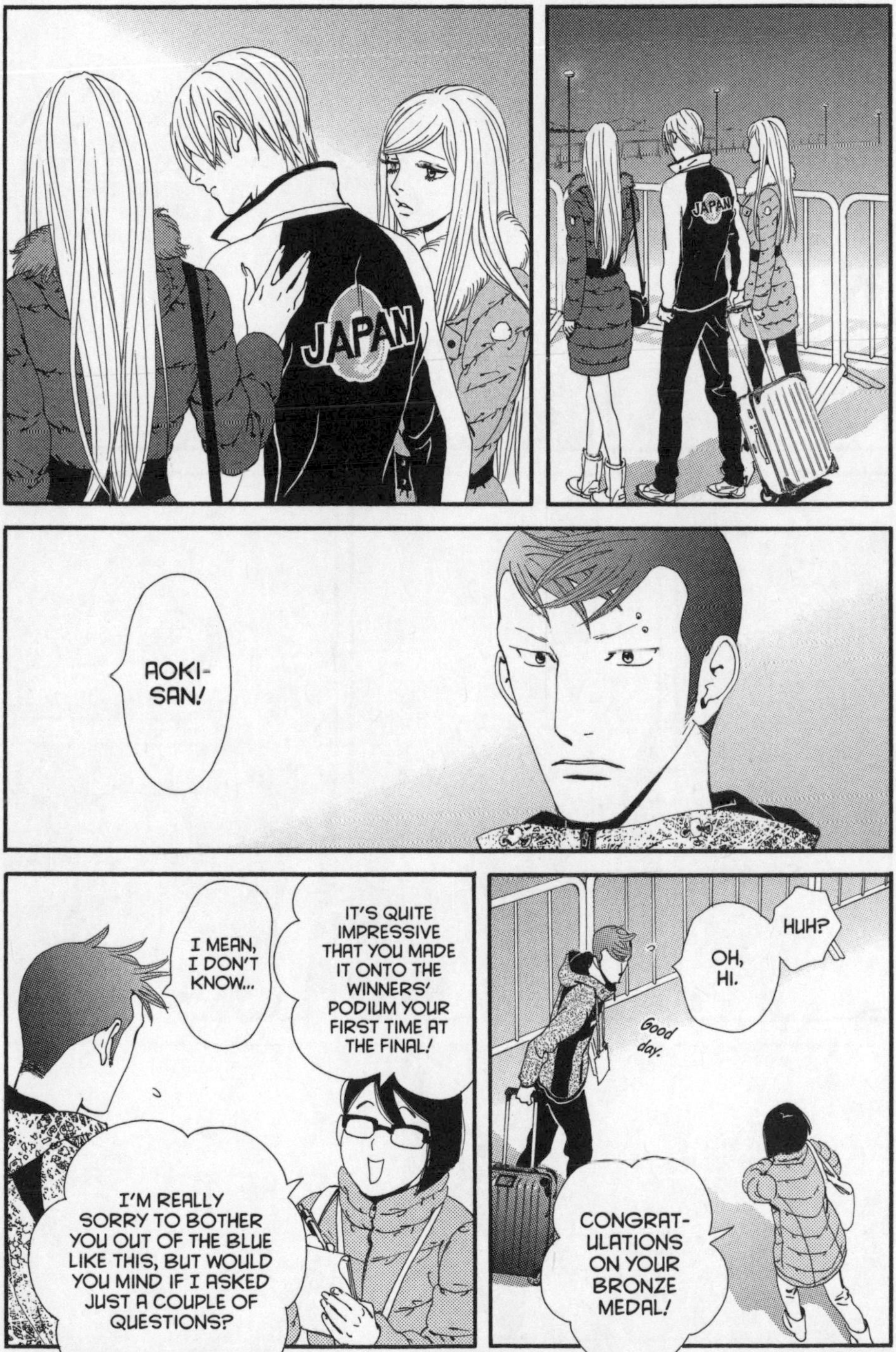
AOKI-SAN!
HUH?
OH, HI.
Good day.
CONGRAT-ULATIONS ON YOUR BRONZE MEDAL!
IT'S QUITE IMPRESSIVE THAT YOU MADE IT ONTO THE WINNERS' PODIUM YOUR FIRST TIME AT THE FINAL!
I MEAN, I DON'T KNOW...
I'M REALLY SORRY TO BOTHER YOU OUT OF THE BLUE LIKE THIS, BUT WOULD YOU MIND IF I ASKED JUST A COUPLE OF QUESTIONS?

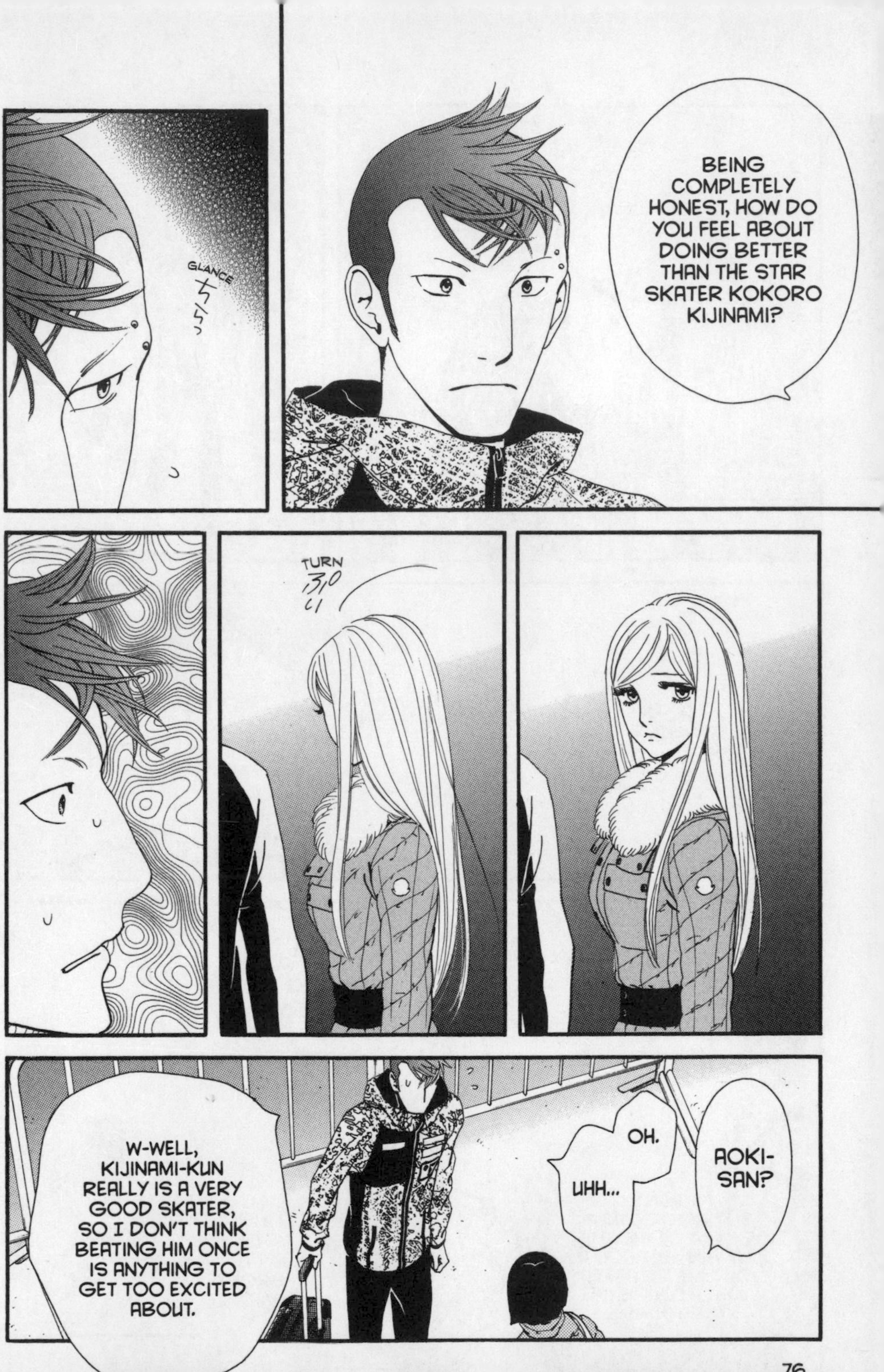
BEING COMPLETELY HONEST, HOW DO YOU FEEL ABOUT DOING BETTER THAN THE STAR SKATER KOKORO KIJINAMI?
GLANCE
ちらっ
TURN
AOKI-SAN?
OH.
UHH...
W-WELL, KIJINAMI-KUN REALLY IS A VERY GOOD SKATER, SO I DON'T THINK BEATING HIM ONCE IS ANYTHING TO GET TOO EXCITED ABOUT.

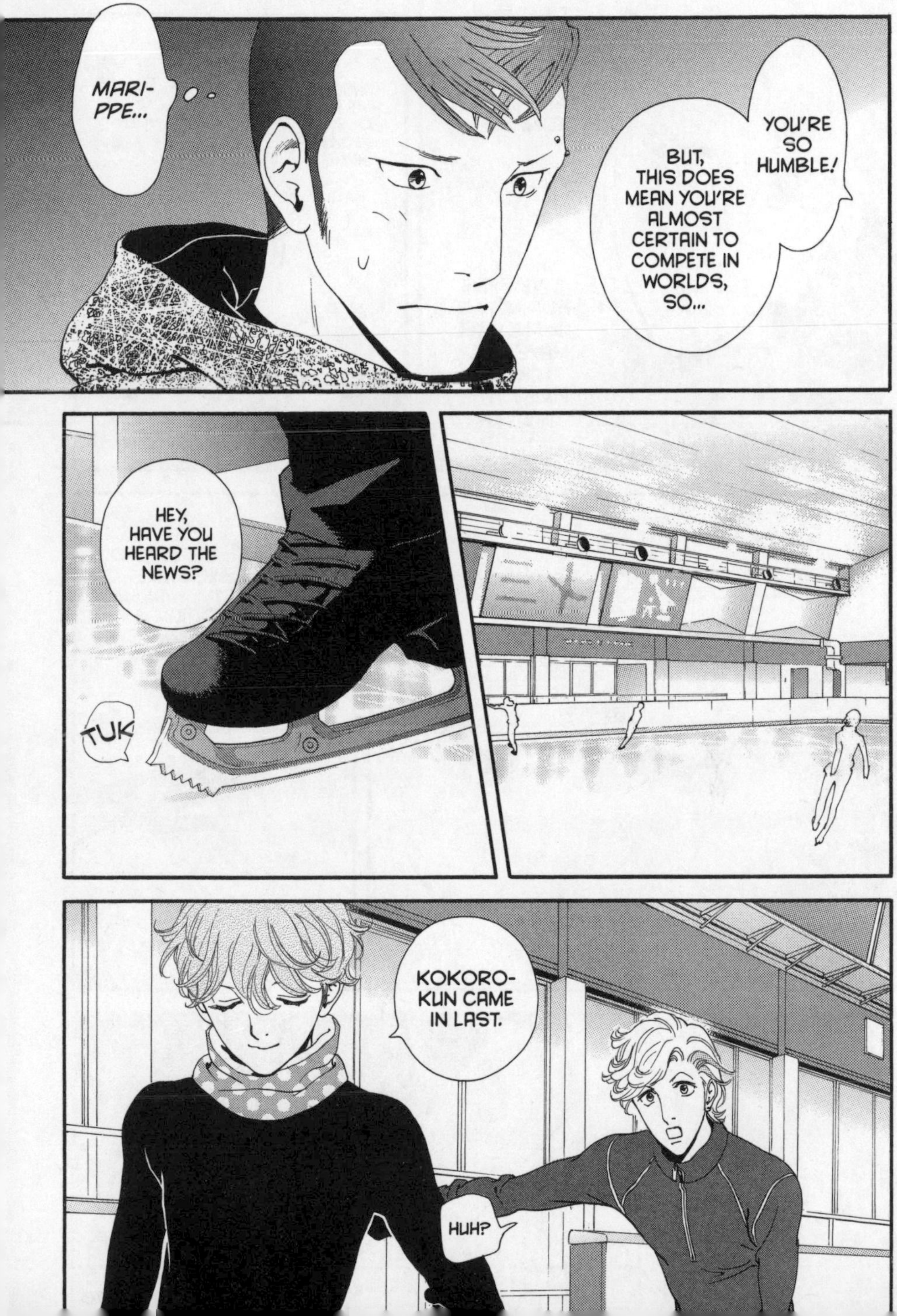
YOU'RE SO HUMBLE!
BUT, THIS DOES MEAN YOU'RE ALMOST CERTAIN TO COMPETE IN WORLDS, SO...
MARI-PPE...
HEY, HAVE YOU HEARD THE NEWS?
TUK
KOKORO-KUN CAME IN LAST.
HUH?

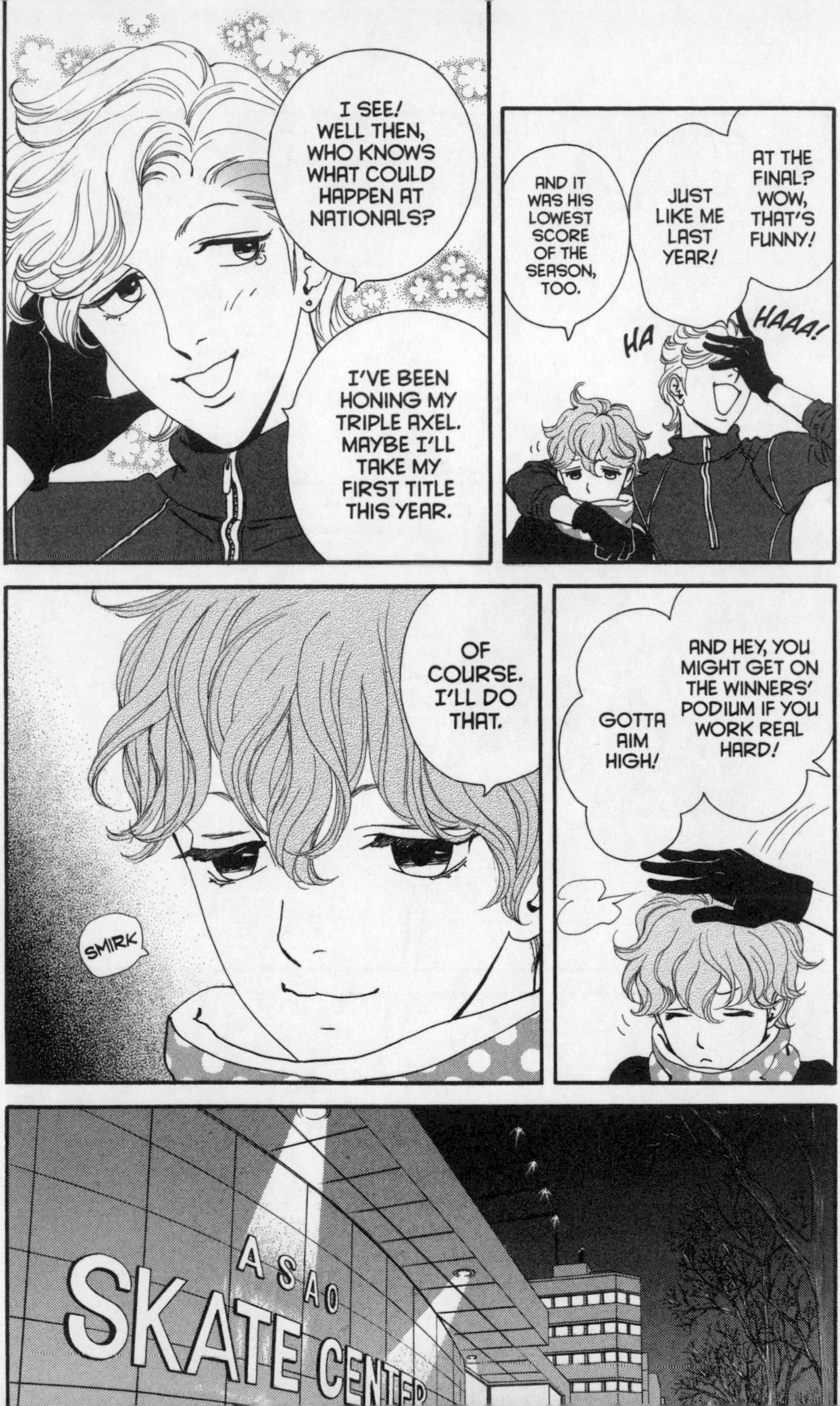
AT THE FINAL? WOW, THAT'S FUNNY!
JUST LIKE ME LAST YEAR!
HAAAA!
HA
AND IT WAS HIS LOWEST SCORE OF THE SEASON, TOO.
I SEE! WELL THEN, WHO KNOWS WHAT COULD HAPPEN AT NATIONALS?
I'VE BEEN HONING MY TRIPLE AXEL. MAYBE I'LL TAKE MY FIRST TITLE THIS YEAR.
AND HEY, YOU MIGHT GET ON THE WINNERS' PODIUM IF YOU WORK REAL HARD!
GOTTA AIM HIGH!
OF COURSE. I'LL DO THAT.
SMIRK
ASAO
SKATE CENTE

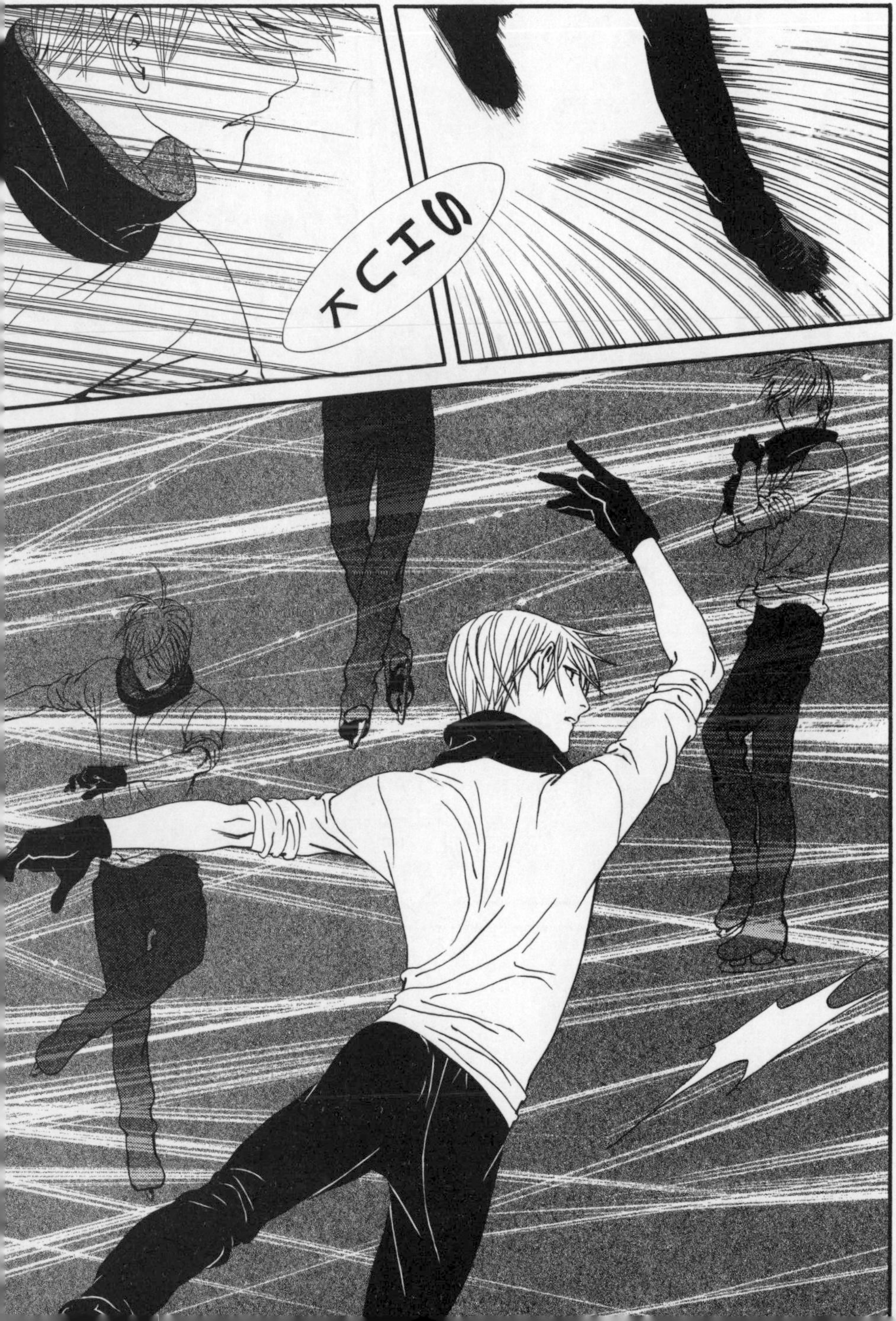

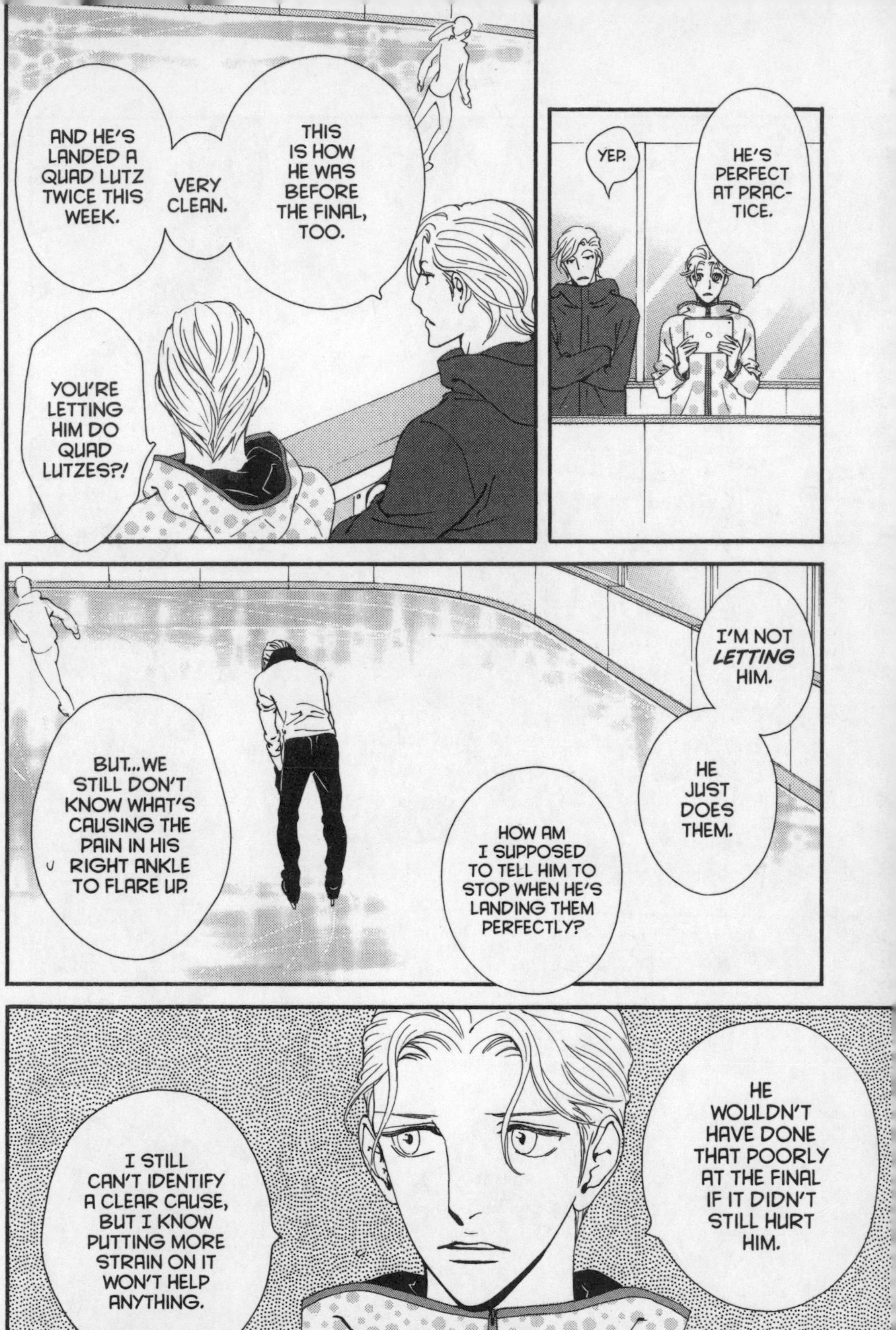
HE'S PERFECT AT PRAC-TICE.
YEP.
THIS IS HOW HE WAS BEFORE THE FINAL, TOO.
VERY CLEAN.
AND HE'S LANDED A QUAD LUTZ TWICE THIS WEEK.
YOU'RE LETTING HIM DO QUAD LUTZES?!
I'M NOT *LETTING* HIM.
HE JUST DOES THEM.
HOW AM I SUPPOSED TO TELL HIM TO STOP WHEN HE'S LANDING THEM PERFECTLY?
BUT...WE STILL DON'T KNOW WHAT'S CAUSING THE PAIN IN HIS RIGHT ANKLE TO FLARE UP.
HE WOULDN'T HAVE DONE THAT POORLY AT THE FINAL IF IT DIDN'T STILL HURT HIM.
I STILL CAN'T IDENTIFY A CLEAR CAUSE, BUT I KNOW PUTTING MORE STRAIN ON IT WON'T HELP ANYTHING.

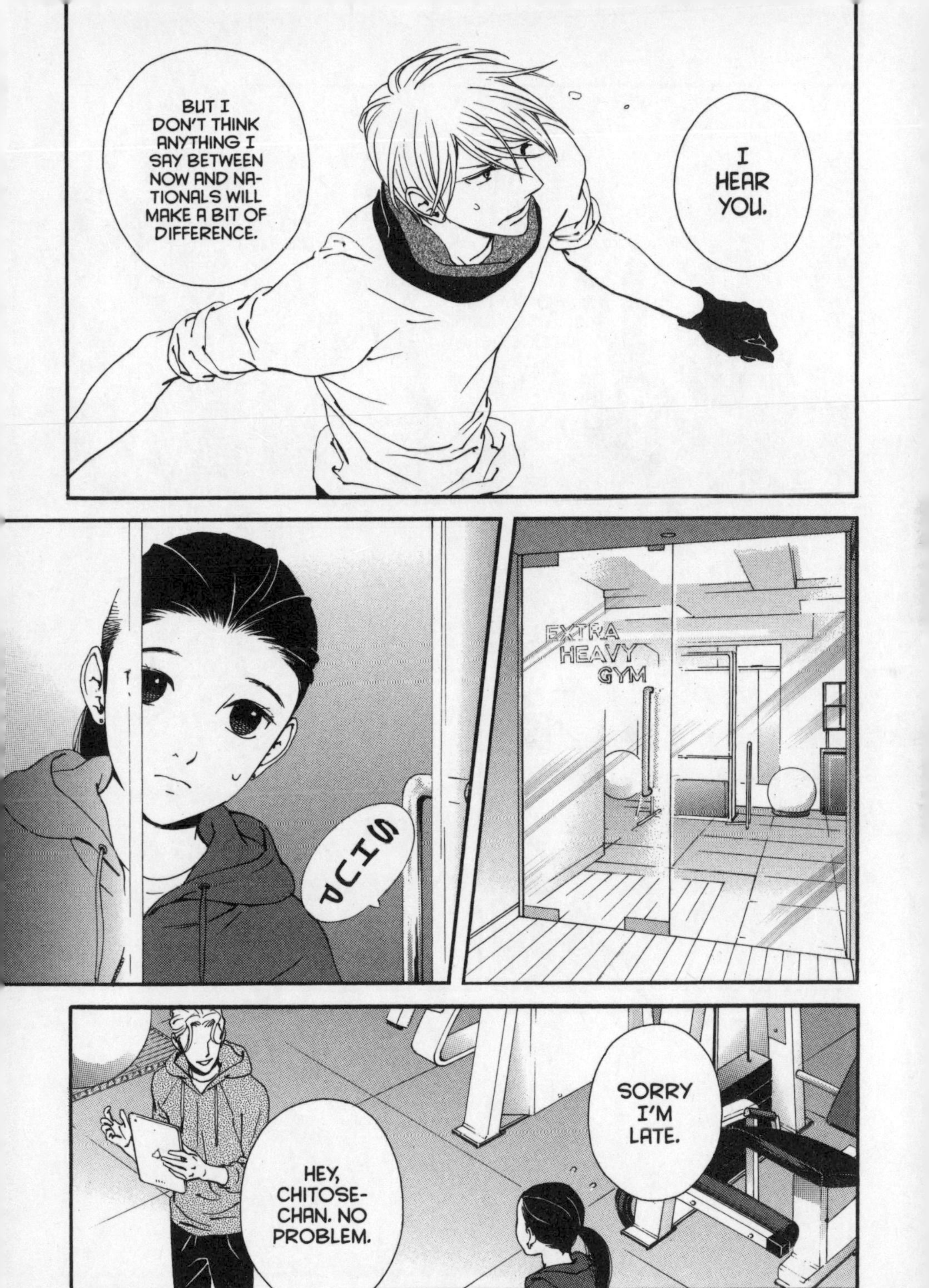
I HEAR YOU.
BUT I DON'T THINK ANYTHING I SAY BETWEEN NOW AND NA-TIONALS WILL MAKE A BIT OF DIFFERENCE.
EXTRA HEAVY GYM
SORRY I'M LATE.
HEY, CHITOSE-CHAN. NO PROBLEM.

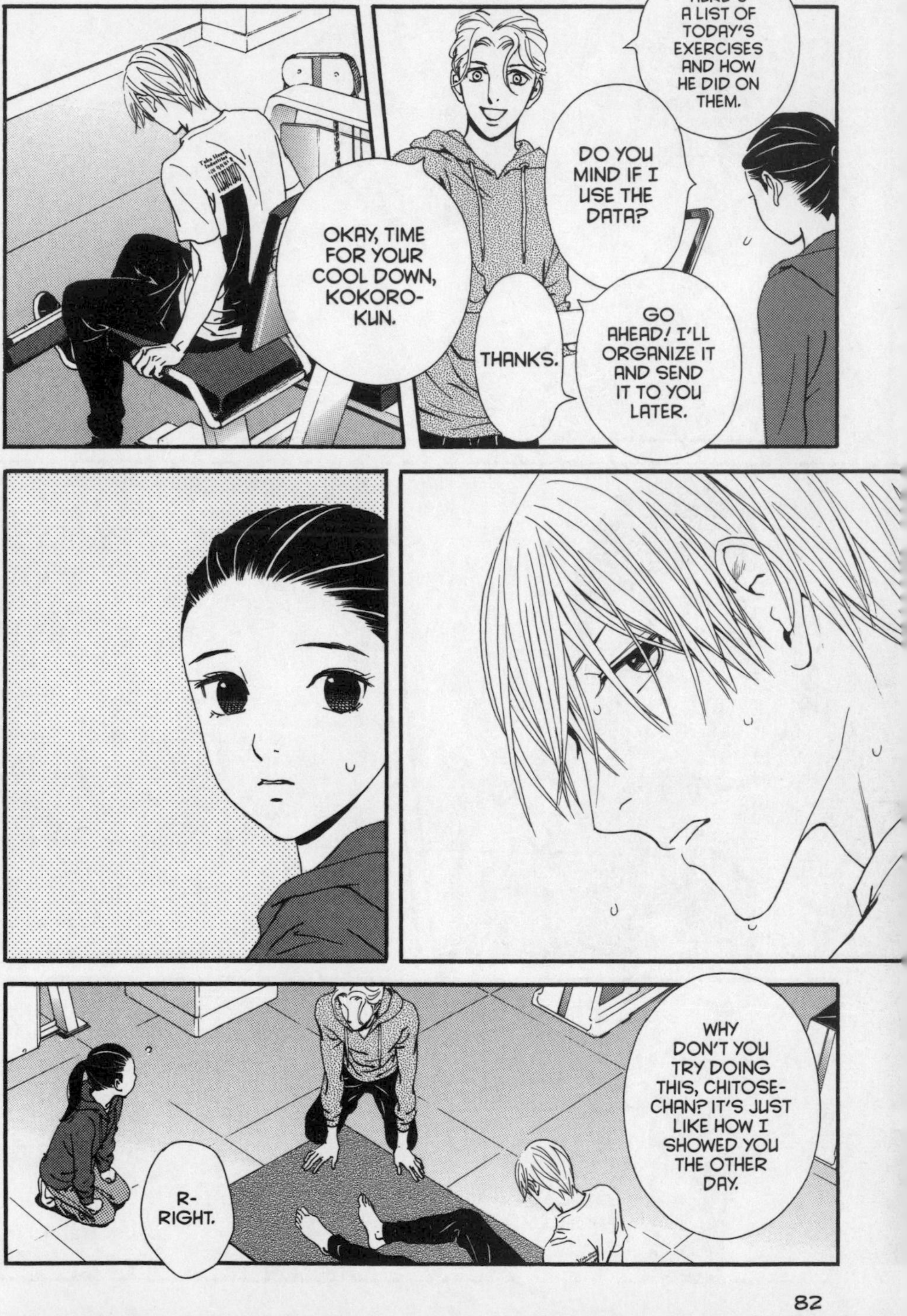
HERE'S A LIST OF TODAY'S EXERCISES AND HOW HE DID ON THEM.
DO YOU MIND IF I USE THE DATA?
GO AHEAD! I'LL ORGANIZE IT AND SEND IT TO YOU LATER.
THANKS.
OKAY, TIME FOR YOUR COOL DOWN, KOKORO-KUN.
WHY DON'T YOU TRY DOING THIS, CHITOSE-CHAN? IT'S JUST LIKE HOW I SHOWED YOU THE OTHER DAY.
R-RIGHT.

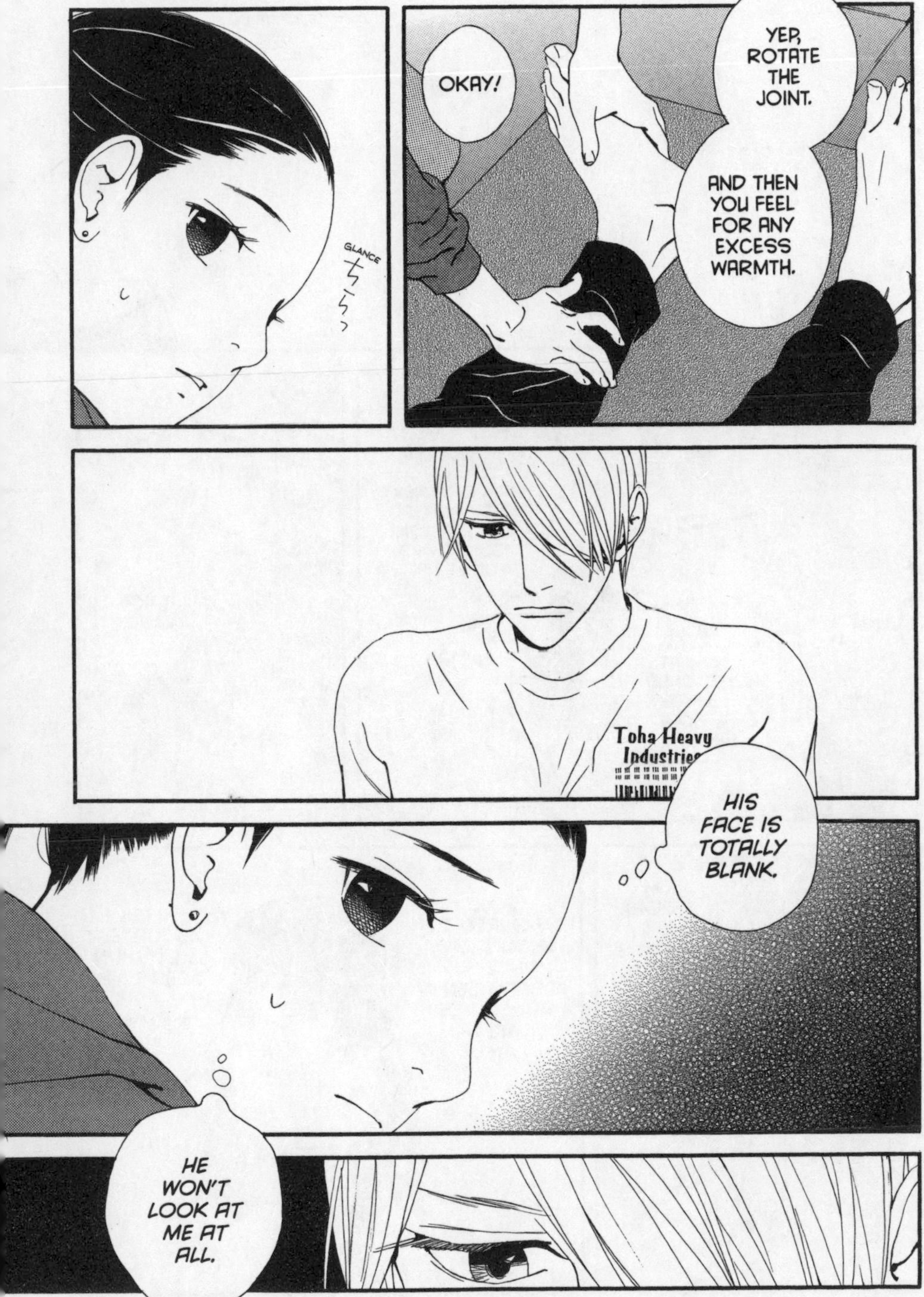
YEP, ROTATE THE JOINT.
AND THEN YOU FEEL FOR ANY EXCESS WARMTH.
OKAY!
GLANCE
Toha Heavy Industries
HIS FACE IS TOTALLY BLANK.
HE WON'T LOOK AT ME AT ALL.

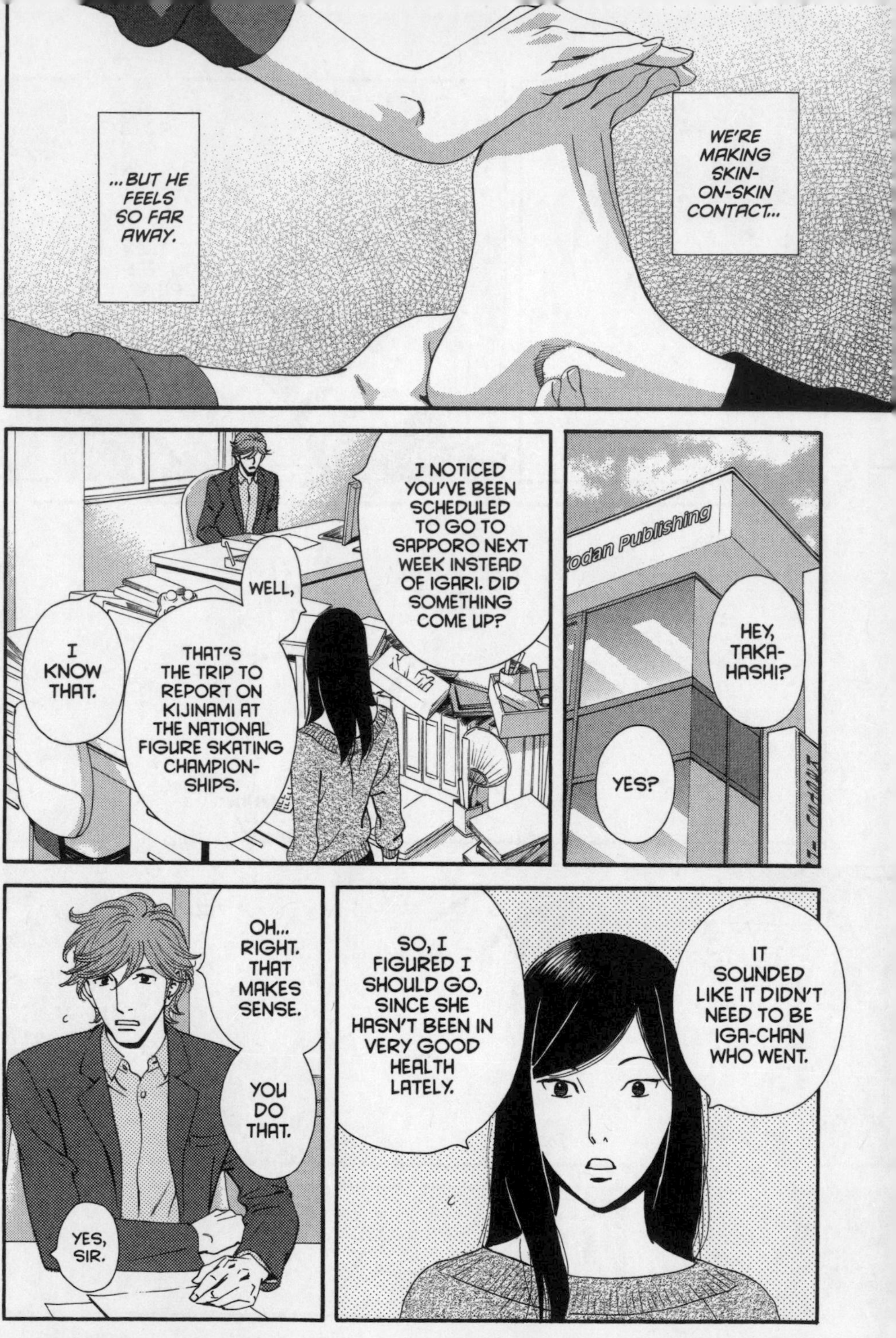
WE'RE MAKING SKIN-ON-SKIN CONTACT...
...BUT HE FEELS SO FAR AWAY.
Kodan Publishing
HEY, TAKA-HASHI?
YES?
I NOTICED YOU'VE BEEN SCHEDULED TO GO TO SAPPORO NEXT WEEK INSTEAD OF IGARI. DID SOMETHING COME UP?
WELL,
THAT'S THE TRIP TO REPORT ON KIJINAMI AT THE NATIONAL FIGURE SKATING CHAMPION-SHIPS.
I KNOW THAT.
IT SOUNDED LIKE IT DIDN'T NEED TO BE IGA-CHAN WHO WENT.
SO, I FIGURED I SHOULD GO, SINCE SHE HASN'T BEEN IN VERY GOOD HEALTH LATELY.
OH... RIGHT. THAT MAKES SENSE.
YOU DO THAT.
YES, SIR.

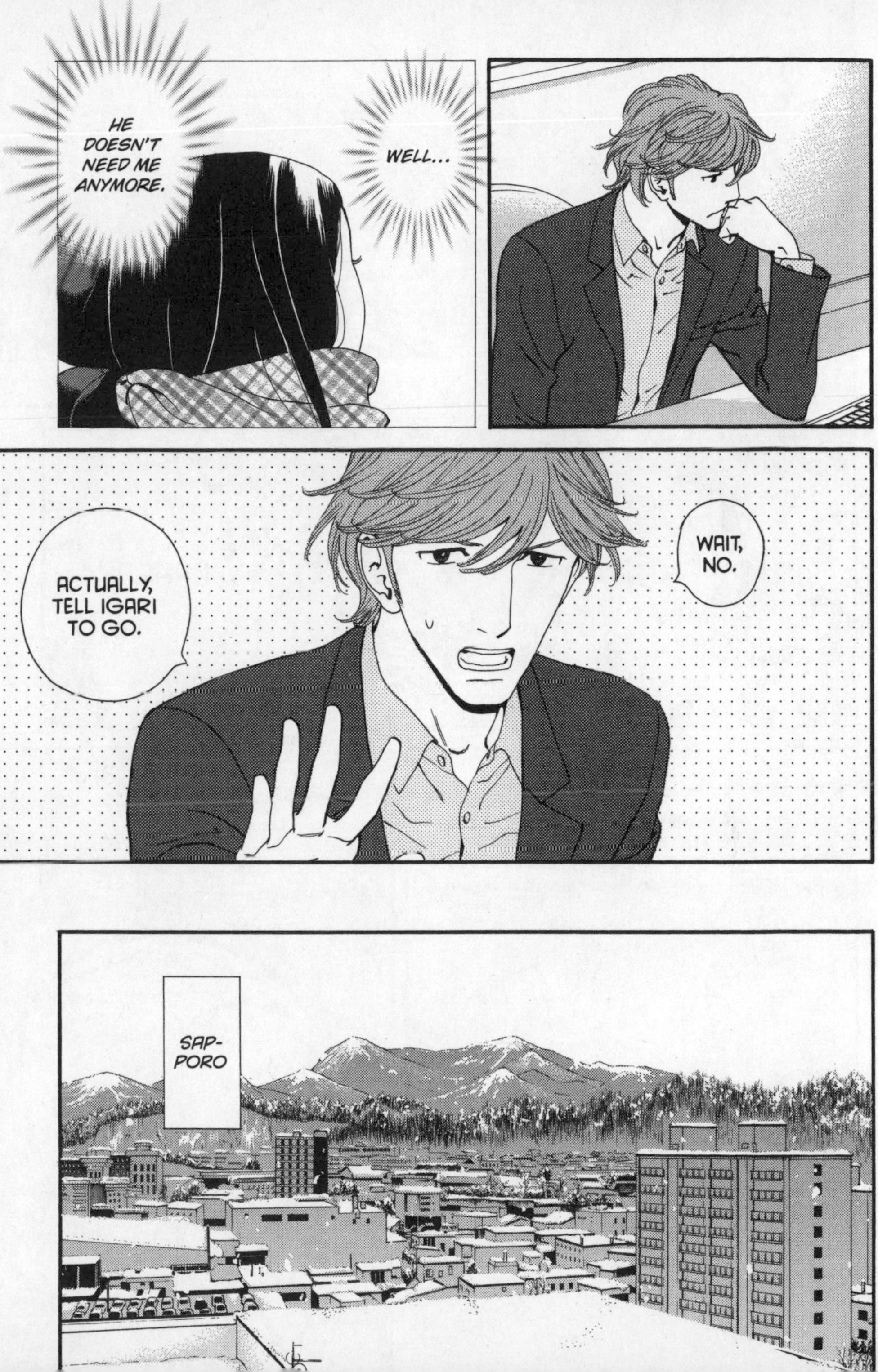
WELL...
HE DOESN'T NEED ME ANYMORE.
WAIT, NO.
ACTUALLY, TELL IGARI TO GO.
SAP-PORO

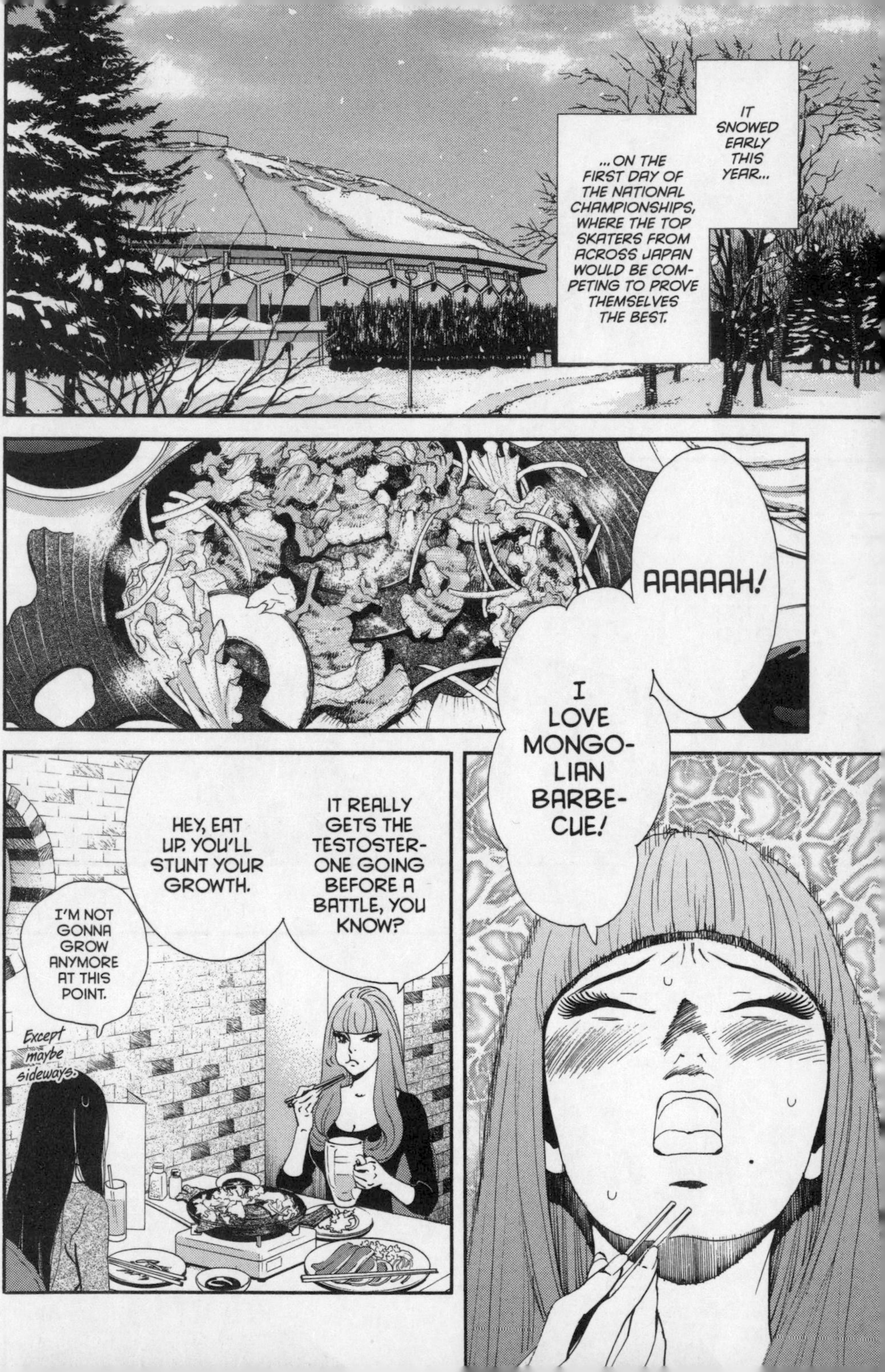
IT SNOWED EARLY THIS YEAR...
...ON THE FIRST DAY OF THE NATIONAL CHAMPIONSHIPS, WHERE THE TOP SKATERS FROM ACROSS JAPAN WOULD BE COMPETING TO PROVE THEMSELVES THE BEST.
AAAAAH!
I LOVE MONGOLIAN BARBECUE!
IT REALLY GETS THE TESTOSTERONE GOING BEFORE A BATTLE, YOU KNOW?
HEY, EAT UP. YOU'LL STUNT YOUR GROWTH.
I'M NOT GONNA GROW ANYMORE AT THIS POINT.
Except maybe sideways.

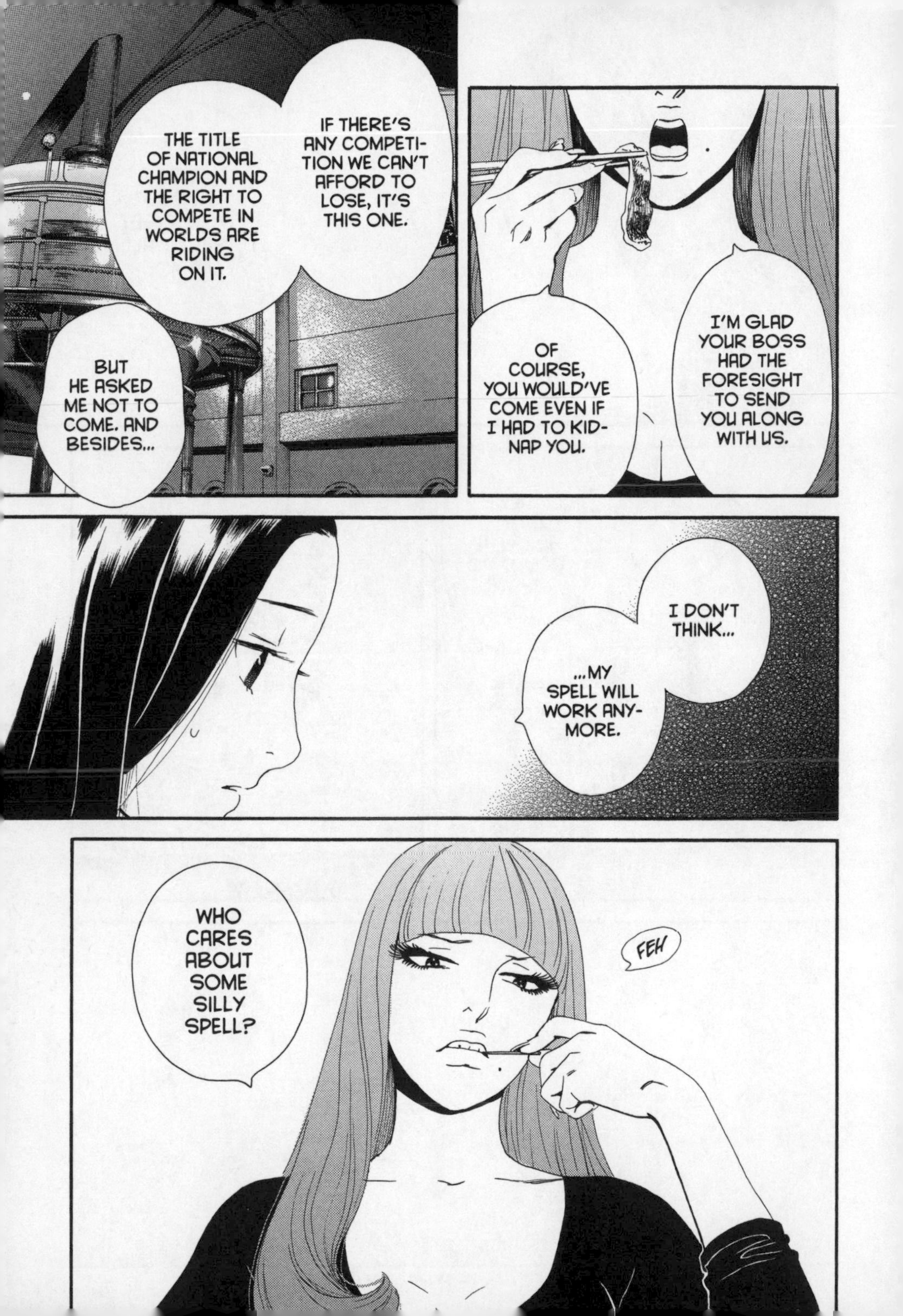
I'M GLAD YOUR BOSS HAD THE FORESIGHT TO SEND YOU ALONG WITH US.
OF COURSE, YOU WOULD'VE COME EVEN IF I HAD TO KID-NAP YOU.
IF THERE'S ANY COMPETI-TION WE CAN'T AFFORD TO LOSE, IT'S THIS ONE.
THE TITLE OF NATIONAL CHAMPION AND THE RIGHT TO COMPETE IN WORLDS ARE RIDING ON IT.
BUT HE ASKED ME NOT TO COME. AND BESIDES...
I DON'T THINK...
...MY SPELL WILL WORK ANY-MORE.
FEH
WHO CARES ABOUT SOME SILLY SPELL?

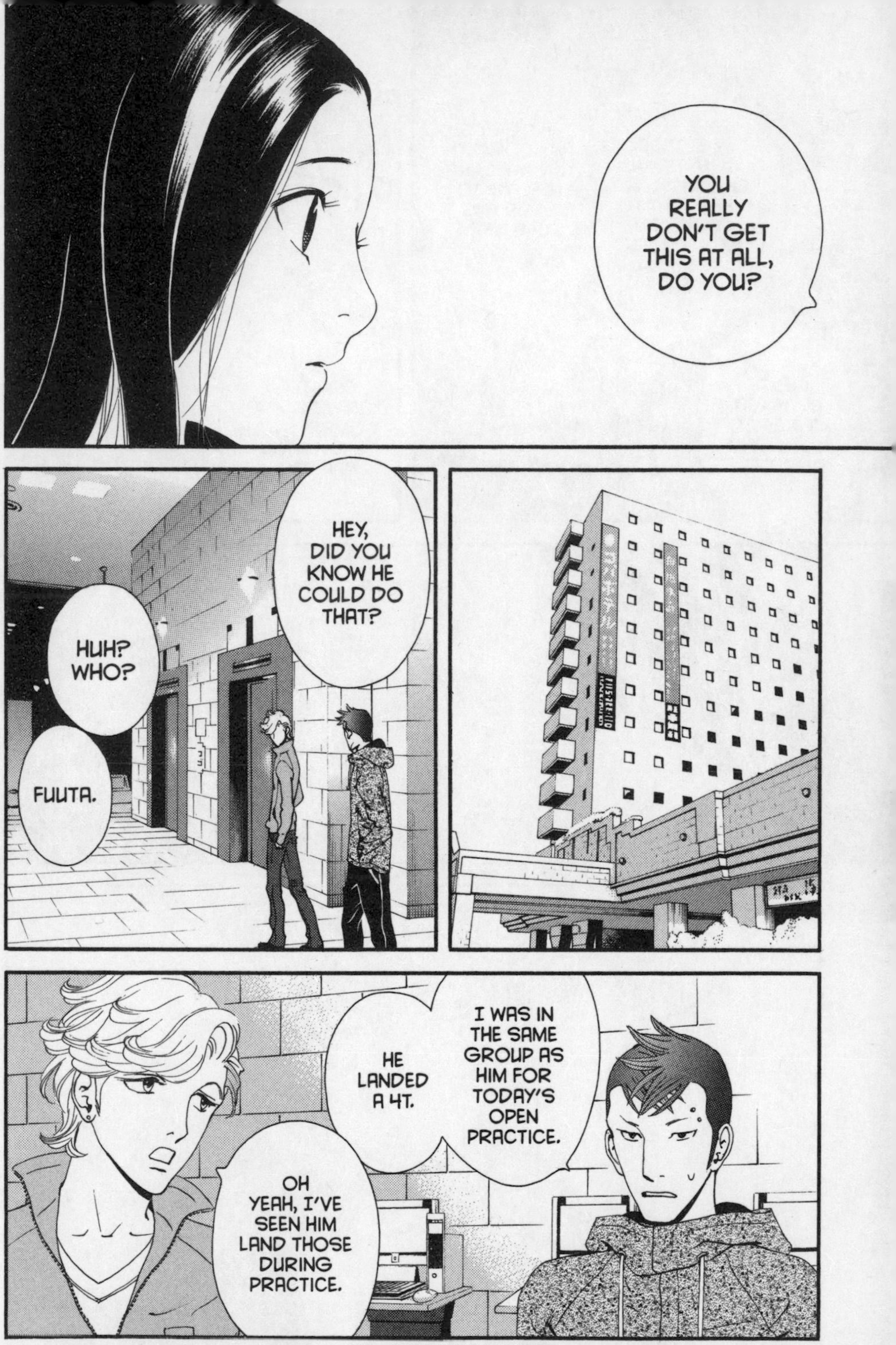
YOU REALLY DON'T GET THIS AT ALL, DO YOU?
HEY, DID YOU KNOW HE COULD DO THAT?
HUH? WHO?
FUUTA.
I WAS IN THE SAME GROUP AS HIM FOR TODAY'S OPEN PRACTICE.
HE LANDED A 4T.
OH YEAH, I'VE SEEN HIM LAND THOSE DURING PRACTICE.

4T = QUADRUPLE TOE LOOP

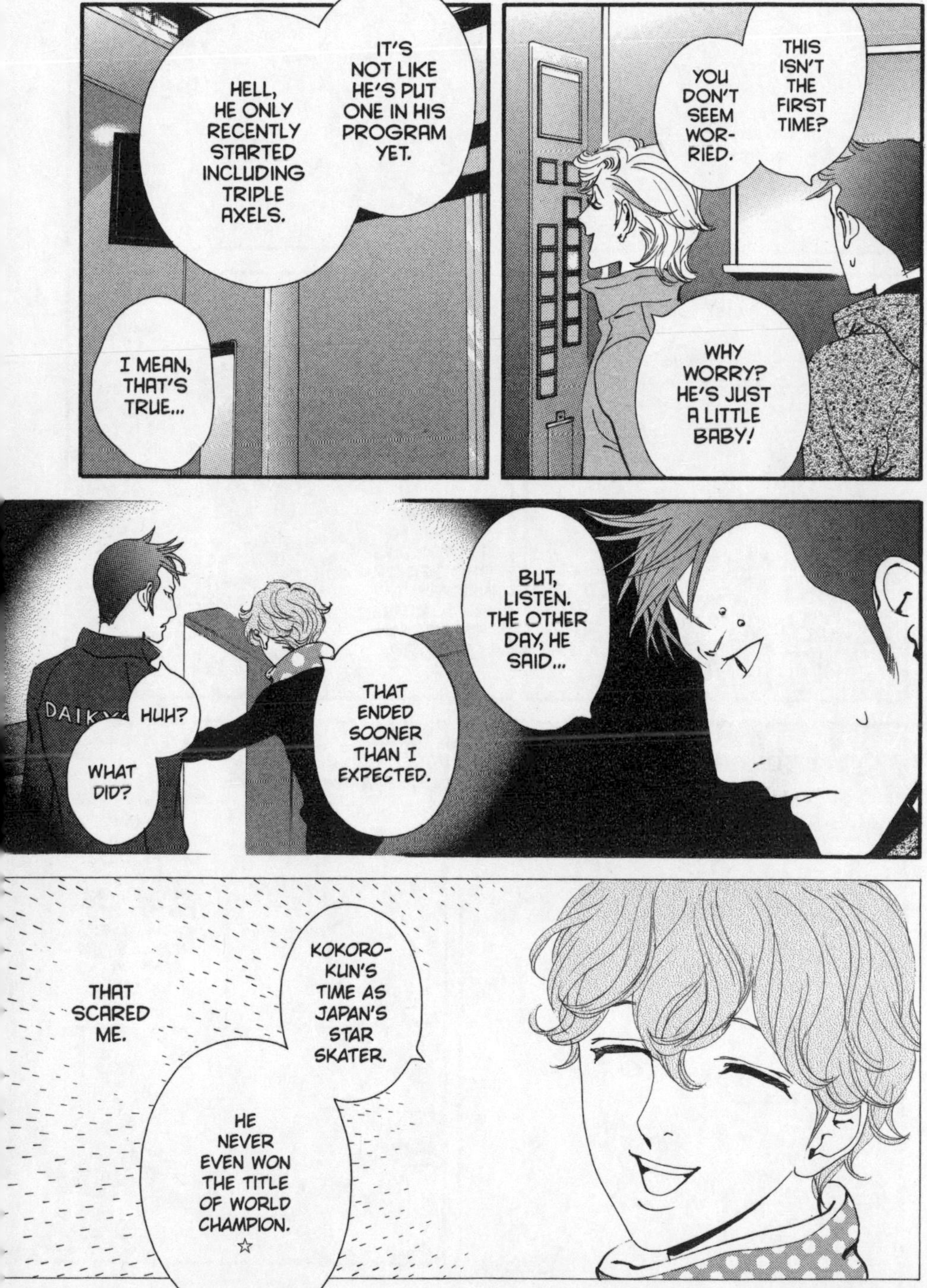
THIS ISN'T THE FIRST TIME?
YOU DON'T SEEM WORRIED.
WHY WORRY? HE'S JUST A LITTLE BABY!
IT'S NOT LIKE HE'S PUT ONE IN HIS PROGRAM YET.
HELL, HE ONLY RECENTLY STARTED INCLUDING TRIPLE AXELS.
I MEAN, THAT'S TRUE...
BUT, LISTEN. THE OTHER DAY, HE SAID...
THAT ENDED SOONER THAN I EXPECTED.
HUH?
WHAT DID?
KOKORO-KUN'S TIME AS JAPAN'S STAR SKATER.
HE NEVER EVEN WON THE TITLE OF WORLD CHAMPION. ☆
THAT SCARED ME.

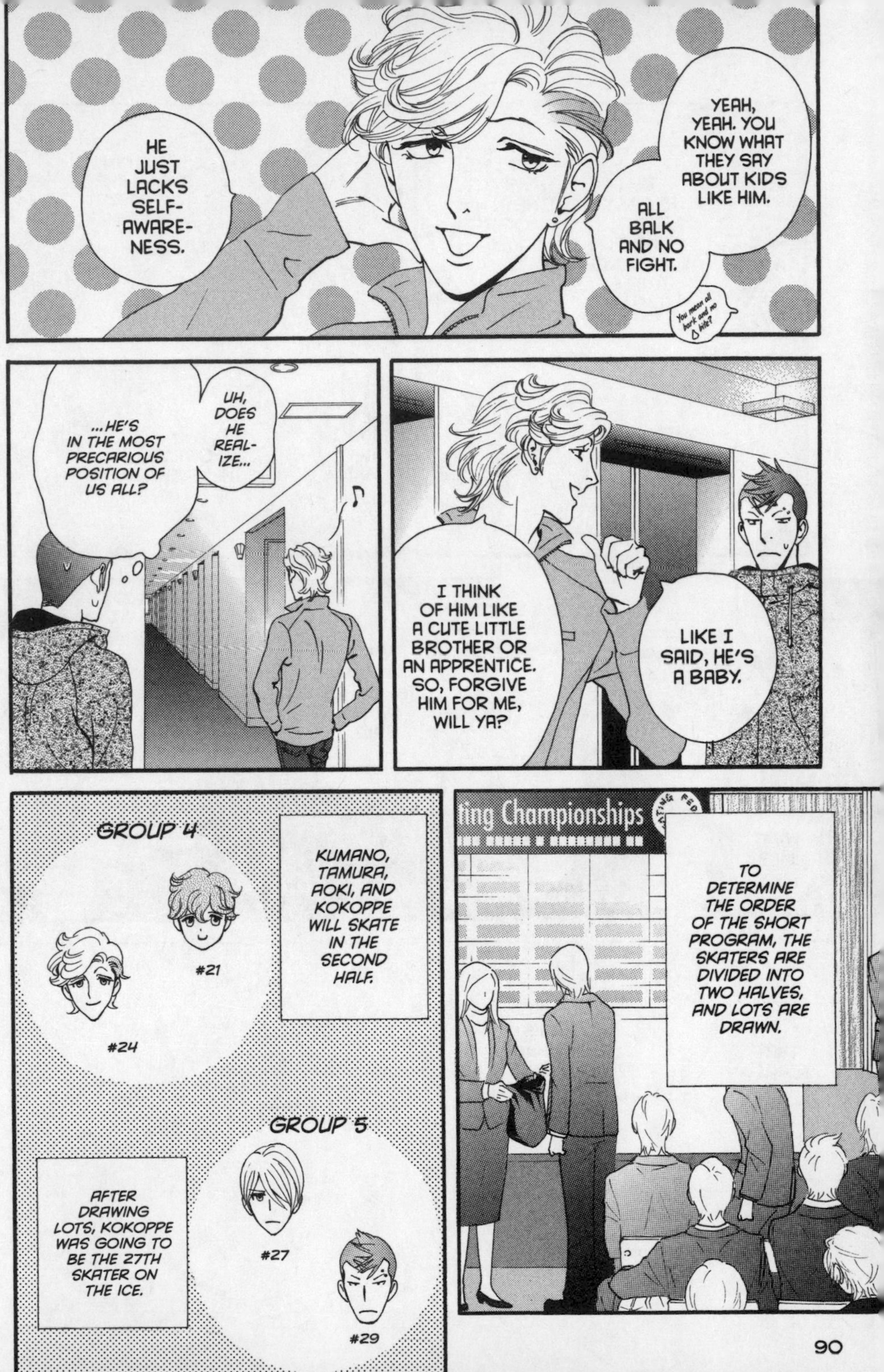
YEAH, YEAH. YOU KNOW WHAT THEY SAY ABOUT KIDS LIKE HIM.
ALL BALK AND NO FIGHT.
You mean all bark and no bite?
HE JUST LACKS SELF-AWARENESS.
LIKE I SAID, HE'S A BABY.
I THINK OF HIM LIKE A CUTE LITTLE BROTHER OR AN APPRENTICE. SO, FORGIVE HIM FOR ME, WILL YA?
UH, DOES HE REAL-IZE...
...HE'S IN THE MOST PRECARIOUS POSITION OF US ALL?
ting Championships
TO DETERMINE THE ORDER OF THE SHORT PROGRAM, THE SKATERS ARE DIVIDED INTO TWO HALVES, AND LOTS ARE DRAWN.
KUMANO, TAMURA, AOKI, AND KOKOPPE WILL SKATE IN THE SECOND HALF.
GROUP 4
#21
#24
GROUP 5
#27
#29
AFTER DRAWING LOTS, KOKOPPE WAS GOING TO BE THE 27TH SKATER ON THE ICE.

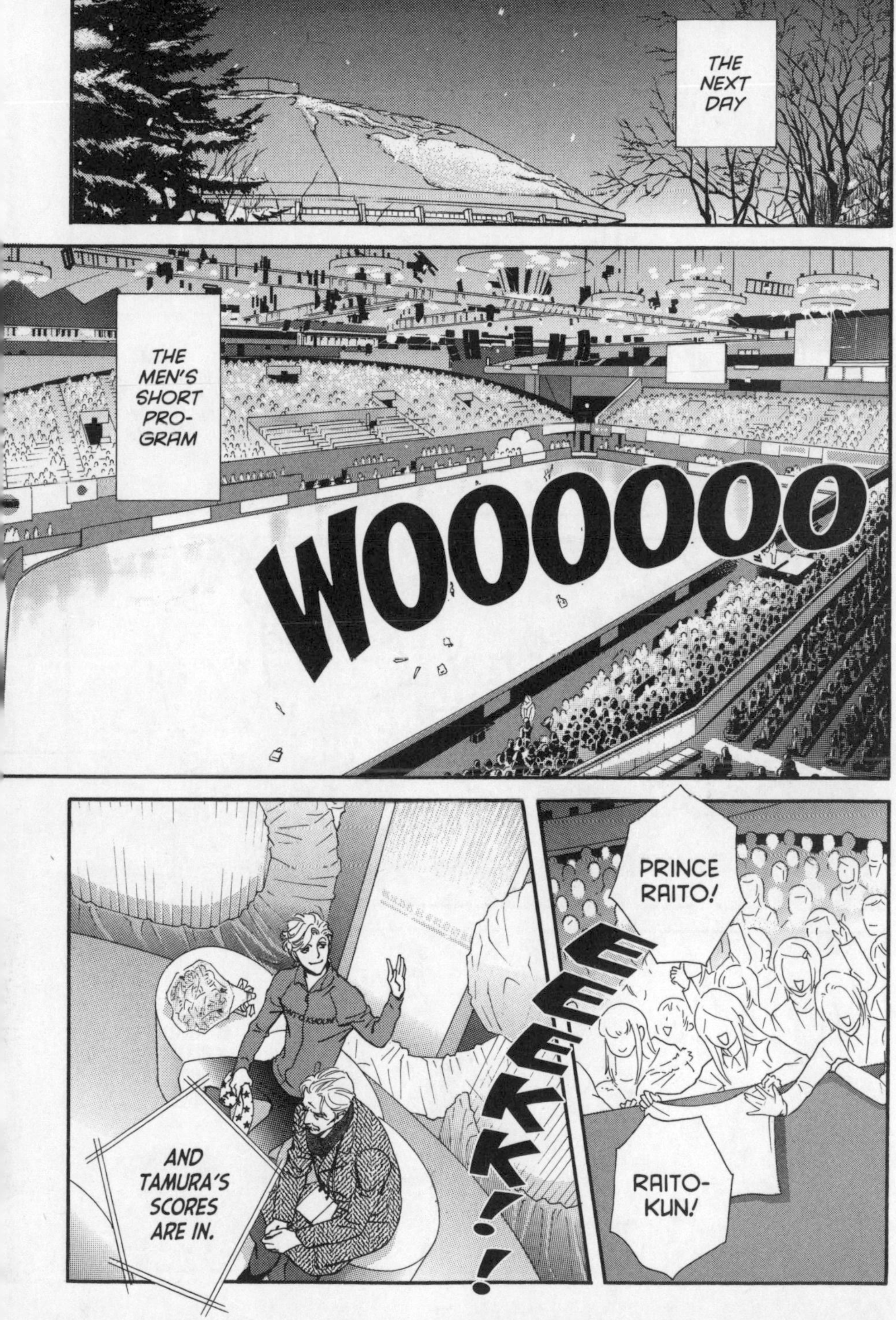
THE NEXT DAY
THE MEN'S SHORT PRO-GRAM
WOOOOOO
PRINCE RAITO!
EEEEKK!!
RAITO-KUN!
AND TAMURA'S SCORES ARE IN.

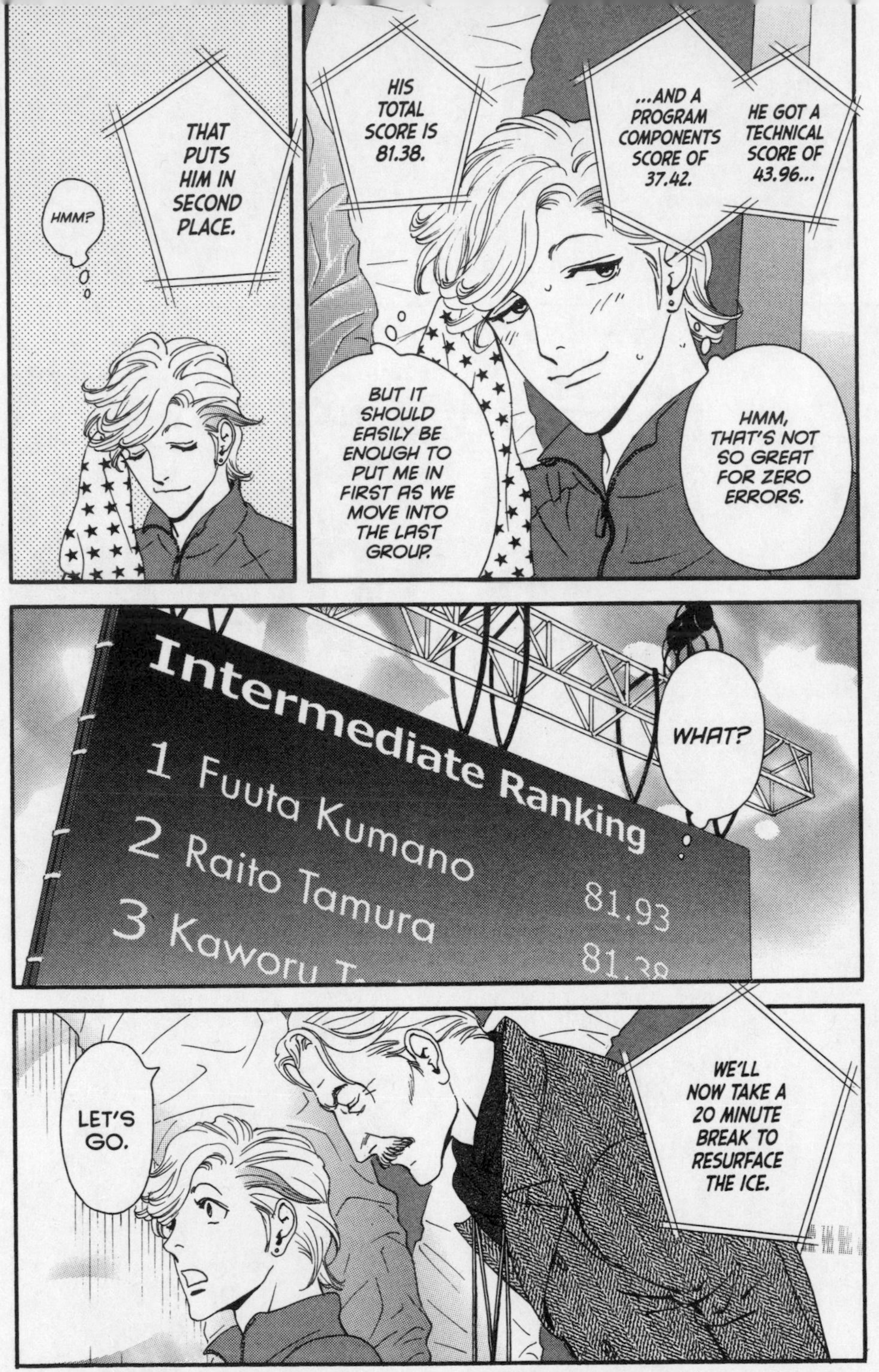
HE GOT A TECHNICAL SCORE OF 43.96...
...AND A PROGRAM COMPONENTS SCORE OF 37.42.
HIS TOTAL SCORE IS 81.38.
HMM, THAT'S NOT SO GREAT FOR ZERO ERRORS.
BUT IT SHOULD EASILY BE ENOUGH TO PUT ME IN FIRST AS WE MOVE INTO THE LAST GROUP.
THAT PUTS HIM IN SECOND PLACE.
HMM?
Intermediate Ranking
1 Fuuta Kumano
2 Raito Tamura
3 Kaworu
81.93
WHAT?
WE'LL NOW TAKE A 20 MINUTE BREAK TO RESURFACE THE ICE.
LET'S GO.

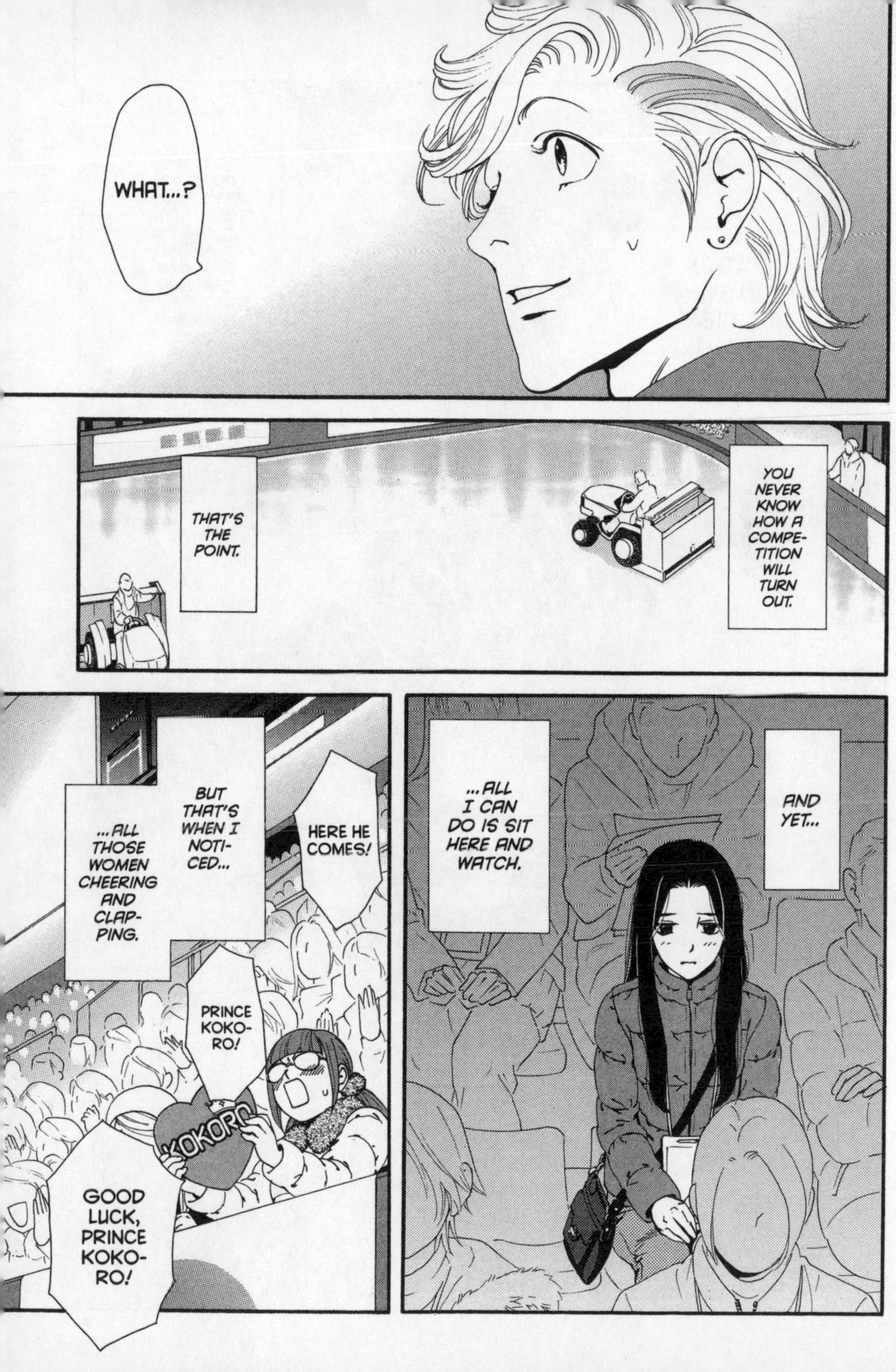
WHAT...?
YOU NEVER KNOW HOW A COMPETITION WILL TURN OUT.
THAT'S THE POINT.
AND YET...
...ALL I CAN DO IS SIT HERE AND WATCH.
HERE HE COMES!
BUT THAT'S WHEN I NOTICED...
...ALL THOSE WOMEN CHEERING AND CLAPPING.
PRINCE KOKORO!
KOKORO
GOOD LUCK, PRINCE KOKORO!

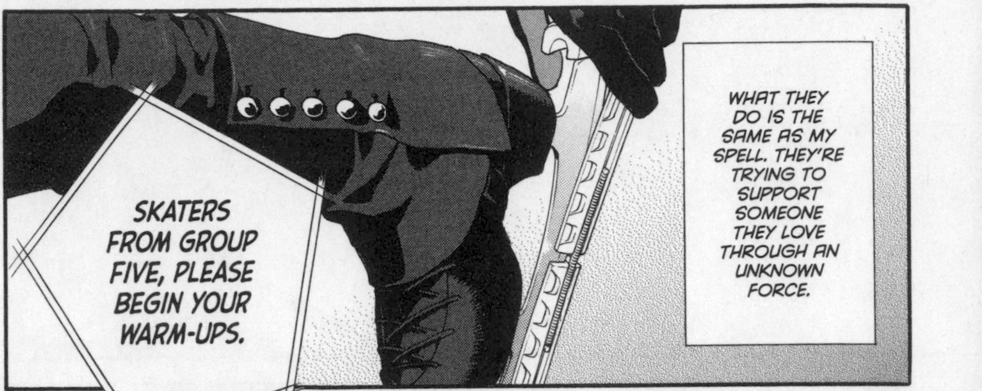
WHAT THEY DO IS THE SAME AS MY SPELL. THEY'RE TRYING TO SUPPORT SOMEONE THEY LOVE THROUGH AN UNKNOWN FORCE.
SKATERS FROM GROUP FIVE, PLEASE BEGIN YOUR WARM-UPS.

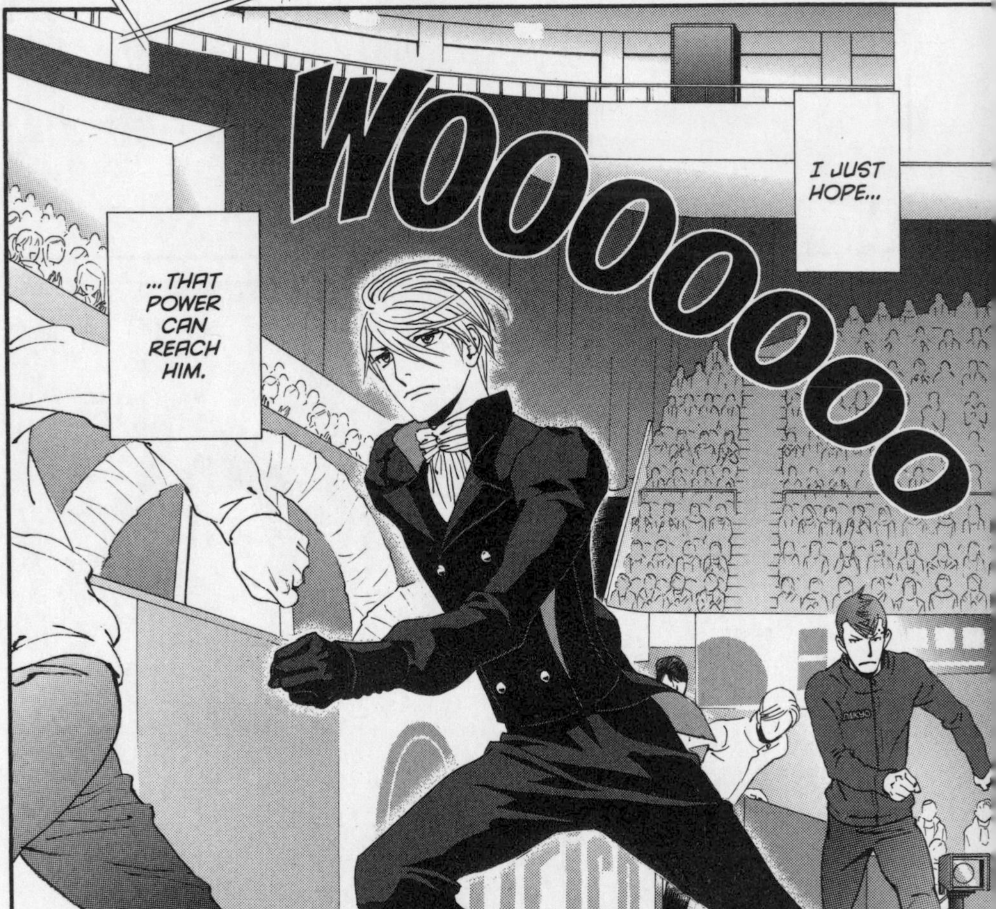
I JUST HOPE...
WOOOOOOOOO
...THAT POWER CAN REACH HIM.

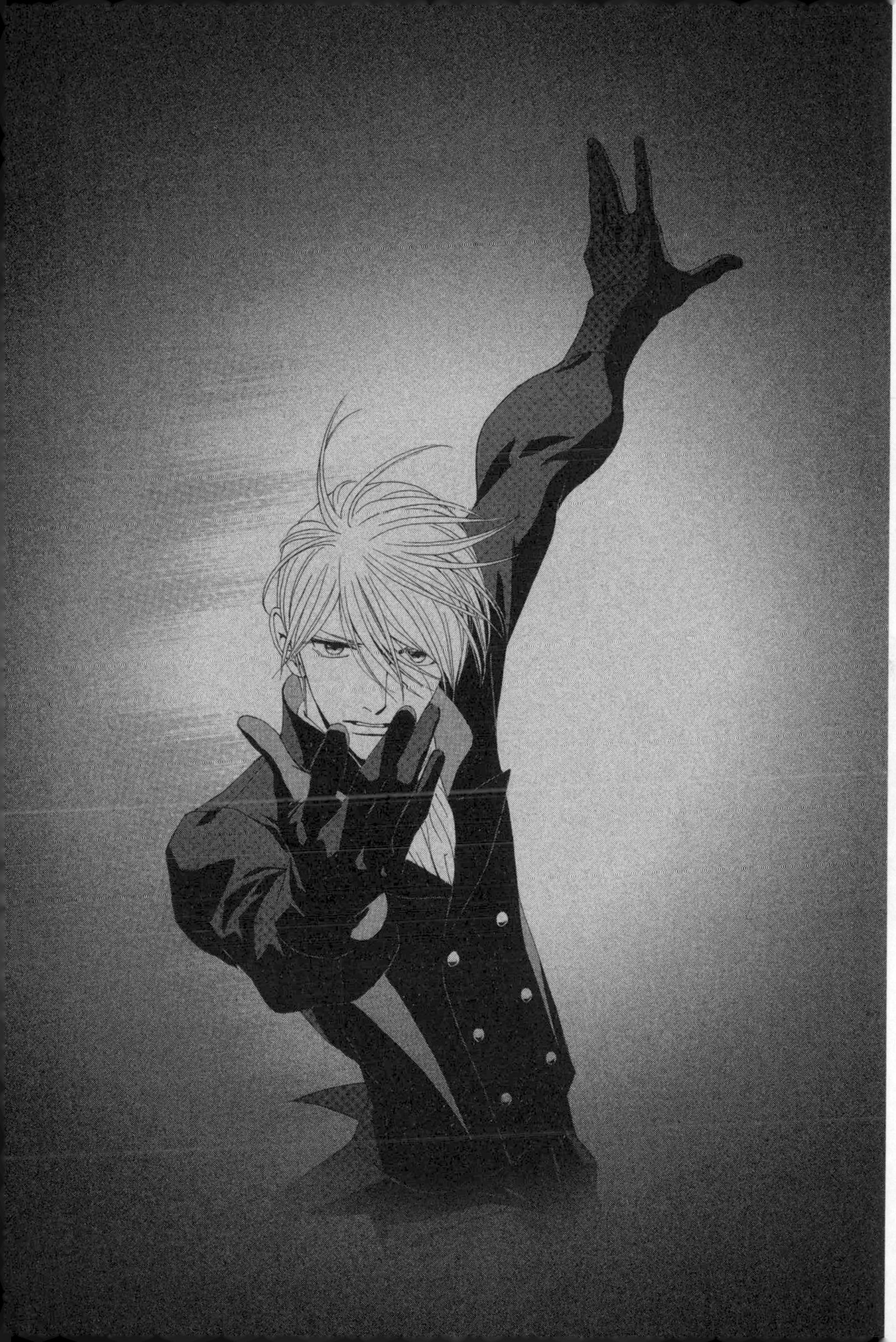

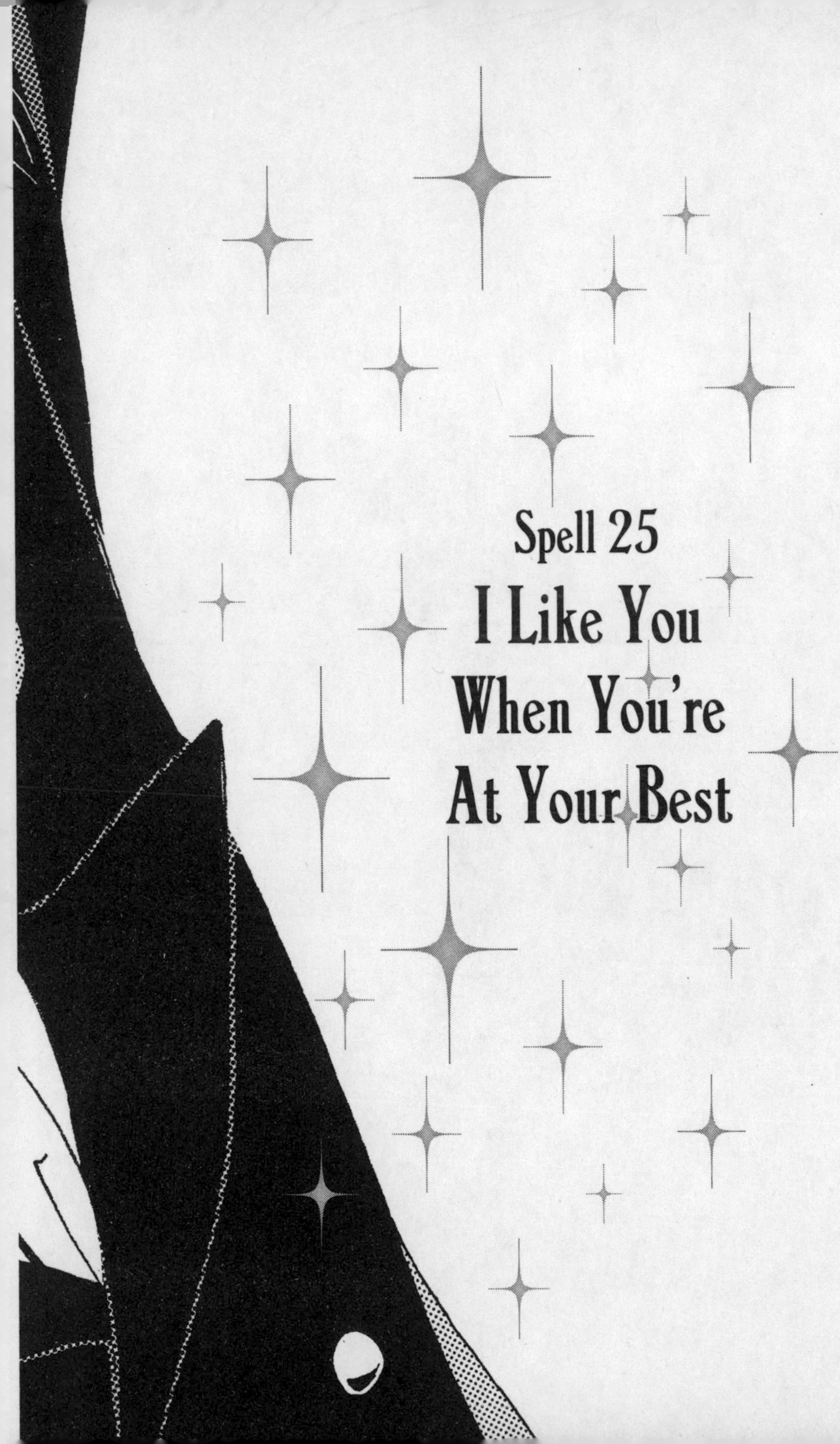

Spell 25
I Like You When You're At Your Best

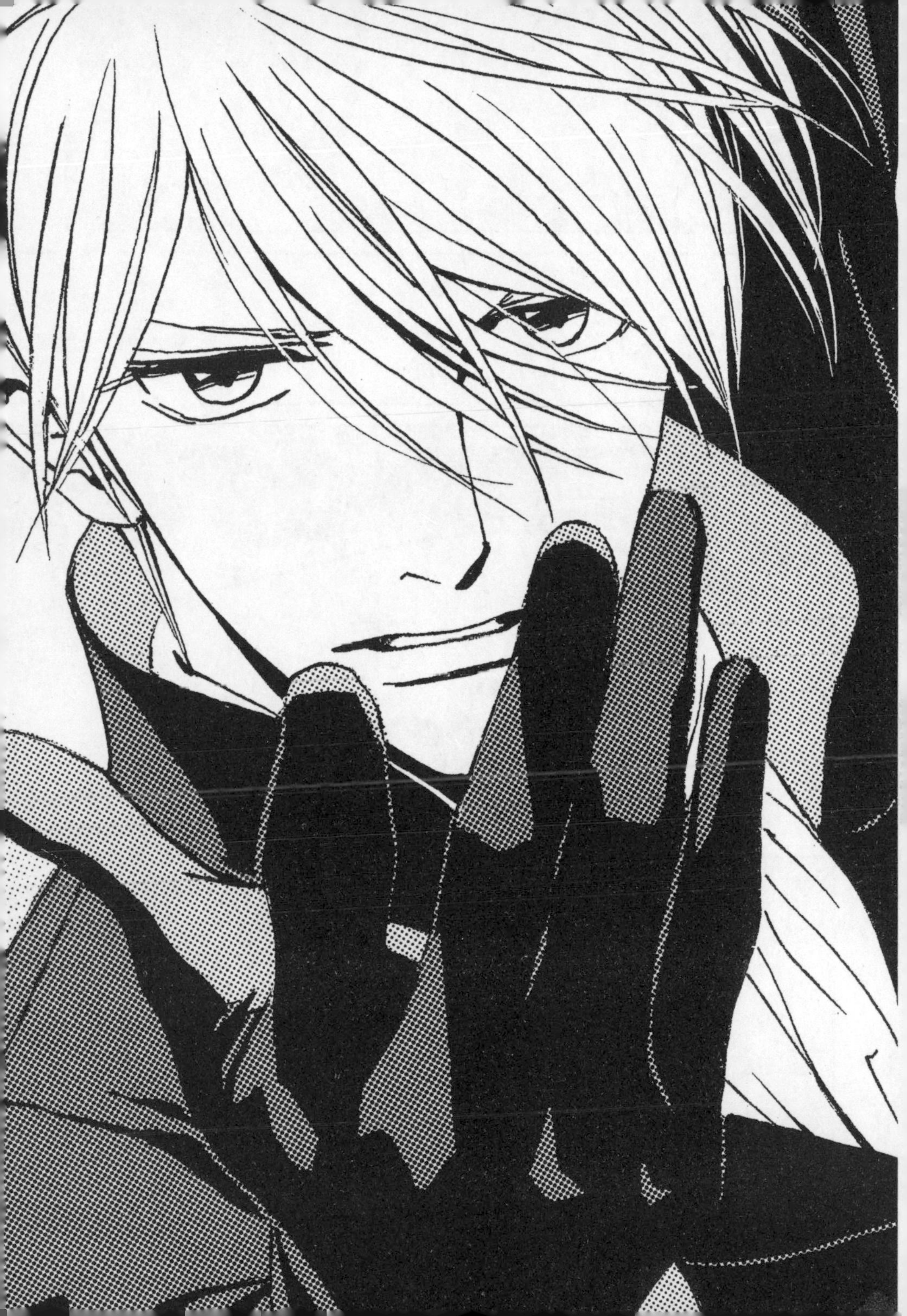

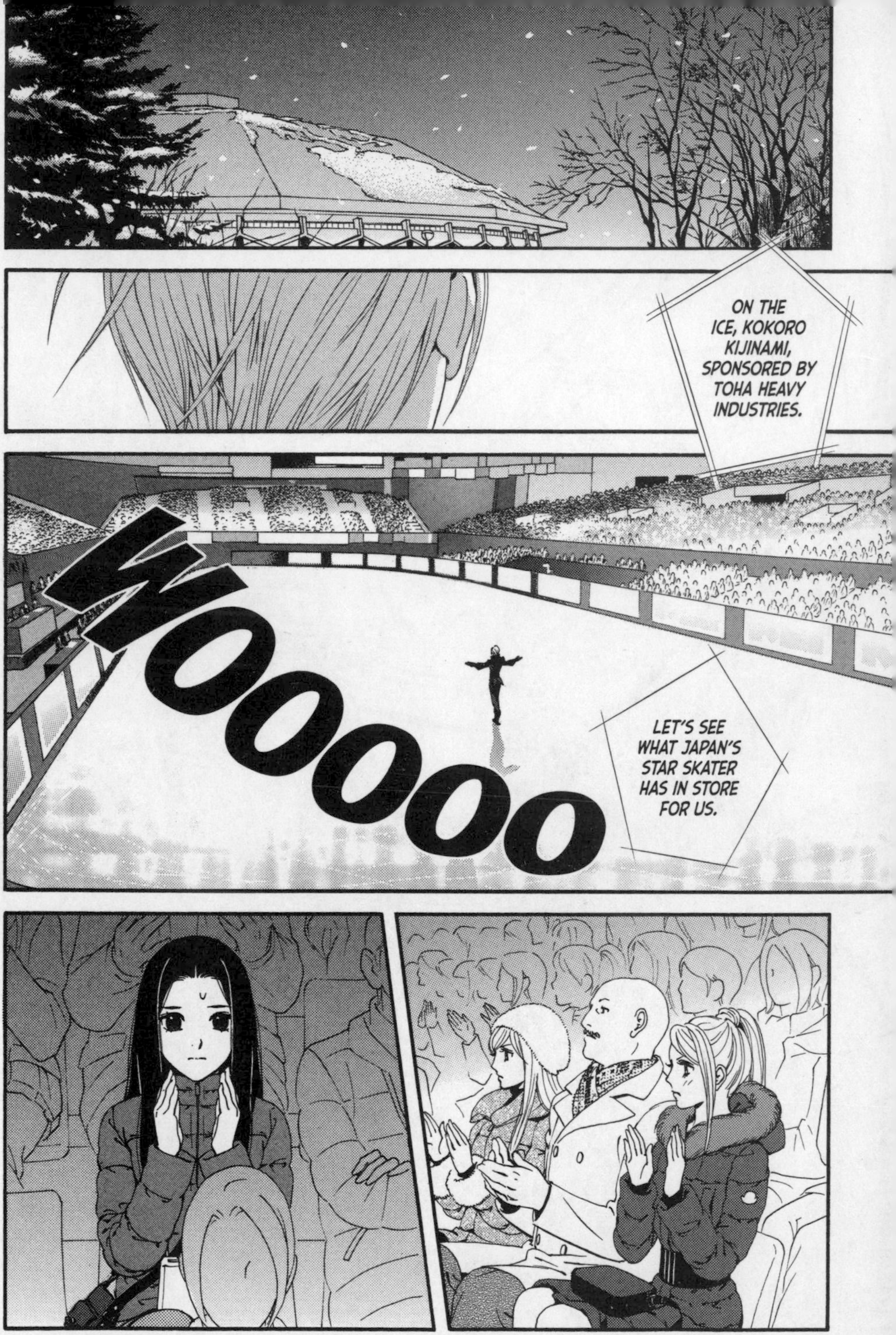
ON THE ICE, KOKORO KIJINAMI, SPONSORED BY TOHA HEAVY INDUSTRIES.
WOOOOOO
LET'S SEE WHAT JAPAN'S STAR SKATER HAS IN STORE FOR US.

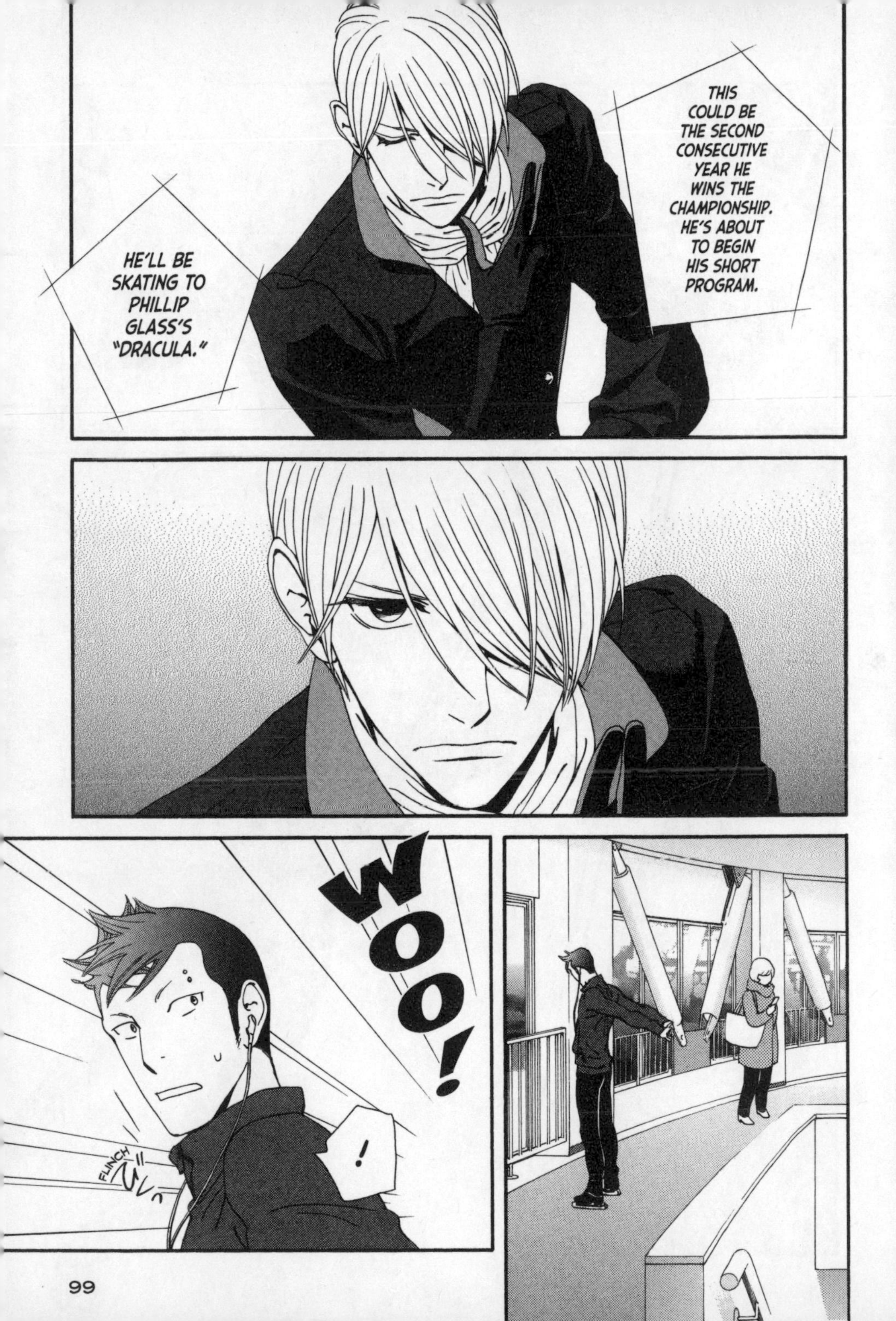
THIS COULD BE THE SECOND CONSECUTIVE YEAR HE WINS THE CHAMPIONSHIP. HE'S ABOUT TO BEGIN HIS SHORT PROGRAM.
HE'LL BE SKATING TO PHILLIP GLASS'S "DRACULA."
WOOO!
!
FLINCH

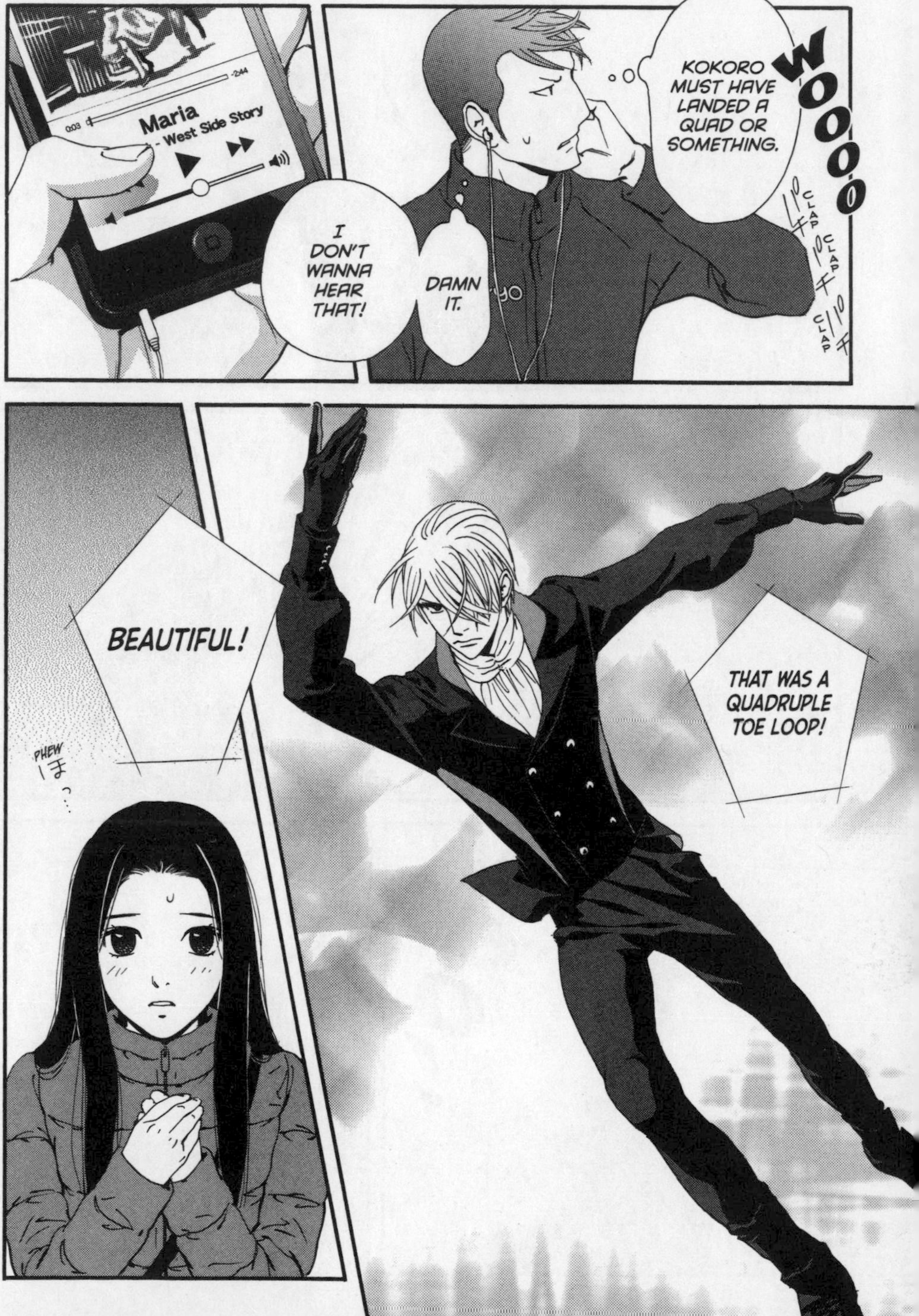
WOOOO
CLAP CLAP CLAP
KOKORO MUST HAVE LANDED A QUAD OR SOMETHING.
DAMN IT.
I DON'T WANNA HEAR THAT!
Maria
- West Side Story
0:03
-2:44
THAT WAS A QUADRUPLE TOE LOOP!
BEAUTIFUL!
PHEW
ほっ…

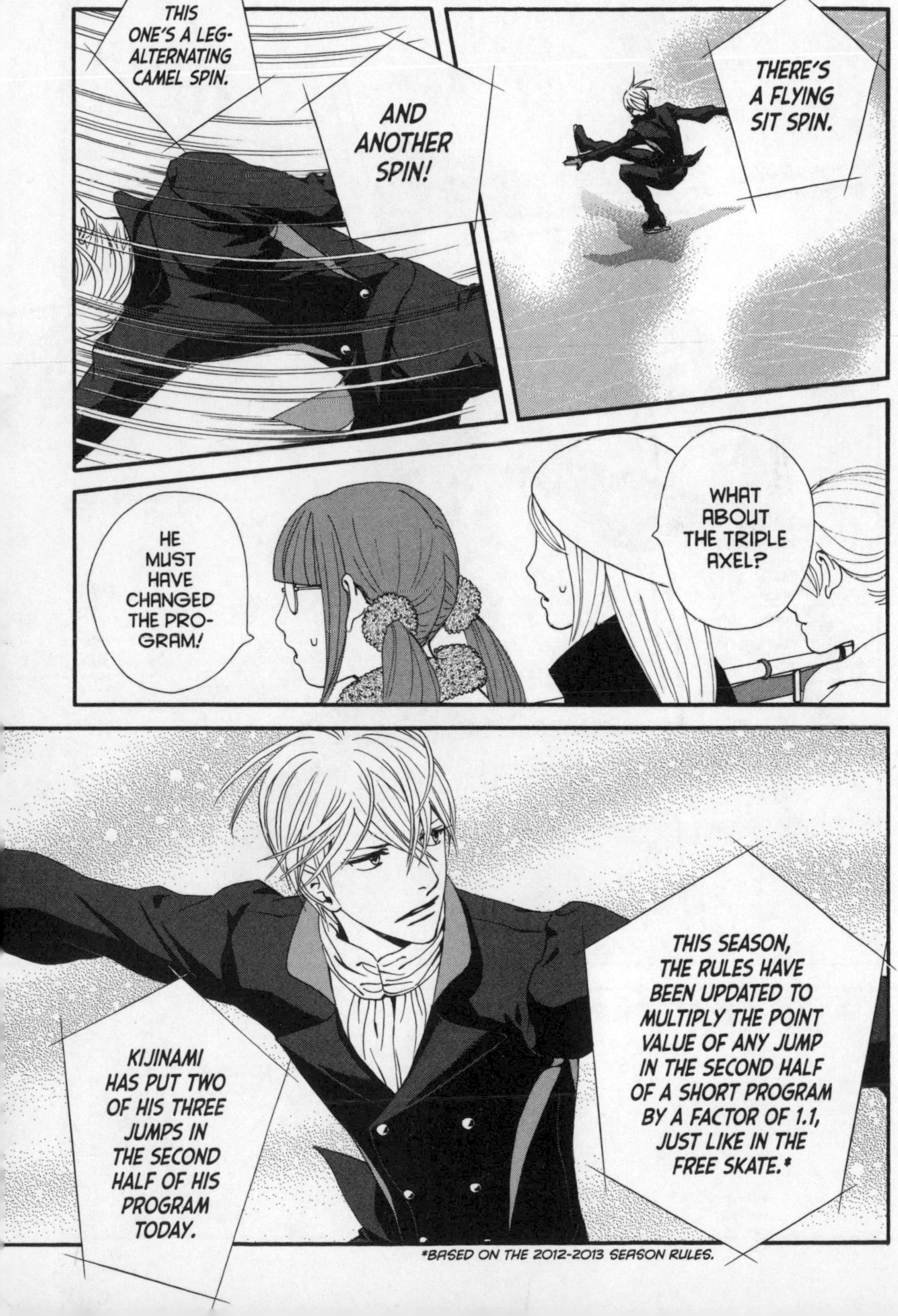
THERE'S A FLYING SIT SPIN.
AND ANOTHER SPIN!
THIS ONE'S A LEG-ALTERNATING CAMEL SPIN.
WHAT ABOUT THE TRIPLE AXEL?
HE MUST HAVE CHANGED THE PROGRAM!
THIS SEASON, THE RULES HAVE BEEN UPDATED TO MULTIPLY THE POINT VALUE OF ANY JUMP IN THE SECOND HALF OF A SHORT PROGRAM BY A FACTOR OF 1.1, JUST LIKE IN THE FREE SKATE.*
KIJINAMI HAS PUT TWO OF HIS THREE JUMPS IN THE SECOND HALF OF HIS PROGRAM TODAY.

*BASED ON THE 2012-2013 SEASON RULES.

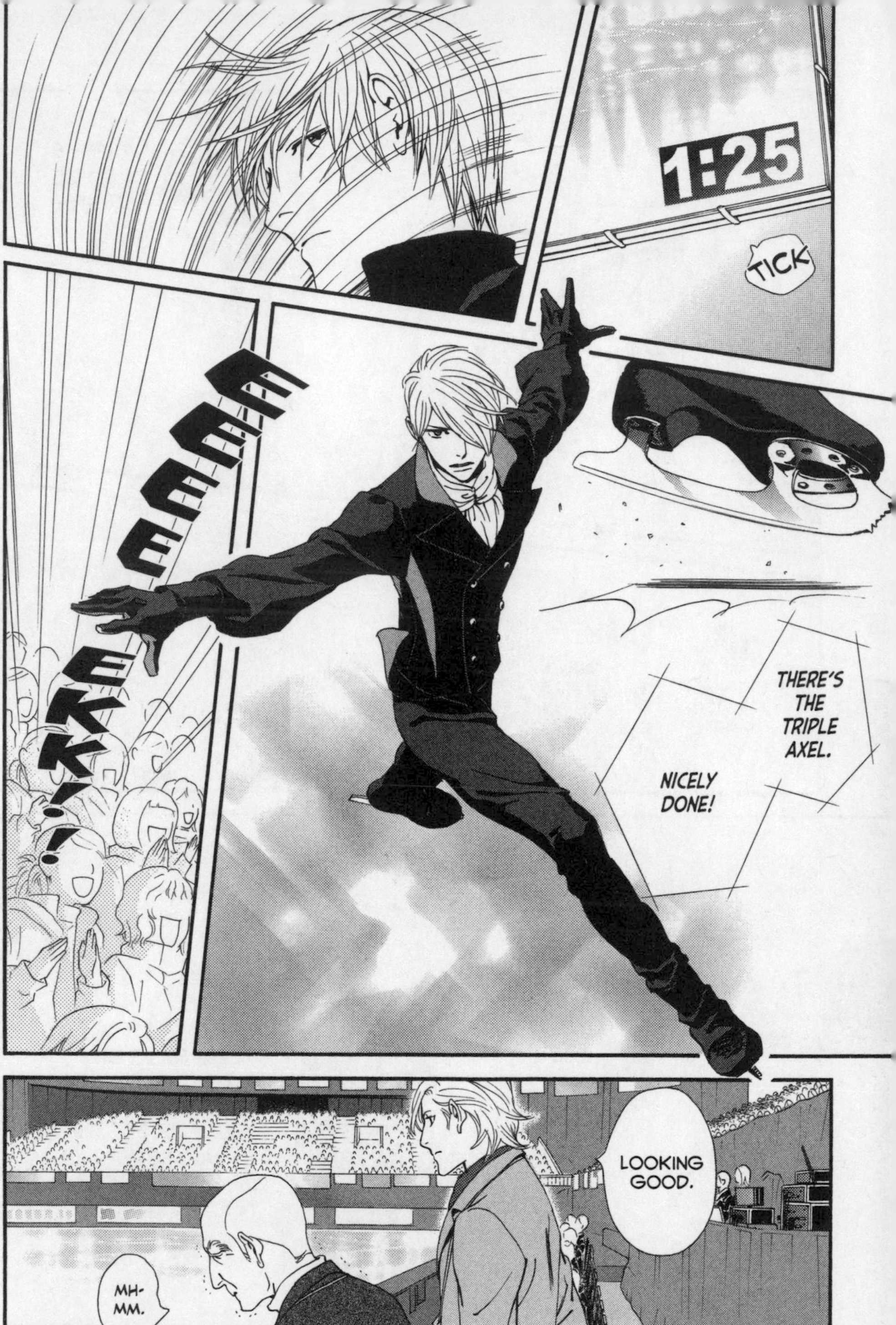
1:25
TICK
THERE'S THE TRIPLE AXEL.
NICELY DONE!
EEEEEKK!!
LOOKING GOOD.
MH-MM.

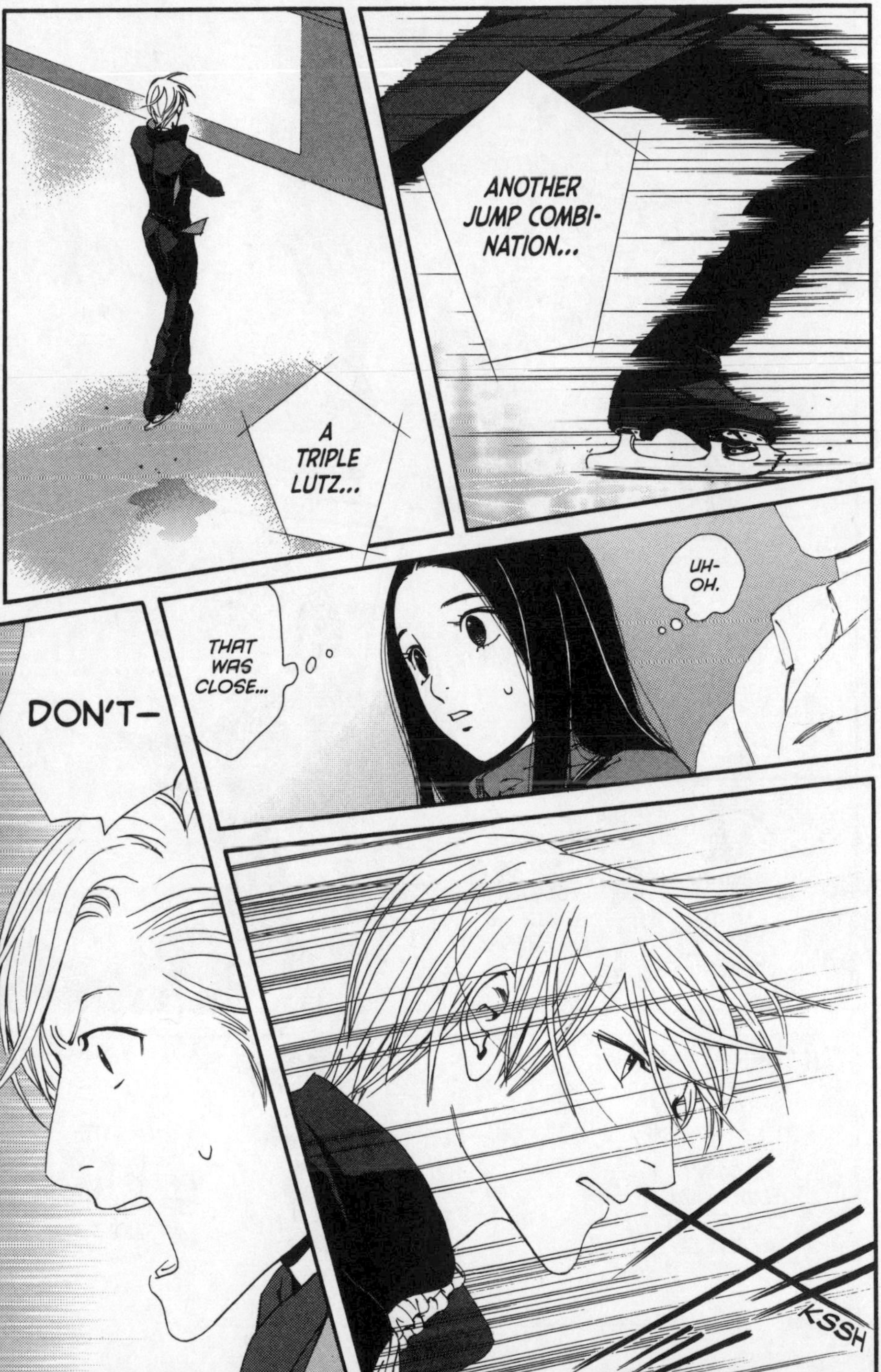
ANOTHER JUMP COMBINATION...
A TRIPLE LUTZ...
UH-OH.
THAT WAS CLOSE...
KSSH
DON'T—

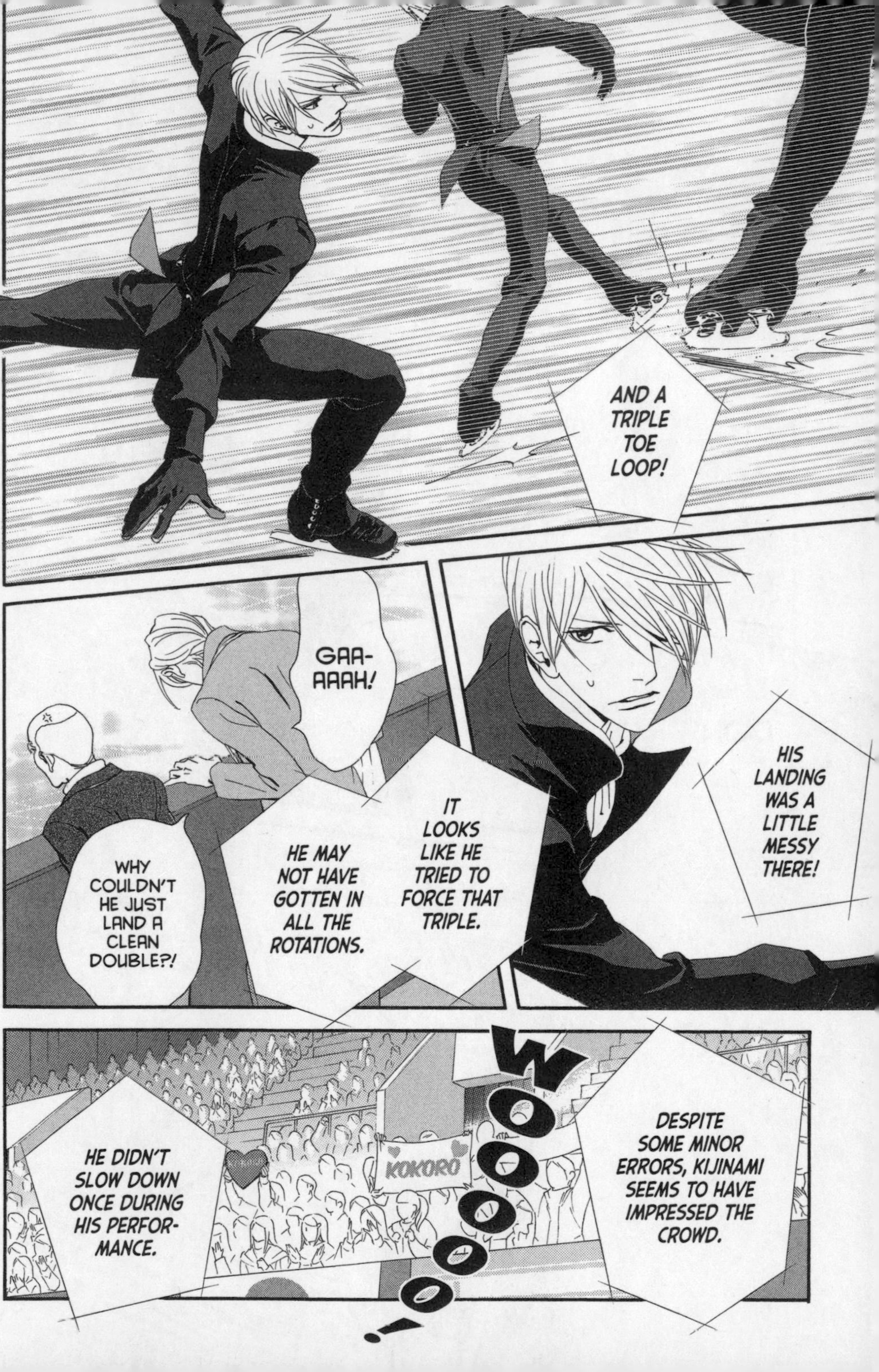
AND A TRIPLE TOE LOOP!
HIS LANDING WAS A LITTLE MESSY THERE!
IT LOOKS LIKE HE TRIED TO FORCE THAT TRIPLE.
HE MAY NOT HAVE GOTTEN IN ALL THE ROTATIONS.
GAA-AAAH!
WHY COULDN'T HE JUST LAND A CLEAN DOUBLE?!
DESPITE SOME MINOR ERRORS, KIJINAMI SEEMS TO HAVE IMPRESSED THE CROWD.
WOOOOOOO!
KOKORO
HE DIDN'T SLOW DOWN ONCE DURING HIS PERFORMANCE.

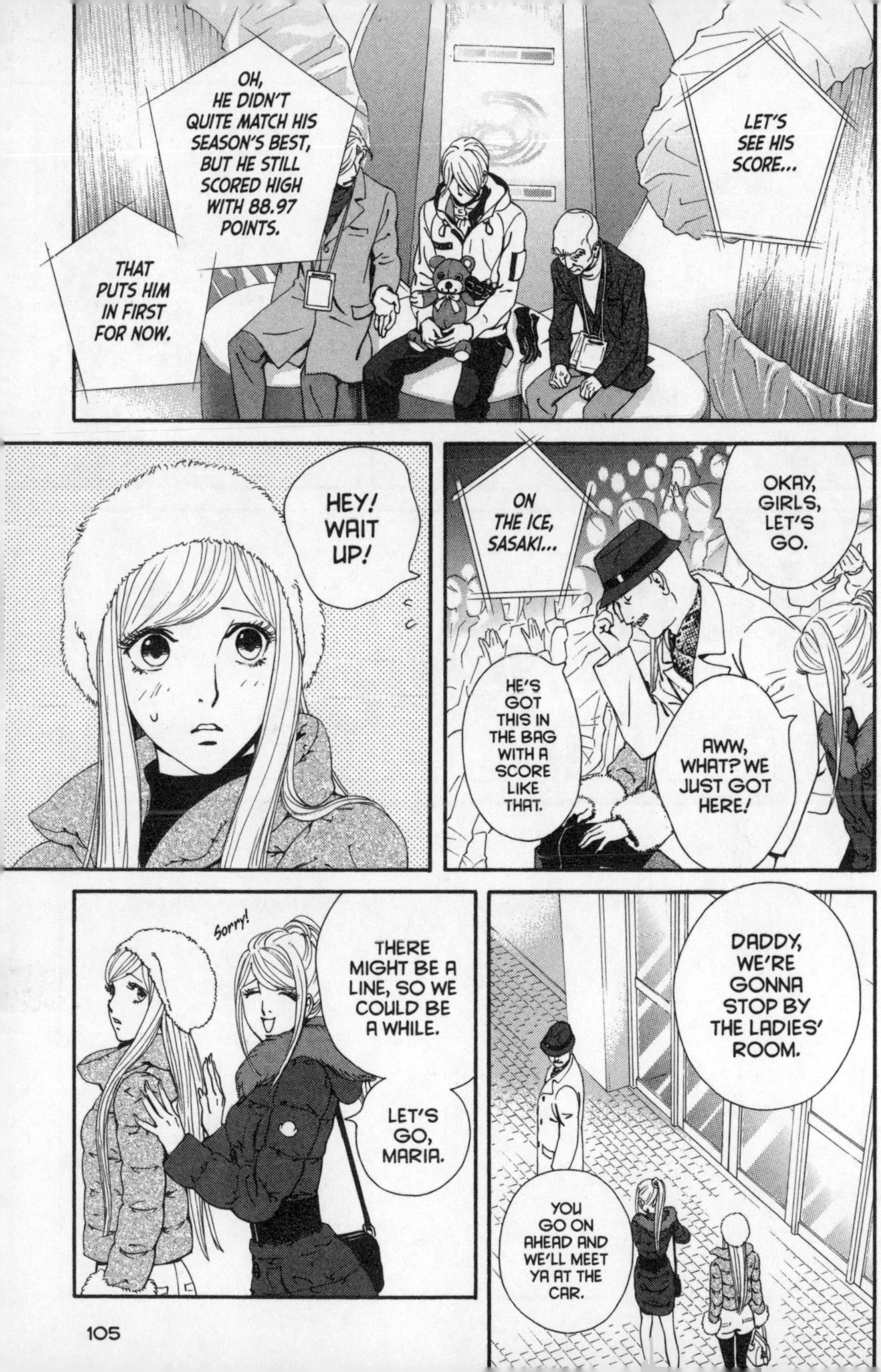
LET'S SEE HIS SCORE...
OH, HE DIDN'T QUITE MATCH HIS SEASON'S BEST, BUT HE STILL SCORED HIGH WITH 88.97 POINTS.
THAT PUTS HIM IN FIRST FOR NOW.
OKAY, GIRLS, LET'S GO.
ON THE ICE, SASAKI...
AWW, WHAT? WE JUST GOT HERE!
HE'S GOT THIS IN THE BAG WITH A SCORE LIKE THAT.
HEY! WAIT UP!
DADDY, WE'RE GONNA STOP BY THE LADIES' ROOM.
YOU GO ON AHEAD AND WE'LL MEET YA AT THE CAR.
THERE MIGHT BE A LINE, SO WE COULD BE A WHILE.
Sorry!
LET'S GO, MARIA.

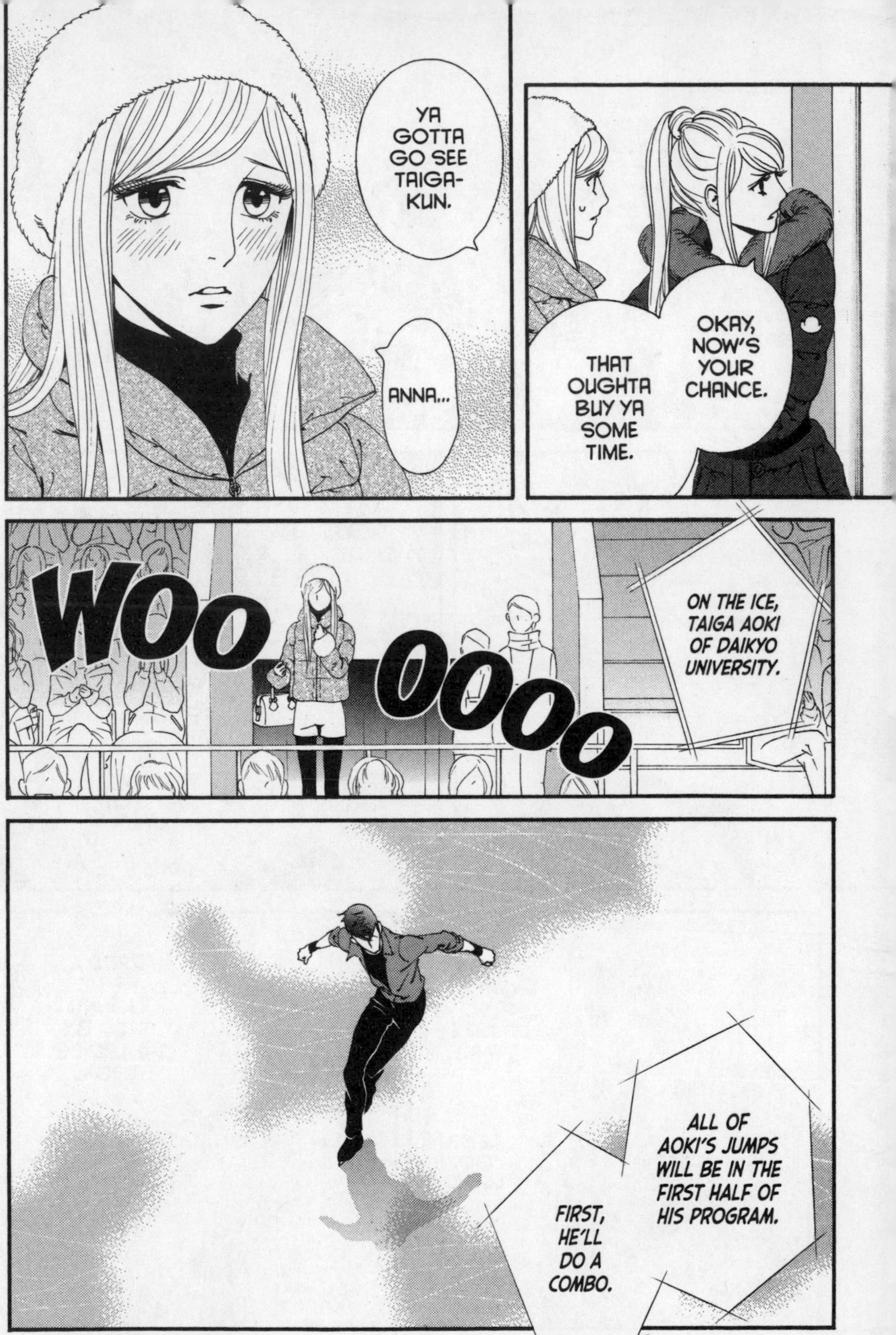
OKAY, NOW'S YOUR CHANCE.
THAT OUGHTA BUY YA SOME TIME.
YA GOTTA GO SEE TAIGA-KUN.
ANNA...
ON THE ICE, TAIGA AOKI OF DAIKYO UNIVERSITY.
WOO OOOOO
ALL OF AOKI'S JUMPS WILL BE IN THE FIRST HALF OF HIS PROGRAM.
FIRST, HE'LL DO A COMBO.

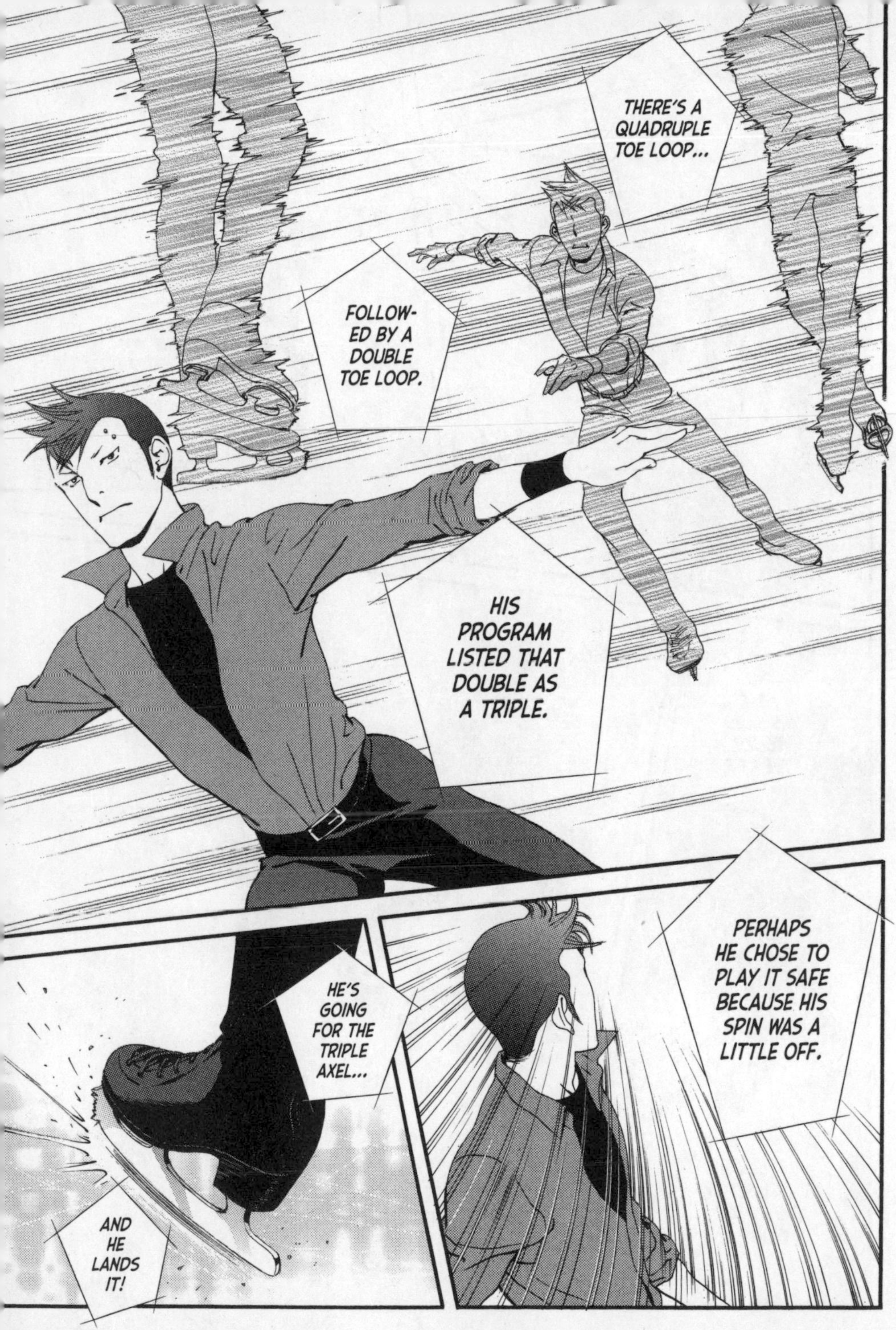
THERE'S A QUADRUPLE TOE LOOP...
FOLLOWED BY A DOUBLE TOE LOOP.
HIS PROGRAM LISTED THAT DOUBLE AS A TRIPLE.
PERHAPS HE CHOSE TO PLAY IT SAFE BECAUSE HIS SPIN WAS A LITTLE OFF.
HE'S GOING FOR THE TRIPLE AXEL...
AND HE LANDS IT!

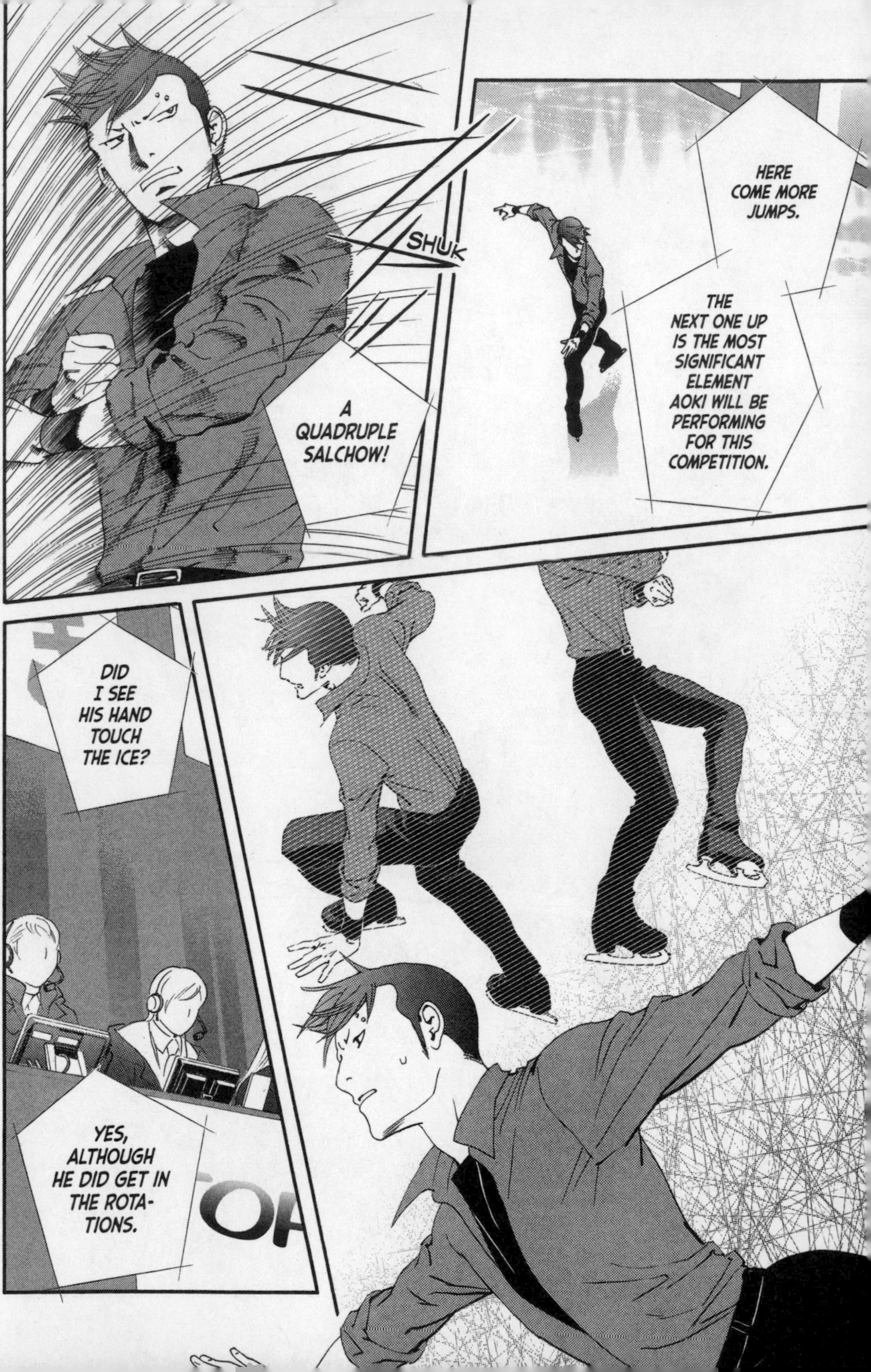
HERE COME MORE JUMPS.
THE NEXT ONE UP IS THE MOST SIGNIFICANT ELEMENT AOKI WILL BE PERFORMING FOR THIS COMPETITION.
SHUK
A QUADRUPLE SALCHOW!
DID I SEE HIS HAND TOUCH THE ICE?
YES, ALTHOUGH HE DID GET IN THE ROTATIONS.

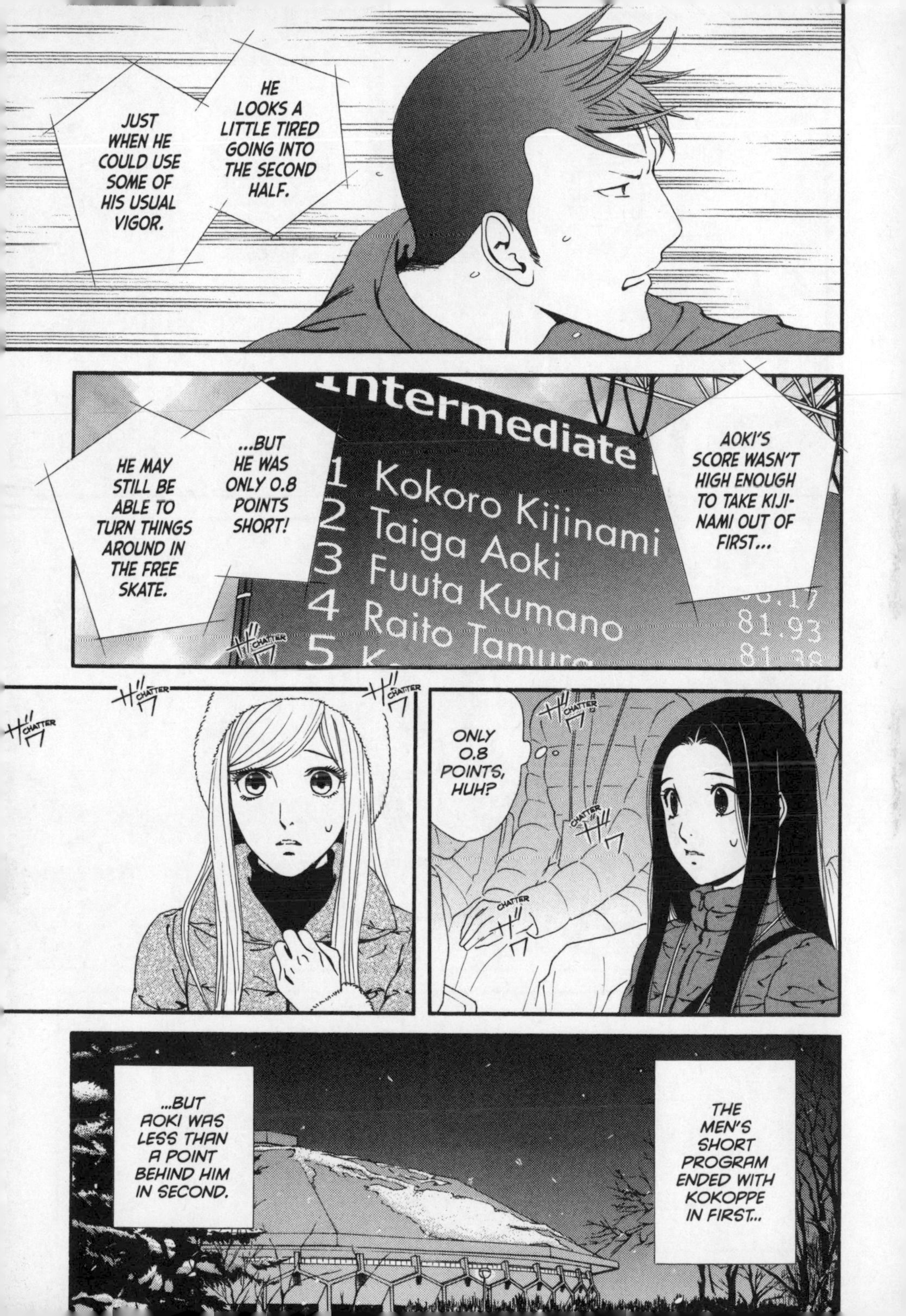
HE LOOKS A LITTLE TIRED GOING INTO THE SECOND HALF.
JUST WHEN HE COULD USE SOME OF HIS USUAL VIGOR.
AOKI'S SCORE WASN'T HIGH ENOUGH TO TAKE KIJINAMI OUT OF FIRST...
Intermediate
1 Kokoro Kijinami
2 Taiga Aoki
3 Fuuta Kumano
4 Raito Tamura
81.93
81.38
...BUT HE WAS ONLY 0.8 POINTS SHORT!
HE MAY STILL BE ABLE TO TURN THINGS AROUND IN THE FREE SKATE.
CHATTER
ONLY 0.8 POINTS, HUH?
CHATTER
CHATTER
CHATTER
CHATTER
CHATTER
CHATTER
THE MEN'S SHORT PROGRAM ENDED WITH KOKOPPE IN FIRST...
...BUT AOKI WAS LESS THAN A POINT BEHIND HIM IN SECOND.

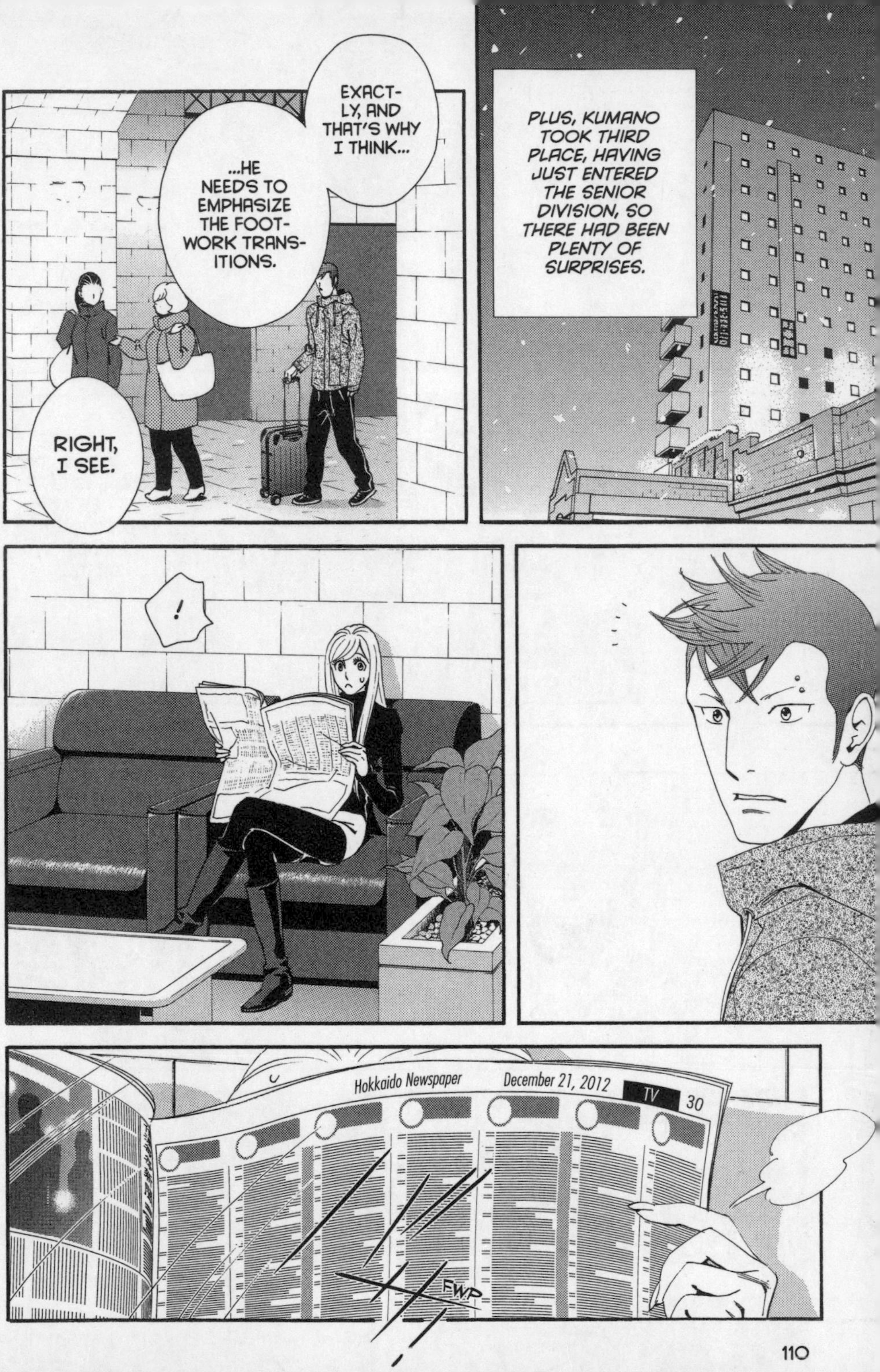
PLUS, KUMANO TOOK THIRD PLACE, HAVING JUST ENTERED THE SENIOR DIVISION, SO THERE HAD BEEN PLENTY OF SURPRISES.
EXACT-LY, AND THAT'S WHY I THINK...
...HE NEEDS TO EMPHASIZE THE FOOT-WORK TRANS-ITIONS.
RIGHT, I SEE.
!
Hokkaido Newspaper
December 21, 2012
TV
30
FWP

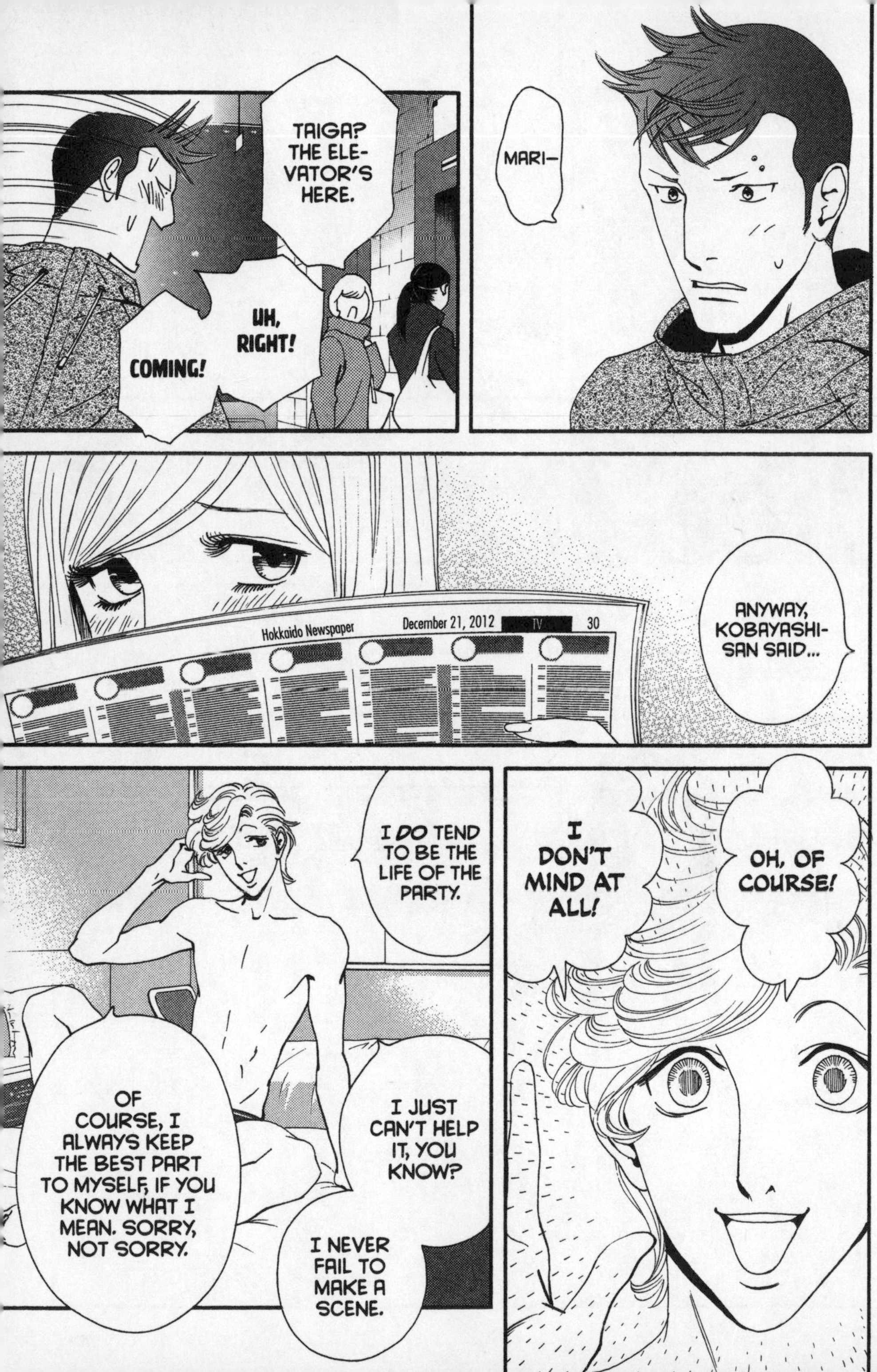
MARI—
TAIGA? THE ELE-VATOR'S HERE.
UH, RIGHT!
COMING!
Hokkaido Newspaper December 21, 2012 TV 30
ANYWAY, KOBAYASHI-SAN SAID...
OH, OF COURSE!
I DON'T MIND AT ALL!
I DO TEND TO BE THE LIFE OF THE PARTY.
I JUST CAN'T HELP IT, YOU KNOW?
I NEVER FAIL TO MAKE A SCENE.
OF COURSE, I ALWAYS KEEP THE BEST PART TO MYSELF, IF YOU KNOW WHAT I MEAN. SORRY, NOT SORRY.

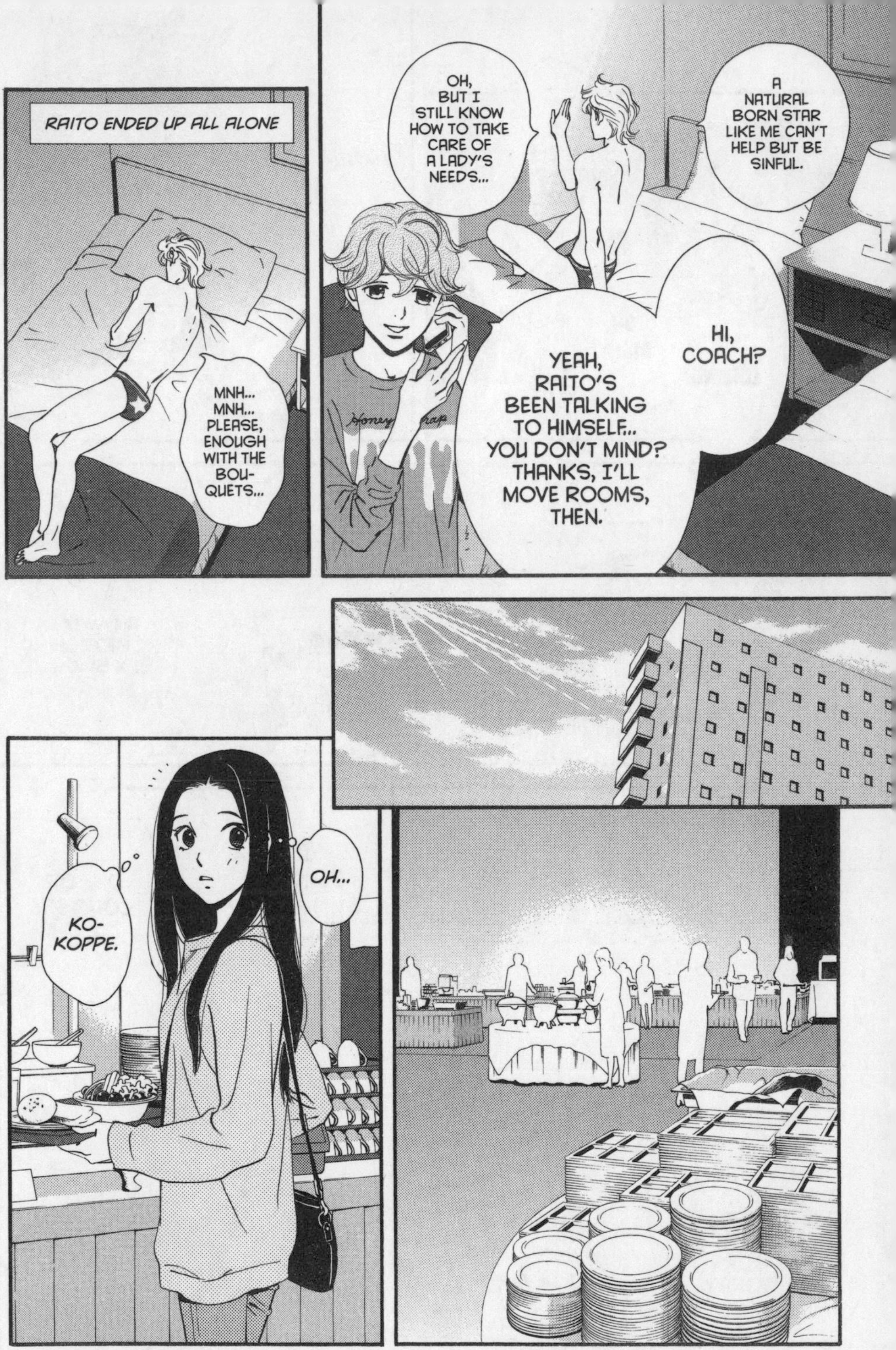
A NATURAL BORN STAR LIKE ME CAN'T HELP BUT BE SINFUL.
OH, BUT I STILL KNOW HOW TO TAKE CARE OF A LADY'S NEEDS...
HI, COACH?
YEAH, RAITO'S BEEN TALKING TO HIMSELF... YOU DON'T MIND? THANKS, I'LL MOVE ROOMS, THEN.
RAITO ENDED UP ALL ALONE
MNH... MNH... PLEASE, ENOUGH WITH THE BOU-QUETS...
OH...
KO-KOPPE.

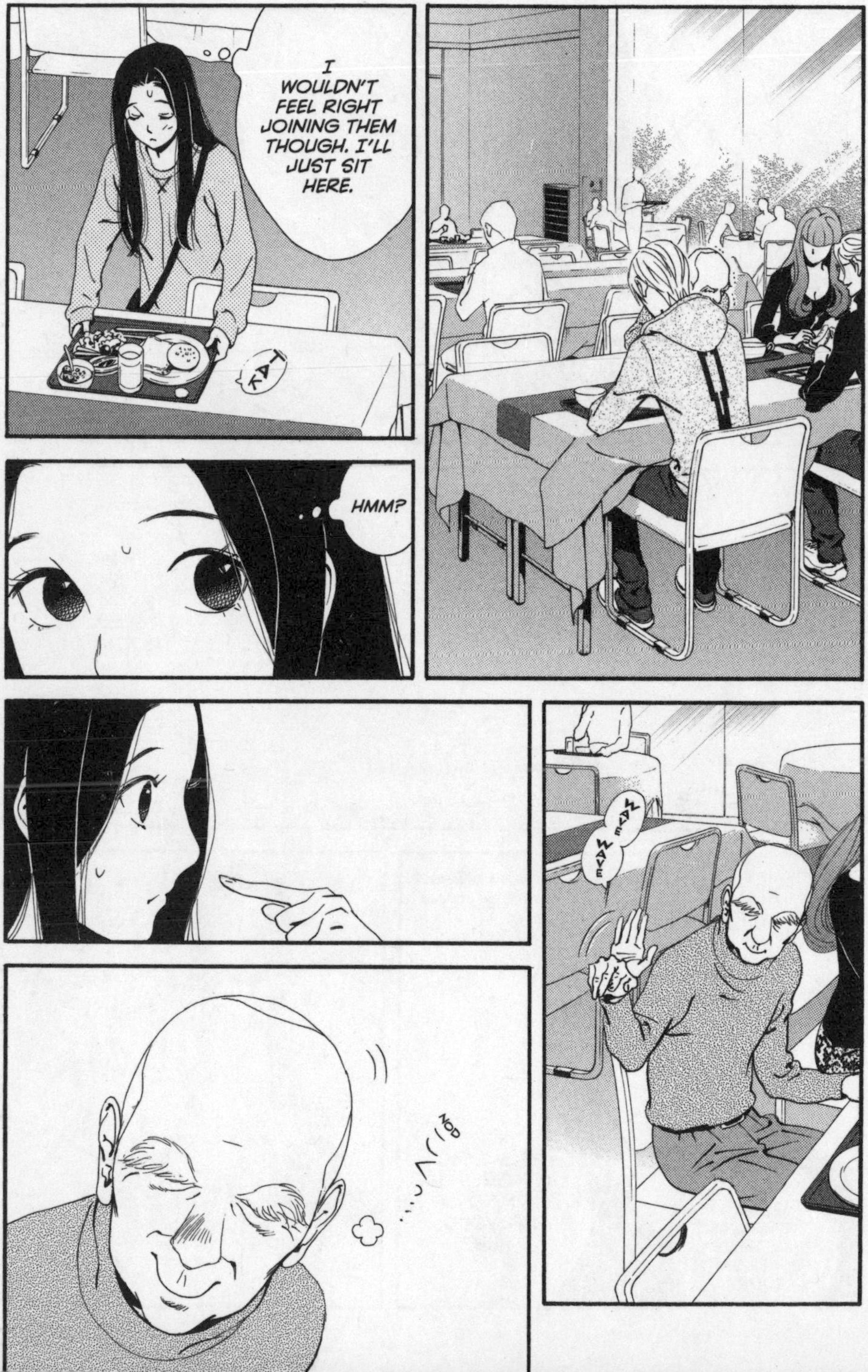
I WOULDN'T FEEL RIGHT JOINING THEM THOUGH. I'LL JUST SIT HERE.
TAK
HMM?
WAVE WAVE
NOD

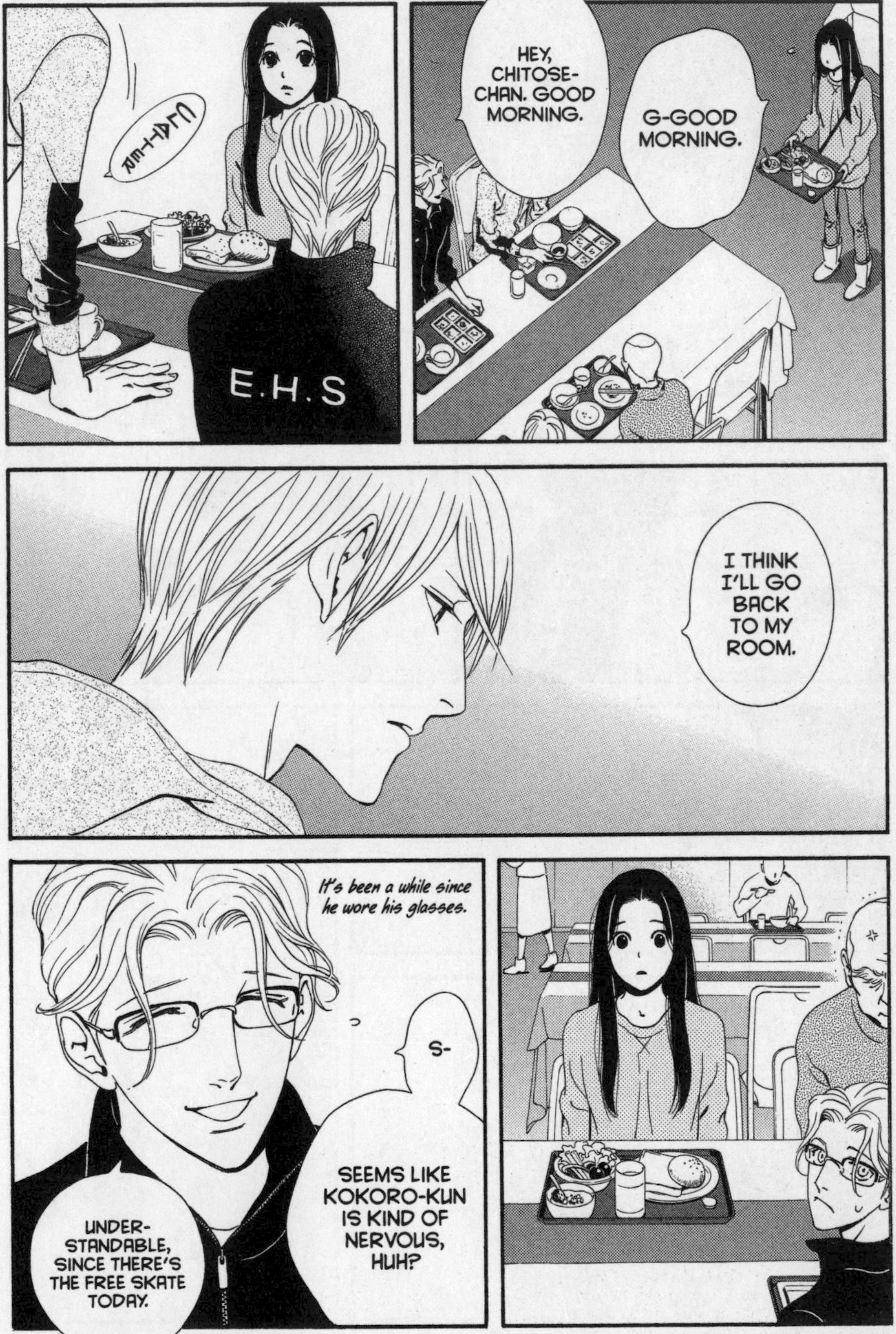
HEY, CHITOSE-CHAN. GOOD MORNING.
G-GOOD MORNING.
E.H.S
I THINK I'LL GO BACK TO MY ROOM.
It's been a while since he wore his glasses.
S-
SEEMS LIKE KOKORO-KUN IS KIND OF NERVOUS, HUH?
UNDER-STANDABLE, SINCE THERE'S THE FREE SKATE TODAY.

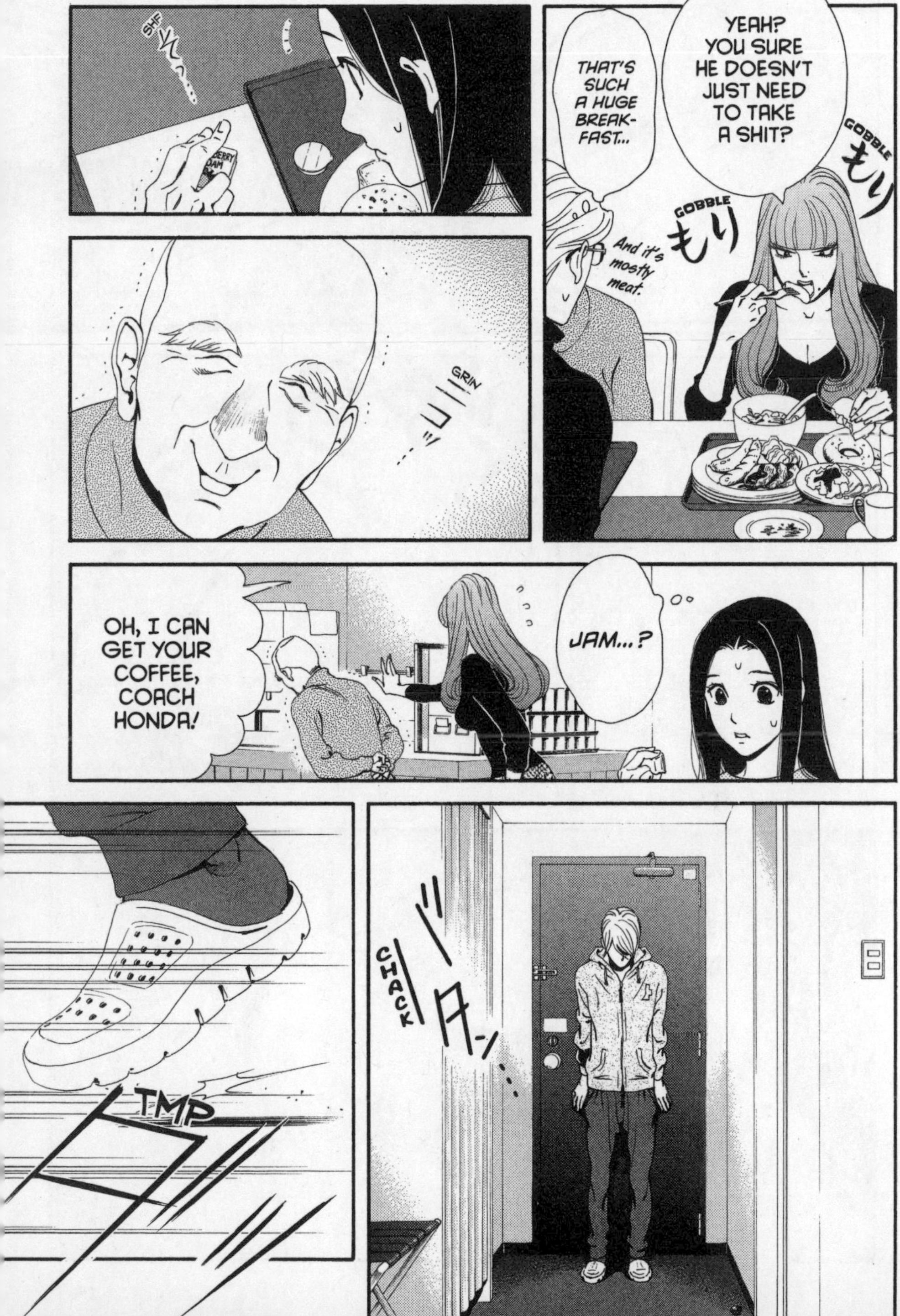
YEAH? YOU SURE HE DOESN'T JUST NEED TO TAKE A SHIT?
THAT'S SUCH A HUGE BREAK-FAST...
GOBBLE
もり
GOBBLE
もり
And it's mostly meat.
SHF
GRIN
JAM...?
OH, I CAN GET YOUR COFFEE, COACH HONDA!
CHACK
TMP

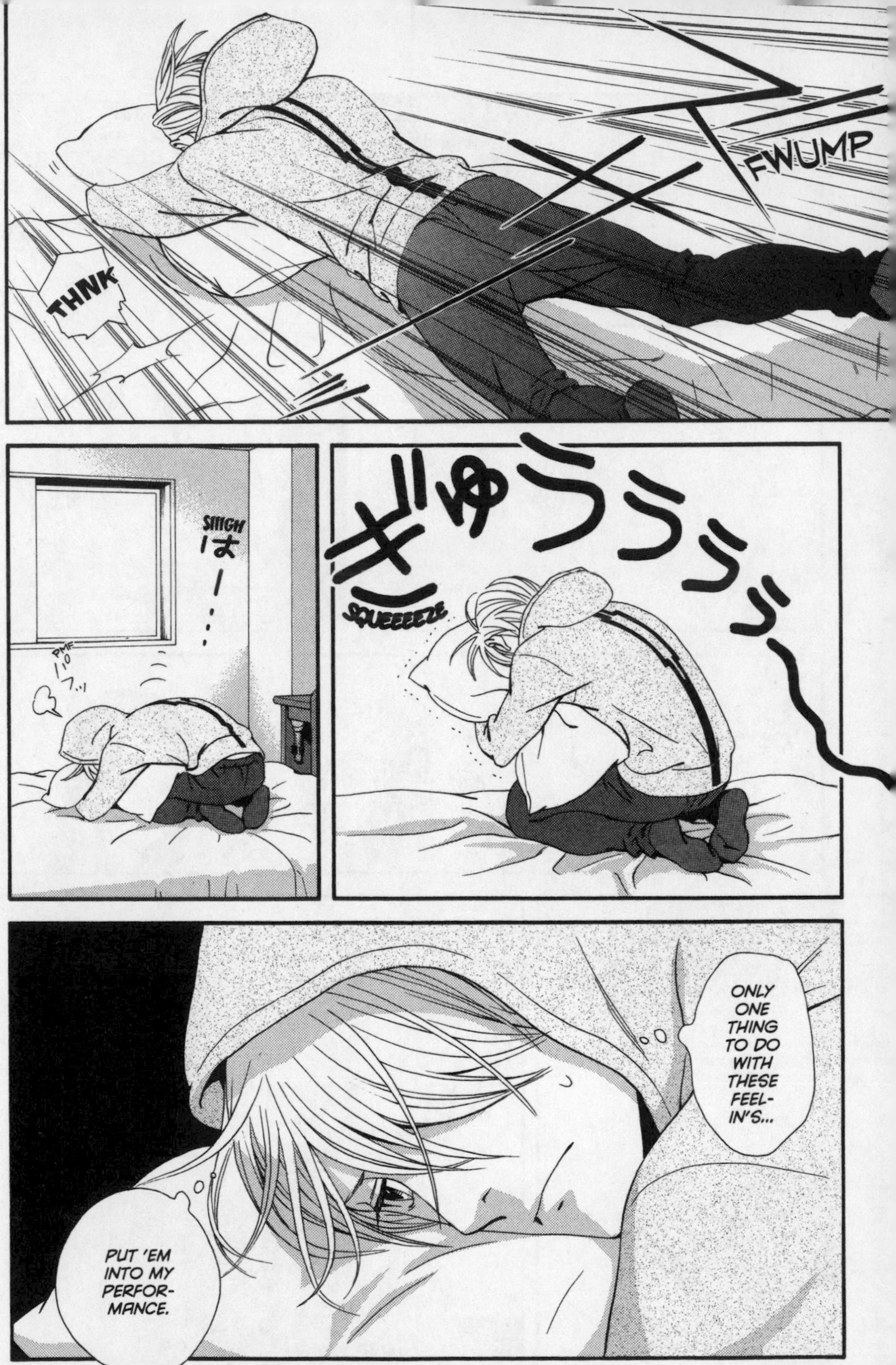
FWUMP
THNK
ぎゅううう～
SQUEEEEZE
SIIIGH
はー…
PMF
ONLY ONE THING TO DO WITH THESE FEEL-IN'S...
PUT 'EM INTO MY PERFOR-MANCE.

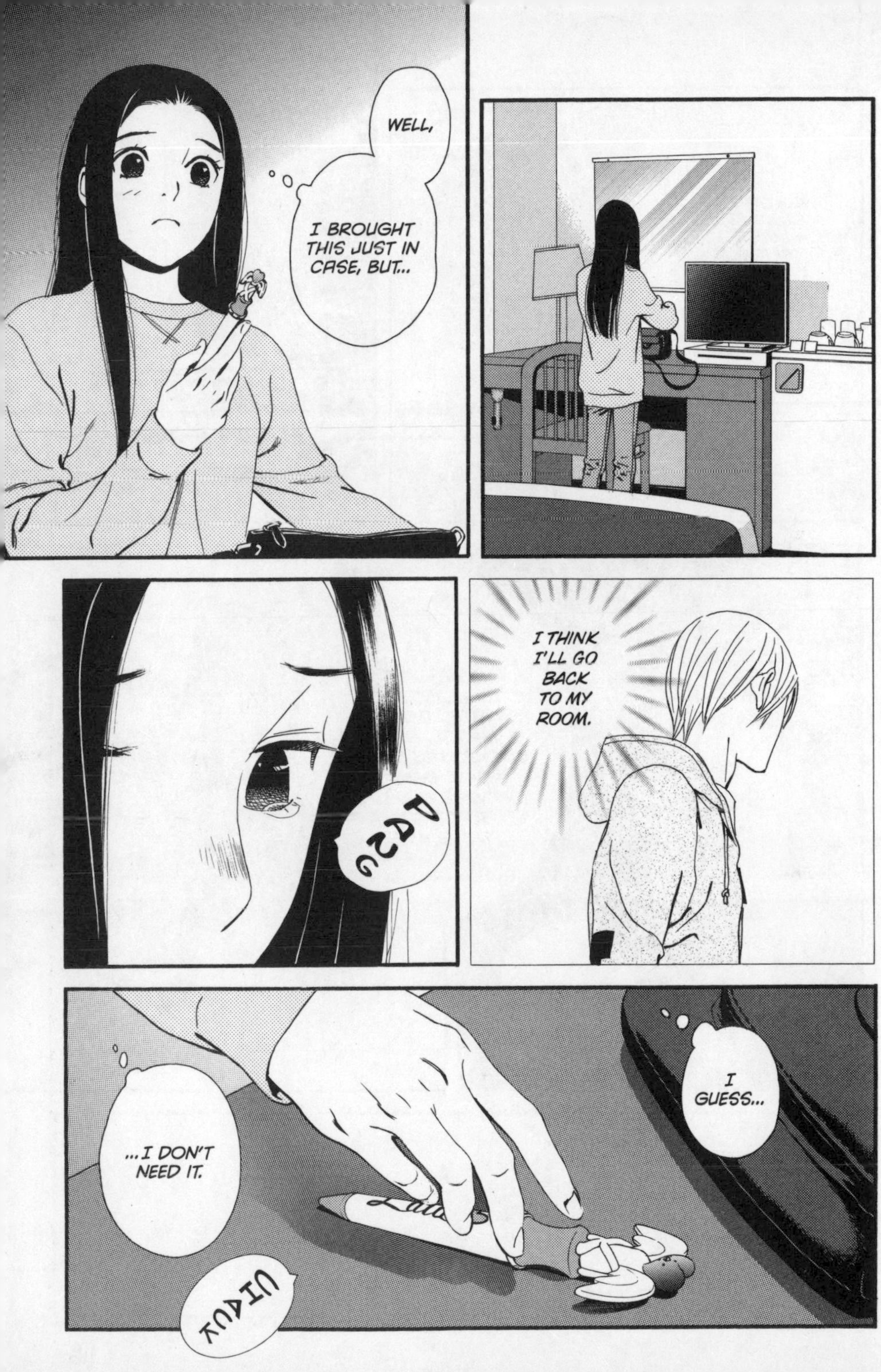
WELL,
I BROUGHT THIS JUST IN CASE, BUT...
I THINK I'LL GO BACK TO MY ROOM.
I GUESS...
...I DON'T NEED IT.

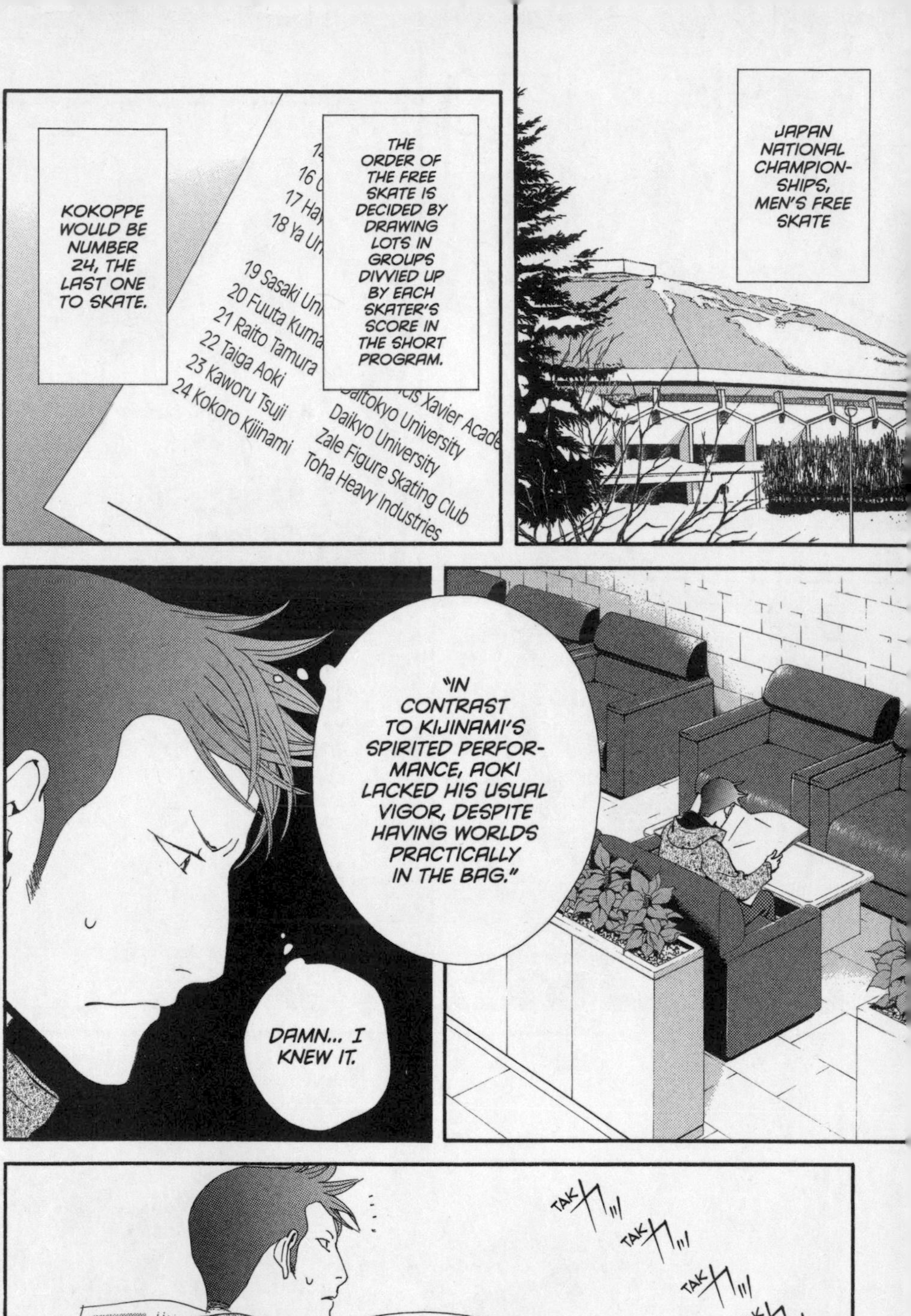
JAPAN NATIONAL CHAMPIONSHIPS, MEN'S FREE SKATE
THE ORDER OF THE FREE SKATE IS DECIDED BY DRAWING LOTS IN GROUPS DIVVIED UP BY EACH SKATER'S SCORE IN THE SHORT PROGRAM.
KOKOPPE WOULD BE NUMBER 24, THE LAST ONE TO SKATE.
21 Raito Tamura
22 Taiga Aoki
23 Kaworu Tsuji
24 Kokoro Kijinami
Daikyo University
Zale Figure Skating Club
Toha Heavy Industries
"IN CONTRAST TO KIJINAMI'S SPIRITED PERFORMANCE, AOKI LACKED HIS USUAL VIGOR, DESPITE HAVING WORLDS PRACTICALLY IN THE BAG."
DAMN... I KNEW IT.
TAK
TAK
TAK
TAK

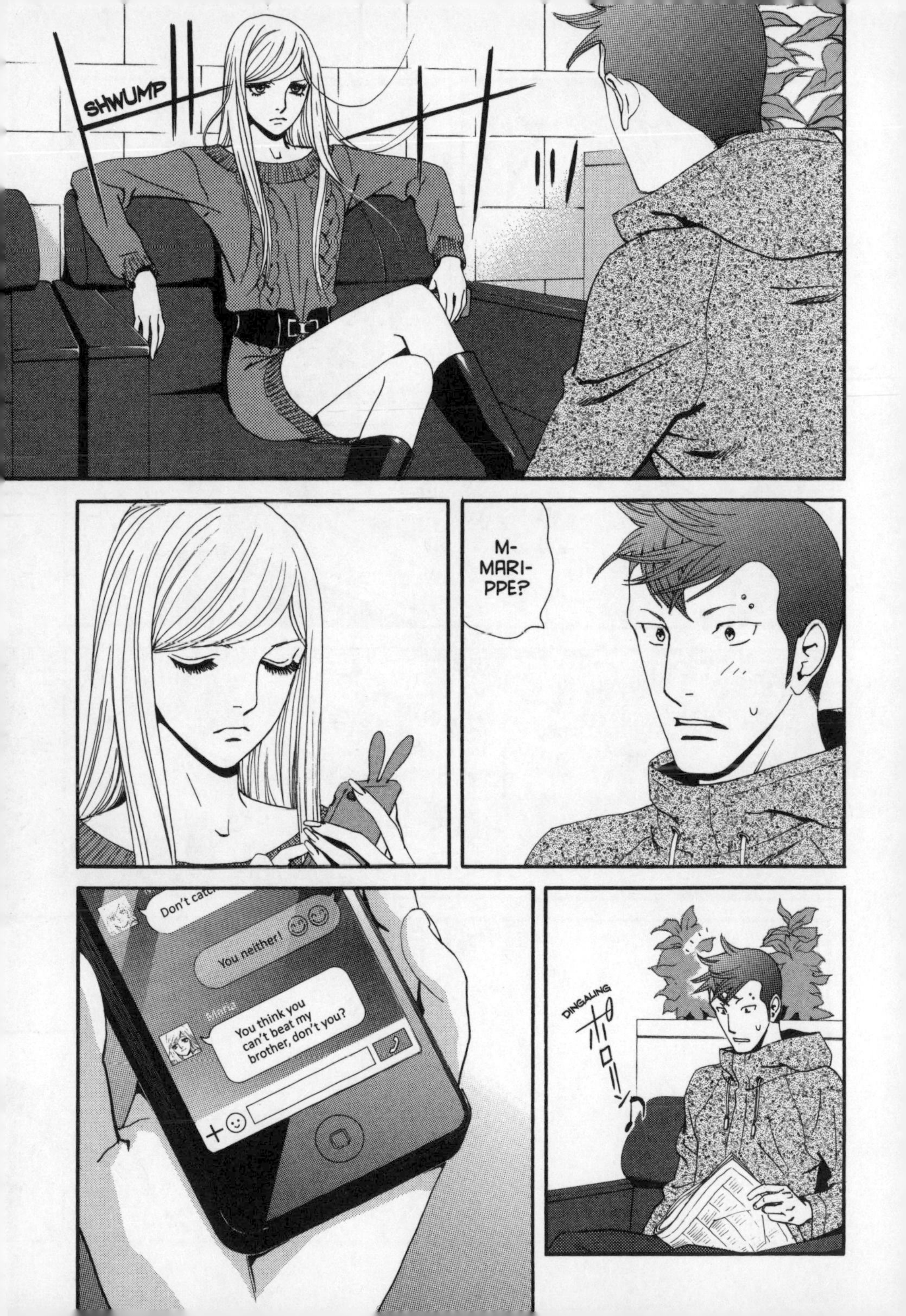
SHWUMP
M-MARI-PPE?
DINGALING
ポロリーン
Don't catc
You neither!
Mari
You think you can't beat my brother, don't you?

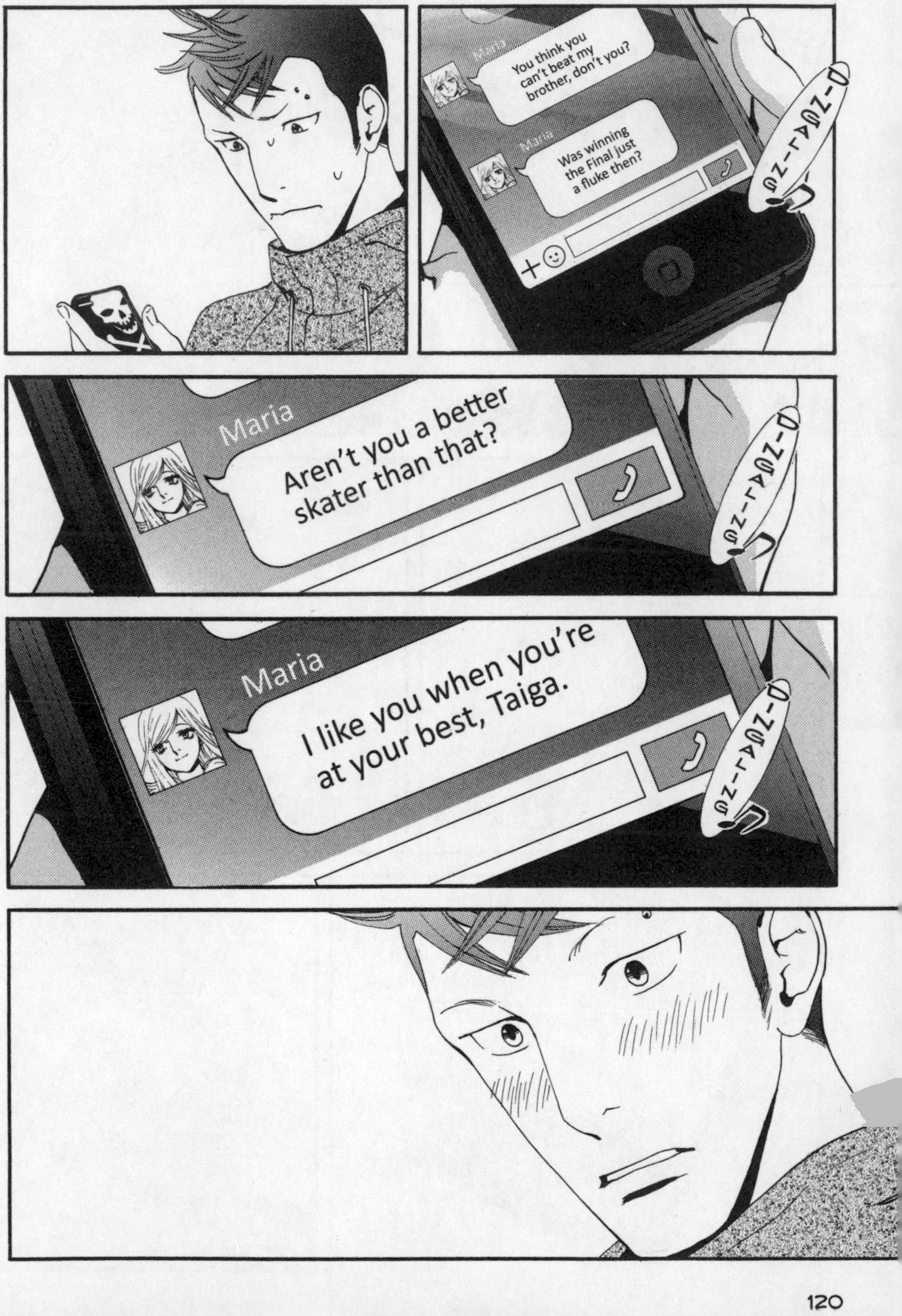
Maria
You think you can't beat my brother, don't you?
Maria
Was winning the Final just a fluke then?
Maria
Aren't you a better skater than that?
Maria
I like you when you're at your best, Taiga.

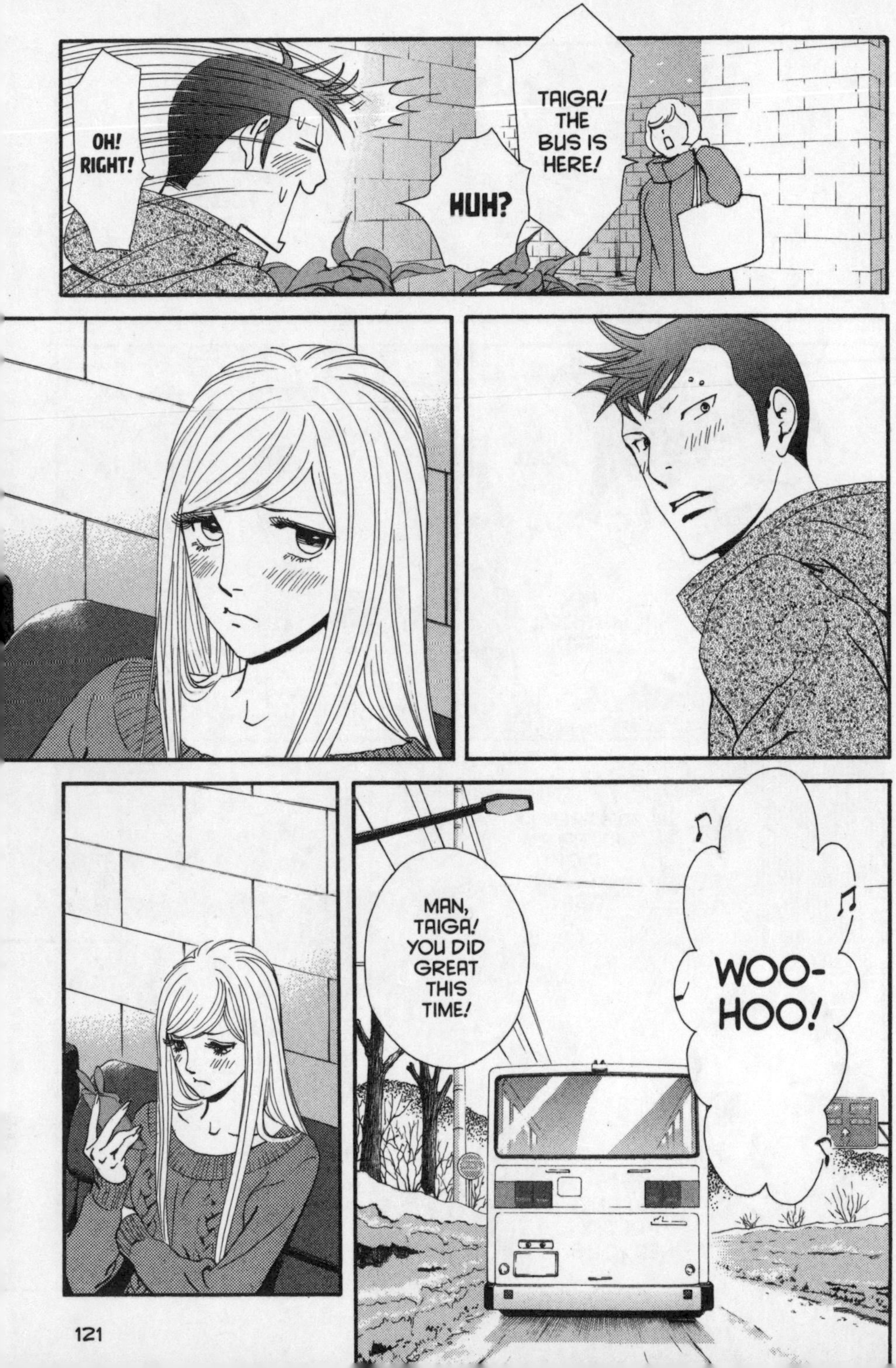
TAIGA! THE BUS IS HERE!
HUH?
OH! RIGHT!
WOO-HOO!
MAN, TAIGA! YOU DID GREAT THIS TIME!

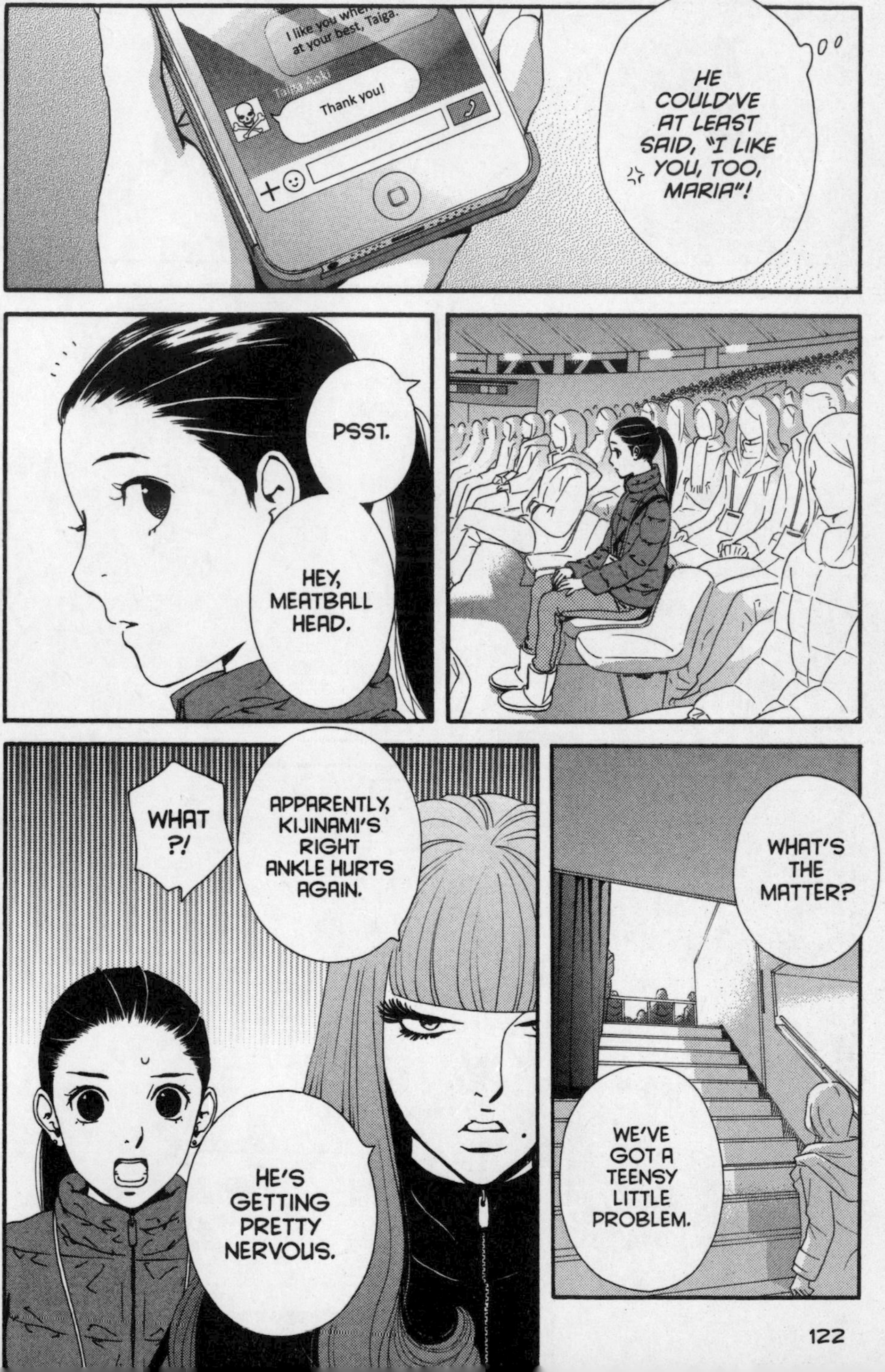
at your best, Taiga.
Thank you!
HE COULD'VE AT LEAST SAID, "I LIKE YOU, TOO, MARIA"!
PSST.
HEY, MEATBALL HEAD.
WHAT'S THE MATTER?
WE'VE GOT A TEENSY LITTLE PROBLEM.
APPARENTLY, KIJINAMI'S RIGHT ANKLE HURTS AGAIN.
WHAT ?!
HE'S GETTING PRETTY NERVOUS.

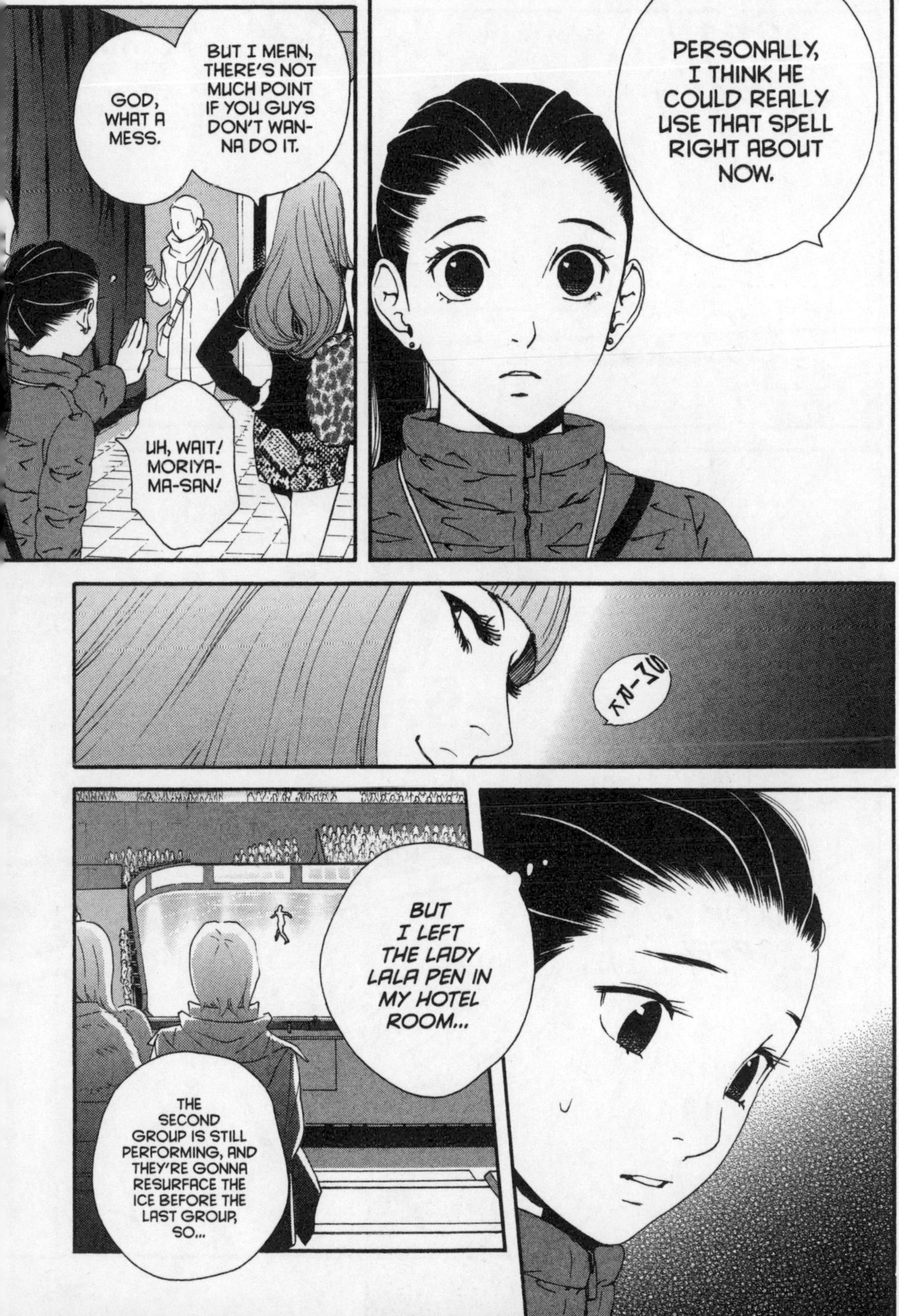
PERSONALLY, I THINK HE COULD REALLY USE THAT SPELL RIGHT ABOUT NOW.
BUT I MEAN, THERE'S NOT MUCH POINT IF YOU GUYS DON'T WAN-NA DO IT.
GOD, WHAT A MESS.
UH, WAIT! MORIYA-MA-SAN!
BUT I LEFT THE LADY LALA PEN IN MY HOTEL ROOM...
THE SECOND GROUP IS STILL PERFORMING, AND THEY'RE GONNA RESURFACE THE ICE BEFORE THE LAST GROUP, SO...

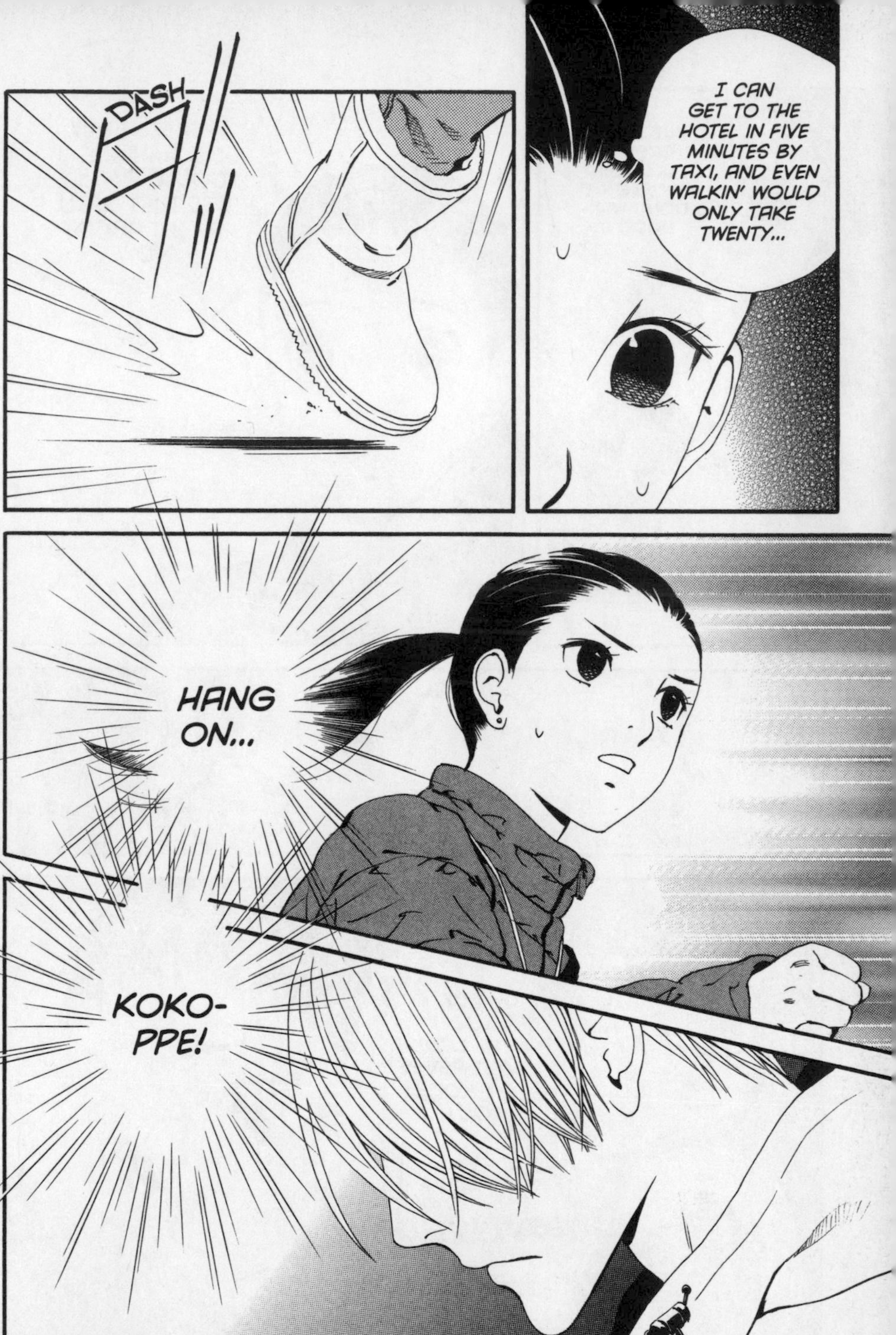
I CAN GET TO THE HOTEL IN FIVE MINUTES BY TAXI, AND EVEN WALKIN' WOULD ONLY TAKE TWENTY...
DASH
HANG ON...
KOKO-PPE!

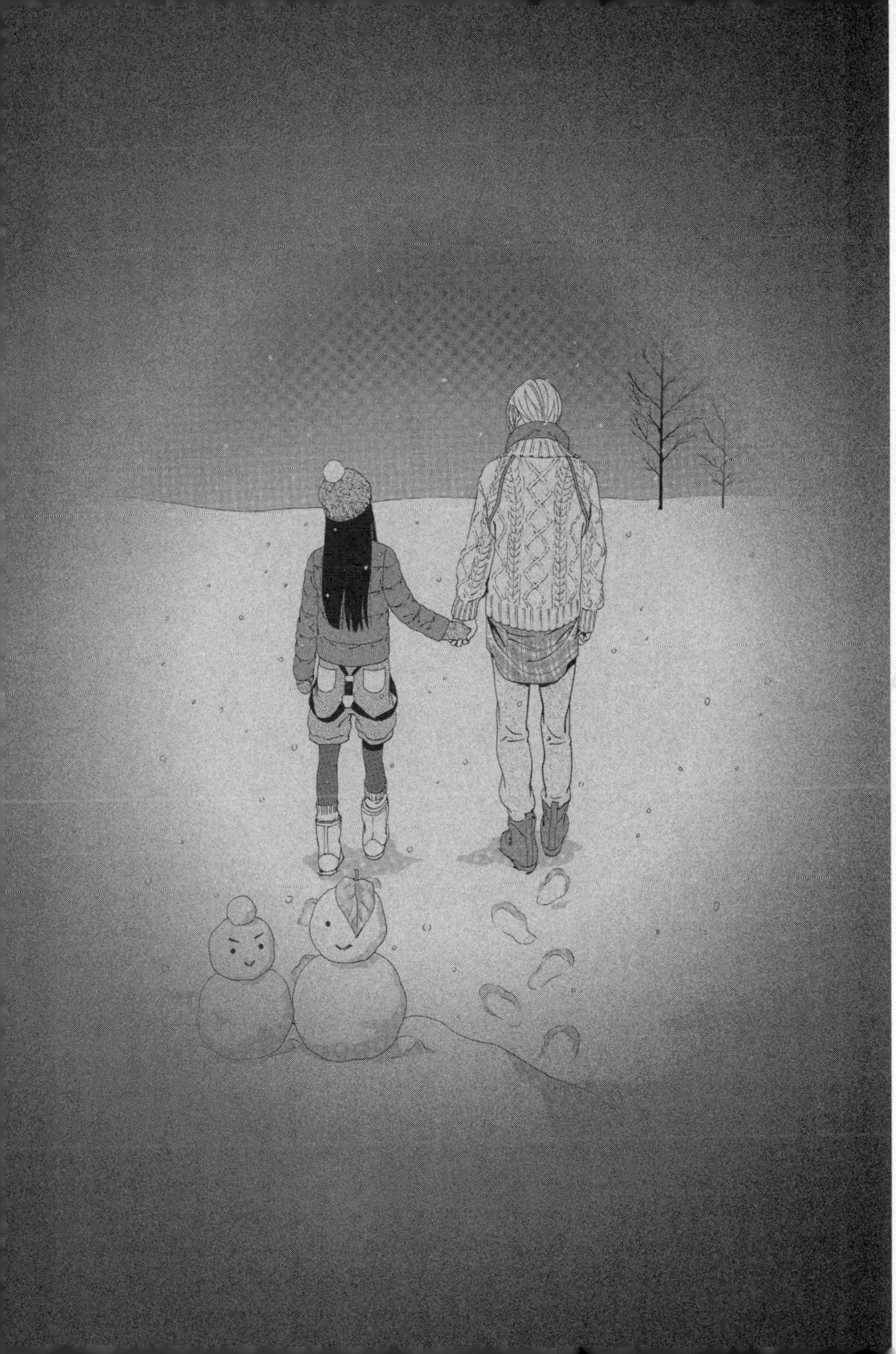

Spell 26
A Kiss From Don Juan

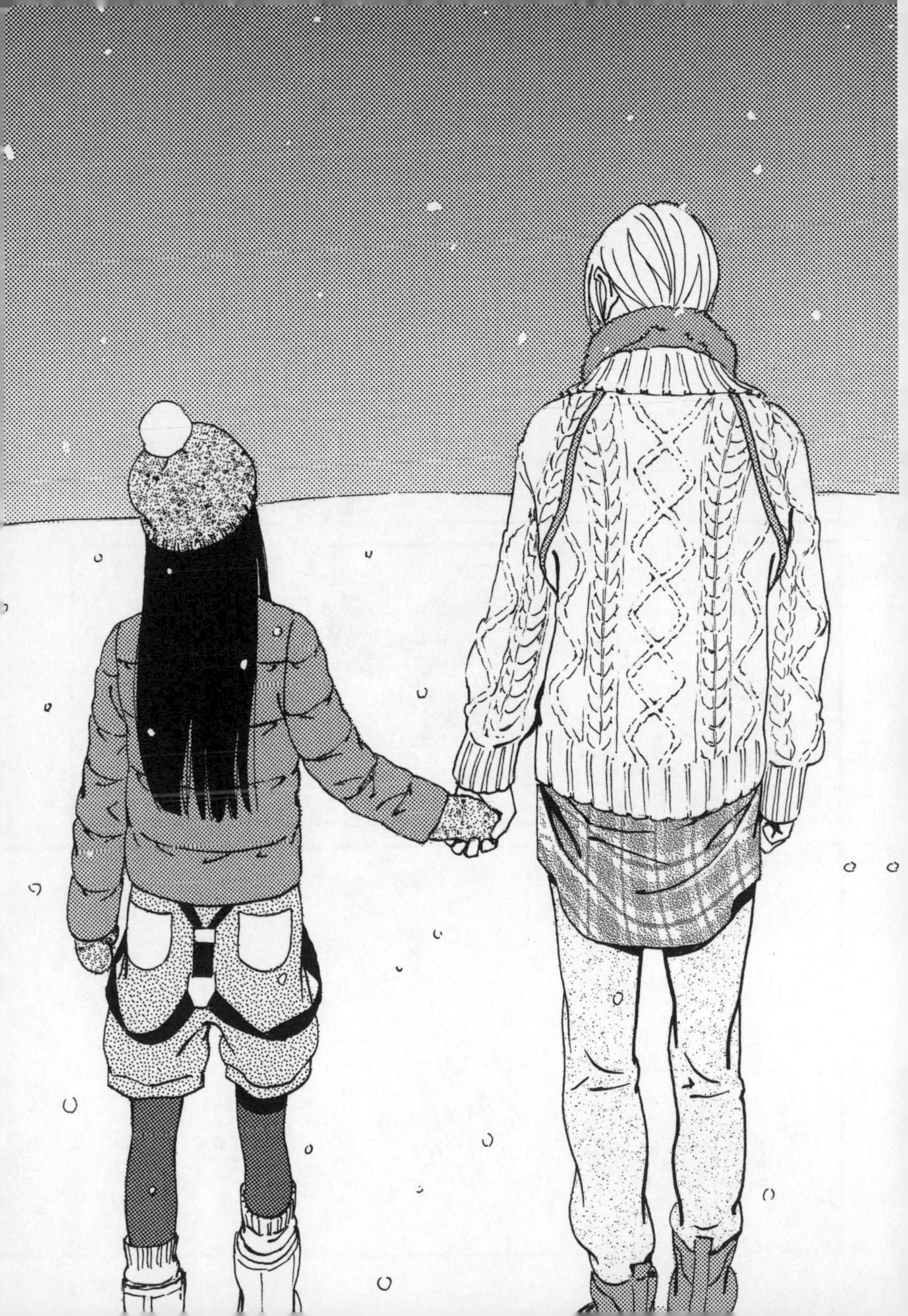

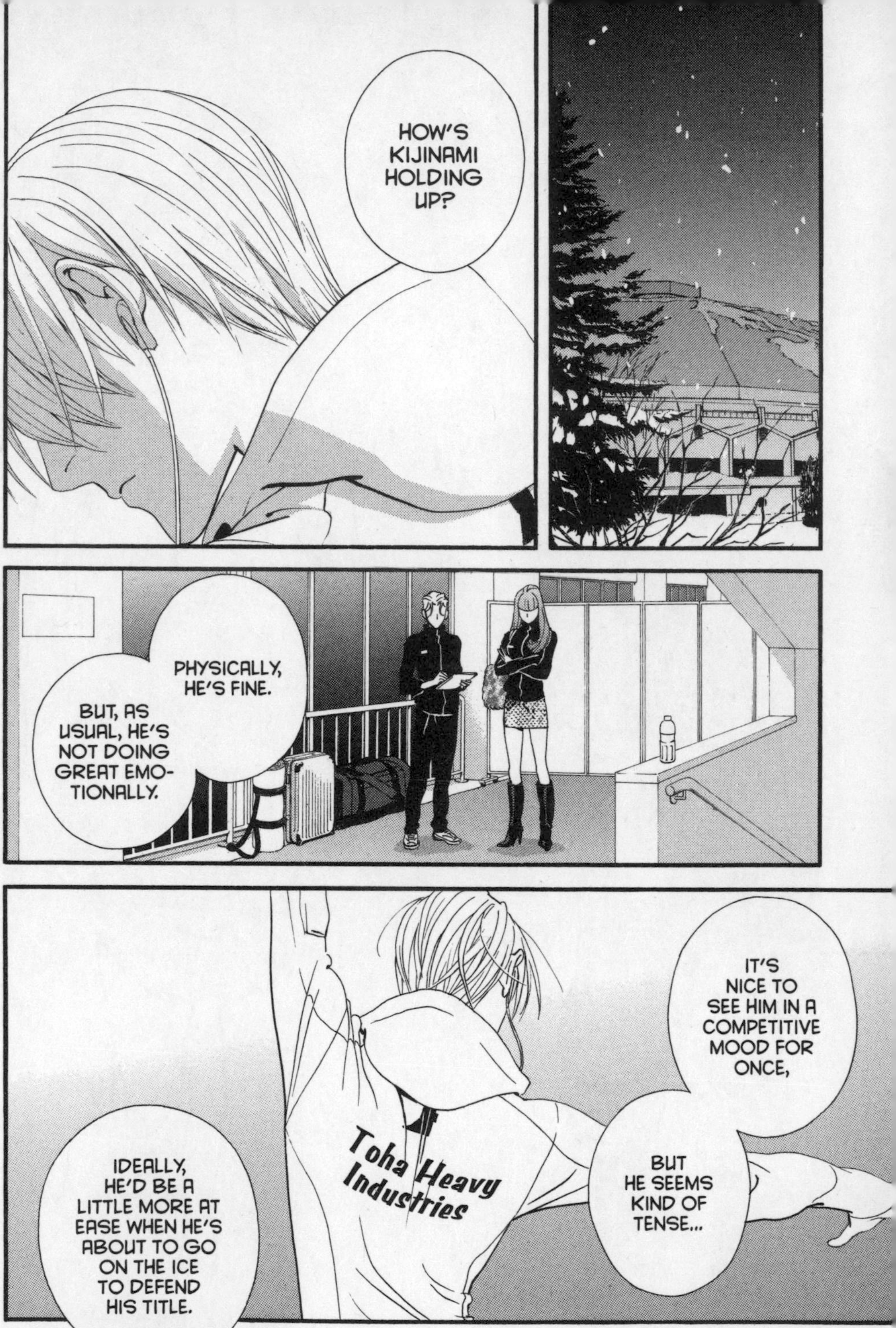
HOW'S KIJINAMI HOLDING UP?
PHYSICALLY, HE'S FINE.
BUT, AS USUAL, HE'S NOT DOING GREAT EMO-TIONALLY.
IT'S NICE TO SEE HIM IN A COMPETITIVE MOOD FOR ONCE,
Toha Heavy Industries
BUT HE SEEMS KIND OF TENSE...
IDEALLY, HE'D BE A LITTLE MORE AT EASE WHEN HE'S ABOUT TO GO ON THE ICE TO DEFEND HIS TITLE.

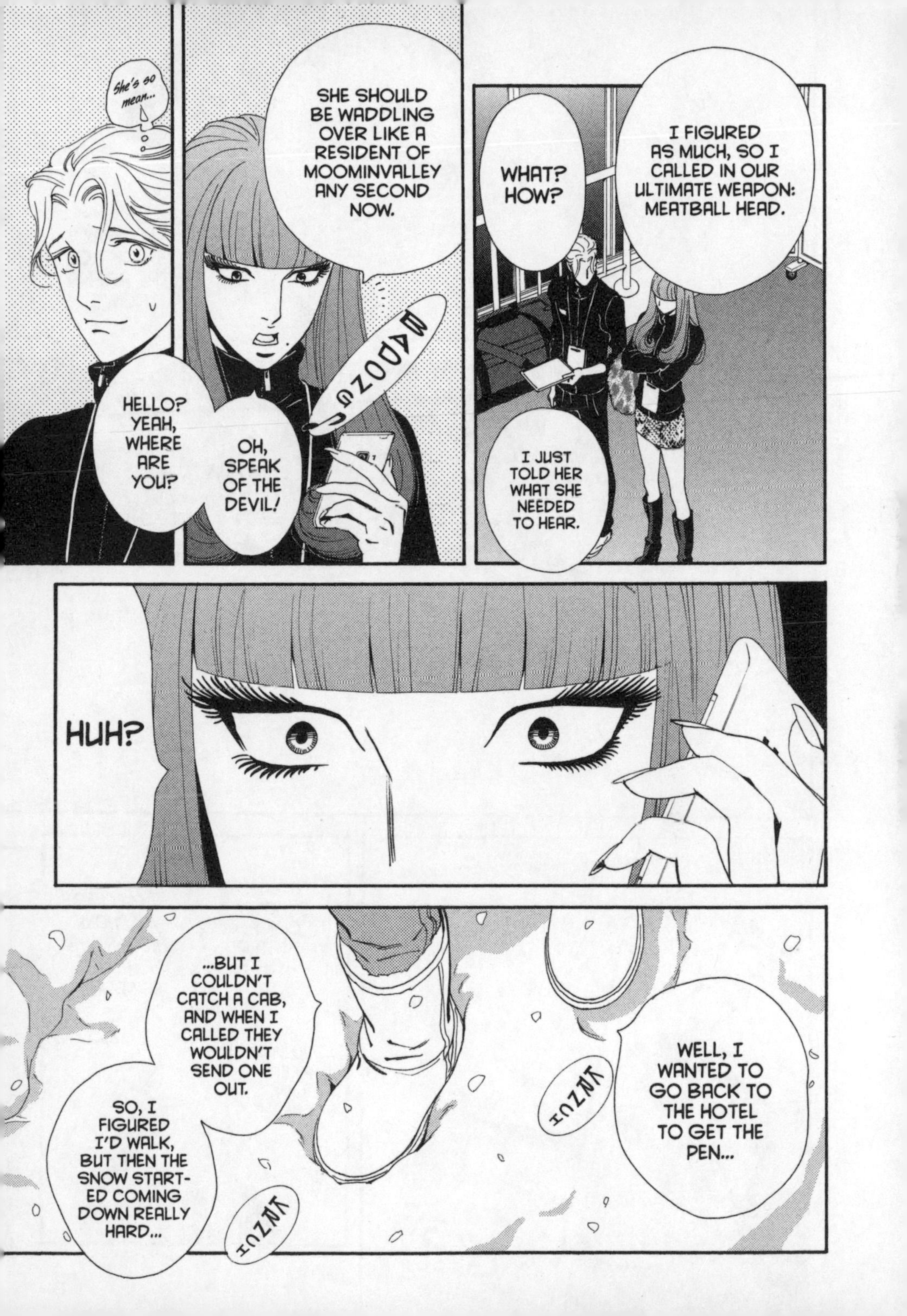
WHAT? HOW?
I FIGURED AS MUCH, SO I CALLED IN OUR ULTIMATE WEAPON: MEATBALL HEAD.
I JUST TOLD HER WHAT SHE NEEDED TO HEAR.
SHE SHOULD BE WADDLING OVER LIKE A RESIDENT OF MOOMINVALLEY ANY SECOND NOW.
OH, SPEAK OF THE DEVIL!
She's so mean...
HELLO? YEAH, WHERE ARE YOU?
HUH?
WELL, I WANTED TO GO BACK TO THE HOTEL TO GET THE PEN...
...BUT I COULDN'T CATCH A CAB, AND WHEN I CALLED THEY WOULDN'T SEND ONE OUT.
SO, I FIGURED I'D WALK, BUT THEN THE SNOW START-ED COMING DOWN REALLY HARD...

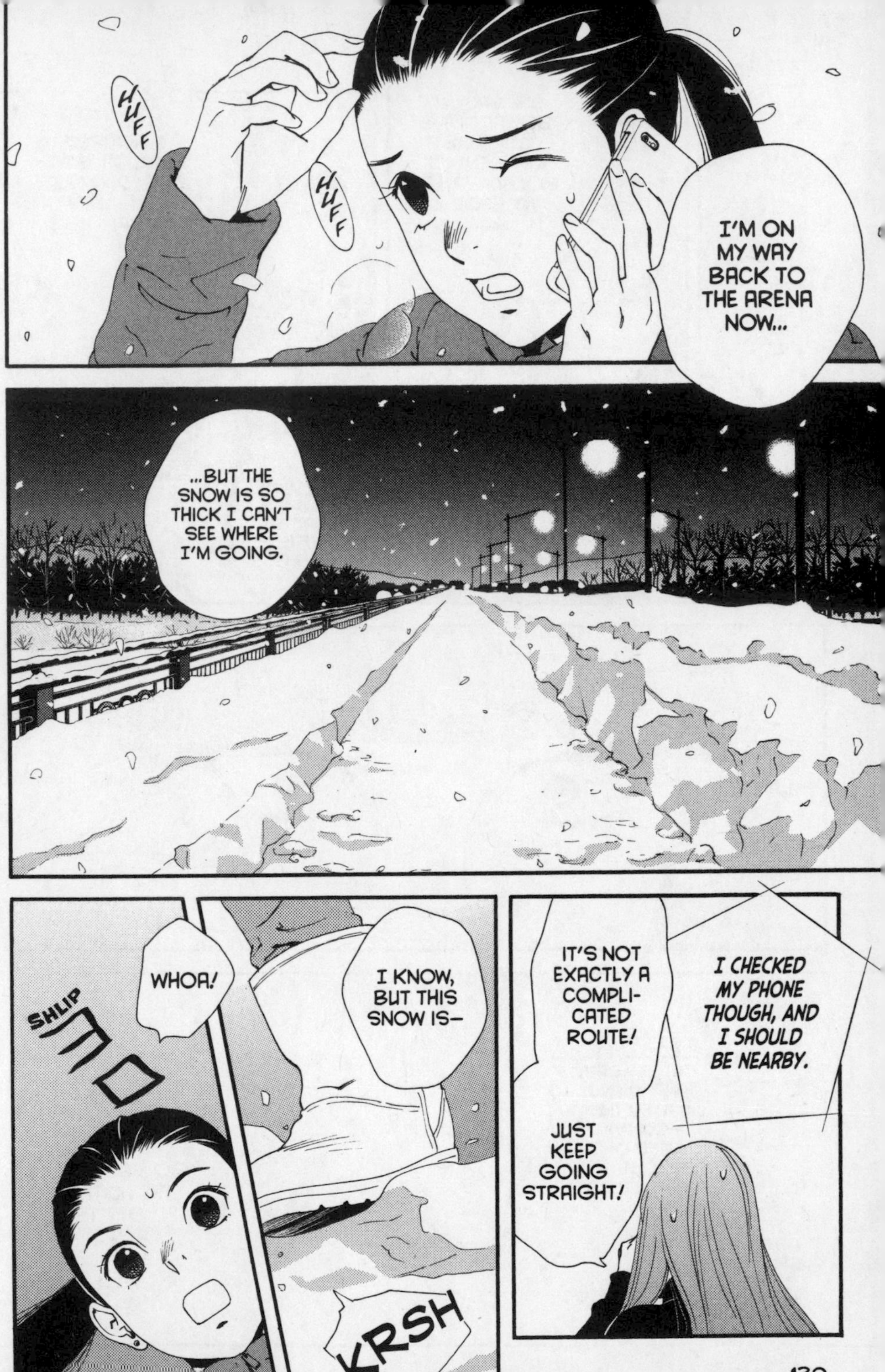
I'M ON MY WAY BACK TO THE ARENA NOW...
HUFF
HUFF
...BUT THE SNOW IS SO THICK I CAN'T SEE WHERE I'M GOING.
I CHECKED MY PHONE THOUGH, AND I SHOULD BE NEARBY.
IT'S NOT EXACTLY A COMPLI-CATED ROUTE!
JUST KEEP GOING STRAIGHT!
I KNOW, BUT THIS SNOW IS—
KRSH
SHLIP
WHOA!

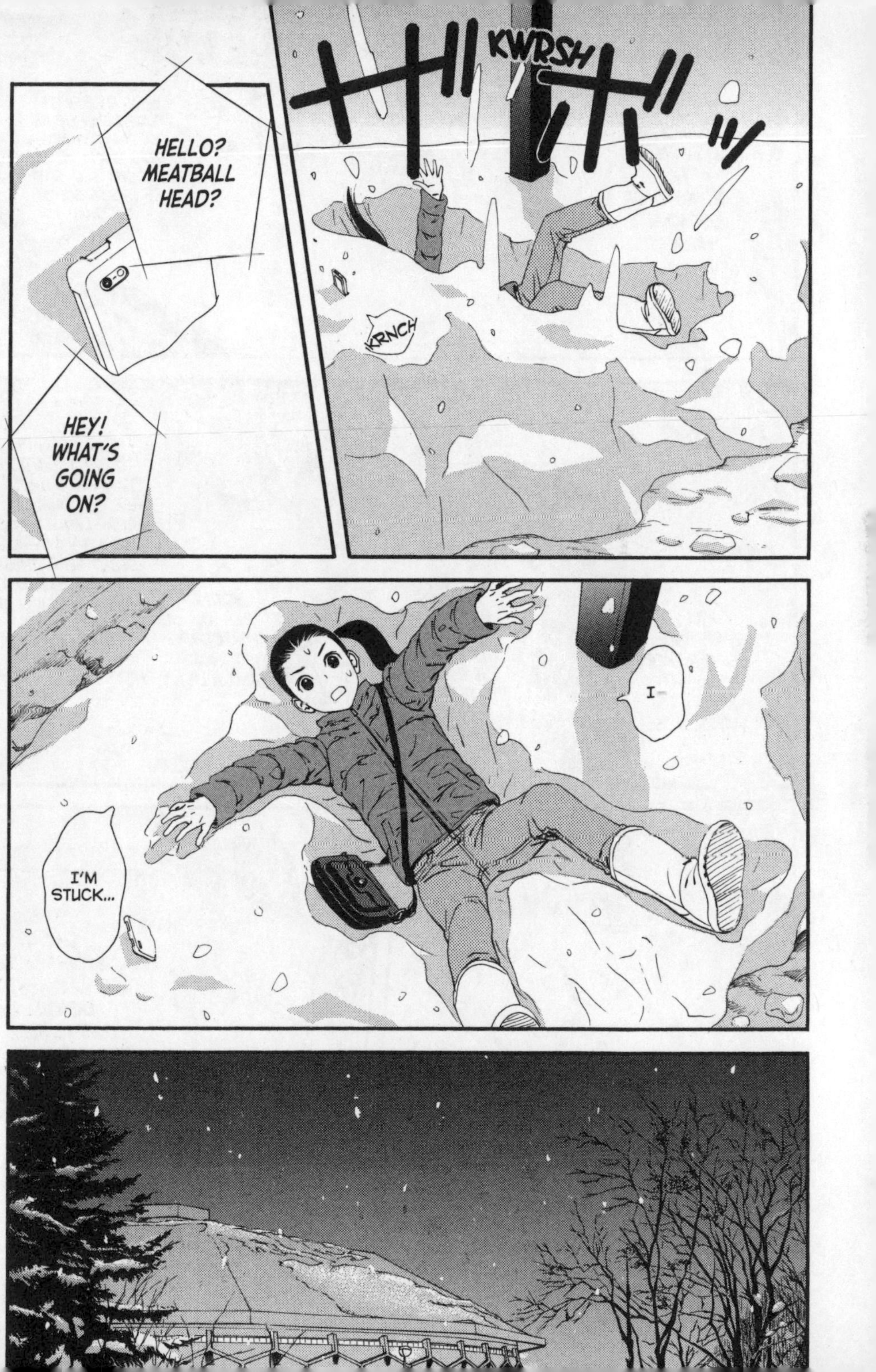
KWRSH
KRNCH
HELLO? MEATBALL HEAD?
HEY! WHAT'S GOING ON?
I—
I'M STUCK...

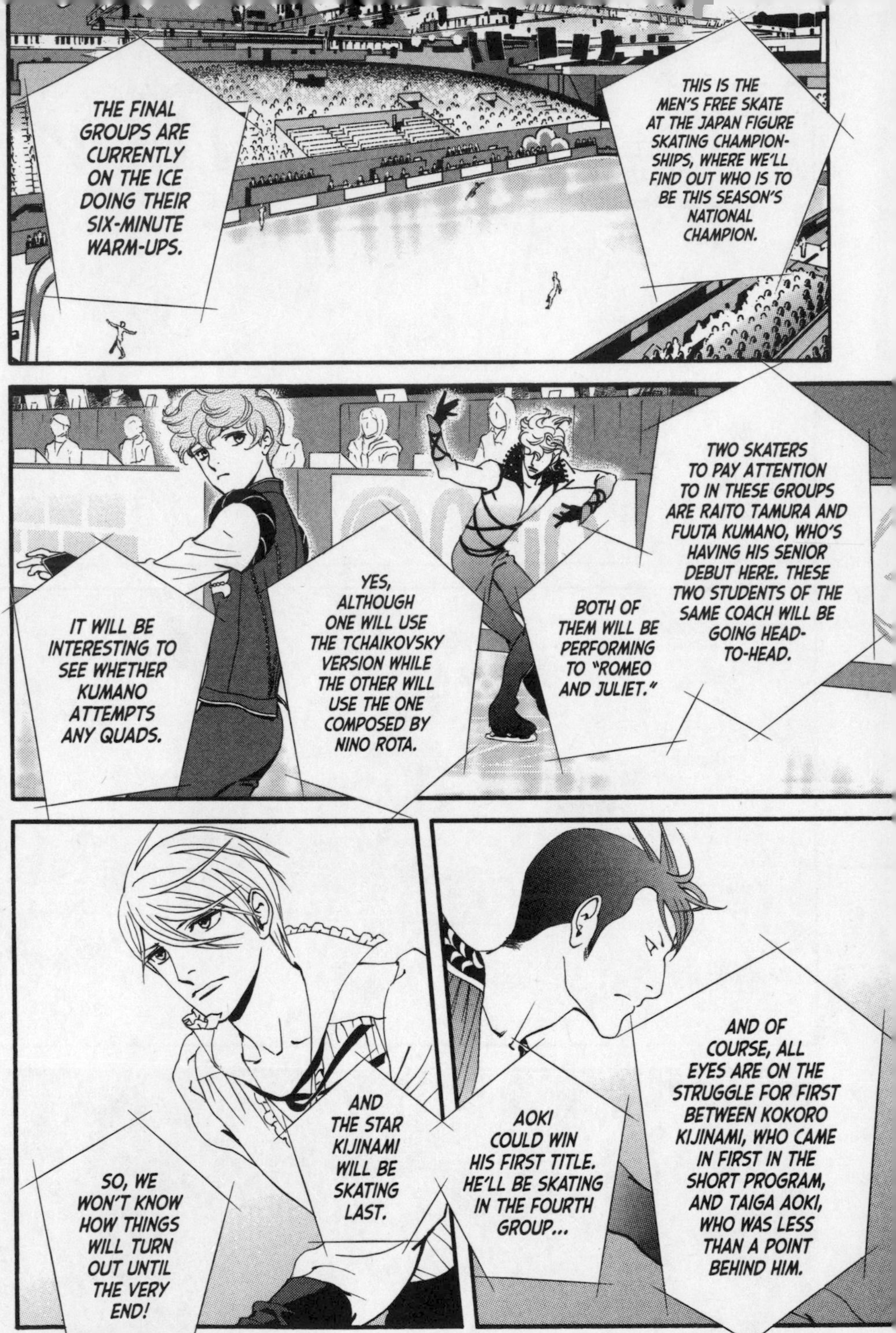
THIS IS THE MEN'S FREE SKATE AT THE JAPAN FIGURE SKATING CHAMPION-SHIPS, WHERE WE'LL FIND OUT WHO IS TO BE THIS SEASON'S NATIONAL CHAMPION.
THE FINAL GROUPS ARE CURRENTLY ON THE ICE DOING THEIR SIX-MINUTE WARM-UPS.
TWO SKATERS TO PAY ATTENTION TO IN THESE GROUPS ARE RAITO TAMURA AND FUUTA KUMANO, WHO'S HAVING HIS SENIOR DEBUT HERE. THESE TWO STUDENTS OF THE SAME COACH WILL BE GOING HEAD-TO-HEAD.
BOTH OF THEM WILL BE PERFORMING TO "ROMEO AND JULIET."
YES, ALTHOUGH ONE WILL USE THE TCHAIKOVSKY VERSION WHILE THE OTHER WILL USE THE ONE COMPOSED BY NINO ROTA.
IT WILL BE INTERESTING TO SEE WHETHER KUMANO ATTEMPTS ANY QUADS.
AND OF COURSE, ALL EYES ARE ON THE STRUGGLE FOR FIRST BETWEEN KOKORO KIJINAMI, WHO CAME IN FIRST IN THE SHORT PROGRAM, AND TAIGA AOKI, WHO WAS LESS THAN A POINT BEHIND HIM.
AOKI COULD WIN HIS FIRST TITLE. HE'LL BE SKATING IN THE FOURTH GROUP...
AND THE STAR KIJINAMI WILL BE SKATING LAST.
SO, WE WON'T KNOW HOW THINGS WILL TURN OUT UNTIL THE VERY END!

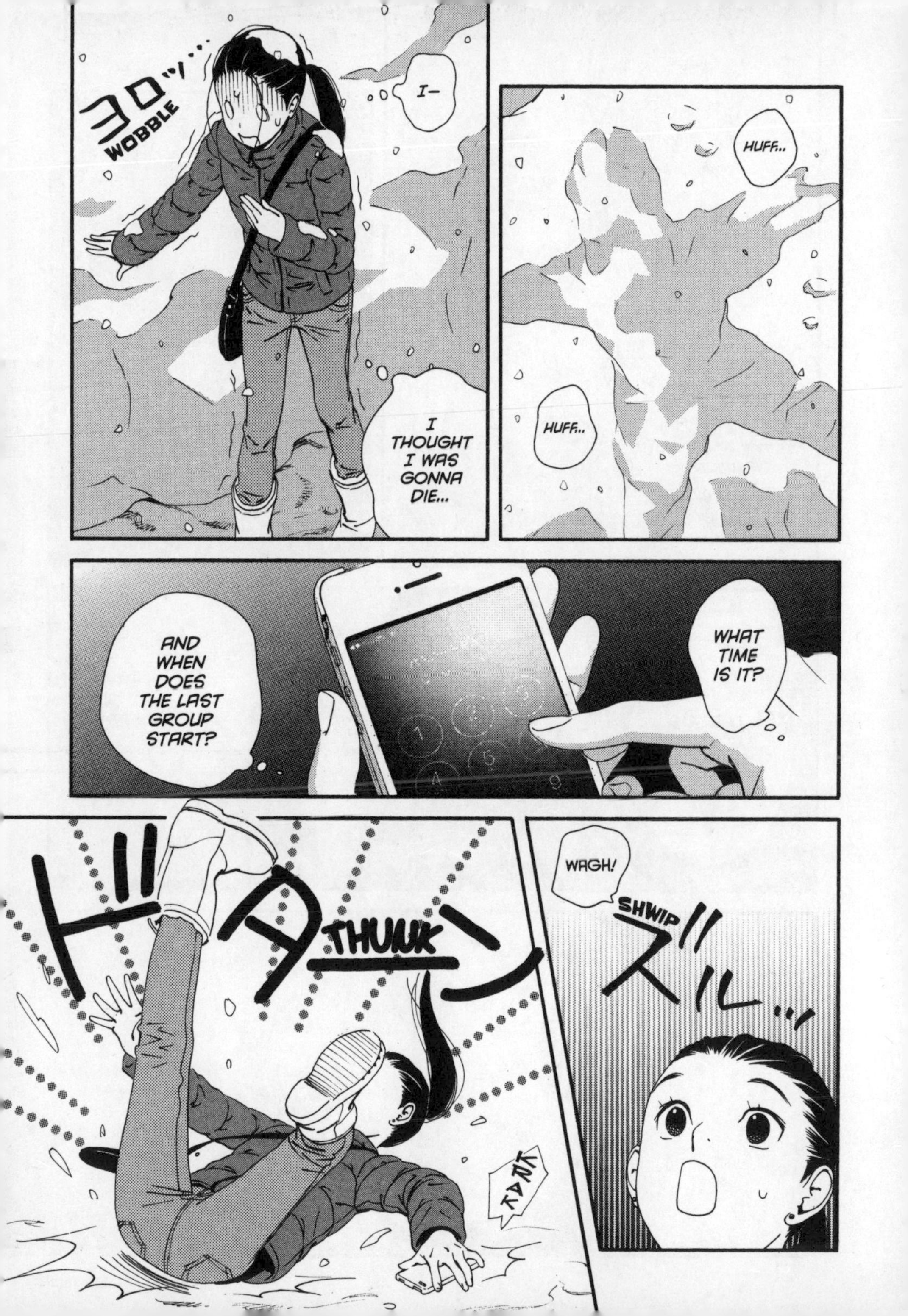

HUFF...
HUFF...
I—
ヨロッ…
WOBBLE
I THOUGHT I WAS GONNA DIE...
WHAT TIME IS IT?
AND WHEN DOES THE LAST GROUP START?
WAGH!
SHWIP
ズル…
ドターン
THUNK

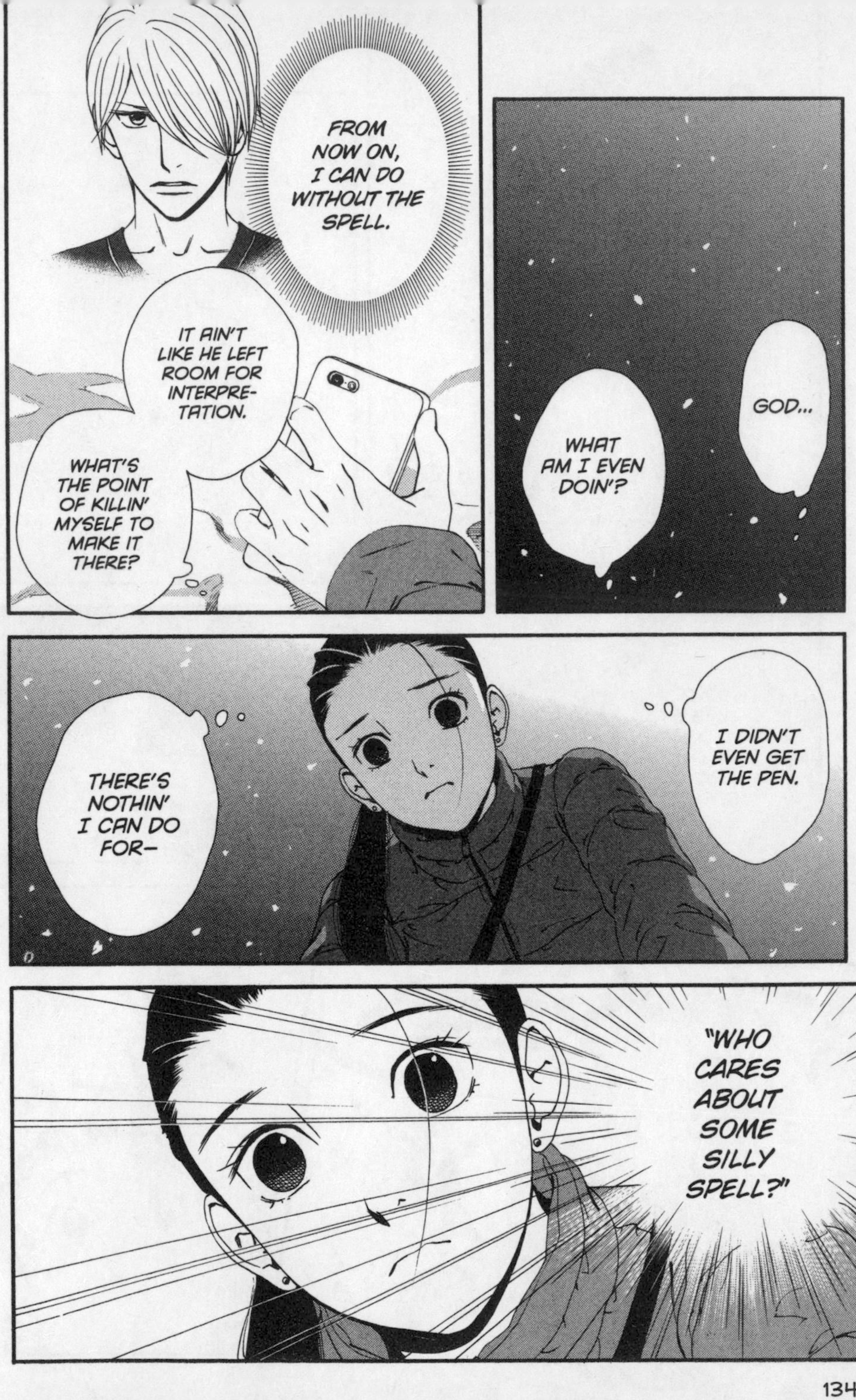
GOD...
WHAT AM I EVEN DOIN'?
FROM NOW ON, I CAN DO WITHOUT THE SPELL.
IT AIN'T LIKE HE LEFT ROOM FOR INTERPRE-TATION.
WHAT'S THE POINT OF KILLIN' MYSELF TO MAKE IT THERE?
I DIDN'T EVEN GET THE PEN.
THERE'S NOTHIN' I CAN DO FOR–
"WHO CARES ABOUT SOME SILLY SPELL?"

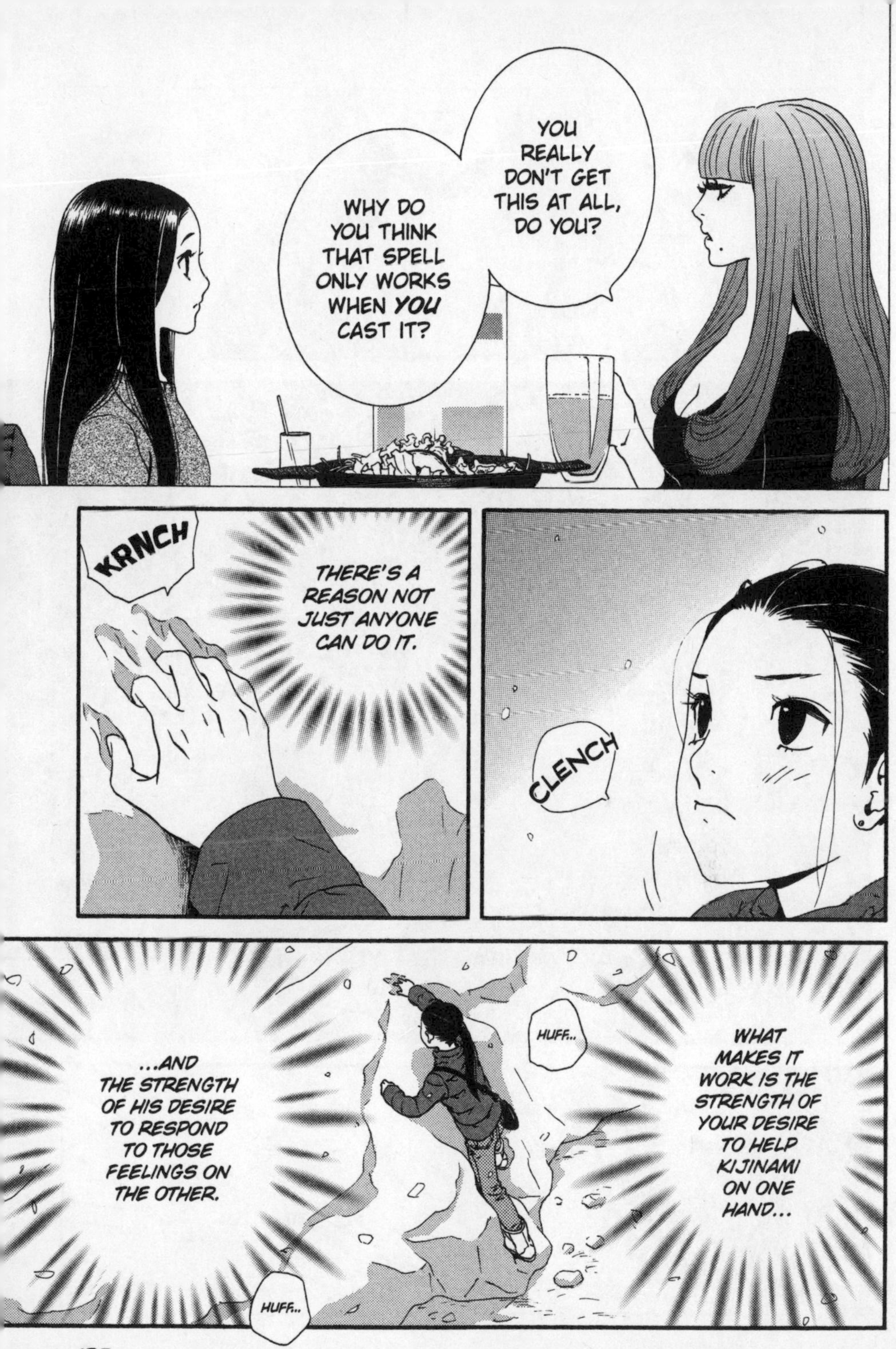
YOU REALLY DON'T GET THIS AT ALL, DO YOU?
WHY DO YOU THINK THAT SPELL ONLY WORKS WHEN *YOU* CAST IT?
CLENCH
KRNCH
THERE'S A REASON NOT JUST ANYONE CAN DO IT.
WHAT MAKES IT WORK IS THE STRENGTH OF YOUR DESIRE TO HELP KIJINAMI ON ONE HAND...
HUFF...
...AND THE STRENGTH OF HIS DESIRE TO RESPOND TO THOSE FEELINGS ON THE OTHER.
HUFF...

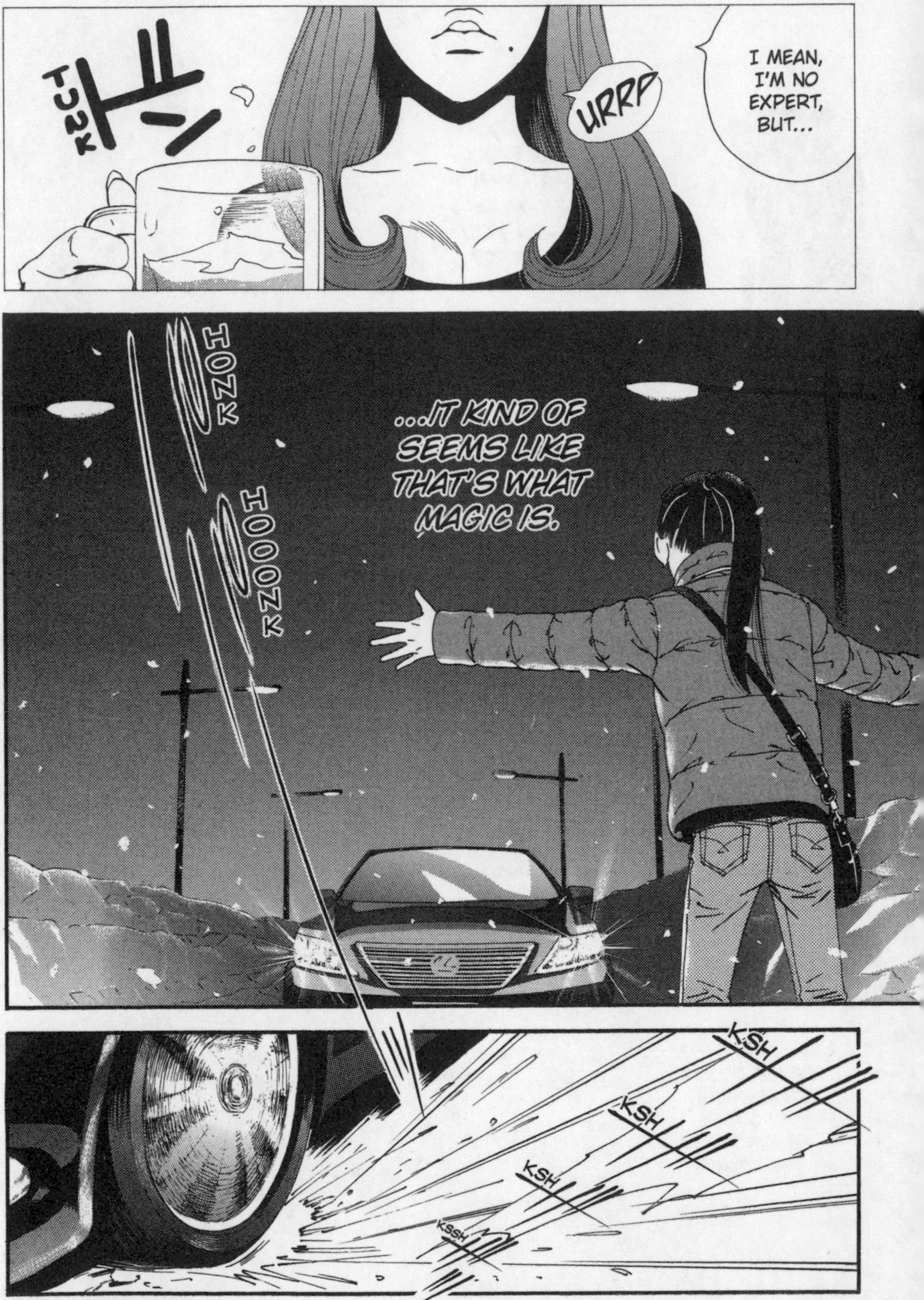
I MEAN, I'M NO EXPERT, BUT...
URRP
TUNK
...IT KIND OF SEEMS LIKE THAT'S WHAT MAGIC IS.
HOOOONK
HONK
KSH
KSH
KSH
KSSH

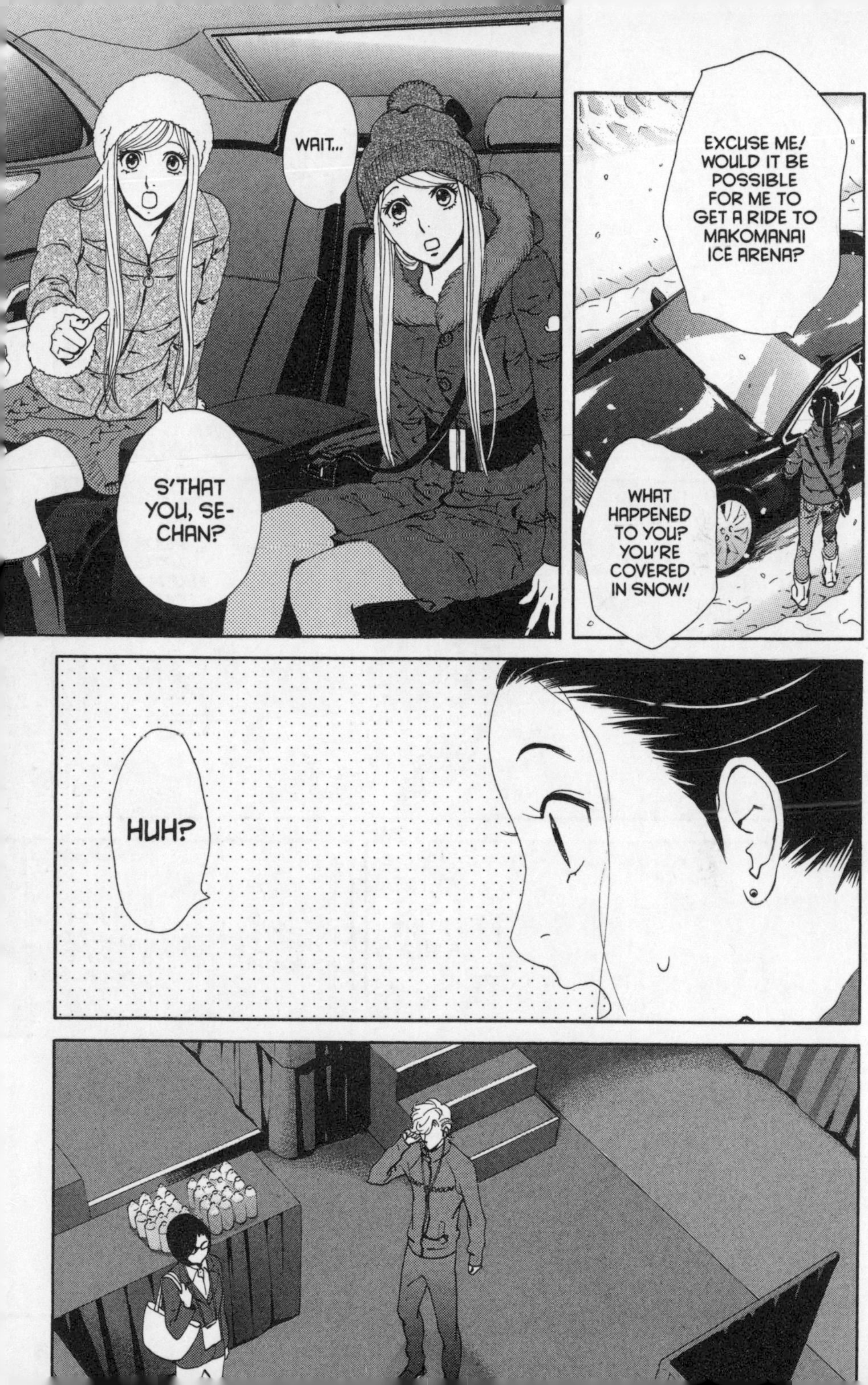
EXCUSE ME! WOULD IT BE POSSIBLE FOR ME TO GET A RIDE TO MAKOMANAI ICE ARENA?
WHAT HAPPENED TO YOU? YOU'RE COVERED IN SNOW!
WAIT...
S'THAT YOU, SE-CHAN?
HUH?

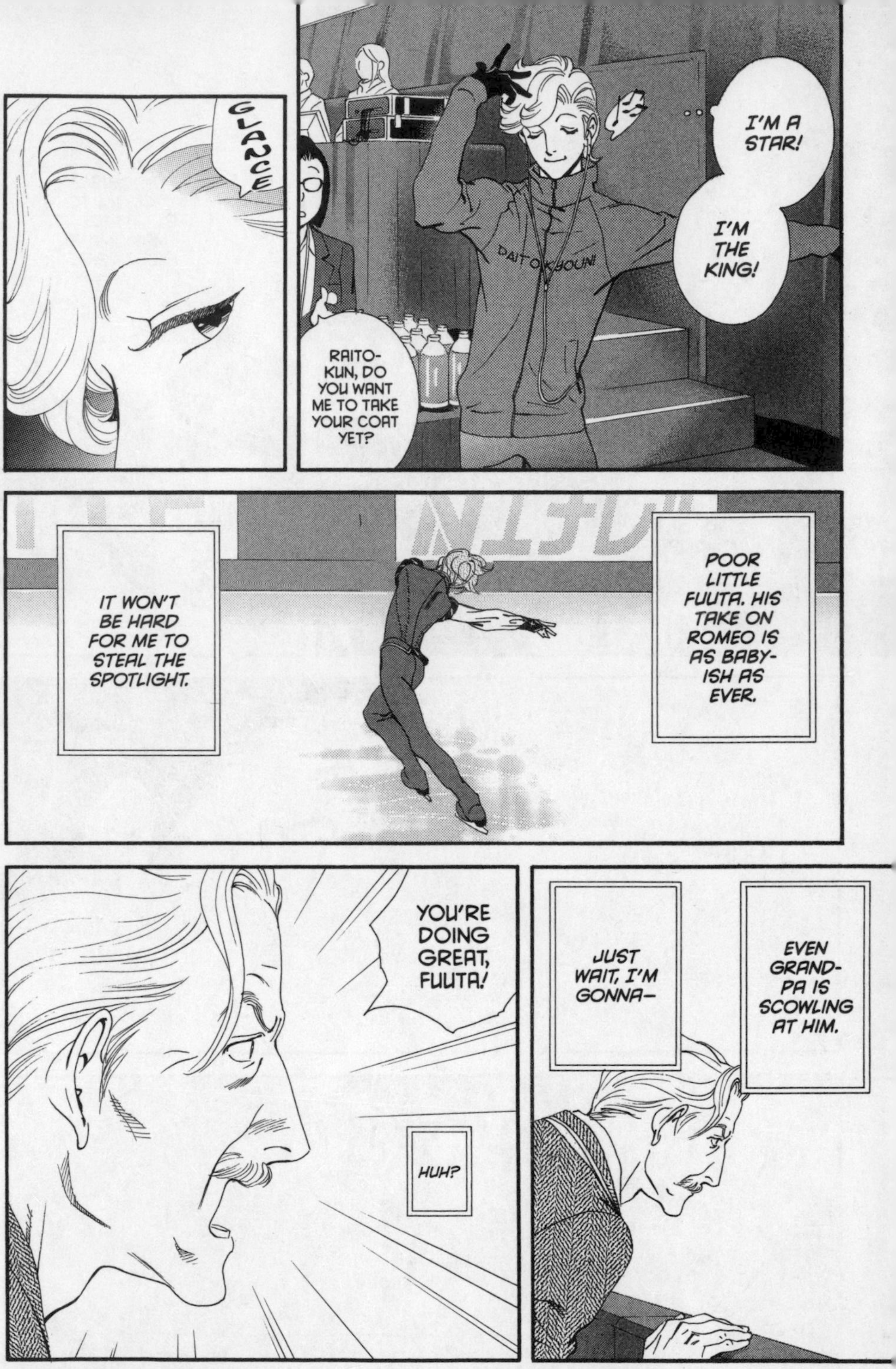
I'M A STAR!
I'M THE KING!
RAITO-KUN, DO YOU WANT ME TO TAKE YOUR COAT YET?
DAITOKYOUNI
GLANCE
POOR LITTLE FUUTA. HIS TAKE ON ROMEO IS AS BABY-ISH AS EVER.
IT WON'T BE HARD FOR ME TO STEAL THE SPOTLIGHT.
EVEN GRAND-PA IS SCOWLING AT HIM.
JUST WAIT, I'M GONNA—
YOU'RE DOING GREAT, FUUTA!
HUH?

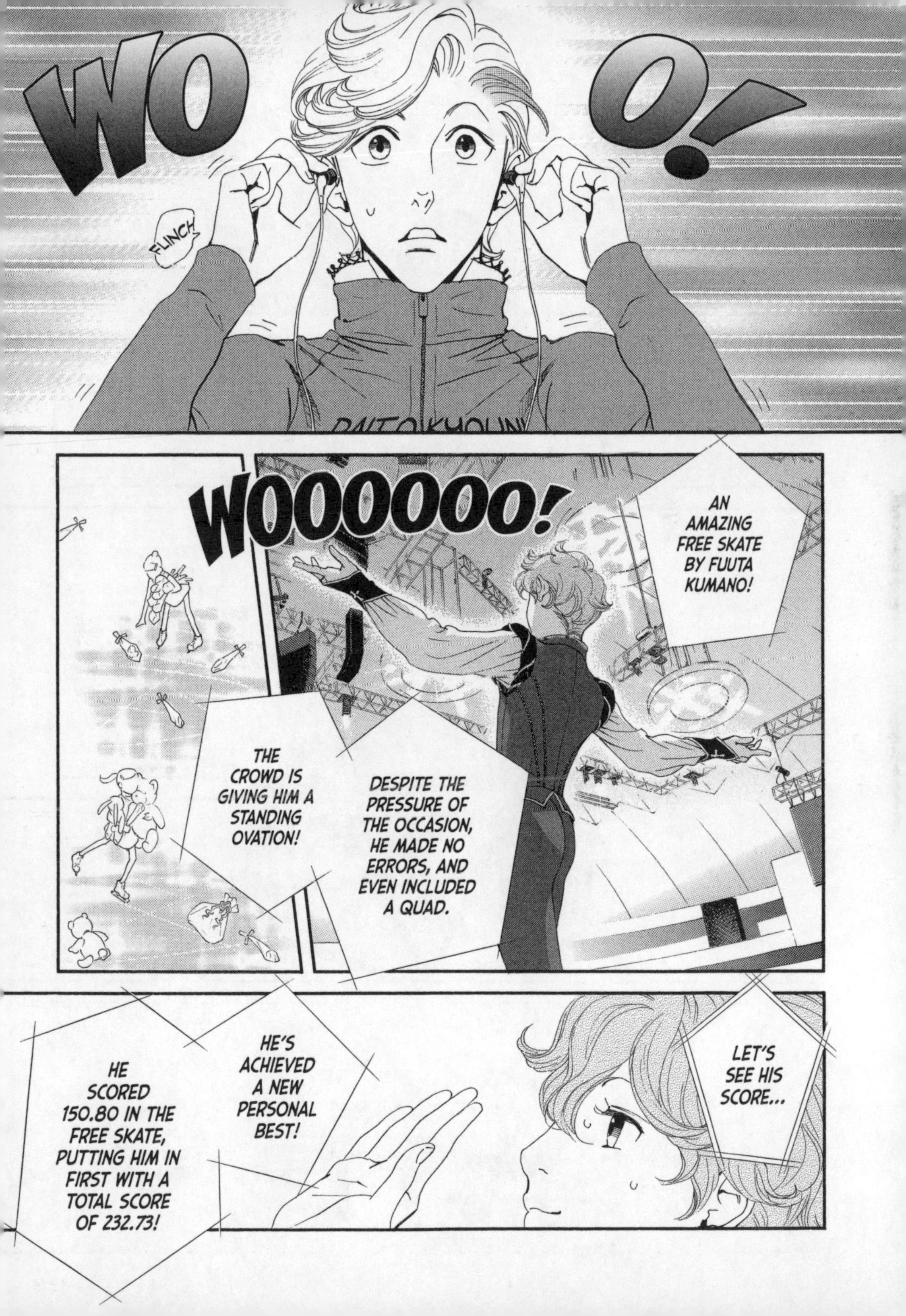
WO O!
FLINCH
AN AMAZING FREE SKATE BY FUUTA KUMANO!
WOOOOOO!
DESPITE THE PRESSURE OF THE OCCASION, HE MADE NO ERRORS, AND EVEN INCLUDED A QUAD.
THE CROWD IS GIVING HIM A STANDING OVATION!
LET'S SEE HIS SCORE...
HE'S ACHIEVED A NEW PERSONAL BEST!
HE SCORED 150.80 IN THE FREE SKATE, PUTTING HIM IN FIRST WITH A TOTAL SCORE OF 232.73!

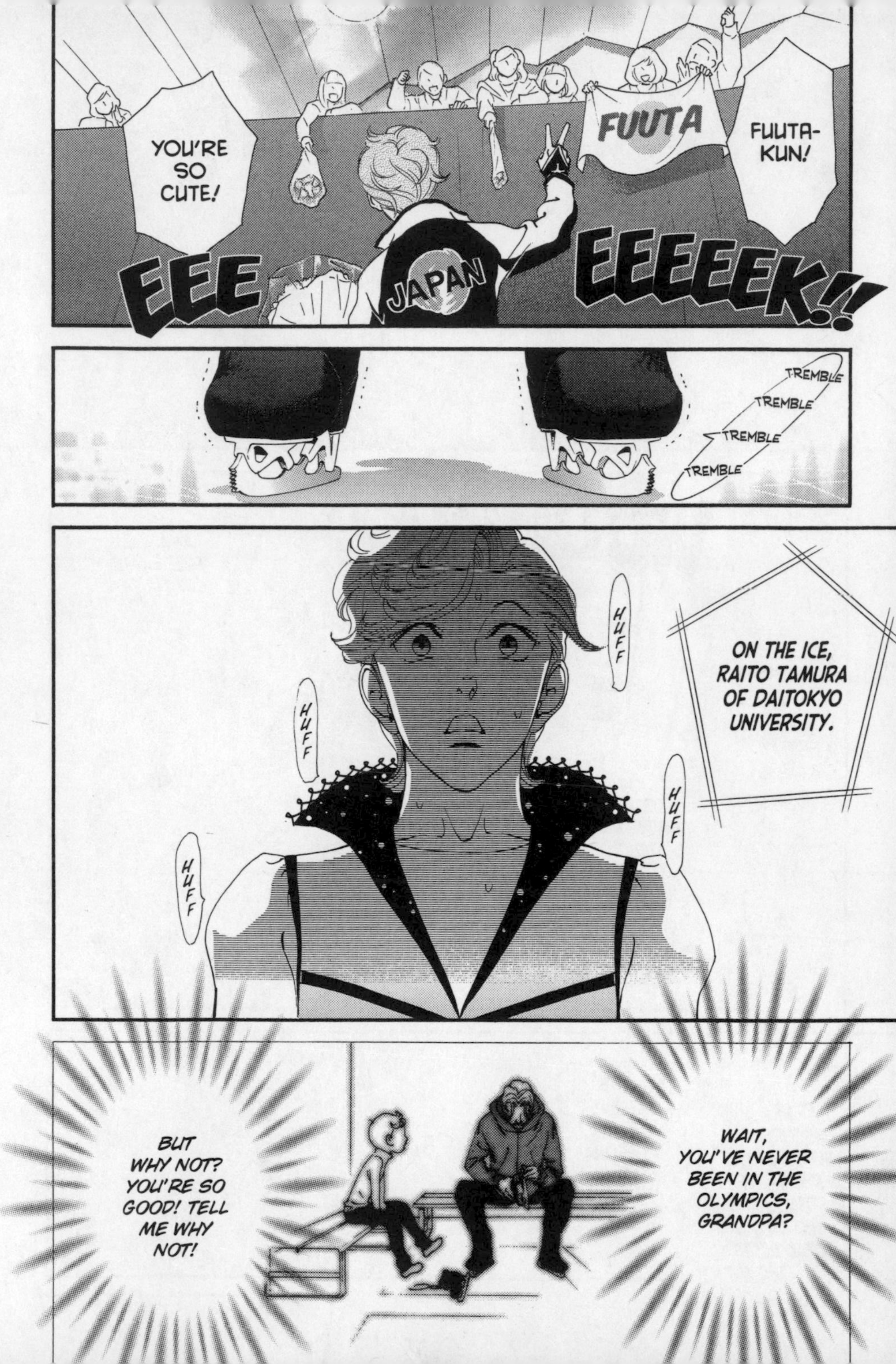
FUUTA-KUN!
FUUTA
YOU'RE SO CUTE!
JAPAN
EEE EEEEEK!!
TREMBLE
TREMBLE
TREMBLE
TREMBLE
ON THE ICE, RAITO TAMURA OF DAITOKYO UNIVERSITY.
HUFF
HUFF
HUFF
HUFF
WAIT, YOU'VE NEVER BEEN IN THE OLYMPICS, GRANDPA?
BUT WHY NOT? YOU'RE SO GOOD! TELL ME WHY NOT!

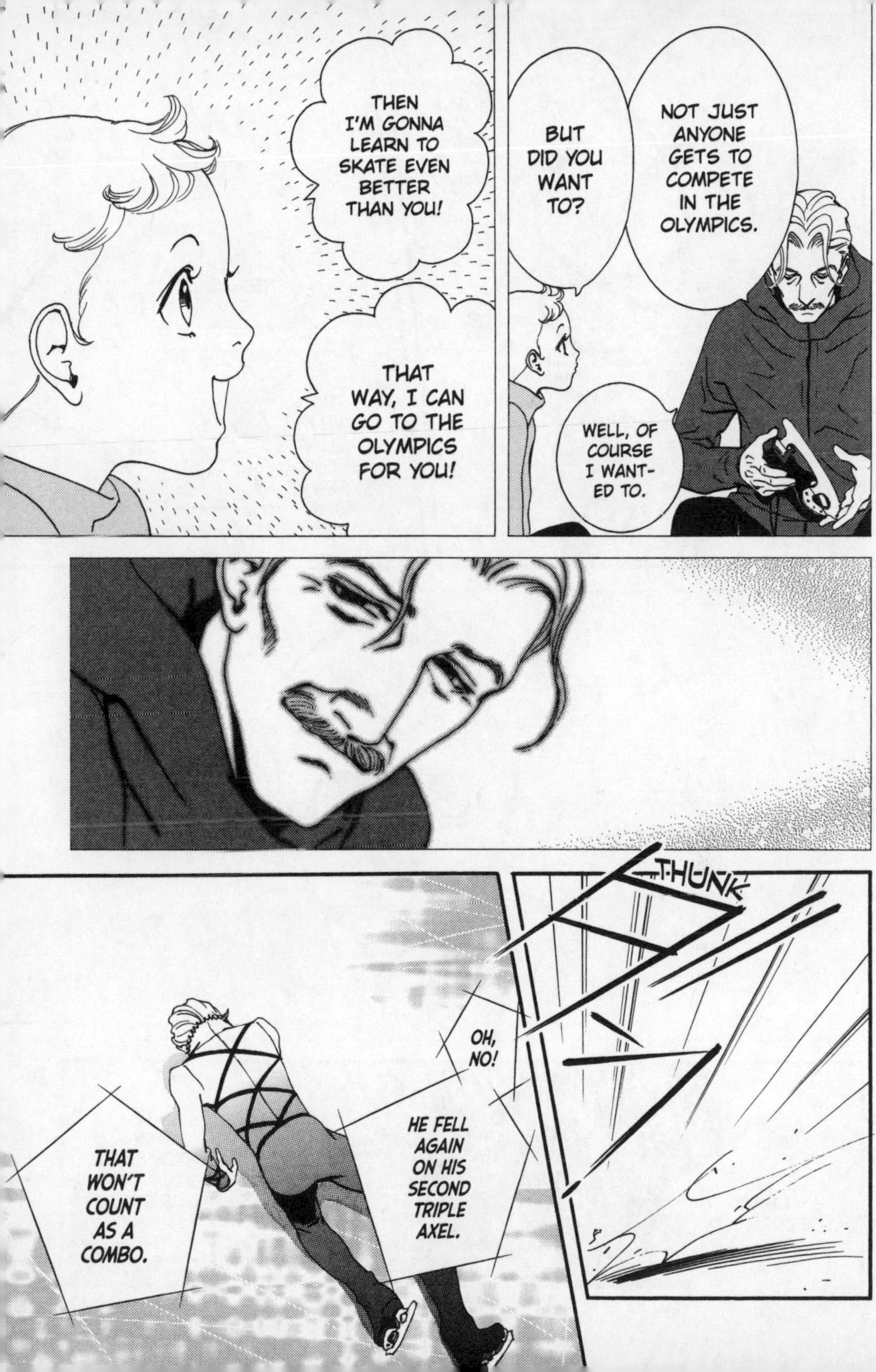
NOT JUST ANYONE GETS TO COMPETE IN THE OLYMPICS.
BUT DID YOU WANT TO?
WELL, OF COURSE I WANT-ED TO.
THEN I'M GONNA LEARN TO SKATE EVEN BETTER THAN YOU!
THAT WAY, I CAN GO TO THE OLYMPICS FOR YOU!
THUNK
OH, NO!
HE FELL AGAIN ON HIS SECOND TRIPLE AXEL.
THAT WON'T COUNT AS A COMBO.

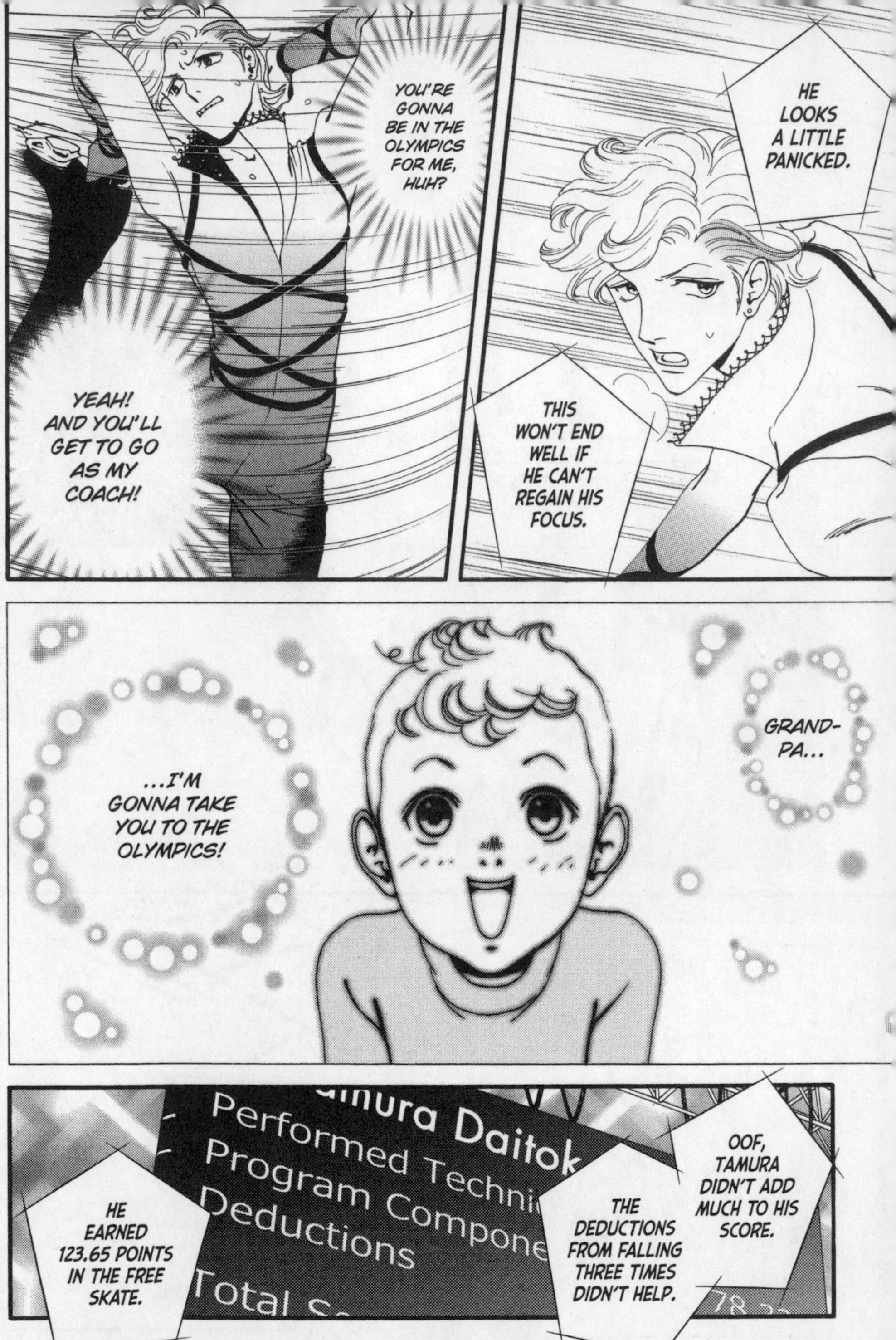
HE LOOKS A LITTLE PANICKED.
THIS WON'T END WELL IF HE CAN'T REGAIN HIS FOCUS.
YOU'RE GONNA BE IN THE OLYMPICS FOR ME, HUH?
YEAH! AND YOU'LL GET TO GO AS MY COACH!
GRAND-PA...
...I'M GONNA TAKE YOU TO THE OLYMPICS!
OOF, TAMURA DIDN'T ADD MUCH TO HIS SCORE.
THE DEDUCTIONS FROM FALLING THREE TIMES DIDN'T HELP.
HE EARNED 123.65 POINTS IN THE FREE SKATE.
amura Daitok
Performed Techni
Program Compone
Deductions

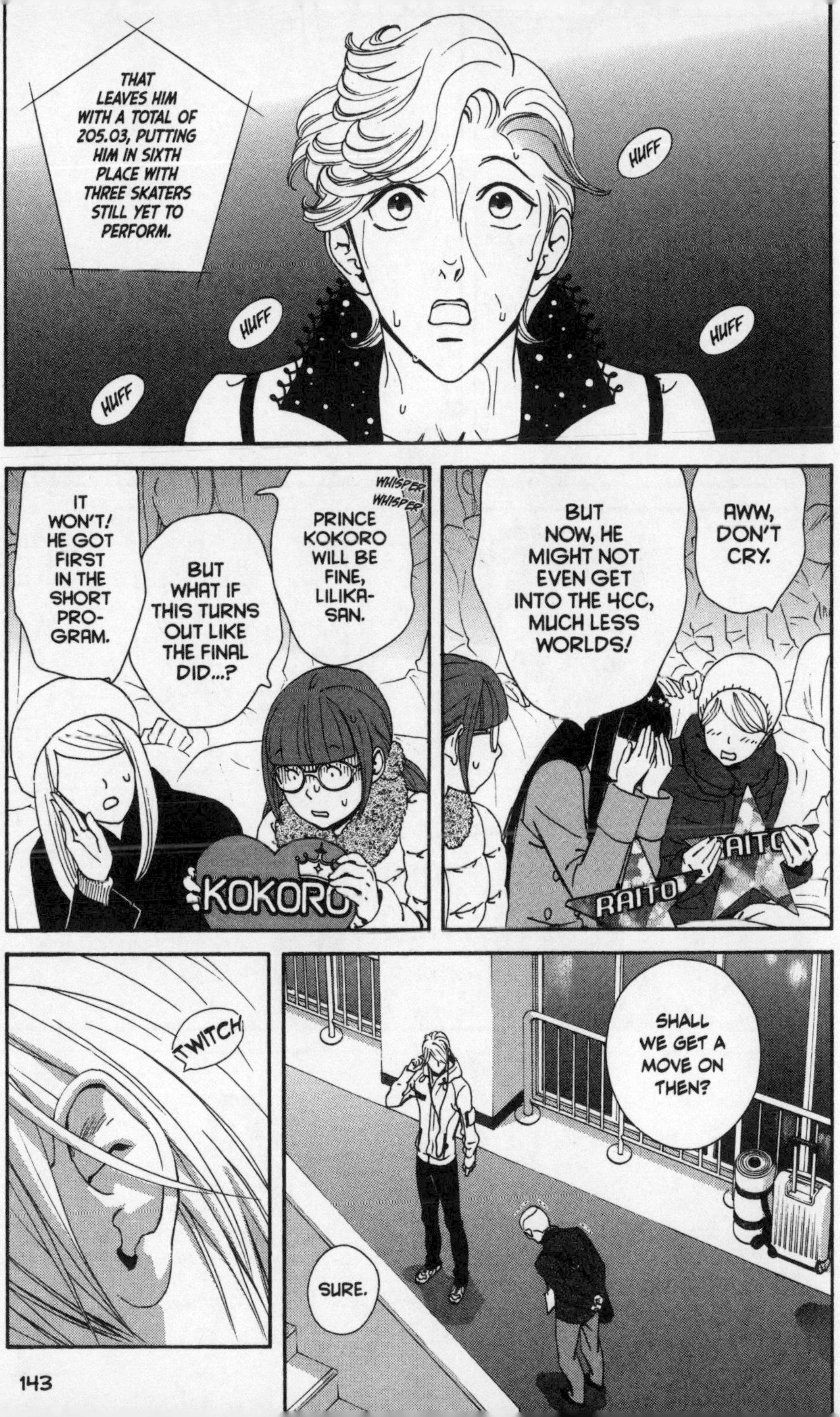
THAT LEAVES HIM WITH A TOTAL OF 205.03, PUTTING HIM IN SIXTH PLACE WITH THREE SKATERS STILL YET TO PERFORM.
HUFF
HUFF
HUFF
HUFF
AWW, DON'T CRY.
BUT NOW, HE MIGHT NOT EVEN GET INTO THE 4CC, MUCH LESS WORLDS!
RAITO
RAITO
WHISPER WHISPER
PRINCE KOKORO WILL BE FINE, LILIKA-SAN.
BUT WHAT IF THIS TURNS OUT LIKE THE FINAL DID...?
IT WON'T! HE GOT FIRST IN THE SHORT PROGRAM.
KOKORO
SHALL WE GET A MOVE ON THEN?
SURE.
TWITCH

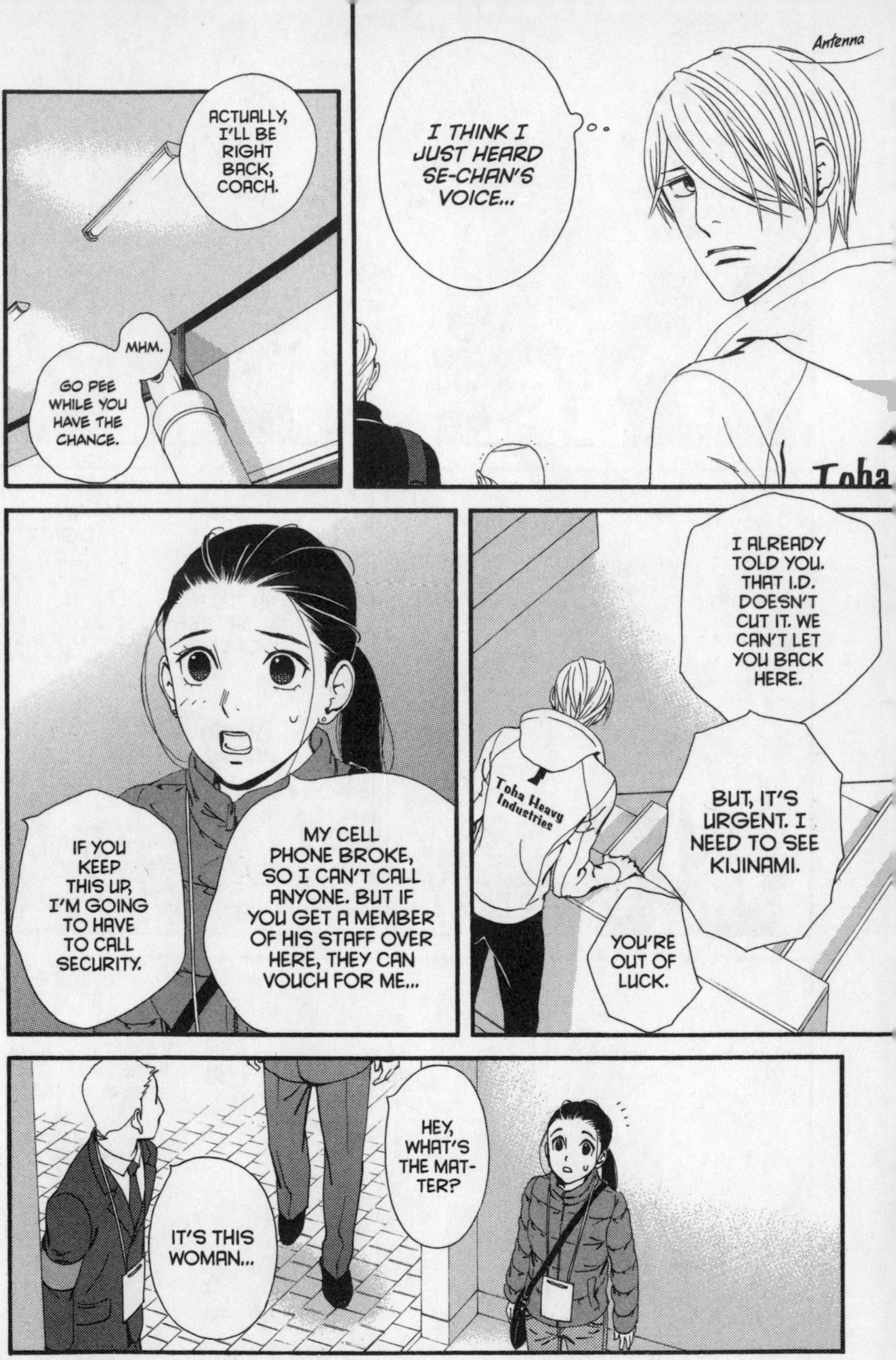
I THINK I JUST HEARD SE-CHAN'S VOICE...
Toha
ACTUALLY, I'LL BE RIGHT BACK, COACH.
MHM.
GO PEE WHILE YOU HAVE THE CHANCE.
I ALREADY TOLD YOU. THAT I.D. DOESN'T CUT IT. WE CAN'T LET YOU BACK HERE.
BUT, IT'S URGENT. I NEED TO SEE KIJINAMI.
YOU'RE OUT OF LUCK.
Toha Heavy Industries
MY CELL PHONE BROKE, SO I CAN'T CALL ANYONE. BUT IF YOU GET A MEMBER OF HIS STAFF OVER HERE, THEY CAN VOUCH FOR ME...
IF YOU KEEP THIS UP, I'M GOING TO HAVE TO CALL SECURITY.
HEY, WHAT'S THE MAT-TER?
IT'S THIS WOMAN...

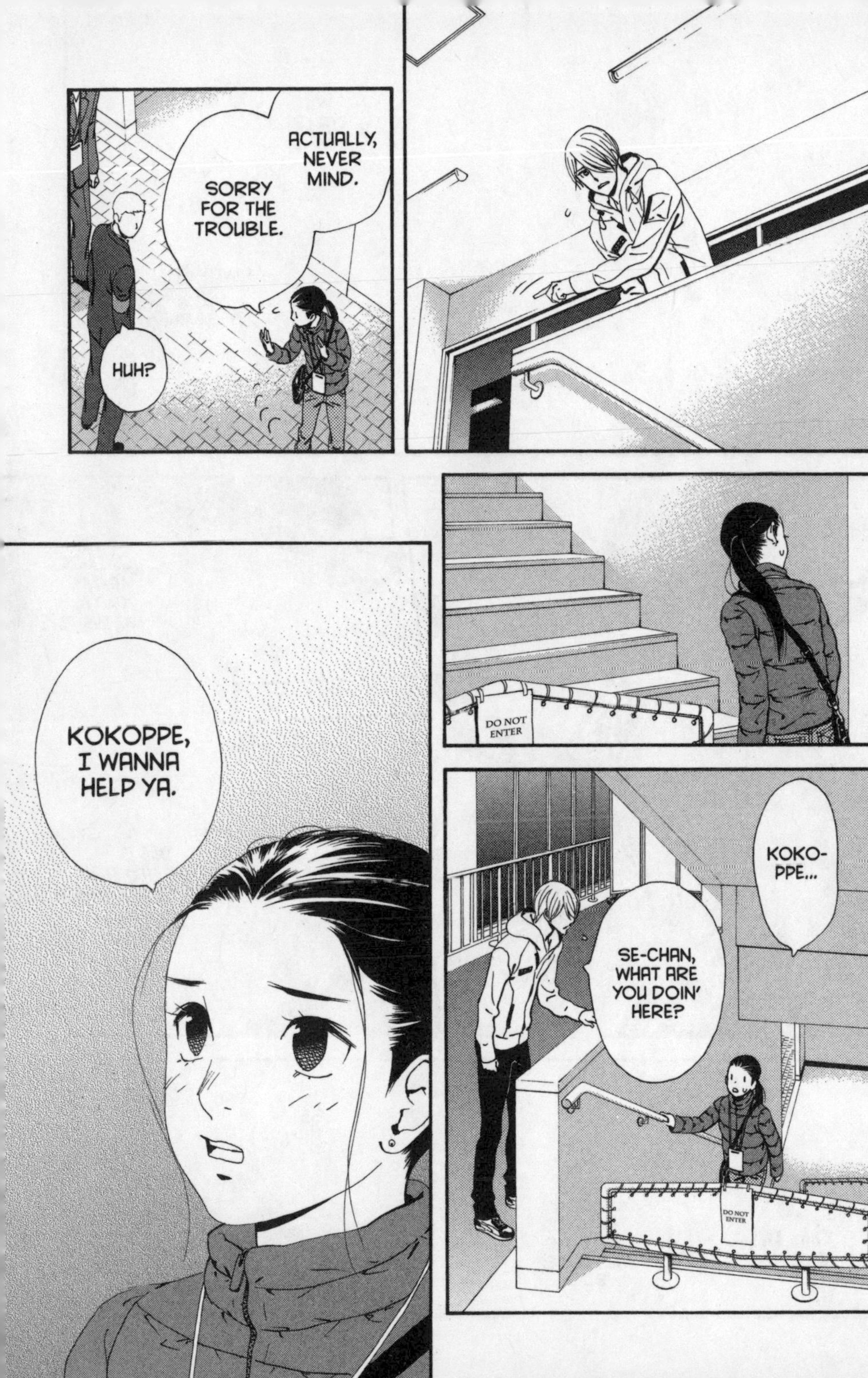
ACTUALLY, NEVER MIND.
SORRY FOR THE TROUBLE.
HUH?
DO NOT ENTER
KOKOPPE...
SE-CHAN, WHAT ARE YOU DOIN' HERE?
DO NOT ENTER
KOKOPPE, I WANNA HELP YA.

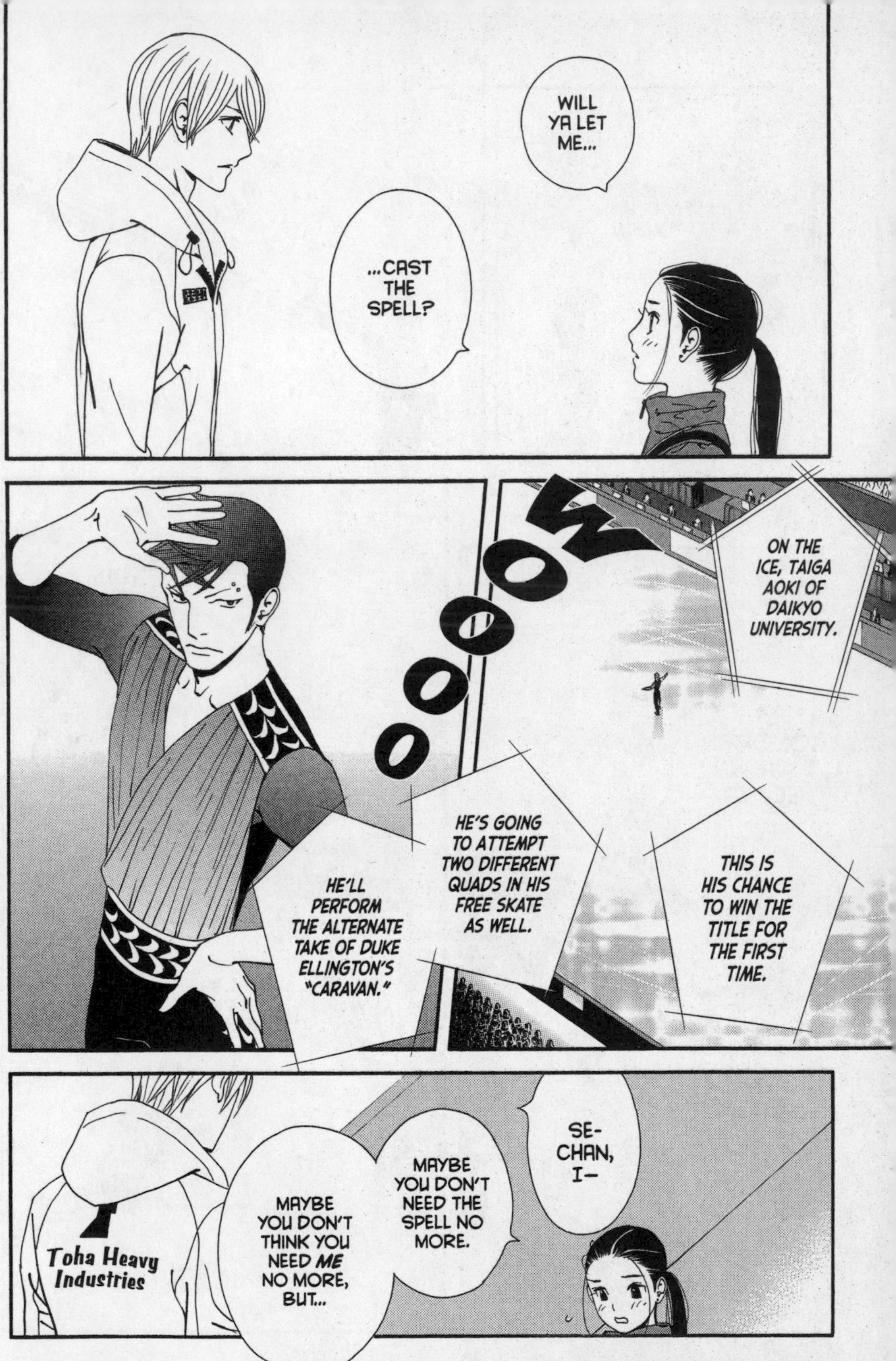
WILL YA LET ME...
...CAST THE SPELL?
WOOOOOO
ON THE ICE, TAIGA AOKI OF DAIKYO UNIVERSITY.
THIS IS HIS CHANCE TO WIN THE TITLE FOR THE FIRST TIME.
HE'S GOING TO ATTEMPT TWO DIFFERENT QUADS IN HIS FREE SKATE AS WELL.
HE'LL PERFORM THE ALTERNATE TAKE OF DUKE ELLINGTON'S "CARAVAN."
SE-CHAN, I—
MAYBE YOU DON'T NEED THE SPELL NO MORE.
MAYBE YOU DON'T THINK YOU NEED *ME* NO MORE, BUT...
Toha Heavy Industries

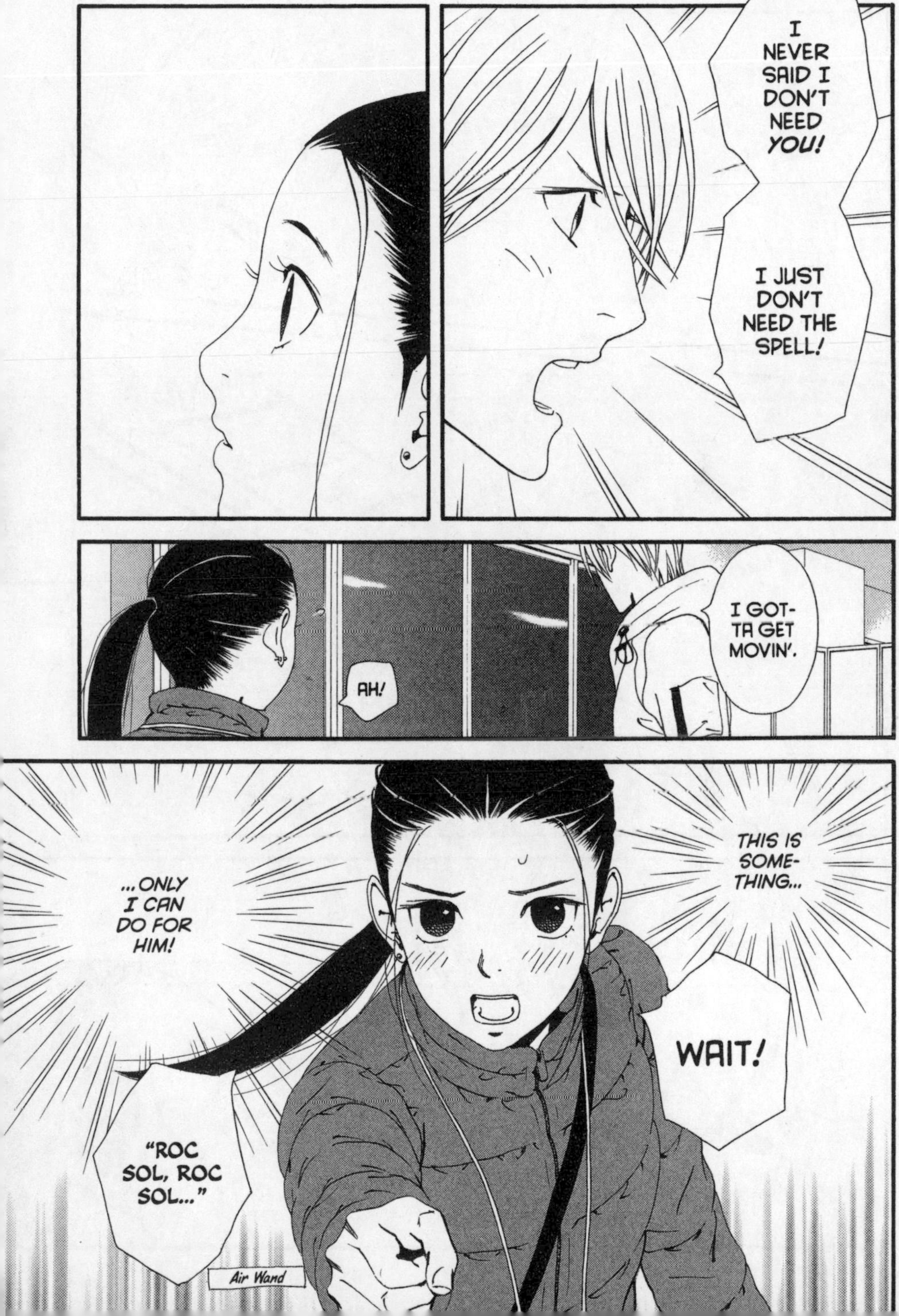
I NEVER SAID I DON'T NEED *YOU!*
I JUST DON'T NEED THE SPELL!
I GOT-TA GET MOVIN'.
AH!
THIS IS SOME-THING...
...ONLY I CAN DO FOR HIM!
WAIT!
"ROC SOL, ROC SOL..."
Air Wand

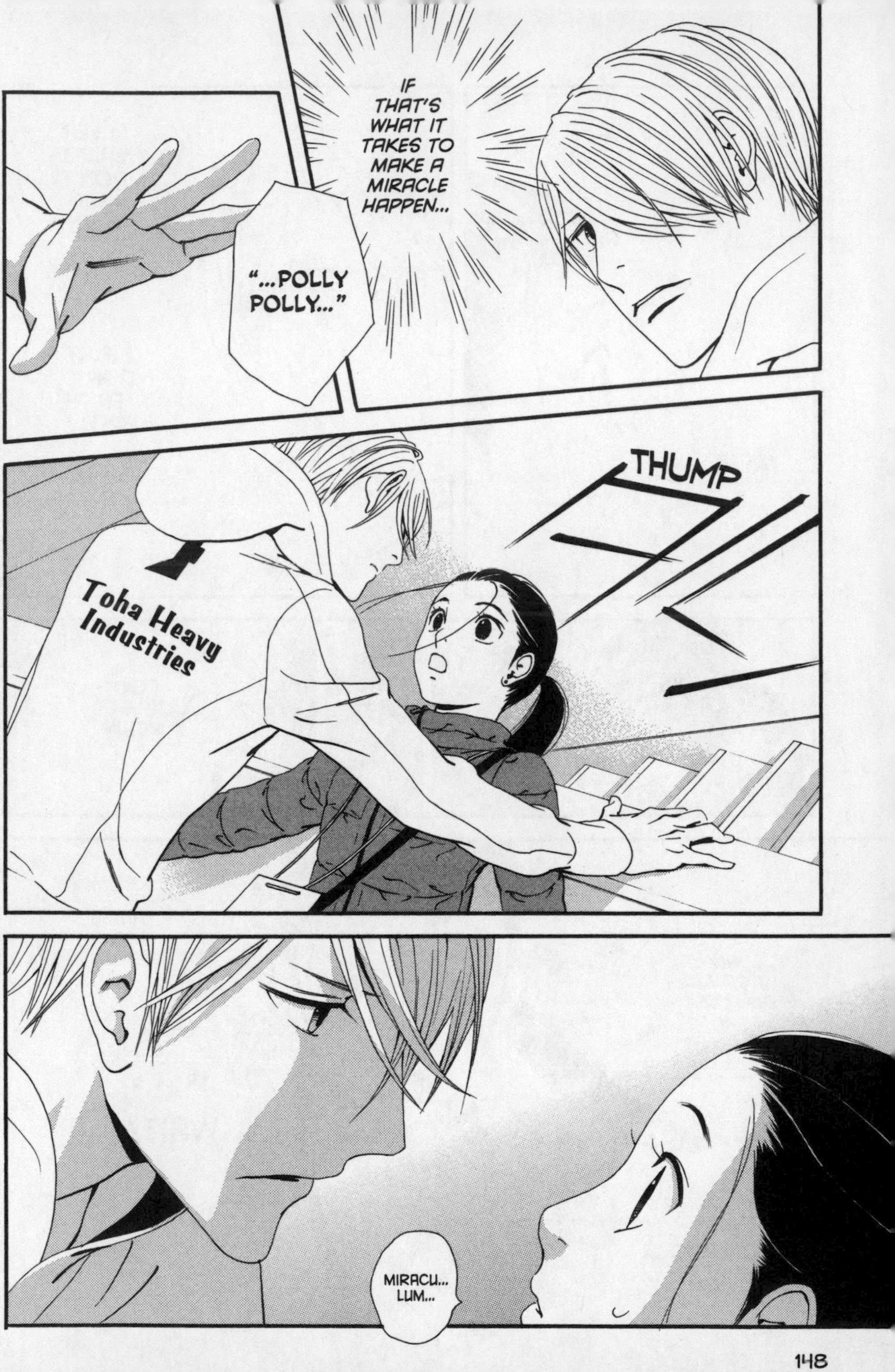
IF THAT'S WHAT IT TAKES TO MAKE A MIRACLE HAPPEN...
"...POLLY POLLY..."
THUMP
Toha Heavy Industries
MIRACU... LUM...

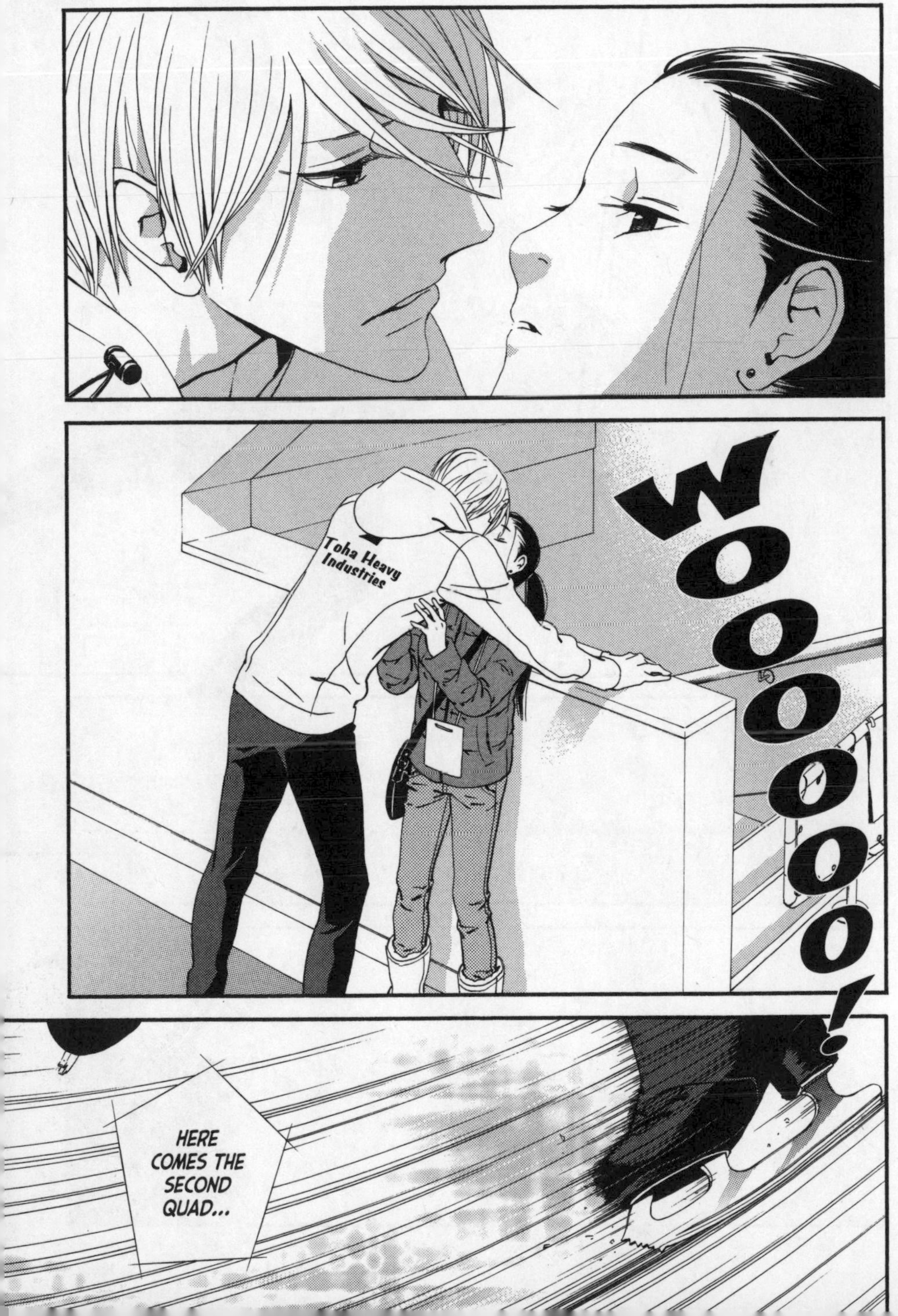
WOOOOOO!
Toha Heavy Industries
HERE COMES THE SECOND QUAD...

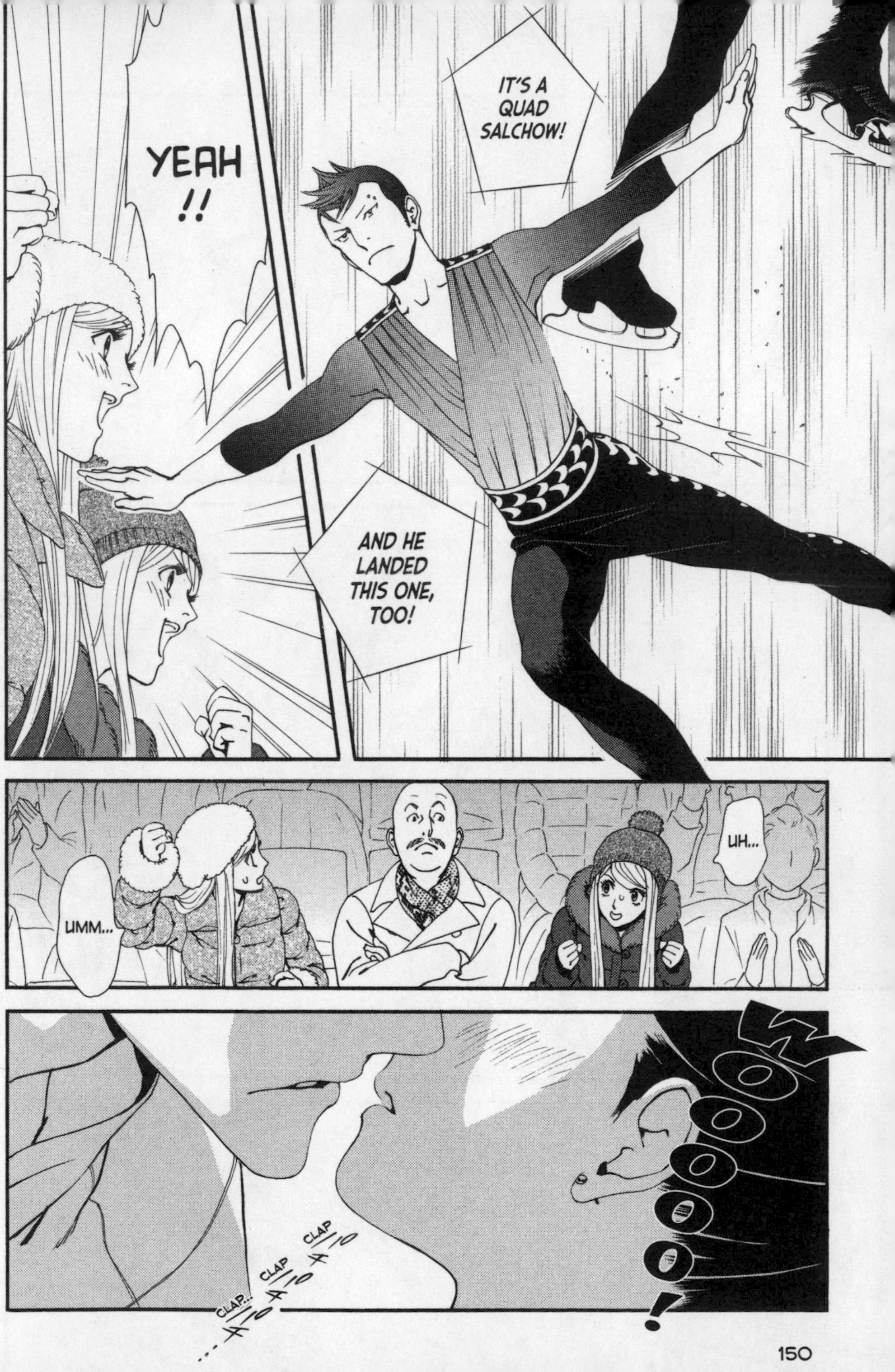
IT'S A QUAD SALCHOW!
YEAH !!
AND HE LANDED THIS ONE, TOO!
UH...
UMM...
WOOOOOOO!
CLAP
CLAP
CLAP...

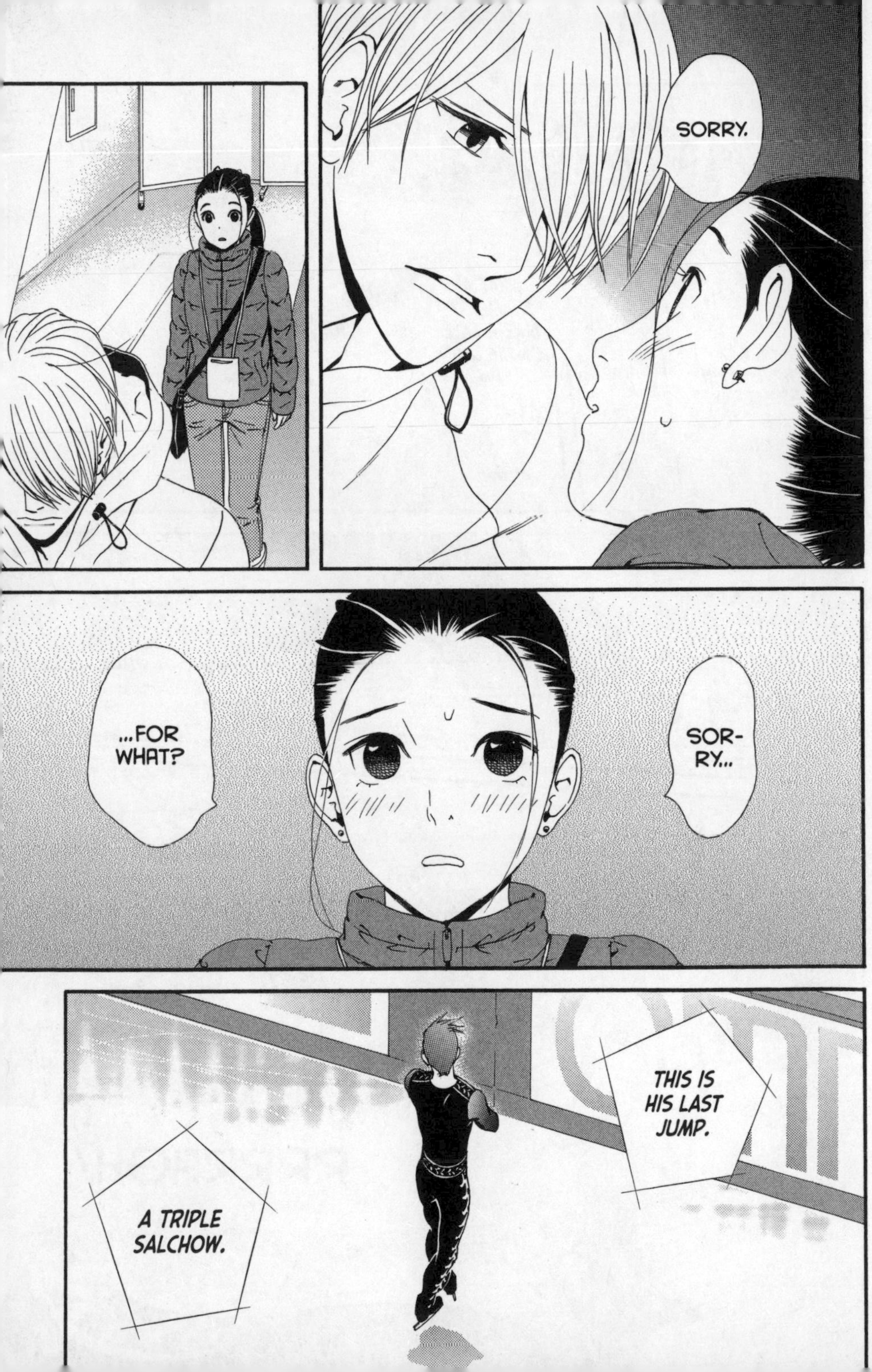
SORRY.
SOR-RY...
...FOR WHAT?
THIS IS HIS LAST JUMP.
A TRIPLE SALCHOW.

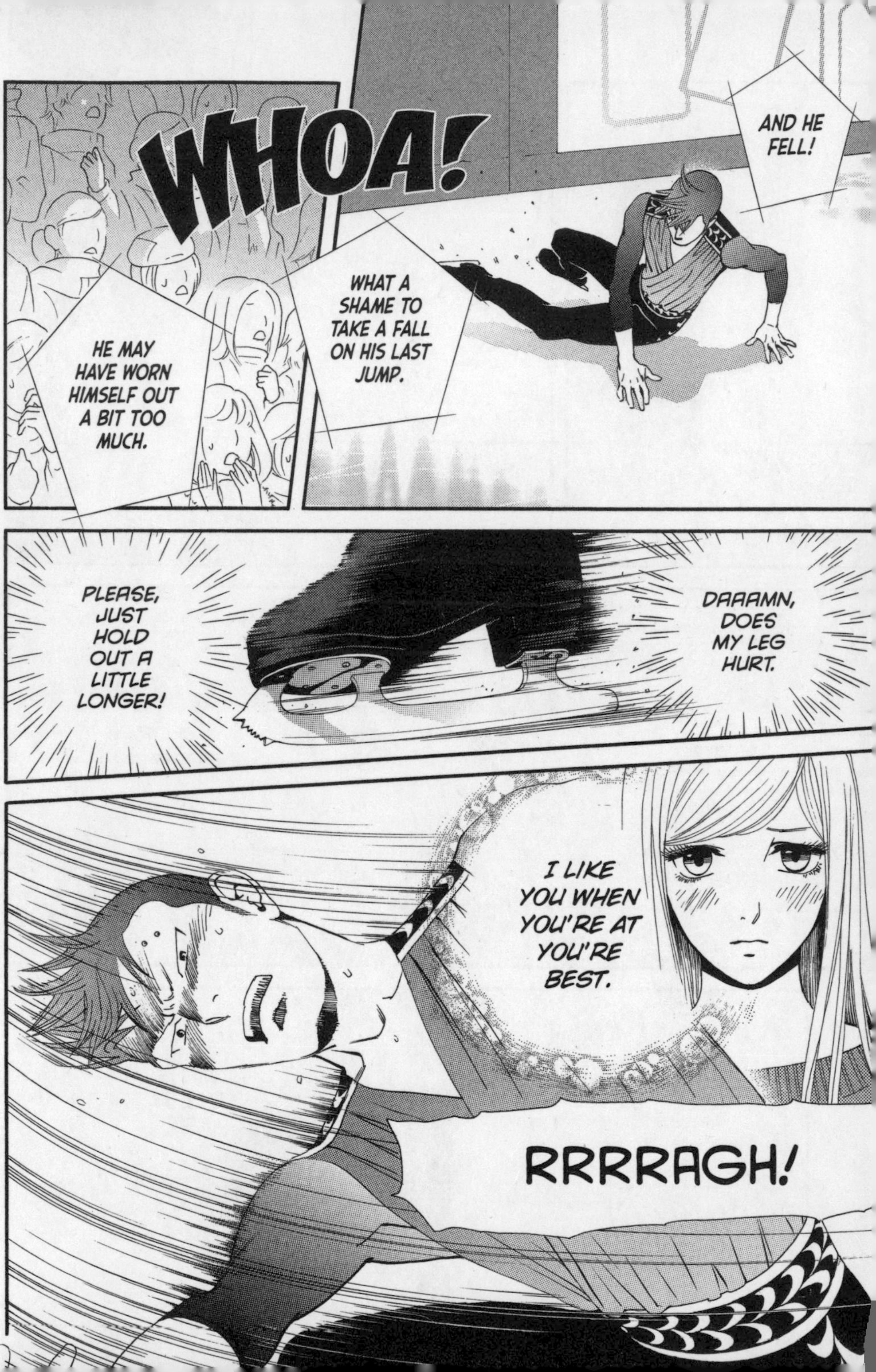
AND HE FELL!
WHAT A SHAME TO TAKE A FALL ON HIS LAST JUMP.
WHOA!
HE MAY HAVE WORN HIMSELF OUT A BIT TOO MUCH.
DAAAMN, DOES MY LEG HURT.
PLEASE, JUST HOLD OUT A LITTLE LONGER!
I LIKE YOU WHEN YOU'RE AT YOU'RE BEST.
RRRRAGH!

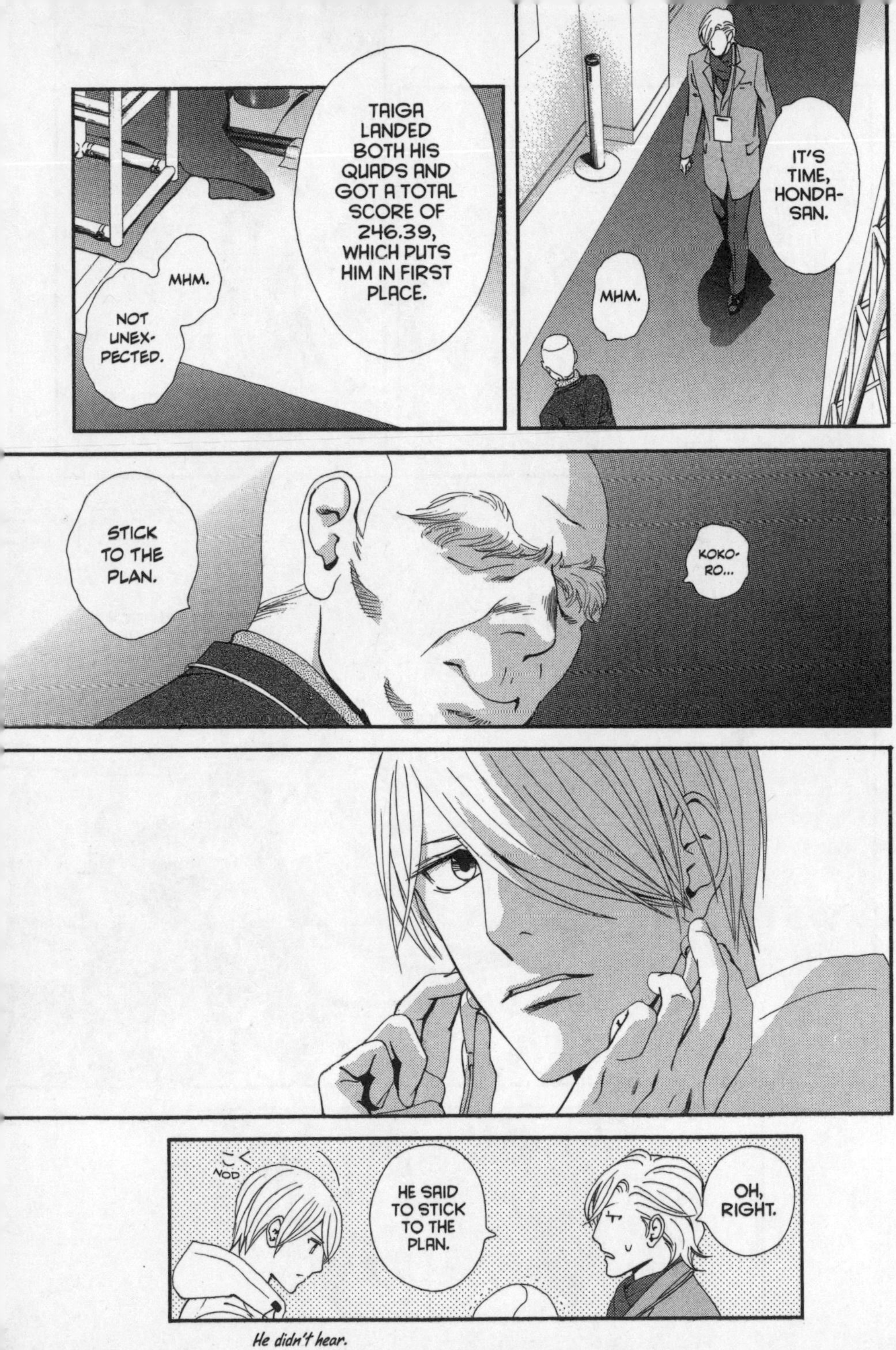
IT'S TIME, HONDA-SAN.
MHM.
TAIGA LANDED BOTH HIS QUADS AND GOT A TOTAL SCORE OF 246.39, WHICH PUTS HIM IN FIRST PLACE.
MHM.
NOT UNEXPECTED.
KOKO-RO...
STICK TO THE PLAN.
OH, RIGHT.
HE SAID TO STICK TO THE PLAN.
こく
NOD
He didn't hear.

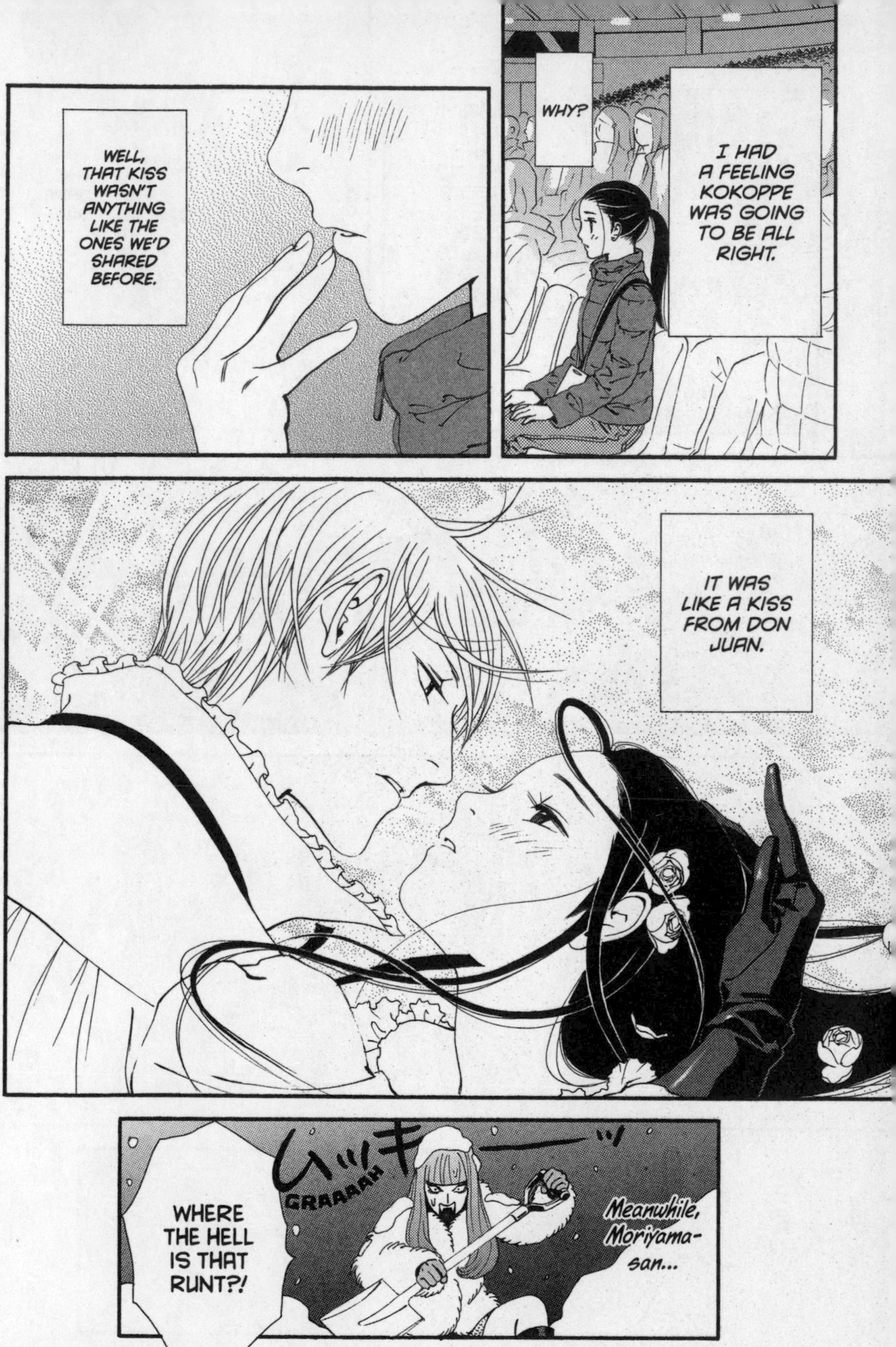
WHY?
I HAD A FEELING KOKOPPE WAS GOING TO BE ALL RIGHT.
WELL, THAT KISS WASN'T ANYTHING LIKE THE ONES WE'D SHARED BEFORE.
IT WAS LIKE A KISS FROM DON JUAN.
Meanwhile, Moriyama-san...
GRAAAAH
WHERE THE HELL IS THAT RUNT?!

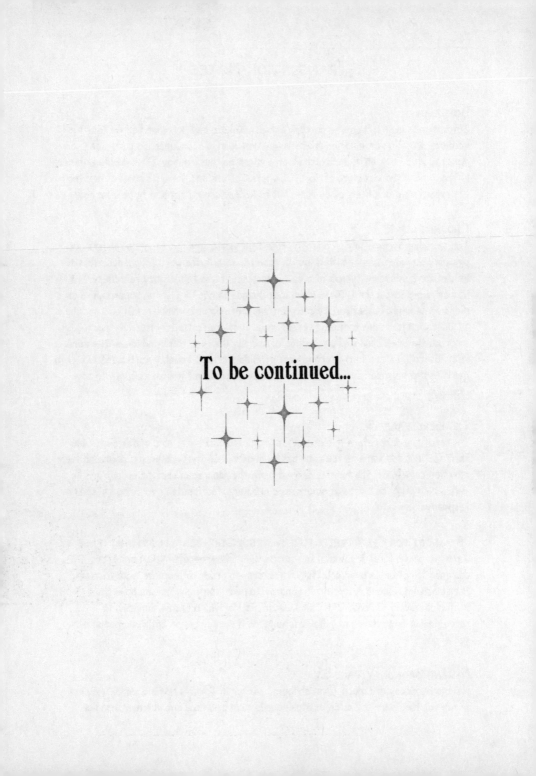

To be continued...

TRANSLATION NOTES

DON JUAN
Since there's been a thematic parallel between Kokoro and Don Juan for the last two volumes now, it's worth noting that the way Don Juan is pronounced in Japanese (*don-fan*) sounds as though it could also mean something like "fanboy." This double entendre is apparent in the structure of Spell 18, where Chitose and Kokoro's coaches and trainers expect him to act like a Don Juan, but he keeps turning out just to be a fanboy.

CHUUNI, PAGE 13
This word has become fairly common around the world, and most manga readers are probably already familiar with it, but in case you're not, the word *chuuni* describes the kind of fantastic ideas typical of a young adolescent who thinks they're mature, but is in many ways still a child. These ideas may include things like having superpowers or being some kind of otherworldly creature like a demon or a vampire. (Of course, who's to judge what ideas are fantastic versus those that are realistic?) Many people today embrace the label *chuuni* as a rejection of socially imposed roles and ideas. The word itself literally refers to the second year of middle school, roughly equivalent to eighth grade in the American system, as this would be a common time for children to have *chuuni* ideas.

TSUNDERE, PAGE 15
The term *tsundere* refers to a character who acts cold or irritable and tries to hide their feelings for someone, but who has moments when that wall breaks down and their affection comes out. The term is derived from the Japanese words *tsun-tsun* and *dere-dere,* which describe states of aloofness and being affectionate in an embarrassed way, respectively.

"A MASCOT FOR CHIBA PREFECTURE WEARS A LIGHT-YELLOW COSTUME," PAGE 52
Japanese prefectures are known for having their own mascots—which are often designed to resemble cute, colorful characters—in order to promote local tourism. Here Moriyama-san is referring to Funassyi, a pear-fairy character who is the unofficial mascot of Funabashi, Chiba, Japan. As Moriyama states, Funassyi is recognizable from its light-yellow costume, as it resembles an anthropomorphic yellow pear.

NAKANO BROADWAY, PAGE 53
Nakano Broadway is a multi-level shopping center in Tokyo's Nakano Ward. They are known for their wide selection of otaku goods such as anime and idol merchandise.

Pointing, page 113

In Japan, when referring to yourself, it's typical to point at your face or nose, as Chitose does here, rather than at your chest, as is common in the US.

Moominvalley, page 129

Moominvalley is the setting of *Moomin,* a comic strip by Tove Jansson that has been adapted into many different forms, including two anime series. Little My, who people often compare Chitose to for her bun and short stature, is one of the series' main characters.

Ice Tsugumori, Remodeled, page 165

This name is a reference to a battle mech from Tsutomu Nihei-sensei's manga *Knights of Sidonia.* The mech's full name is Type 17 Garde Shiratsuki Remodeled Ver. Tsugumori.

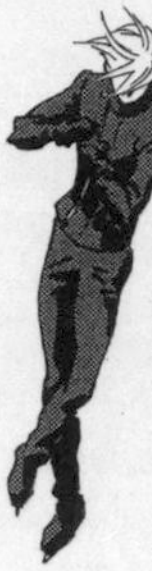

Glossary by Coach Akiyuki Kido

(based on May 2014 rules)

Open practice (page 11)
Open practice is typically held on the day before or the day of a competition. It's the skaters' last chance to polish their routines, and they're free to participate or not at their discretion. The technical panel—which consists of a technical specialist, an assistant technical specialist, and a technical controller—is required to watch and familiarize themselves with the skaters' programs.

Banquet (page 11)
Banquets are often held for everyone involved after the opening or closing ceremonies of skating events.

ISU Grand Prix (page 27)
The ISU Grand Prix is a series of six competitions held between October and December, including Skate America, Skate Canada, the Cup of China, the Trophée Eric Bompard (France), the Rostelecom Cup (Russia), and the NHK Trophy (Japan). The order they're held in varies by year.

Free skate (page 27)
In the free skating competition, skaters get to choose what elements and moves to use. Still, to ensure a well-rounded program, there are rules about what jumps, spins, and steps are required, as well as restrictions on the number of them allowed. In women's singles, this segment lasts four minutes, and in men's singles, it lasts four minutes and thirty seconds.

Short program (page 27)
The short program is a segment in which the shaters have up to two minutes and fifty seconds to perform eight predetermined elements, such as jumps, spins, or steps.

Toe loop (page 29)
The toe loop is considered the easiest jump out of the six. The skater uses their left toe to launch themselves into the air from their right skate's back outside edge. To date, no one has managed to execute this jump with more than four revolutions, and only a select few skaters can do even that.

Footwork (page 31)
A skater's footwork is the way they weave together steps with elements such as turns. Moves such as the Mohawk, the chasse, the crossroll, and the Choctaw are steps, whereas the three turn, loop turn, rocker, counter, bracket, and twizzle are turns. A combination of steps and turns is called a step sequence. For their steps to earn a high level grade, the skater has to use a variety of them and move both left and right. Because of the difficulty of doing footwork when your upper body is not aligned with your center of gravity, skaters can also use that as a means of increasing their level grade.

Exhibition gala (page 38)
After a competition, the winning skaters and other special guests may sometimes perform in a kind of ice show called an exhibition gala. This gives them an opportunity to skate without having to worry about rules, so they often do things like use props or play music with lyrics. It's also common for singers or other celebrities to participate as guests. (Editor's Note: Originally, skaters were not allowed to perform to music with lyrics. In 2014, the International Skating Union announced that they would allow skaters to perform to music with lyrics during figure skating competitions.)

Final (page 49)
The six highest-ranking skaters in the ISU Grand Prix go on to compete for first in the Grand Prix Final.

Japan Open (page 55)

The Japan Open is an international competition held at the start of the skating season. Japan, North America, and Europe all compete. Each region is represented by two women, two men, one pair, and one ice dancing couple. The only category is the free skate. This is also where Japan's skaters usually debut their new programs. An exhibition gala with an extravagant ice show is held after the competition, so it is like a festival that christens the beginning of the new season.

Jumps in a program (page 56)

The six jumps in figure skating are the toe loop, Salchow, loop, flip, Lutz, and Axel. In the short program, the following jumps are required: 1) a triple-triple or triple-double jump combination, 2) a quadruple or triple jump following footwork, and 3) a double or triple Axel. In the free skate, the skater may perform up to eight jumps, one of which must be an Axel. No more than three jump combinations are allowed, and only one of those can consist of three jumps.

Program components score (PCS, or presentation score) (page 56)

For this score, skaters are evaluated on the basis of five program components: skating skills, transitions, performance, composition, and interpretation. A skater's final score is the total of their program components score (PCS) and their technical score.

World Figure Skating Championships (page 77)

Also known as Worlds, this competition is the biggest event of the skating season and draws in skaters from all over the world. The winner earns the title of world champion for that season.

National Championships (page 78)

The Japan Figure Skating Championships are held every year near the end of December to determine the best skater in Japan. The results of this competition largely determine who will represent Japan at the Olympics and World Championships.

Axel (page 78)

There are six different jumps in figure skating. An Axel is the only one that begins with the skater facing directly forward (on their forward outside edge). It's the most difficult jump, and a triple Axel requires three and a half midair rotations. Midori Ito was the first woman in Japan to successfully execute this jump.

Lutz (page 80)

The Lutz is considered the second hardest jump after the Axel. To perform this jump, a skater uses their right toe pick (the front of the skate's blade where it has teeth) to launch themselves into the air from their left skate's back outside edge. Because of the difficulty of skating on this edge, many skaters make an edge error. It is named after the Austrian skater Alois Lutz, the first person to perform this jump. Note that the roles of each foot are reversed for skaters who spin clockwise.

4T (page 88)

This is an abbreviation of quadruple toe loop.

Technical score (page 92)

The technical score is determined by the technical elements included in the program and their quality. Jumps, spins, steps, and other elements each have a base value, which is modified by a grade of execution (GOE) to get the technical score. The GOE is the average of the modifiers assigned by the judges, excluding the highest and lowest. These modifiers have one of seven values between negative and positive three.

Flying sit spin (page 101)
To perform a flying sit spin, a skater leaps into a one-legged squat in which they spin with their free leg extended out.

Camel spin (page 101)
In a camel spin, the skater holds their upper body and free leg a little higher than parallel with the ice to form a T shape while spinning.

Jump combination (page 103)
A jump combination is when a skater performs a jump and then immediately performs another from the foot they land on. Since jumps are landed on the right skate's back outside edge (or the left skate's if you're spinning clockwise), all jumps after the first in a combination are limited to either the toe loop or the loop jump. If the skater weaves footwork between their jumps, it's called a jump sequence instead.

Salchow (page 108)
This jump is executed from the left foot's back inside edge by lifting the right foot forward and to the left. The way both feet face outward just before takeoff is a unique feature of the Salchow jump. It was named after the Swedish skater Ulrich Salchow.

Senior (page 110)
There are three age divisions in figure skating: novice, junior, and senior. The senior division includes skaters age 15 or older, based on their age on June 30th before the competition.

Footwork transitions (page 110)
This term refers to the footwork that connects one element of a program to another.

Deduction (page 142)
Each element—such as a jump, spin, step sequence, or spiral sequence—has a base value for use in scoring. The judges assign a modifier with one of seven values between negative and positive three to this base value, resulting in either a deduction or bonus points. Today, these deductions and bonuses are clearly defined in the rules, and there is a checklist of features that will earn one or the other (e.g., particularly high or low jumps, the overall flow, and speed).

4CC (page 143)
The 4CC, or Four Continents Figure Skating Championships, is an international competition open to skaters from four continents: Africa, Asia, the Americas, and Oceania. Europe is excluded.

Akiyuki Kido
Born on August 28th, 1975, Akiyuki Kido represented Japan in ice dancing at the 2006 winter Olympics in Turin, Italy. He took fifteenth place, the highest Japan had ever placed in ice dancing at the time. Today, he works as a coach at the Shin-Yokohama Skate Center.

Knight of the ICE

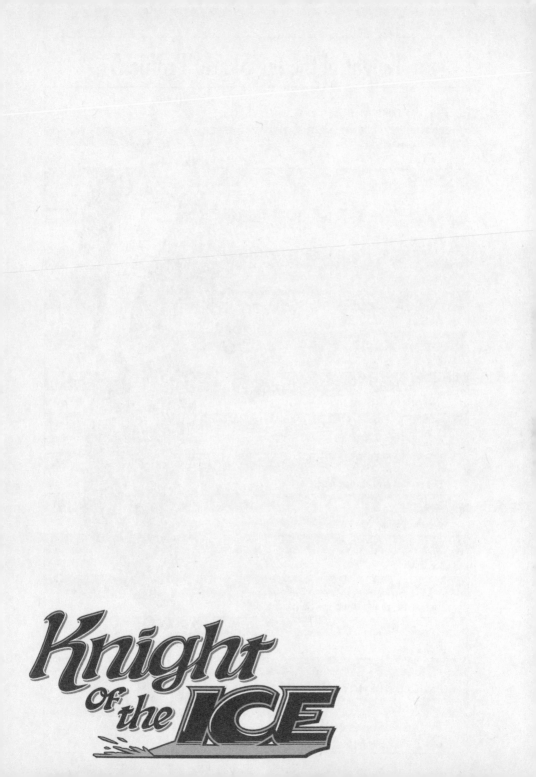

Knight of the Ice Skater Profile 5

5 Louis Claire

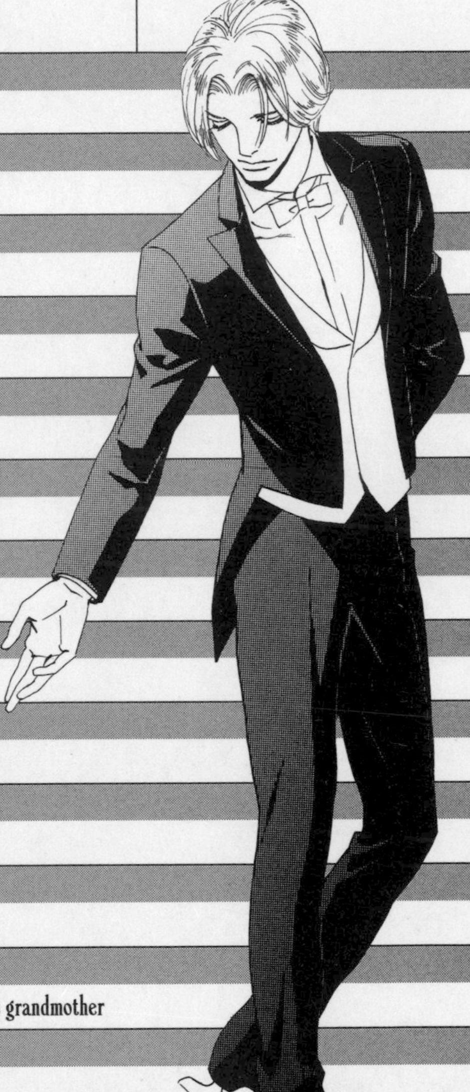

Height:

173 cm

Blood type:

0

Birthday:

February 14th

Place of origin:

Montreal

Strongest element:

Footwork

Strongest jump:

Flip

Most difficult jump performed to date:

Quadruple toe loop

Strength:

His smooth skating

Weakness:

He's not that good at triple Axels

Hobby:

Horseback riding

Talent:

Ice dancing

Family composition:

Two parents, an older sister, and his grandmother

Favorite food:

French fries

Least favorite food:

Mochi (he can't tell when it's safe to swallow)

Notes:

When Kokoro was living abroad in Canada, Louis trained at the same rink he did.
Louis is also known for the bad blood between him and Kyle Miller.

About Toha
Heavy Industries

The company sponsoring Kokoppe, Toha Heavy
Industries, is a fictional corporation from the
works of Tsutomu Nihei-sensei, including Blame!,
Biomega, and Knights of Sidonia. I'm a big fan of
these manga, and Nihei-sensei was kind enough
to allow this small collaboration!

Seu-san

Dhomo-san

Also, I think Kokoppe and Taiga's designs were
influenced by Seu and Dhomochevsky from Blame!...

Divided Opinion

Episode 5
Heavy Industry

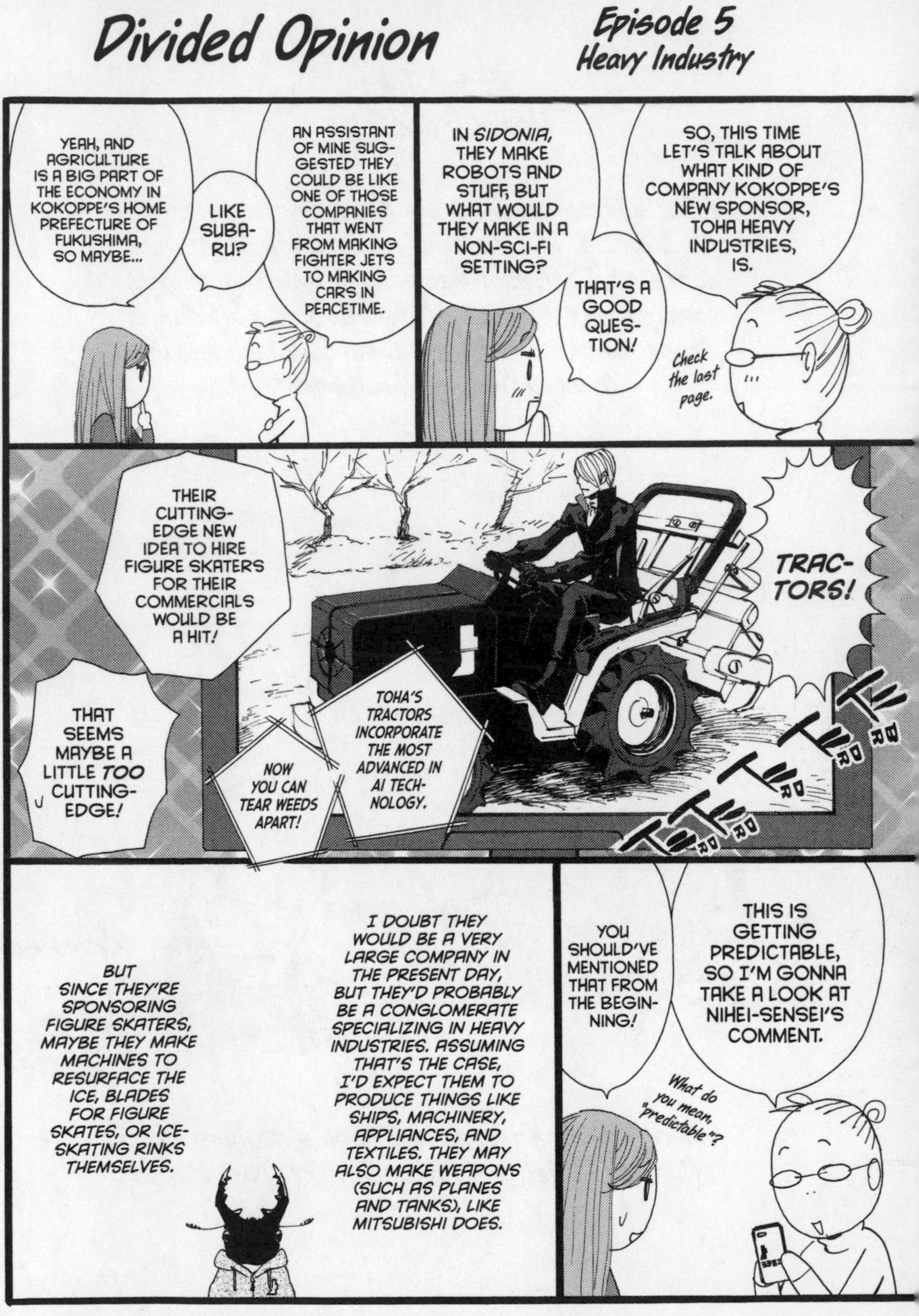

SO, THIS TIME LET'S TALK ABOUT WHAT KIND OF COMPANY KOKOPPE'S NEW SPONSOR, TOHA HEAVY INDUSTRIES, IS.
IN *SIDONIA*, THEY MAKE ROBOTS AND STUFF, BUT WHAT WOULD THEY MAKE IN A NON-SCI-FI SETTING?
THAT'S A GOOD QUES-TION!
Check the last page.
AN ASSISTANT OF MINE SUG-GESTED THEY COULD BE LIKE ONE OF THOSE COMPANIES THAT WENT FROM MAKING FIGHTER JETS TO MAKING CARS IN PEACETIME.
LIKE SUBA-RU?
YEAH, AND AGRICULTURE IS A BIG PART OF THE ECONOMY IN KOKOPPE'S HOME PREFECTURE OF FUKUSHIMA, SO MAYBE...
TRAC-TORS!
BRR DRR DRR DRR
THEIR CUTTING-EDGE NEW IDEA TO HIRE FIGURE SKATERS FOR THEIR COMMERCIALS WOULD BE A HIT!
TOHA'S TRACTORS INCORPORATE THE MOST ADVANCED IN AI TECH-NOLOGY.
NOW YOU CAN TEAR WEEDS APART!
THAT SEEMS MAYBE A LITTLE *TOO* CUTTING-EDGE!
THIS IS GETTING PREDICTABLE, SO I'M GONNA TAKE A LOOK AT NIHEI-SENSEI'S COMMENT.
YOU SHOULD'VE MENTIONED THAT FROM THE BEGIN-NING!
What do you mean, "predictable"?
I DOUBT THEY WOULD BE A VERY LARGE COMPANY IN THE PRESENT DAY, BUT THEY'D PROBABLY BE A CONGLOMERATE SPECIALIZING IN HEAVY INDUSTRIES. ASSUMING THAT'S THE CASE, I'D EXPECT THEM TO PRODUCE THINGS LIKE SHIPS, MACHINERY, APPLIANCES, AND TEXTILES. THEY MAY ALSO MAKE WEAPONS (SUCH AS PLANES AND TANKS), LIKE MITSUBISHI DOES.
BUT SINCE THEY'RE SPONSORING FIGURE SKATERS, MAYBE THEY MAKE MACHINES TO RESURFACE THE ICE, BLADES FOR FIGURE SKATES, OR ICE-SKATING RINKS THEMSELVES.

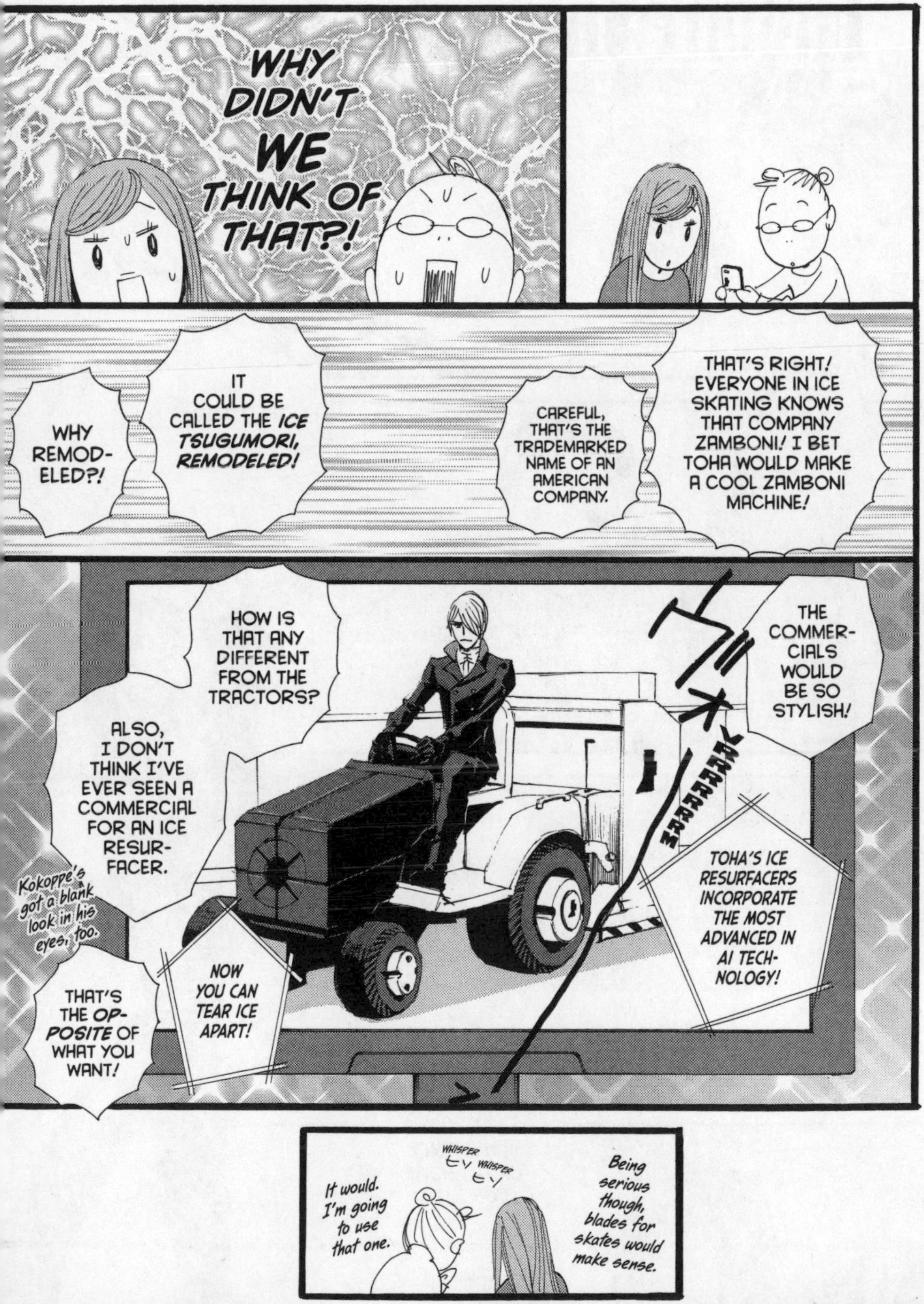
WHY DIDN'T WE THINK OF THAT?!
THAT'S RIGHT! EVERYONE IN ICE SKATING KNOWS THAT COMPANY ZAMBONI! I BET TOHA WOULD MAKE A COOL ZAMBONI MACHINE!
CAREFUL, THAT'S THE TRADEMARKED NAME OF AN AMERICAN COMPANY.
IT COULD BE CALLED THE *ICE TSUGUMORI, REMODELED!*
WHY REMODELED?!
THE COMMERCIALS WOULD BE SO STYLISH!
VRRRRRRRM
TOHA'S ICE RESURFACERS INCORPORATE THE MOST ADVANCED IN AI TECHNOLOGY!
HOW IS THAT ANY DIFFERENT FROM THE TRACTORS?
ALSO, I DON'T THINK I'VE EVER SEEN A COMMERCIAL FOR AN ICE RESURFACER.
NOW YOU CAN TEAR ICE APART!
Kokoppe's got a blank look in his eyes, too.
THAT'S THE *OPPOSITE* OF WHAT YOU WANT!
Being serious though, blades for skates would make sense.
WHISPER WHISPER
It would. I'm going to use that one.

Thank you, Nihei-sensei!

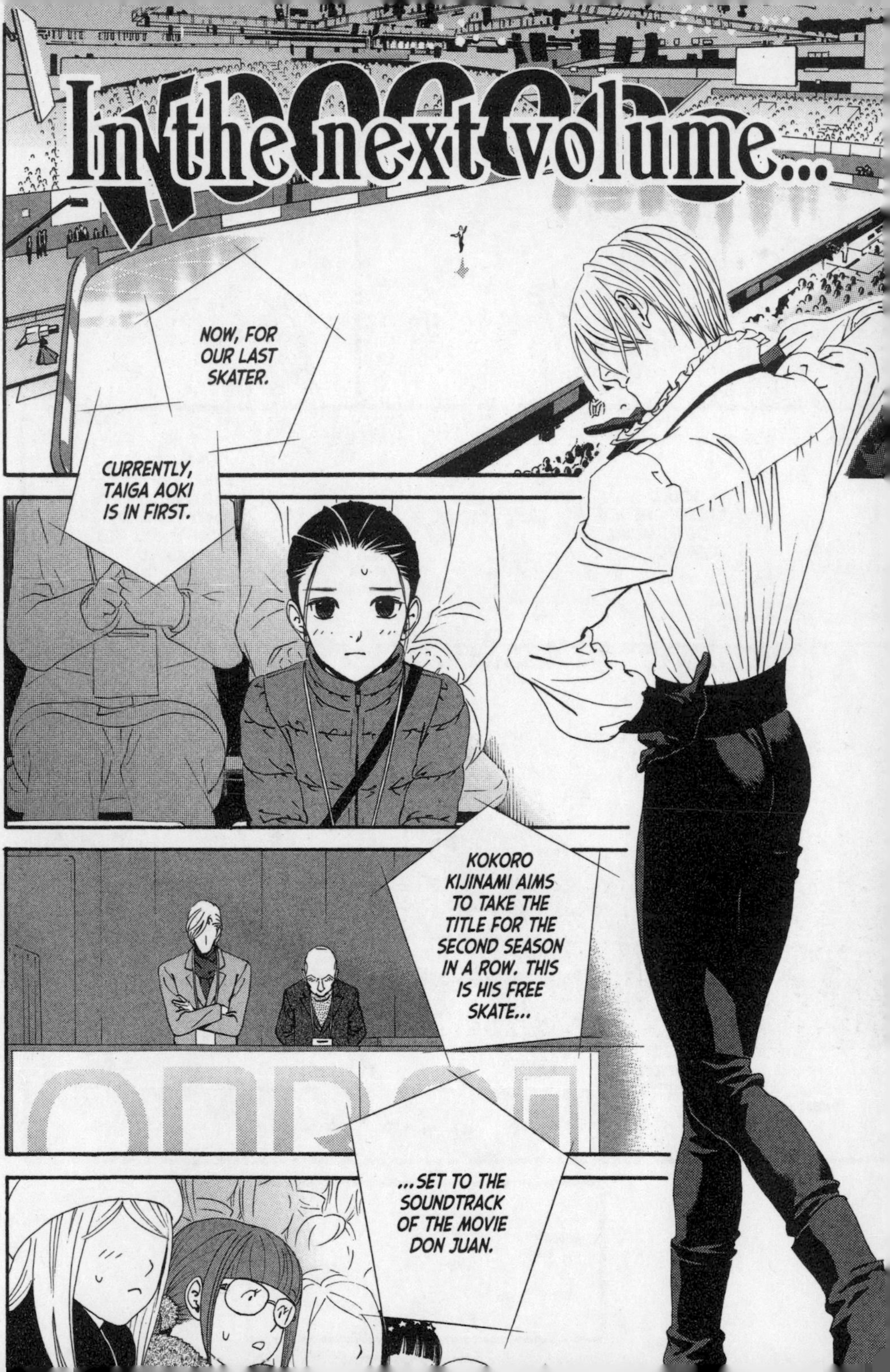
In the next volume...
NOW, FOR OUR LAST SKATER.
CURRENTLY, TAIGA AOKI IS IN FIRST.
KOKORO KIJINAMI AIMS TO TAKE THE TITLE FOR THE SECOND SEASON IN A ROW. THIS IS HIS FREE SKATE...
...SET TO THE SOUNDTRACK OF THE MOVIE DON JUAN.

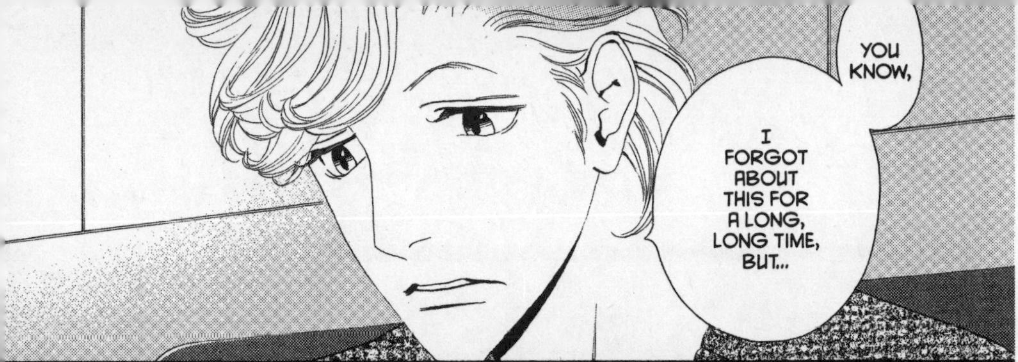
YOU KNOW,
I FORGOT ABOUT THIS FOR A LONG, LONG TIME, BUT...

What could Kokoro have meant when he interrupted Chitose's spell to kiss her and apologize?! What's this plan of Coach Honda's? And what is the meaning of Kokoro's father's words for Chitose?

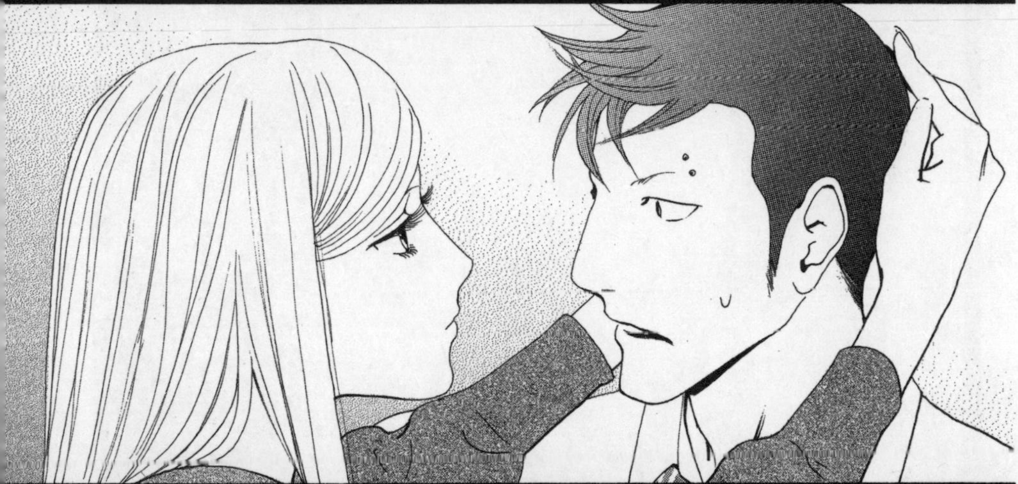

Knight of the Ice vol. 6

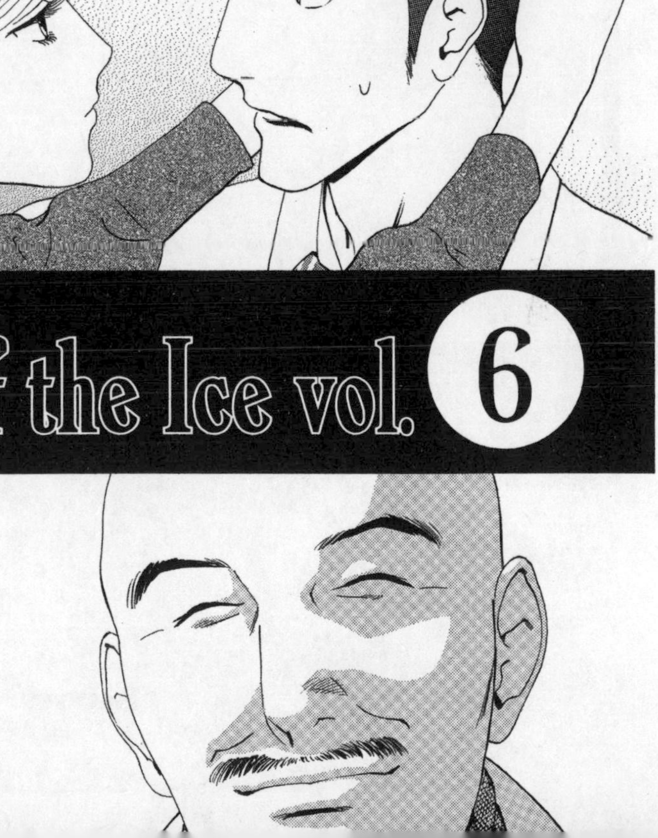

Coming soon!

A SMART, NEW ROMANTIC COMEDY FOR FANS OF *SHORTCAKE CAKE* AND *TERRACE HOUSE*!

A romance manga starring high school girl Meeko, who learns to live on her own in a boarding house whose living room is home to the odd (but handsome) Matsunaga-san. She begins to adjust to her new life away from her parents, but Meeko soon learns that no matter how far away from home she is, she's still a young girl at heart — especially when she finds herself falling for Matsunaga-san.

PERFECT WORLD

Rie Aruga

A TOUCHING NEW SERIES ABOUT LOVE AND COPING WITH DISABILITY

An office party reunites Tsugumi with her high school crush Itsuki. He's realized his dream of becoming an architect, but along the way, he experienced a spinal injury that put him in a wheelchair. Now Tsugumi's rekindled feelings will butt up against prejudices she never considered — and Itsuki will have to decide if he's ready to let someone into his heart...

"Depicts with great delicacy and courage the difficulties some with disabilities experience getting involved in romantic relationships... Rie Aruga refuses to romanticize, pushing her heroine to face the reality of disability. She invites her readers to the same tasks of empathy, knowledge and recognition."
—Slate.fr

"An important entry [in manga romance]... The emotional core of both plot and characters indicates thoughtfulness... [Aruga's] research is readily apparent in the text and artwork, making this feel like a real story."
—Anime News Network

KC KODANSHA COMICS

In love, there are
no save points.

ヲタクに恋は難しい

WOTAKOI:
LOVE IS HARD FOR OTAKU

by FUJITA

Narumi has had it rough: Every boyfriend she's had dumped her once they found out she was an otaku, so she's gone to great lengths to hide it. At her new job, she bumps into Hirotaka, her childhood friend and fellow otaku. When Hirotaka almost gets her secret outed at work, she comes up with a plan to keep him quiet. But he comes up with a counter-proposal: Why doesn't she just date him instead?

CARDCAPTOR SAKURA
COLLECTOR'S EDITION
C L A M P

Cardcaptor Sakura Collector's Edition © CLAMP • Shigatsu Tsuitachi Co., Ltd. / Kodansha Ltd.

Ten-year-old Sakura Kinomoto lives a pretty normal life with her older brother, Tōya, and widowed father, Fujitaka—until the day she discovers a strange book in her father's library, and her life takes a magical turn...

- A deluxe large-format hardcover edition of CLAMP's shojo manga classic
- All-new foil-stamped cover art on each volume
- Comes with exclusive collectible art card

KODANSHA COMICS

THE WORLD OF CLAMP!

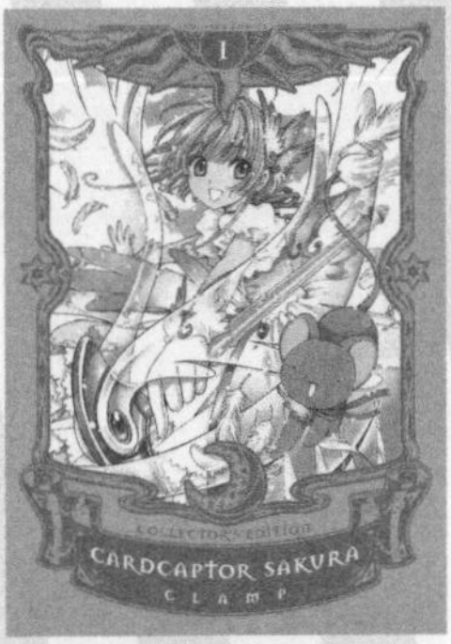
CARDCAPTOR SAKURA
CLAMP

Cardcaptor Sakura
Collector's Edition

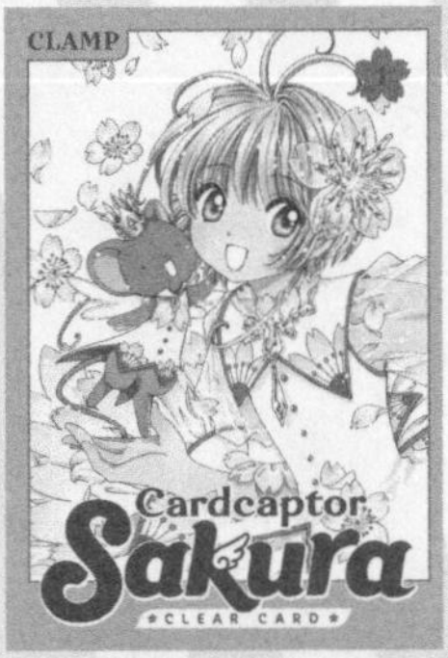
CLAMP
Cardcaptor Sakura
CLEAR CARD

Cardcaptor Sakura:
Clear Card

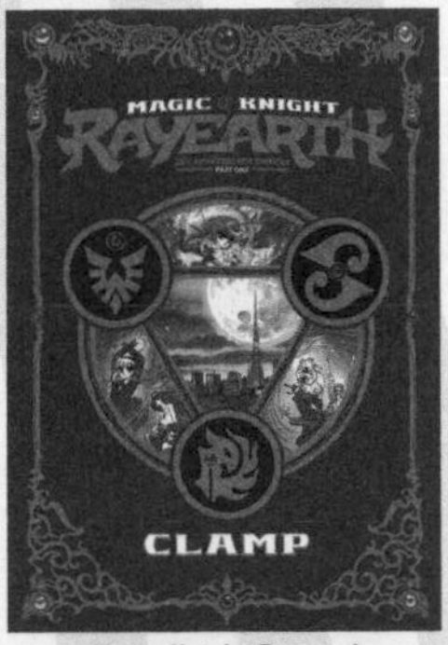
MAGIC KNIGHT RAYEARTH
CLAMP

Magic Knight Rayearth
25th Anniversary Box Set

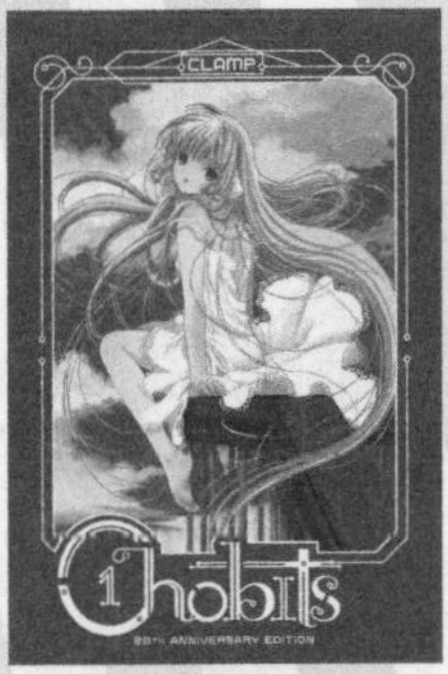
CLAMP
Chobits

Chobits

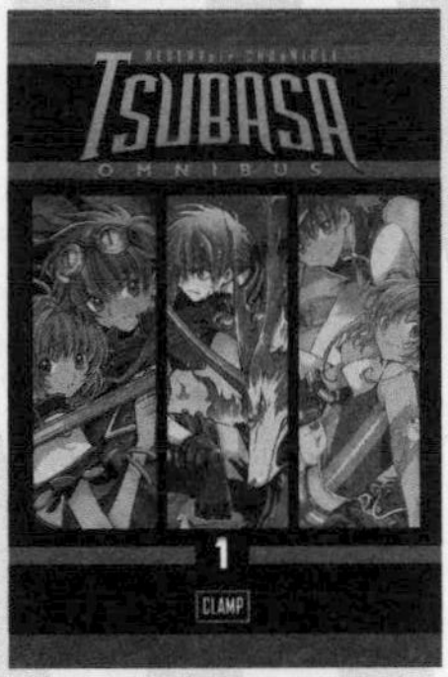
TSUBASA
OMNIBUS
1
CLAMP

TSUBASA Omnibus

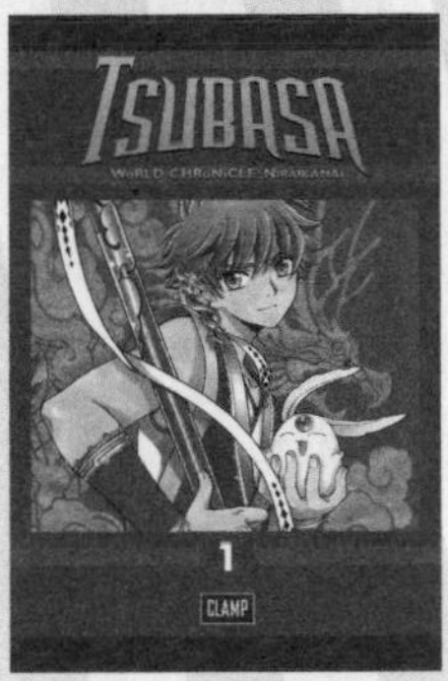
TSUBASA
1
CLAMP

TSUBASA WoRLD CHRoNiCLE

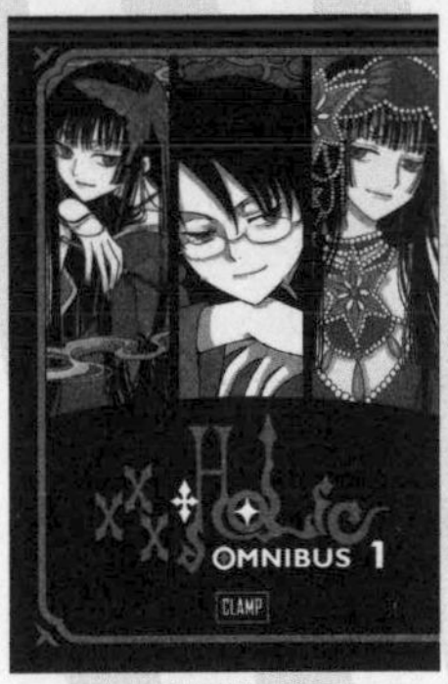
xxxHOLiC
OMNIBUS 1
CLAMP

xxxHOLiC Omnibus

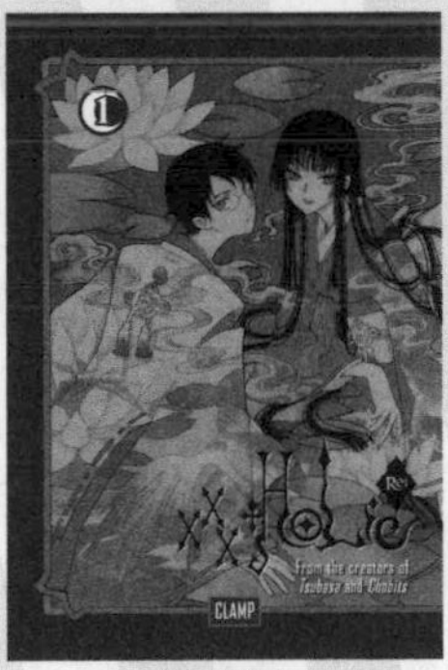
xxxHOLiC
From the creators of Tsubasa and Chobits
CLAMP

xxxHOLiC Rei

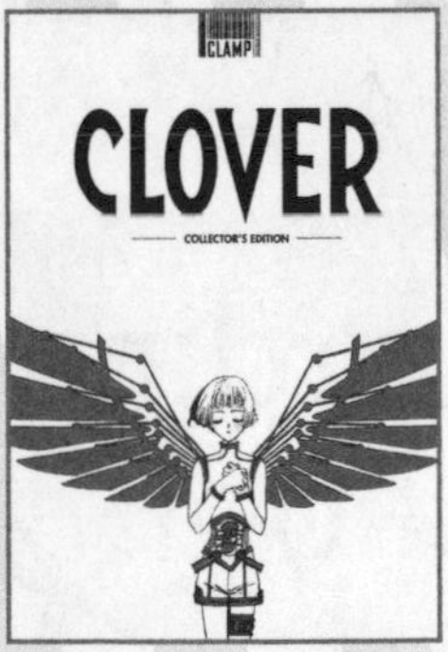
CLAMP
CLOVER
COLLECTOR'S EDITION

CLOVER Collector's Edition

KC KODANSHA COMICS

Kodansha Comics welcomes you to explore the expansive world of CLAMP, the all-female artist collective that has produced some of the most acclaimed manga of the century. Our growing catalog includes icons like *Cardcaptor Sakura* and *Magic Knight Rayearth*, each crafted with CLAMP's one-of-a-kind style and characters!

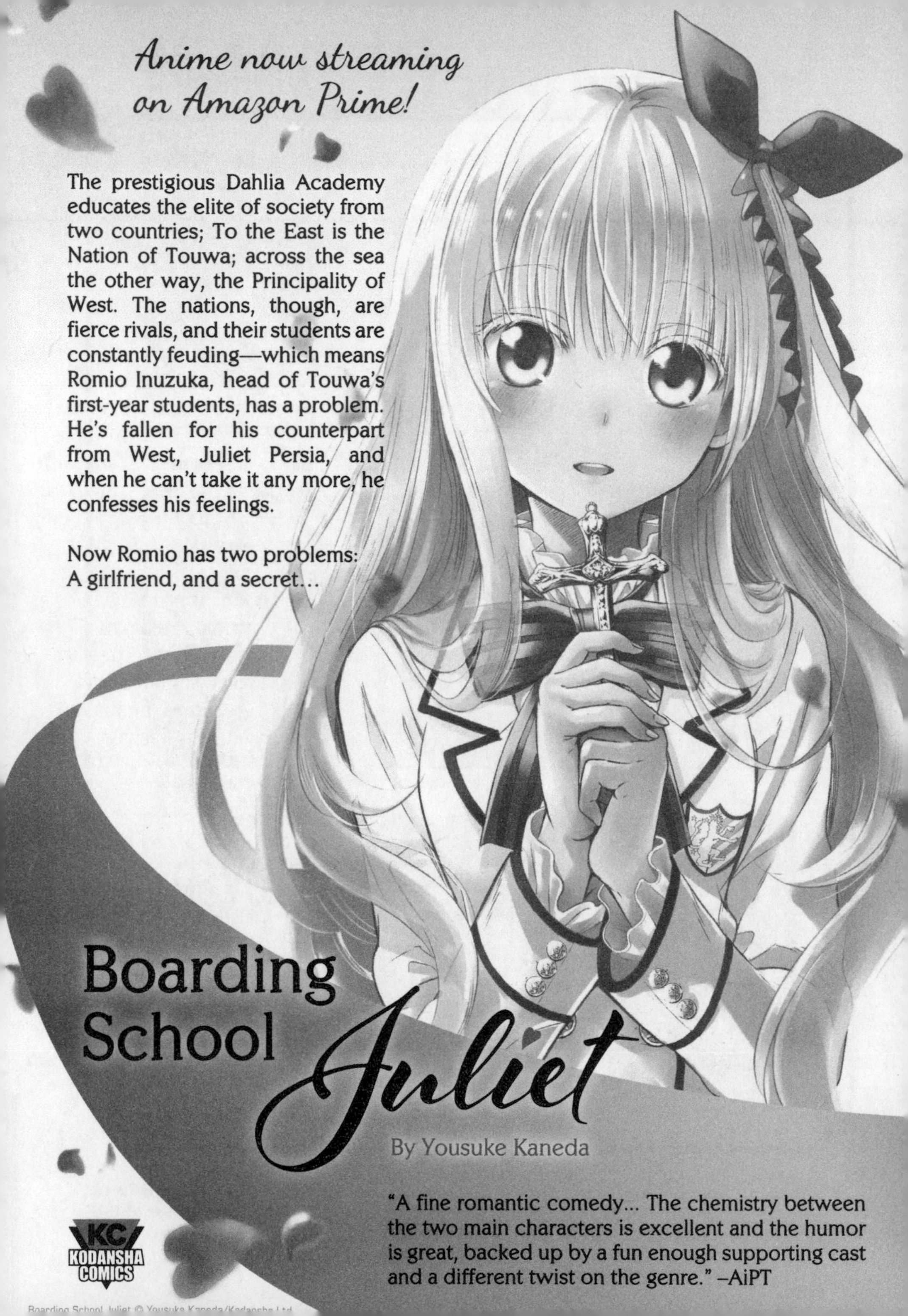
Anime now streaming on Amazon Prime!
The prestigious Dahlia Academy educates the elite of society from two countries; To the East is the Nation of Touwa; across the sea the other way, the Principality of West. The nations, though, are fierce rivals, and their students are constantly feuding—which means Romio Inuzuka, head of Touwa's first-year students, has a problem. He's fallen for his counterpart from West, Juliet Persia, and when he can't take it any more, he confesses his feelings.
Now Romio has two problems: A girlfriend, and a secret…
Boarding School Juliet
By Yousuke Kaneda
"A fine romantic comedy… The chemistry between the two main characters is excellent and the humor is great, backed up by a fun enough supporting cast and a different twist on the genre." –AiPT
KC KODANSHA COMICS
Boarding School Juliet © Yousuke Kaneda/Kodansha Ltd.

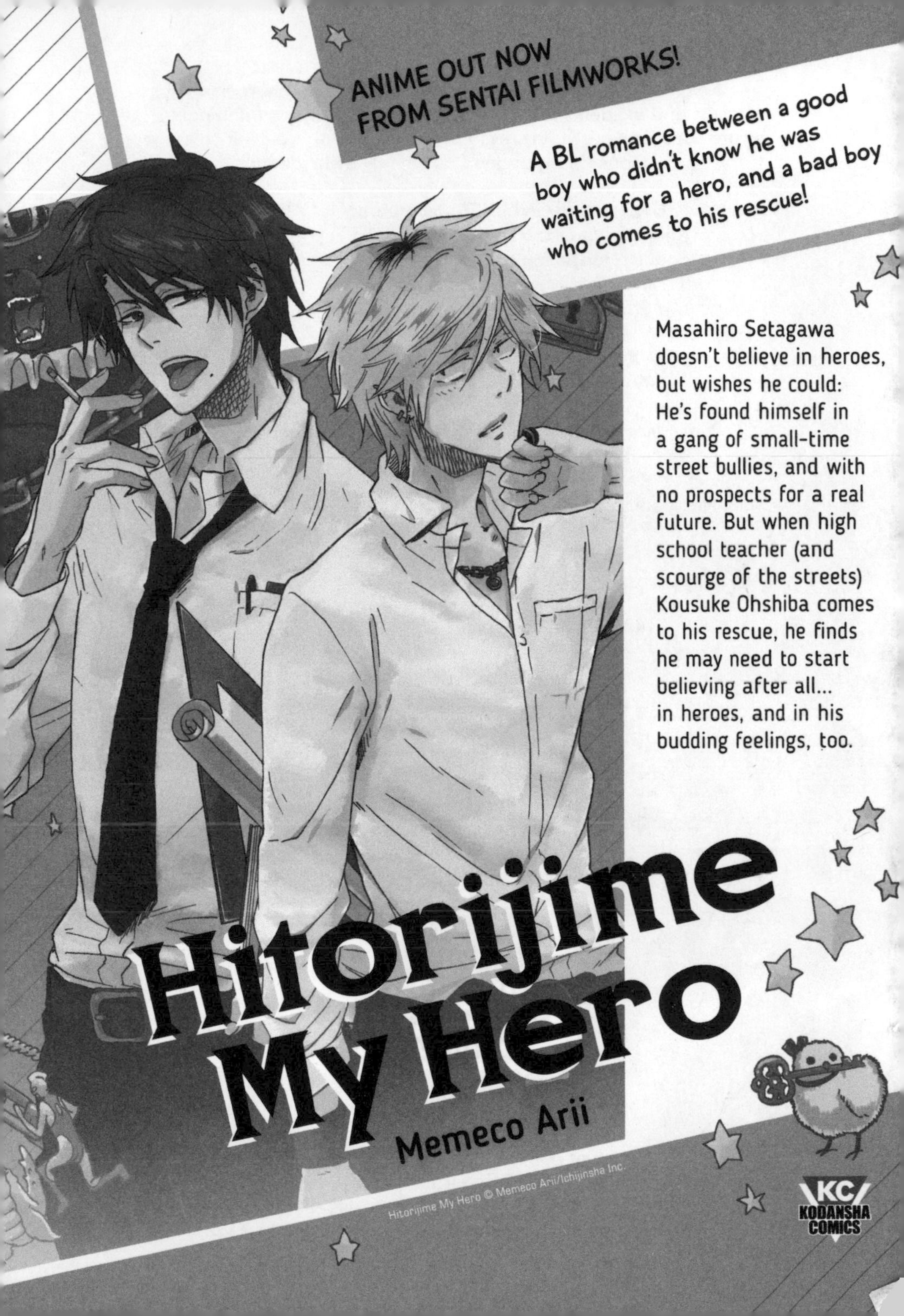
ANIME OUT NOW FROM SENTAI FILMWORKS!
A BL romance between a good boy who didn't know he was waiting for a hero, and a bad boy who comes to his rescue!
Masahiro Setagawa doesn't believe in heroes, but wishes he could: He's found himself in a gang of small-time street bullies, and with no prospects for a real future. But when high school teacher (and scourge of the streets) Kousuke Ohshiba comes to his rescue, he finds he may need to start believing after all... in heroes, and in his budding feelings, too.
Hitorijime My Hero
Memeco Arii
Hitorijime My Hero © Memeco Arii/Ichijinsha Inc.
KC KODANSHA COMICS

A Kodansha Comics Trade Paperback Original
Knight of the Ice 5 copyright © 2015 Yayoi Ogawa
English translation copyright © 2021 Yayoi Ogawa

Published in the United States by Kodansha Comics, an imprint of
Kodansha USA Publishing, LLC, New York.

Publication rights for this English edition arranged through
Kodansha Ltd., Tokyo.

First published in Japan in 2015 by Kodansha Ltd., Tokyo
as *Ginban Kishi*, volume 5.

ISBN 978-1-64651-052-8

Printed in the United States of America.

www.kodanshacomics.com

9 8 7 6 5 4 3 2 1
Translation: Rose Padgett
Lettering: Jennifer Skarupa
Editing: Tiff Ferentini
Kodansha Comics edition cover design by Phil Balsman

▼

Publisher: Kiichiro Sugawara

Director of publishing services: Ben Applegate
Associate director of operations: Stephen Pakula
Publishing services managing editor: Noelle Webster
Assistant production manager: Emi Lotto, Angela Zurlo